The Decline of Employment of People with Disabilities

A Policy Puzzle

The Decline in Employment of People with Disabilities

A Policy Puzzle

David C. Stapleton
Richard V. Burkhauser
Editors

2003

W.E. Upjohn Institute for Employment Research
Kalamazoo, Michigan

Library of Congress Cataloging-in-Publication Data

The decline in employment of people with disabilities : a policy puzzle / David C. Stapleton and Richard V. Burkhauser, editors.
   p. cm.
  Includes bibliographical references and index.
   ISBN 0-88099-259-X (pbk. : alk. paper) — ISBN 0-88099-260-3 (hardcover : alk. paper)
   1. People with disabilities—Employment—United States. 2. People with disabilities—Employment—United States—Statistics. 3. People with disabilities—Employment—Government policy—United States. I. Stapleton, David C. II. Burkhauser, Richard V.
   HD7256.U5D413 2003
   331.5'9'0973—dc22
                                              2003015636

© 2003

W.E. Upjohn Institute for Employment Research
300 S. Westnedge Avenue
Kalamazoo, Michigan 49007–4686

The facts presented in this study and the observations and viewpoints expressed are the sole responsibility of the authors. They do not necessarily represent positions of the W.E. Upjohn Institute for Employment Research.

Cover design by Alcorn Publication Design.
Index prepared by Nancy Humphreys.
Printed in the United States of America.
Printed on recycled paper.

Contents

Acknowledgments	xv

1 Introduction — 1
  Richard V. Burkhauser and David C. Stapleton

The Employment and Economic Well-Being of Working-Aged People with Disabilities	2
Is the Decline in Employment a Measurement Aberration?	5
Comparing Trends in the Employment of People with Disabilities Across Data Sets and Disability Population Definitions	8
Is the Overall Employment Rate of People with Disabilities the Appropriate Policy Success Measure?	9
Alternative Explanations of the Overall Decline in Employment Rates	10
Who Is Right?	20
Note	20
References	20

2 A User's Guide to Current Statistics on the Employment of People with Disabilities — 23
  Richard V. Burkhauser, Andrew J. Houtenville, and David C. Wittenburg

Data Description	26
Conceptualizing Disability	28
Empirical Analysis	34
Explaining the Differences in Employment Trends in Other Studies	41
Other Labor Market Success Measures	47
Conclusion	52
Notes	54
Appendix 2A	59
References	85

3 Employment Declines among People with Disabilities — 87
  Andrew J. Houtenville and Mary C. Daly

Data and Measurement	88
Shifts in Population Composition	90
Isolated Occurrence or Widespread Decline?	95
Decomposition of Employment Decline	101
Within-Group Changes in Health	108
Conclusion	110

Notes	111
Appendix 3A	113
References	123

**4 Have Changes in the Nature of Work or the Labor Market   125
Reduced Employment Prospects of Workers with Disabilities?**
David C. Stapleton, Nanette Goodman, and
Andrew J. Houtenville

The Static Aspects of Work	128
The Dynamic Aspects of Work	156
Conclusion	160
Notes	161
Appendix 4A	165
Appendix Notes	175
References	176

**5 Rising Health Care Expenditures and the Employment   181
of People with High-Cost Chronic Conditions**
Steven C. Hill, Gina A. Livermore, and *Andrew J. Houtenville*

Background	183
Data and methods	188
Findings	198
Discussion	208
Summary of Findings	209
Notes	211
References	212

6 Employment and the Changing Disability Population   217
H. Stephen Kaye

Employment Measures for the Disability Population	219
The Changing Size and Composition of the Disability Population	224
Increased Prevalence of Chronic Conditions and Impairments	234
What Risk Factors Might Have Led to These Increases?	242
Conclusion	253
Notes	254
References	254

**7 The Americans with Disabilities Act and the Employment   259
of People with Disabilities**
Thomas DeLeire

Background	260

The A Priori Case Against the ADA	263
Empirical Studies—the Weight of the Evidence Against the ADA	265
What Needs To Be Done?	273
Notes	275
References	275

8 Does the Definition Affect the Outcome? 279
Douglas Kruse and *Lisa Schur*

Problems in Defining and Measuring Disability	282
Estimates of Employment Patterns and Trends	291
Conclusion	295
Notes	296
References	298

9 Is It Time to Declare the ADA a Failed Law? 301
Peter Blanck, Susan Schwochau, and *Chen Song*

Economic Models of Employment Discrimination	303
Effect of ADA Title I	307
Does the ADA Exacerbate the Employment Problem?	314
Conclusion	328
Notes	329
References	332

10 Social Security Disability Insurance and the Recent Decline in the Employment Rate of People with Disabilities 339
Nanette Goodman and *Timothy Waidmann*

Background	341
Findings	348
Discussion	362
Notes	365
References	367

11 A Review of the Evidence and Its Implications for Policy Change 369
Richard V. Burkhauser and David C. Stapleton

Did the Employment Rate Decline?	372
Which Measure of the Employment Rate Should We Focus On?	375
What Caused the Employment Rate Decline?	377
Policy Implications	393
Notes	403
References	404

The Authors	407
Index	413
About the Institute	431

Figures

2.1	Disability Conceptualizations	32
2.2	Disability Prevalence Rates in 1996 Using Alternative Disability Definitions from the NHIS, CPS, and SIPP	35
2.3	Employment Rates in 1996 of Alternatively Defined Disability Populations from the NHIS, CPS, and SIPP	37
2.4	Yearly Employment Rate Trends of Men with Disabilities in Alternatively Defined Disability Populations from the NHIS, CPS, and SIPP	39
2.5	Yearly Employment Rate Trends of Women with Disabilities in Alternatively Defined Disability Populations from the NHIS, CPS, and SIPP	40
2.6	Yearly Employment Rate Trends of Men without Disabilities in Alternatively Defined Disability Populations from the NHIS, CPS, and SIPP	42
2.7	Yearly Employment Rate Trends of Women without Disabilities in Alternatively Defined Disability Populations from the NHIS, CPS, and SIPP	43
2.8	Employment Rate Trends of the Subsample of the Work-Limitation-Based Disability Population Who Report Being Able to Work from the NHIS, CPS, and SIPP	45
2.9	Trends in the Proportion of the Work-Limitation-Based Disability Population Who Report Being Able to Work from the NHIS, CPS, and SIPP	46
2.10	Unemployment Rate Trends in the Work-Limitation-Based Disability Population from the NHIS, CPS, and SIPP	48
2.11	Labor Force Participation Rate Trends in the Work-Limitation-Based Disability Population from the NHIS, CPS, and SIPP	50
2.12	SSI and SSDI Beneficiary Rate Trends in the Work-Limitation-Based Disability Population from the CPS and SIPP	51

2A.1 Annual Disability Prevalence Rates of Men in Alternatively   81
       Defined Disability Populations from the NHIS, CPS, and SIPP
2A.2 Annual Disability Prevalence Rates of Women in Alternatively   83
       Defined Disability Populations from the NHIS, CPS, and SIPP

3.1   Employment Rates in 2000 of Those Reporting Work Limitations,   90
       by Gender, Age, Race, and Education
3.2   Prevalence of Work Limitations in Employment in 2000, by   92
       Gender, Age, Race, and Education
3.3   Yearly Trends (1980–2000) of Those Reporting Work Limitations,   93
       by Gender
3.4   Yearly Trends (1980–2000) of Those Reporting Work Limitations,   94
       by Age
3.5   Yearly Trends (1980–2000) of Those Reporting Work Limitations,   95
       by Race
3.6   Yearly Trends (1980–2000) of Those Reporting Work Limitations,   96
       by Education
3.7   Yearly Employment Rate Trends (1980–2000) of Those Reporting   97
       Work Limitations, Total and by Gender
3.8   Yearly Employment Rate Trends (1980–2000) of Those Reporting   98
       Work Limitations, by Age
3.9   Yearly Employment Rate Trends (1980–2000) of Those Reporting   99
       Work Limitations, by Race
3.10 Yearly Employment Rate Trends (1980–2000) of Those Reporting   99
       Work Limitations, by Education
3.11 Yearly Trends of Those Reporting Work Limitations, by   109
       Self-Reported Health Status
3.12 Yearly Employment Rate Trends (1980–2000) of Those Reporting   110
       Work Limitations, by Self-Reported Health Status

4.1   Three-Year Moving Average of Percentage of Jobs Filled by   126
       Workers with Work Limitations
4.2   Distribution of Employment by Industry, 1954–2000   128
4.3   Mean of GED-Language, 1985–2000   134
4.4   Mean of Specific Vocational Preparation   135
4.5   Percent of Jobs that Require Repetitive Tasks, 1985–2000   136
4.6   Percent of Jobs that Require Employee to Direct the Actions   137
       of Others, 1985–2000
4.7   Percent of Jobs that Require Bachelor's Degree or Higher   139
4.8   Percent of Jobs that Are Dead-End   140
4.9   Mean Value of Strength Score   141

4.10	Percent of Jobs that Are Full-Time/Full-Year	144
4.11	Percent of Jobs with Employer-Subsidized Health Insurance	146
4.12	Employer Size	148
4.13	Involuntary Job Loss as a Percent of Total Unemployment	159
6.1	NHIS Employment Rates among Working-Age Adults with Disabilities, 1988–1996	220
6.2	CPS Employment Rates among Working-Age Adults with Disabilities, 1994–2000	222
6.3	NHIS Disability Rate and Rate of Inability to Work among Working-Age Adults, 1988–1996	225
6.4	Disability Rate and Rate of Inability to Work among Working-Age Adults, 1994–2000	226
6.5	Proportion of Working-Age Adults with Disabilities Reported as Unable to Work, 1988–2000	227
6.6	Proportion of Working-Age Adults Reporting Poor or Fair Health, by Disability Status, 1988–1996 (NHIS) and 1996–2000 (CPS)	228
6.7	Need for Personal Assistance among Working-Age Adults with Disabilities, by Ability to Work, 1988–1996	230
6.8	Functional Limitations among Working-Age Adults with Disabilities by Ability to Work, 1994–1995	230
6.9	Proportion of Working-Age Adults Needing Personal Assistance in Self-Care and Home-Management Activities, 1988–1996	231
6.10	Leading Body System Sources of Disability among Working-Age Adults, 1988–1996	232
6.11	Prevalence of Back Problems, Overall and as a Cause of Disability or Inability to Work, Ages 18–64, 1988–1996	236
6.12	Rates of Disability, Inability to Work, and Physician Contact Due to Depression or Bipolar Disorder, ages 18–64, 1988–1996	237
6.13	Condition-Specific Disability Rates for Selected Conditions among Working-Age Adults, 1988–1996	239
6.14	Prevalence of Disabling and Nondisabling Chronic Conditions among Working-Age Adults, 1988–1996	240
6.15	Actual and Predicted Rates of Disability and Inability to Work from Chronic Condition Prevalence, Ages 18–64, 1988–1996	242
6.16	Proportion of Working-Age Adults Considered Overweight or Obese, 1988–1996	243
6.17	Prevalence of Disability among Working-Age Adults, by Body System and Body Mass Index, 1988–1996	244
6.18	Rate of Disability Due to Back Problems or Diabetes, Actual and Expected from Body Mass Index Model, 1988–1996	246

6.19 Average Duration of Unemployment at Time of Interview, Seasonally Adjusted, 1988–1996 — 247
6.20 Chronic Conditions and Disability among Working-Age Adults, Seasonally Adjusted, 1988–1996 — 248
6.21 Proportion of Working-Age Adults Discussing a Chronic Condition with a Physician in Prior Two Weeks, Seasonally Adjusted, 1988–1996 — 49
6.22 Proportion of Working-Age Adults Seeing Doctor for Depression or Stress in Prior Two Weeks, Seasonally Adjusted, 1988–1996 — 251
6.23 Chronic Condition Prevalence among Working-Age Adults, by Body System, Seasonally Adjusted, 1988–1996 — 252

7.1 Employment Rates of Men With and Without Work Limitations Disabilities, Aged 18–64: SIPP Data — 267

10.1 Applications Respond to Program Changes — 349
10.2 SSDI Applications, Awards, and Beneficiaries — 350
10.3 Work Limited and Not Employed and SSDI Enrollment (Men, aged 45–54) as a Percent of Population, 1969–1996 — 352
10.4 Fraction of Men (Aged 45–54) with Work Limitations and Fraction Predicted by SSDI Enrollment 1969–1996 — 353
10.5 SSDI Application per Population for a One-Unit Demand Shock, 1978–1998 — 360
10.6 Percent of Nonelderly Adults Aged 25–64 Receiving Disability Benefits, 1984 and 1999 — 361

11.1 Percentage of Persons with Affective Disorders Who Report an Activity Limitation or Inability to Work — 384

Tables

1.1 Mean and Median Household-Size-Adjusted Real Income of Civilians, Aged 25–61, by Gender and Disability Status — 3
1.2 Employment Rates of Civilians Aged 25–61, by Gender and Disability Status — 4
1.3 Mean Real Income from Own Labor Earnings and Own Social Security Disability Insurance (SSDI) and Supplemental Security Income (SSI) for Civilians Aged 25–61, by Gender and Disability Status — 6

2.1	Summary of Disability in the NHIS, CPS, and SIPP	29
2A.1	Comparison Data Sets and Variable Definitions	61
2A.2	Disability Prevalence Rates Using Alternative Disability Definitions from the NHIS, CPS, and SIPP, by Gender	70
2A.3	Yearly Employment Rate Trends of Those with Disabilities in Alternatively Defined Disability Populations from the NHIS, CPS, and SIPP, by Gender	72
2A.4	Yearly Employment Rate Trends of Those without Disabilities in Alternatively Defined Disability Populations from the NHIS, CPS, and SIPP, by Gender	74
2A.5	Employment Rate Trends of the Subsample of the Work-Limitation-Based Disability Population Who Report Being "Able to Work" from the NHIS, CPS, and SIPP, by Gender	76
2A.6	Trends in the Proportion of the Work-Limitation-Based Disability Population Who Report Being "Able to Work" from the NHIS, CPS, and SIPP, by Gender	77
2A.7	Unemployment Rate and Labor Force Participation Trends of Those in the Work-Limitation-Based Disability Population from the NHIS, CPS, and SIPP, by Gender	78
2A.8	SSI and SSDI Beneficiary Rate Trends in the Work-Limitation-Based Disability Population from the CPS and SIPP, by Gender	80
3.1	Population Shares and Employment Rates of Those Reporting Work Limitation, by Gender, Age, Race, and Education (16 mutually exclusive groups) (percentages and percentage point changes)	103
3.2	Decomposition of the Percentage Point Change in the Employment Rate of Those Reporting Work Limitation, by Changes in Population Shares and Employment Rates and by Gender, Age, Race, and Education	105
3A.1	Prevalence of Work Limitation, by Gender, Age, Race, and Education	115
3A.2	Share Composition of Those Reporting Work Limitation, by Gender, Age, Race, and Education	116
3A.3	Share Composition of Those Reporting No Work Limitation, by Gender, Age, Race, and Education	117
3A.4	Employment Rates of Those Reporting Work limitations, by Gender, Age, Race, and Education	118
3A.5	Employment Rates of Those Reporting No Work Limitation, by Gender, Age, Race, and Education	119

3A.6 Population Shares and Employment Rates of Those Reporting   120
        No Work Limitations, by Gender, Age, Race, and Education
3A.7 Decomposition of the 1.8 Percentage Point Increase in the   121
        Employment Rate of Those Reporting No Work Limitations, by
        Changes in Population Shares and Employment Rates and by
        Gender, Age, Race, and Education
3A.8 Population Shares and Employment Rates of Those Reporting   122
        No Work Limitations, by Self-Reported Health

 4.1 Summary of Findings for Six Dimensions of Static   130
        Job Characteristics
4A.1 Job Requirements in the 1991 *Dictionary of Occupational Titles* 168
4A.2 Job Characteristics Used in the Analysis   171
4A.3 Regression Coefficients, 1990–2000, Dependent Variable   174
4A.4 Estimated Components of Change in the Proportion of Workers   175
        with Limitations, 1990–2000

 5.1 Condition Data Collection in Three Surveys   192
 5.2 Summary of Chronic Condition Categories   195
 5.3 Reported Prevalence of Chronic Conditions, by Costliness,   199
        Persons Aged 25–61
 5.4 Reported Prevalence of High-Cost Chronic Conditions among   199
        People with Work Limitations, Aged 25–61
 5.5 Annual Expenditures per Person, Aged 25–61, by Costliness   201
        of Chronic Conditions
 5.6 Health Insurance by Costliness of Chronic Conditions for   202
        Persons Aged 25–61
 5.7 Percent of Persons Aged 25–61 Employed Any Time During the   204
        Year, by Costliness of Chronic Conditions
 5.8 People with Work Limitations, Aged 25–61, Employed in the   205
        Past Two Weeks
 5.9 Decomposition of Change in Employment Rate for People with   207
        Work Limitations, Aged 25–61

 7.1 Summary of Empirical Studies of the Effects of Disability   268
        Discrimination Laws

 8.1 Alternative Disability Measures and Employment Change   288

10.1 Potential SSDI Income as a Percent of Current Earnings for Nonelderly Males at Various Percentiles of the Wage Distribution, 1979 and 1999   347

10.2 Change in Fraction (per 1,000) of Men Unable to Work, by Cause, 1983–1996   355

10.3 Change in Fraction (per 1,000) on SSDI, by Diagnostic Group, 1986–1996   356

Acknowledgments

In large part in response to the grass-roots disability empowerment movement, a sea change occurred in the goals of United States disability policy in the 1990s. The key insight of this movement is that a significant physical or mental impairment need not lead to a work disability. Rather, it is the interaction of a person's impairment with the social environment he or she faces that leads to an inability to work. Hence, changes in the social environment may be as effective, or even more effective, in increasing the employment of working-aged people with disabilities as medical or vocational rehabilitation efforts. Further, programs that help people with impairments to support themselves through productive use of their abilities (i.e., through work) are preferred to programs that provide income support and in-kind support to those with serious impairments on the condition that they severely limit the use of those abilities for work.

The Americans with Disabilities Act of 1990 is the most prominent change in social policy that focuses on the integration of working-aged people with disabilities into the workforce and away from dependence on disability benefits. In 1998, the Director of the National Institute for Disability and Rehabilitation Research (NIDRR), Kate Seelman, called for a new kind of Rehabilitation Research and Training Center that would measure the impact of the social environment on the employment of working-aged people with disabilities. This eventually led to the establishment of the Cornell Rehabilitation Research and Training Center (RRTC) for Economic Research on Employment Policy for People with Disabilities, under the leadership of Susanne Bruyère and the two editors of this volume, which was funded by a five-year cooperative agreement with NIDRR.

Early on, our RRTC's researchers were drawn into an ongoing dispute over the quality of the data used to measure the employment of working-aged people with disabilities. One result of this dispute is that much of the recent empirical analysis on the employment of people with disabilities done by social scientists has been called into question. Based on feedback from representatives of the disability community on our RRTC's Advisory Board, we believed that the lack of confidence in these data by government policymakers, as well as by the disability community, required that we investigate their validity before we carried out some of the research that we had proposed to NIDRR. After consultation with NIDRR, it was agreed that we would use RRTC funding to invite the leading social science scholars in this area to meet with policymakers, advocates, and leaders of grass-root disability organizations to: 1) examine the usefulness of the data; 2) assess what we could and could not learn about employment rate trends for people with disabilities from it; and 3) consider the implications of what we could learn for public policy.

The meeting, held in Washington, DC, in October 2001, was so successful in both the number and breadth of attendees and the quality of the discussion that, encouraged by NIDRR, we asked conference presenters to revise their work for inclusion in a book. The result is the first book to consider the validity of current data for measuring trends in the employment rate of people with disabilities in a comprehensive way, and to investigate the causes and consequences of the declining rate of employment shown in the data. The book uses rigorous empirical methods to document in a straightforward manner the importance of the social environment for the employment of working-aged people with disabilities, and points the way for future policies that will better achieve the disability policy goals established in the 1990s.

Much of the work on the book was funded by our cooperative agreement with NIDRR. The Social Security Administration generously provided additional support for our effort, through an inter-agency agreement with NIDRR. We thank the new Director of NIDRR, Steven Tingus, as well as our Project Officer, Ruth Brannon, for encouraging us to focus our NIDDR resources on this book. We also thank Kenneth McGill of the Social Security Administration for his role in providing additional support.

Many people were involved with the development of the content of this book, beginning with the development of the conference, and all deserve credit for it. Foremost among them are Susanne Bruyère, the Principle Investigator for the Cornell RRTC, who worked closely with us in organizing and carrying out the conference and who has provided constant encouragement to us in our efforts to complete this book, and Ruth Brannon, who has given us valuable guidance throughout the project. The members of our RRTC Advisory Board provided ongoing feedback and input for the conference and the book, through quarterly meetings: Monroe Berkowitz, Rutgers University; Robert A. Burns, Maryland Division of Rehabilitation Services; Bruce Flynn, Watson Wyatt Worldwide; Lex Frieden, Independent Living Research Utilization and Baylor College of Medicine; Deborah Kaplan, World Institute on Disability; Donald Kewman, University of Michigan Hospital; Corinne Kirchner, American Foundation for the Blind; John Kosciulek, University of Missouri-Columbia; Douglas Kruse, Rutgers University; Mitchell LaPlante, University of California-San Francisco; Michael Morris, Community Options, Inc.; Pat Owens, Independent Consultant; William Talley, Assumption College; Paul Wehman, Virginia Commonwealth University; and Tony Young, NISH.

We received very valuable help in planning the conference from an external committee set up for that purpose, consisting of: Susan Daniels, Daniels and Associates; Lex Frieden; Andy Imparato, American Association of People with Disabilities; Deborah Kaplan, World Institute on Disability; Corinne Kirchner; Pat Owens; Sue Suter, Consultant on Public Policy Issues; and Tony Young. The following organizations helped us obtain the visibility we sought for the conference in the disability community by becoming official sponsors for the conference and dissemination information about the conference to their members: The American Association of People with Disabilities, The American Foundation for the Blind, The Arc of the United States, The Association of Educators in Rehabilitation Community Programs, The International Association of Psychosocial Rehabilitation Services, The National Alliance for the Mentally Ill, The National Association of Rehabilitation Research and Training Centers, The National Council on Rehabilitation Education, The National Organization on Disability, NISH, The Paralyzed Veterans of America, The Society for Disability Studies, The SSI Coalition For a Responsible Safety Net, and The World Institute on Disability.

We are greatly indebted to the authors of the individual chapters for their efforts to substantially rework their original conference presentations in ways that would increase their accessibility to a broad audience and help us integrate them into a cohesive book. Two chapters, based primarily on material presented by others at the conference, were written especially for this book, and we would like to thank their authors for agreeing to write them: Thomas DeLeire (Chapter 7), and Nanette Goodman and Timothy Waidmann (Chapter 10). We would also like to thank three researchers who are not chapter authors, but who contributed through reviews of drafts of the same two chapters, which drew heavily on their earlier papers: Joshua Angrist (Massachusetts Institute of Technology, Chapter 7), David Autor (Harvard University, Chapter 10) and John Bound (University of Michigan, Chapter 10); Angrist and Autor also made presentations at the conference.

We also wish to thank Nanette Goodman for assisting us in all aspects of preparing the manuscript, with special appreciation for her help in making the chapters more consistent in language and reducing the professional jargon that is the unwanted bi-product of social science policy research, and Jennifer Duffy, for her proofreading and checking of stylistic requirements.

Ultimately, we take responsibility for the views expressed in the introduction and conclusion of this volume and the authors take responsibility for their individual chapters. The views expressed in this volume do not necessarily reflect those of NIDRR, SSA, or any of the various other organizations that provided support for individual chapters.

1
Introduction

Richard V. Burkhauser
David C. Stapleton
Cornell University

A major debate has begun over reports of an unprecedented decline in the employment rate of working-aged people with disabilities during the 1990s business cycle (1989–2000) by those using currently available data sources to track the employment and economic well-being of the U.S. population. The debate is occurring at two overlapping levels. The first is over the quality of the data, with some calling on the federal government to end its financial support for disseminating employment estimates for people with disabilities using currently available data (National Council on Disability 2002). Others argue that although the current data are usable within certain limits, the major findings on employment using these data are quite sensitive to the definitions used to capture the "relevant" population with disabilities, and have been used in a way that understates the employment success of public policies such as the Americans with Disabilities Act of 1990 (ADA). The second level of debate is over the specific causes of the decline found in the data. Researchers have made conflicting judgments over the relative importance of health and the social environment, especially public policies, in explaining this decline.

In the background of the academic debate over these issues are the concerns of policymakers, disability advocates, and people with disabilities over the success of their efforts to better integrate working-aged people with disabilities into the workforce, increase their employment, and reduce their dependence on disability-based income support programs. There is especially concern that the ADA—the centerpiece of the political movement to increase labor market access of people with disabilities—will be unfairly judged a failure based on partial and inappropriate measures of its success.

In October 2001, Cornell University's Rehabilitation Research and Training Center for Economic Research on Employment Policy for

Persons with Disabilities, funded by the U.S. Department of Education's National Institute on Disability and Rehabilitation Research (NIDRR), conducted a two-day conference in Washington, DC, to address the issues surrounding the decline in the employment rate of people with disabilities. The conference for the first time brought together the leading researchers on these issues and members of the policymaking and disability advocacy communities, including working-aged people with disabilities.

This book grew out of that conference, with support from both NIDRR and the Social Security Administration (SSA). The book is not, however, a traditional academic conference volume. Instead, we worked with the authors to make the final version of their work responsive both to the criticisms of their initial presentation by their fellow researchers and the more general audience at the conference. Our objective was to provide information that was accessible and credible to researchers and to the broader policymaking, advocacy, and grassroots disability communities. The result is a cohesive book that presents the latest research on the employment decline of working-aged people with disabilities in a way that is tightly focused on documenting this decline, evaluating the conflicting evidence of its causes, and spelling out the implications for public policy.

THE EMPLOYMENT AND ECONOMIC WELL-BEING OF WORKING-AGED PEOPLE WITH DISABILITIES

Table 1.1 uses data from the Current Population Survey (CPS) to revise Burkhauser, Daly, and Houtenville (2001). It shows that mean household income of (working-aged) men without disabilities increased by 9.4 percent and mean household income of women without disabilities increased by 12.6 percent between 1989, the peak year of the 1980s business cycle, and 2000, the peak of the 1990s business cycle. In contrast, the mean household income of men with disabilities fell by 2.9 percent and the mean household income of women with disabilities increased by 5.6 percent during the period.

The proximate reason for this dramatic difference in the fortunes of the working-aged population with and without disabilities was the even

Table 1.1 Mean and Median Household-Size-Adjusted Real Income of Civilians, Aged 25–61, by Gender and Disability Status[a]

Population[b]	Year			Percentage change[c]		
	1989	1992	2000	1989–92	1992–2000	1989–2000
Mean household income ($2,000)						
Men without disabilities	35,863	33,968	39,401	−5.4	14.8	9.4
Men with disabilities	21,178	19,774	20,572	−6.9	4.0	−2.9
Women without disabilities	32,430	31,247	36,774	−3.7	16.2	12.6
Women with disabilities	19,629	18,401	20,762	−6.5	12.1	5.6
Median household income ($2,000)						
Men without disabilities	31,899	30,253	34,146	−5.3	12.1	6.8
Men with disabilities	16,905	15,741	16,063	−7.1	2.0	−5.1
Women without disabilities	28,921	27,933	32,042	−3.5	13.7	10.2
Women with disabilities	14,939	13,589	15,633	−9.5	14.0	4.5

[a] Those younger than 25 or older than 61 or in the Armed Forces are excluded. Persons are considered to have a disability if they report having a health problem or disability that prevents them from working or limits the kind or amount of work they can do. Because top coding rules have varied over the history of the CPS, we consistently top code all income at the lowest common income percentile in all years across the CPS data from 1976–2001. Burkhauser, Daly, and Houtenville (2001) handled this problem by excluding the top and bottom 1 percent of the distribution.

[b] Disability status is for the year following the income year. In 1994, there were several changes to the CPS. It moved fully to computer-assisted survey interviews. Sample weights based on the 1980 Census were replaced with sample weights based on the 1990 Census. The Monthly Basic Survey was revised, and three new disability questions were added. It is possible that these changes affected the measurement of the population with disabilities either through changes in the sample weights or in the way respondents answered disability questions.

[c] When calculating percentage change, we use the average of the two years as the base.

SOURCE: Revised and updated calculations of Burkhauser, Daly, and Houtenville (2001) using March Current Population Survey, 1990–2001.

more dramatic divergence in their employment rates during the period (Table 1.2). The employment rate of men without disabilities was procyclical (i.e., followed the business cycle), declining during the recession years of the early 1990s, but then growing during the later recovery years. In contrast, the employment rate of men with disabilities fell both during the recession years and even more so during the recovery years of the 1990s. The long-term secular growth in the employment rate of women muted some of the cyclical effects on their employment rate. The employment rate of women without disabilities grew during both the recession and recovery years, but grew much more during the growth years. Women with disabilities experienced declines in their employment rate during the entire period, although the decline was smaller during the growth years. As Burkhauser et al. (2002) show, the failure of the employment rates of both men and women with disabilities to increase during the growth years of the 1990s business cycle (after 1992) was a complete reversal of the procyclical behavior of their employment rates during the 1980s business cycle.

Table 1.2 Employment Rates of Civilians Aged 25–61, by Gender and Disability Status[a]

	Year			Percentage change[c]		
Population[b]	1989	1992	2000	1989–92	1992–2000	1989–2000
Men without disabilities	96.1	94.8	95.2	−1.4	0.4	−1.0
Men with disabilities	44.0	41.6	33.1	−5.5	−22.9	−28.4
Women without disabilities	77.1	77.6	81.3	0.7	4.6	5.3
Women with disabilities	37.5	34.3	32.6	−8.9	−4.9	−13.8

[a] Those younger than 25 or older than 61 or in the Armed Force are excluded. Persons are considered to have a disability if they report having a health problem or disability that prevents them from working or limits the kind or amount of work they can do.

[b] Disability status is for the year following the income year. In 1994, there were several changes to the CPS. It moved fully to computer-assisted survey interviews. Sample weights based on the 1980 Census were replaced with sample weights based on the 1990 Census. The Monthly Basic Survey was revised, and three new disability questions were added. It is possible that these changes affected the measurement of the population with disabilities either through changes in the sample weights or in the way respondents answered disability questions.

[c] When calculating percentage change, we use the average of the two years as the base.

SOURCE: Revised and updated calculations of Burkhauser, Daly, and Houtenville (2001) using March Current Population Survey, 1990–2001.

The reason this unprecedented decline in employment did not have an even greater effect on the household income of those with disabilities during the period was that mean income from Social Security Disability Insurance (SSDI) and Supplemental Security Income (SSI) rose by 33.8 percent for men with disabilities, and rose by 48.6 percent for women with disabilities from 1989 to 2000 (Table 1.3). Those increases nearly offset the 34.6 percent decline in mean labor earnings for men with disabilities and added substantially to the gain of 13.8 percent in the labor earnings of women with disabilities, during the period.

During the 1990s business cycle (1989–2000), the employment rate of the population with disabilities was below its 1989 business cycle peak for both men and women with disabilities, and their income was more dependent on federal government programs. Given the robust economic expansion of the 1990s and the promise of greater independence that is embodied in the ADA, this decline in both employment and its importance for household income might reasonably be considered a social disaster for the working-aged population with disabilities. Hence, it is not surprising that this decline in measured employment has generated a major debate, represented in this book, over the quality of the numbers produced by current data sets and, if credible, the causes for this unprecedented decline.

IS THE DECLINE IN EMPLOYMENT A MEASUREMENT ABERRATION?

Although at face value the decline in the employment rates of men and women with disabilities generated by data from the CPS is unprecedented, there are those who would argue that either it is impossible to measure trends in the employment rate of people with disabilities in a meaningful way with these data, or that it is the wrong measure for assessing progress toward better employment outcomes for people with disabilities. In short, they would question whether this decline in employment of the working-aged population with disabilities in the CPS is a real phenomenon or simply an artifact of faulty or misapplied data.

Table 1.3 Mean Real Income from Own Labor Earnings and Own Social Security Disability Insurance (SSDI) and Supplemental Security Income (SSI) for Civilians Aged 25–61, by Gender and Disability Status[a]

Income source/ population[b]	Year			Percentage change[c]		
	1989	1992	2000	1989–1992	1992–2000	1989–2000
Own labor earnings						
Men without disabilities	31,434	37,046	37,046	−7.3	16.4	9.1
Men with disabilities	8,058	6,793	5,680	−17.0	−17.8	−34.6
Women without disabilities	16,065	16,632	20,240	3.5	19.6	23.0
Women with disabilities	4,250	4,092	4,880	−3.8	17.6	13.8
Own SSDI/SSI						
Men without disabilities	50	71	76	33.5	7.0	40.3
Men with disabilities	3,013	3,356	4,237	10.8	23.2	33.8
Women without disabilities	164	150	149	−8.7	−1.1	−9.8
Women with disabilities	2,004	2,380	3,292	17.2	32.1	48.6

[a] Those less than age 25 or more than age 61 or in the Armed Forces are excluded. Persons are considered to have a disability if they report having a health problem or disability that prevents them from working or limits the kind or amount of work they can do. All dollar amounts are in 2000 dollars. Because top coding rules have varied over the history of the CPS, we consistently top code all income at the lowest common income percentile in all years across the CPS data from 1976–2001. Burkhauser, Daly, and Houtenville (2001) handled this problem by excluding the top and bottom 1 percent of the distribution.

[b] Disability status is for the year following the income year. In 1994, there were several changes in the CPS. It moved fully to compter-assisted survey interviews. Sample weights based on the 1980 Census were replaced with sample weights based on the 1990 Census. The Monthly Basic Survey was revised, and three new disability questions were added. It is possible that these changes affected the measurement of the population with disabilities either through changes in the sample weights or in the way respondents answered disability questions.

[c] When calculating percentage change, we use the average of the two years as the base.

The root causes of the disagreement are the conceptual and practical difficulties in measuring disability in surveys. The seemingly esoteric debate about the definition of the population of people with disabilities has made it to the front pages of the nation's newspapers as courts grapple with the issue in response to ADA litigation. (The ADA defines disability as a "physical or mental impairment that substantially limits one or more of the major life activities.")

The old medical model, which posits that a disability is a deficiency within the individual, has been replaced by the widely held view that a disability is caused by an interaction between the individual's functional limitation and the social environment. When one asks a person if he or she has a "disability," or, more specifically, a "work disability," the answer might depend on the person's current employment status. A person who works despite a significant physical or mental impairment might say no, but the identical person might say yes if he or she is not employed. Burkhauser et al. (2002) show that work-limitation-based measures of the population with disabilities from the CPS and the National Health Interview Survey (NHIS) significantly underestimate the number of persons in the broader population with impairments and overrepresent those with impairments who are not employed. Hence, work-limitation-based measures of disabilities are potentially sensitive to changes in the social environment in which the questions are asked, such as the passage of the ADA, easing of the eligibility standards for SSDI or SSI, availability of private health insurance, or any factor that could influence employment prospects and, hence, the likelihood that a person with an impairment will report a work limitation in response to a survey question.

Concerns of this type have led some researchers to argue that the CPS and its work-limitation-based measure of the population with disabilities cannot be used to provide credible information to policymakers with respect to the employment of working-aged people with disabilities (Hale 2001). Along these lines, the National Council on Disability, in its report of July 26, 2002, recommends that "The Federal Government should not encourage or support the dissemination of employment data until a methodology for assessing employment rates among people with disabilities that is acceptable to leading researchers and demographers in the field and credible to persons with disabilities can be developed" (National Council on Disability 2002, p. 20).

However, Burkhauser et al. (2002) show that the employment trends for working-aged men and women found in the CPS and NHIS surveys based on a work-limitation definition of disability yield trends in employment rates between 1983 and 1996 are not significantly different from the employment trends for the broader population of people with an impairment. This is an important finding because a population defined on the basis of having an impairment is presumably less sensitive to changes in the social environment. The authors argue that work-limitation-based questions from the CPS as well as from other continuous and representative samples of the U.S. population can be used to evaluate trends in the employment of working-aged people with disabilities, and their causes.

Although all the authors in this book recognize the limitations of currently available data in defining the working-aged population with disabilities, and in evaluating the employment of this population, they all believe it is valid to use these current data for evidence-based policy analysis. Nonetheless, they have conflicting views on the most appropriate current data and the most appropriate subsamples of the data to use in that analysis.

COMPARING TRENDS IN THE EMPLOYMENT OF PEOPLE WITH DISABILITIES ACROSS DATA SETS AND DISABILITY POPULATION DEFINITIONS

The research on trends in the employment rate of people with disabilities is restricted by the questions asked in three large nationally representative surveys conducted in a consistent fashion during the 1980s and 1990s. Much of the research presented in this book is based on data from these data sets: the CPS, the NHIS, and the SIPP.

Burkhauser, Houtenville, and Wittenburg (Chapter 2) describe the strengths and limitations of each of these surveys and how the disability measures that can be constructed from their questions relate to medical and sociopolitical definitions of disability. They compare trends in employment rates for people with disabilities, based on the various surveys and the disability measures available in them. They find that although the level of the employment rate is sensitive to the survey and measure used, trends in the employment rate are much less sensitive. Employment rate trends based on functional limitation measures of the population with disabilities are very similar to those for the more problematic work-limitation measures of this population, indicating that the latter are capturing a stable population over a long period. Importantly, they point out that what seem to be differences in research findings based on differences in the original data, in fact stem from differences in the choice of disability populations that were drawn from these data sets. Hence, they argue that it is not differences in the quality of current data, but in the judgments of the researchers on how the data are used that explains the differences reflected in the various chapters of this book. (Compare, especially, how Kaye, Chapter 6, Kruse and Schur, Chapter 8, and Blanck, Schwochau, and Song, Chapter 9, define the relevant populations with disabilities with the definitions in DeLeire, Chapter 7, and Goodman and Waidmann, Chapter 10.)

IS THE OVERALL EMPLOYMENT RATE OF PEOPLE WITH DISABILITIES THE APPROPRIATE POLICY SUCCESS MEASURE?

Even if the employment rate of the overall population with disabilities is measured consistently over time, and employment trends across differing definitions of this population are similar, is the overall employment rate of this population the appropriate measure to assess the performance of current social policies? The population represented in the employment rate (i.e., the denominator of the rate) includes people who report being unable to work at all. Although, theoretically, all people with disabilities are able to work with appropriate accommodations, most would acknowledge that there is a group for which work is not a meaningful alternative. Including this group in the analysis may be misleading.

All the authors who have contributed to this book agree that:
- the overall employment rate of working-aged people with disabilities, as measured in various ways across several surveys, declined during the 1990s, or at least did not increase, while the overall employment rate of working-aged people without disabil-

ities grew during the period;
- the proportion of working-aged people with disabilities who say they are unable to work at all, or are unavailable for work, also measured in various ways, increased during the 1990s; and
- among those working-aged people with disabilities who say they are available or able to work, an increasing proportion is employed.

The authors are not, however, in agreement on whether those who say they are unable to work at all should be included in the measurement of employment rates for purposes of evaluating the general social welfare of working-aged people with disabilities, or the success of public policy in integrating them into the labor force. Nor do they agree on the reasons for the changes in the employment rates. The bulk of this book is devoted to providing a detailed examination of the various possible explanations for the overall employment rate decline among working-aged people with disabilities found in the data and its importance for policy analysis. Although some of the authors argue that it is the result of the unintended consequence of public policy and programs, others argue the decline is because of factors that mask the actual success of these same policies and programs.

ALTERNATIVE EXPLANATIONS OF THE OVERALL DECLINE IN EMPLOYMENT RATES

Demographic Factors and Education

One possible explanation for the decline in the overall employment rate of working-aged people with disabilities is a shift in the demographic composition of this population. If, for example, over time there are proportionally more women in this population, who traditionally have less attachment to the labor force, or older workers, who are less likely to undertake retraining after the onset of a disability, or less educated workers, who are less productive in the labor force, then the overall employment rate for the population with disabilities would show a decline that had little to do with changes in public policy. Alternatively, it may be that only one subpopulation within the overall population with disabilities is experiencing a dramatic drop in employment and masking the success of public policies on the majority of the population with disabilities.

Houtenville and Daly (Chapter 3), using data from the CPS during the 1980s and 1990s business cycles, find no credible evidence that composition changes of this sort or the dramatic decline in employment of a specific subpopulation "artificially" caused the decline in the 1990s.

They use a formal analytical method to separate, or "decompose," the employment rate decline into a component owing to changes in the composition of the population and a component owing to changes in the employment rate within demographic and educational subgroups during the two business cycles. They find that a downward trend in employment is apparent during the 1990s in each of the gender, age, race and education subgroups of people with disabilities they investigate, with no one subgroup explaining a substantial part of the decline. In contrast, they find that compositional changes in these subgroups had a much more important influence on the increases in the employment of working-aged people with disabilities during the 1980s business cycle.

Houtenville and Daly also conduct a decomposition by health status. Data availability limits the analysis to the years 1995–2000. During this short period, there is no significant change in the distribution of health status of people with disabilities, and the employment rate declines as much, or more, for those who report being in relatively good health as for others.

Changing Job Characteristics

Although changes in the composition of demographic and education groups within the working-aged population with disabilities cannot explain the dramatic decline in the employment rates of this group in the 1990s, it is possible that changes in the job market might offer such an explanation. Stapleton, Goodman, and Houtenville (Chapter 4) consider the possibility that changes in the nature of work (substantive complexity, relational or interactive nature, autonomy/control, task scope, physical demands, and terms of employment) have, on average, made it more difficult for people with work limitations to compete with others.

Using data from the CPS during the 1980s and 1990s, they show that although changes in the composition of jobs might have contributed to a long-term decline in the employment of people with work limitations, such changes are too small to explain the dramatic decline in their employment found in these data. Further, similar changes were occurring in the 1980s, when the employment rate for people with work limitations was not declining. Although this exercise provides some evidence that changes in the composition of jobs cannot explain much of the decline, it is possible that changes within these jobs could. That is, the jobs themselves might have changed in ways that make it more difficult for people with work limitations to compete. The authors point out, however, that the literature on this subject does not provide any indication of a sharp departure from long-term trends in the nature of work that could explain the decline during the 1990s in the employment rate for people with work limitations.

It is also possible that declines in job security, which result in more frequent job changes and reduced attachment to a specific employer, might have contributed to the employment rate decline because, on average, it is more difficult for workers with limitations to change jobs than for others. The literature provides some evidence that job security has declined, but the authors conclude that the decline has been very gradual, and began well before the decline in the employment rate for people with disabilities.

Health Care Costs

Many working-aged people with disabilities have chronic conditions that require substantial medical care, and growth in the cost of this care, coupled with how it is financed, might explain some of the decline in their employment rate. Most private medical insurance is purchased via employers. People with disabilities may obtain public insurance through SSDI (Medicare) or SSI (Medicaid). Although access to Medicaid for those not receiving SSI has been expanding in recent years, it is still quite limited. Rising health care costs have made it more expensive for employers to employ people with disabilities. Most have passed on a significant share of the higher costs for health insurance to employees and, to reduce premium growth, have elected to purchase plans that have an increasing number of use restrictions. Thus, increases in the relative costs of treating high-cost conditions over time may have both made employers more reluctant to hire people with these conditions and reduced the attractiveness of employment for people with such conditions as a way to obtain health insurance relative to participation in SSDI or SSI.

Hill, Livermore, and Houtenville (Chapter 5) use data from the 1987 National Medical Expenditure Survey (NMES) and the 1996 and 1997 Medical Expenditure Panel Survey (MEPS) to test this possible explanation for the employment decline of working-aged people with disabilities between the 1980s and the 1990s. They divide individuals in their samples in 1987 and in 1996–1997 by the cost of treating their chronic health conditions—high-cost, medium-cost, low-cost, very low-cost and no chronic conditions—and show that the average expenditures on high-, medium-, and low-cost chronic conditions significantly increased during the period, as did the share of the samples that had high- and medium-cost chronic conditions. Furthermore, they show that the employment rate of those with high-cost chronic conditions fell relative to the rate for those without such conditions.

To further test the importance of increases in health care costs on employment, they repeat this exercise using samples of people with work limitations in the NHIS. They compare the employment rates of those with and without high-cost chronic conditions in 1984–1987 with those same groups in 1993–1996, using the condition groups developed with the MEPS and NMES data. They hypothesize that if growth in health care costs contributed to the employment rate decline, the employment rate for those with work limitations and high-cost conditions should fall relative to the rate for those with work limitations but no high-cost conditions. The finding for women is consistent with this hypothesis, but the finding for men is not. If growth in health care costs explains the result for women, it is difficult to explain the finding for men.

Finally, as done in some of the earlier chapters, they conduct a decomposition exercise to assess the extent to which the increase in the prevalence of high-cost chronic conditions among people with work limitations and the decline in their employment rate might account for the decline in the employment rate for all people with work limitations.

They find a negative effect for both men and women, but the size is small relative to changes in employment rates during the period they study.

Increasing Severity of Disabilities

Rather than focusing on the cost of health care service for chronic conditions or changes in the social environment, one could argue that it is simply a rise in the share of very severe, work-limiting impairments and chronic conditions within the overall population that is responsible for the decline in the overall employment rate of working-aged people with disabilities. Once this shift in underlying medically based factors is taken into consideration, it might be that the employment of those with disabilities who are "able to work at all" greatly improved in the 1990s.

Kaye (Chapter 6) considers this possibility. He first uses NHIS and CPS data to show that the overall employment rates of working-aged people with disabilities did not rise in the 1990s, focusing on those who report a limitation in any major activity, including work. Similar to Burkhauser and coauthors (Chapter 2), and Kruse and Schur (Chapter 8), however, Kaye then shows that the employment rate of the subset of the population with activity limitations who reported being "able to work at all" rose in the 1990s. Although the exact employment rates reported in these three chapters vary because of differences in the years used and in their definition of the population with disabilities (and its "able to work at all" subpopulation), what is consistent across the three studies is that the significant, although declining, share of the overall population with disabilities who describe themselves as "able to work at all" saw increased employment rates during the 1990s while the employment rate of the overall population with disabilities declined. Where Kaye departs from Burkhauser and coauthors (Chapter 2), DeLeire (Chapter 7), and Goodman and Waidmann (Chapter 10) is in his explanation for the dramatic decline in the share of the working-aged population with disabilities that self-report being able to work at all.

Although Kaye does not perform a formal decomposition exercise, it is helpful to think of the arguments in his chapter as similar in design to those in the previous three chapters. Using NHIS data, Kaye finds that the prevalence of impairments and chronic conditions increased during the period. Like Burkhauser and coauthors (Chapter 2), he argues that a population definition based on impairment or chronic health condition questions is less subject to changes in the social environment and, hence, provides a better continuous measure of the "population with disabilities" than do other population definitions (e.g., work-limitation-based definitions). The two chapters also agree that the vast majority of the working-aged population with impairments and chronic conditions work and do not report a work limitation.

Kaye then argues that it is the rise and change in the mix of these underlying impairments and chronic conditions that have caused the decline in the share of those with activity limitations who say they are able to work at all. Kaye examines data on major chronic conditions and concludes that, for those reporting each of the conditions he considers, the proportion reporting an activity limitation (work limitation or limitation in other major life activity) and the proportion reporting they are unable to work at all have both remained constant. Thus, for each condition, there has been no change in the proportion of those with activity limitations who report they are able to work at all. This is a critical finding because, Kaye argues, this would not be the case if the social environment were causing changes in the ability to work over time among those with chronic conditions. If this conclusion is correct, it is not changes in the social environment, but rather the increase in the share of chronic conditions that result in low "able to work at all" rates among those with activity limitations that is driving the overall decline in the population with these activity limitations who are able to work at all.

Kaye further considers the possible causes of the rapid growth in the prevalence of conditions that result in low "able to work at all" rates—musculoskeletal, respiratory, nervous system, and mental health conditions. He argues that the major increases in these chronic conditions are linked to the obesity epidemic and stress-related disorders caused by the 1991 recession.

Most important from a policy perspective, Kaye argues that, "If the goal is to measure improvements in the level of *employment opportunity* for people with disabilities, as the ADA's goal statement suggests, one should use a measure that includes those people who are likely to take advantage of such opportunities and leaves out everyone else" (page 226). When he and others omit those who report they are unable to work at all, on the grounds that they cannot take advantage of employment opportunities, the employment rate of those remaining (those people with disabilities who report they can work at all) has risen since the passage of ADA.

The Americans with Disabilities Act

We would expect that the declining unemployment rates during the growth years of the 1990s business cycle would have caused employers to look beyond their traditional workforce to the millions of working-aged people with disabilities. Yet, as we have seen, the overall employment rates of those with disabilities declined during this period. Some argue that the ADA impeded this process. The ADA, passed in 1990 and effective in 1992, was intended, among other things, to increase the employment of people with disabilities by requiring firms to make reasonable accommodations for "qualified" employees and by banning discrimination against people with disabilities in hiring, firing and pay. Proponents claimed the ADA would induce companies to make adjustments necessary to employ workers with disabilities, and would reduce unlawful discrimination. Critics argued that the unintended consequence of the increased costs of accommodation and the increased threat of litigation resulting from the act would be a decline in the employment of the very people the ADA was meant to protect.

DeLeire (Chapter 7) makes the case that the ADA is responsible for the decline in the employment of working-aged people with disabilities. DeLeire first lays out the conditions under which protective labor laws could induce employers, on net, to employ more or fewer protected workers, and the methods used to measure the net effect of such protective laws. He explains that models in the economics literature used to test the relative importance of the ADA are the same as those that were used to show that the 1964 Civil Rights Act improved the employment rates of African Americans in the 1960s and beyond. In the case of the ADA, however, the results using these models show the opposite outcome. He concludes that, after controlling for all other factors, the employment of working-aged people with disabilities fell after the ADA went into effect.

Based on data from the CPS and SIPP, Acemoglu and Angrist (2001) and DeLeire (2000) use econometric modeling to show that the employment of the working-aged population with disabilities fell after passage of the ADA in 1990 and after its effective starting date in 1992. Importantly, both of these studies define the population with disabilities as all working-aged persons reporting a work limitation. DeLeire defends the use of this population rather than a subset of it that reports being "able to work at all" because, he believes, the answer to the "able to work at all" question is affected by the social environment that he is examining. That is, he believes that the social environment can influence whether a person with work limitations will report being able to work at all, and that to focus only on those with disabilities who so report will understate the effects that the ADA and other social factors have on employment of the larger population with disabilities who could have worked at all.

DeLeire concludes that the difference in the employment outcome of the 1964 Civil Rights Act and the ADA is likely the result of the burden that accommodation costs place on employers, and urges that policies to lighten that load be considered to reverse this outcome.

Kruse and Schur (Chapter 8) agree with the basic theoretical model described by DeLeire, but argue that both the DeLeire (2000) and the Acemoglu and Angrist (2001) papers are flawed because they fail to control for all other factors in their empirical models. Similar to Kaye (Chapter 6), Kruse and Schur focus on the dramatic changes that have occurred in the severity of impairments and chronic conditions in the overall population with disabilities. They report that their own work (Kruse and Schur 2003) using SIPP data replicates the DeLeire (2000) finding of a fall in the employment of the overall working-aged population with work limitations, but they go on to show that the employment rate of the work-limited population who report being able to work at all rises following passage of the ADA. They show that the results are quite sensitive to alternative definitions of the population with disabilities.

In effect, Kruse and Schur, although acknowledging the criticisms of others in this book, line up with Kaye in their conclusions that those who self-report being unable to work at all should not be included in policy analysis of the ADA. Thus, they conclude that increases in the severity of impairments in the working-aged population with disabilities reduced the overall employment rate, and that the ADA, or possibly other changes in the social environment, had a positive effect on the employment of working-aged people with disabilities.

Blanck, Schwochau, and Song (Chapter 9) approach the economics-based discussion in DeLeire and Kruse and Schur from the broader perspective of the law. They criticize the theoretical model used to analyze protective legislation such as the 1964 Civil Rights Act and the ADA as too narrow in its assumptions about competitive labor and product markets. They provide a review of the theoretical literature that explicitly accounts for market failures via imperfect information and difference in the productivity of workers with and without disabilities. They argue that simple competitive models fail to take into account additional possible reasons why firms that are not constrained by perfectly competitive markets would be willing to employ additional workers following the passage of protective legislation. Like both DeLeire and Kruse and Schur, they conclude that theoretical models are ambiguous in their predictions of the impact of the ADA on employment. Ultimately, the only way to assess the impact is through empirical research.

Blanck, Schwochau, and Song go on to provide a more detailed institutional argument for the use of the kind of subpopulations discussed by both Kaye and Kruse and Schur to study the consequences of the ADA on the employment of its specific protected class. They argue that because the ADA was intended to focus on only a small subset of the population with chronic conditions or work limitations, empirical analysis of its consequences should focus solely on the outcomes in its intended protected class. They conclude that such research has not yet been done, and that it is premature to implicate the ADA as the main cause of the decline in the employment rate for people with disabilities.

Changes in Income Support Policies

The SSDI and SSI programs are designed to provide cash benefits to individuals who have impairments that prevent "any substantial gainful activity." A large economics-based literature links changes in the size of the SSDI and SSI populations to changes in program eligibility criteria and their enforcement and to the generosity of program benefits relative to market wages (see Bound and Burkhauser 1999 for a review of this literature with respect to SSDI, and Daly and Burkhauser forthcoming for a review with respect to SSI). Because not being "able to work at all" is essentially a precondition for receiving benefits, some argue that changes in program rules might have induced a greater proportion of those with work limitations to leave the labor force in the 1990s and declare themselves unable to work at all so they could receive benefits. That is, some people with disabilities might rationally choose SSDI or SSI benefits over work or continuing to look for work if unemployed, given their expected wages and the costs, both monetary and nonmonetary, of working.

Goodman and Waidmann (Chapter 10) review the evidence that the expansion of the SSDI program during the late 1980s and early 1990s played a central role in the rise in the fraction of men who had work limitations and reported being unable to work at all. They primarily focus on two papers, Autor and Duggan (2003) and Bound and Waidmann (2002), which use data from the CPS and a work-limitation measure of disability, to argue that changes in SSDI eligibility and benefits are primarily responsible for the decline in the employment of working-aged people with disabilities. They show, using data from the CPS and NHIS, a close correlation between increased enrollment in the SSDI program and decreased employment during the past 30 years. The authors then argue that program expansions, which began in 1984, reduced the employment rate of working-aged people with disabilities in the early 1990s in two ways. First, many workers made eligible by the easing of eligibility standards in the mid 1980s began applying for SSDI benefits when the economy began deteriorating between 1990 and 1992. Second, the wage indexing method used in the formula for determining benefit levels had the unintended consequence of increasing the value of the benefit, relative to wages, for low-wage workers. They argue that it was the change in SSDI eligibility rules and benefit growth for low-wage workers during the period, rather than a change in the underlying severity of impairment or chronic conditions, that led to the sharp decline in the employment rates of those who reported work limitations in the CPS data. Empirically, they show that increases in the SSDI rolls account for the entire rise in the fraction of the population who both report that they have a work limitation and are not employed.

WHO IS RIGHT?

Although the authors agree that the employment rate for all people with disabilities declined during the 1990s, they sharply disagree on the main cause. We are left with three main contenders:

- increases in the severity of impairments and health conditions among those with work limitations or activity limitations, as argued by Kaye (Chapter 6) and Kruse and Schur (Chapter 8);
- the passage and implementation of the ADA, as argued by DeLeire (Chapter 7); and
- easing of the eligibility standards and increases in the relative benefits of the SSDI and SSI programs, as argued by Goodman and Waidmann (Chapter 10).

At this point, we leave the reader to weigh the evidence and arguments presented in Chapters 2–10. We provide our own assessment of the evidence in the book's concluding chapter. We also consider the implications that the findings have for public policy.

Note

The authors wish to thank Ludmila Robka for her research assistance in updating the Burkhauser, Daly, and Houtenville (2001) tables used in this chapter as well as Andrew Houtenville for his help in assuring the accuracy of these values. We also thank the National Institute on Disability and Rehabilitation Research (NIDRR) and the Social Security Administration (SSA) for supporting our work on this chapter. We would also like to thank NIDRR's Ruth Brannon and our colleague Susanne Bruyère for their encouragement and guidance. The opinions we express are our own and do not represent official positions of NIDRR, SSA, or Cornell University.

References

Acemoglu, Daron, and Joshua Angrist. 2001. "Consequences of Employment Protection? The Case of the Americans with Disabilities Act." *Journal of Political Economy* 109(5): 915–957.

Autor, David, and Mark Duggan. 2003. "The Rise in Disability Recipiency and the Decline in Unemployment." *Quarterly Journal of Economics* 118(1): 157–205.

Bound, John, and Richard Burkhauser. 1999. "Economic Analysis of Transfer Programs Targeted on People with Disabilities." In *Handbook of Labor Economics,* Vol. 3c, Orley Ashenfelter and David Card, eds. Amsterdam: Elsevier Science, pp. 3417–3528.

Bound, John, and Timothy Waidmann. 2002. "Accounting for Recent Declines in Employment Rates among the Working-Aged Disabled." *Journal of Human Resources* 37(2): 231–250.

Burkhauser, Richard V., Mary C. Daly, and Andrew J. Houtenville. 2001. "How Working Age People with Disabilities Fared Over the 1990s Business Cycle." In *Ensuring Health and Income Security for an Aging Workforce*, P. Budetti, R.V. Burkhauser, J. Gregory, and H.A. Hunt, eds. Kalamazoo, MI: W.E. Upjohn Institute for Employment Research, pp. 291–346.

Burkhauser, Richard V., Mary C. Daly, Andrew J. Houtenville, and Nigar Nargis. 2002. "Self-Reported Work-Limitation Data: What They Can and Cannot Tell Us." *Demography* 39(3): 541–555.

Daly, Mary C., and Richard V. Burkhauser. Forthcoming. "The Supplemental Security Income Program." In *Means-Tested Transfer Programs in the United States*, Robert Moffitt, ed. Chicago: University of Chicago Press.

DeLeire, Thomas. 2000. "The Wage and Employment Effects of the Americans with Disabilities Act." *Journal of Human Resources* 35(4): 693–715.

Hale, Thomas. 2001. "Lack of a Disability Measure in Today's Current Population Survey." *Monthly Labor Review* 124(7): 38–40.

Kruse, Douglas, and Lisa Schur. 2003. "Employment of People with Disabilities Following the ADA." *Industrial Relations* 42(1): 31–66.

National Council on Disability. 2002. National Disability Policy: A Progress Report (December 2000–December 2001). Available at: <http://www.ncd.gov/newsroom/publications/progressreport_07-26-02.html>. (Accessed: August 20, 2002.)

2
A User's Guide to Current Statistics on the Employment of People with Disabilities

Richard V. Burkhauser
Cornell University

Andrew J. Houtenville
Cornell University

David C. Wittenburg
The Urban Institute

The passage of the American with Disabilities Act (ADA) of 1990 was a major political victory for those who believe that working-aged people with disabilities should be fully integrated into the workforce. The intellectual underpinnings of this belief are first, that the path to economic independence is through market work, and second, that the social environment is a more powerful factor in determining employment outcomes than is an individual's impairment. The ADA aims to change the workplace environment and hence increase the employment of people with disabilities by mandating that their employers provide them with reasonable accommodations and protecting them from employment discrimination.[1]

This recognition by social policymakers of the centrality of work for people with disabilities increases the need for reliable statistics to monitor their workforce outcomes and to determine the degree to which social policies aimed at fully integrating people with disabilities into the workforce are succeeding. To do so requires nationally representative survey information that can track the size of the working-aged population with disabilities, its employment success, and the factors that influence such outcomes.

A new and highly controversial literature using currently available, nationally representative employment data sets—the National Health

Interview Survey (NHIS), the Current Population Survey (CPS), and the Survey of Income and Program Participation (SIPP)—argues that the employment of working-aged people with disabilities fell dramatically relative to the rest of the working-aged population after the passage of the ADA (see especially Acemoglu and Angrist 2001; Bound and Waidmann 2002; Burkhauser, Daly, and Houtenville 2001; DeLeire 2000). Even more controversially, Acemoglu and Angrist (2001) and DeLeire (2000) argue that the ADA is primarily responsible for the decline. Critics of this literature, using alternative definitions of the working-aged population with disabilities, argue that the employment rate of working-aged people with disabilities has actually increased since the passage of the ADA, and that the unemployment rate of this population has declined (see especially Kaye 2002 and Chapter 6; Kruse and Schur Chapter 8). Still others dismiss all of these results as fundamentally flawed given that they are based on self-reported work-limitation data that capture neither the actual working-aged population with disabilities nor its employment trends over time (see especially Hale 2001; Kirchner 1996).

Here, we step back from the controversy surrounding the impact of the ADA on employment and focus on two fundamental questions related to measuring the employment outcomes of people with disabilities. First, can a reasonable operational definition of disability be developed from current surveys that will enable policymakers to track the size and employment outcomes of that population? And if yes, are the findings sensitive to alternative definitions of disability and employment?

To address the first question, we use a conceptualization of disability based on Nagi (1965, 1991) and the World Health Organization (Jette and Bradley 2002) to put alternative operational definitions of the working-aged population with disabilities into a consistent context. We argue that questions contained in current data sets are sufficient to determine trends in the prevalence and employment success of working-aged people with disabilities based on reasonable definitions of disability, although efforts should be pursued to improve questions in existing surveys.

To address the second question, we present estimates of the size and employment success of alternatively measured populations of working-aged men and women with disabilities during the 1980s and the 1990s using data from the NHIS, CPS, and SIPP. We find that the employment rates of working-aged (aged 25–61) men with disabilities fell sharply in the 1990s, while the employment rates of working-aged women with disabilities showed a somewhat smaller decline. The size of the working-aged population with disabilities and its employment success are sensitive to the data we use to capture it, as well as to the types of questions available within a given data set. Nonetheless, we find declining employment trends regardless of whether we define disability based on impairment (NHIS) or activity limitations (NHIS, CPS, or SIPP).

We also examine the potential differences between our findings and those of others who find a more positive employment outlook for people with disabilities (Kaye 2002 and Chapter 6; Kruse and Schur Chapter 8). We show that such differences in employment success are primarily caused by differences in the disability population followed and the employment success measure used, rather than by differences in the survey data itself. Specifically, we show that although our findings of declining employment in the 1990s are robust across impairment- and activity-limitation populations, more positive employment trends can be found using a subcategory of these populations that excludes those who also report being unable to do any work. We argue that using this narrower measure of employment is inappropriate for measuring the success of public policies because the goal of these policies is the integration of all working-aged people with disabilities into employment. The same is true with respect to focusing on the unemployment rate rather than the employment rate. Both these narrower success measures ignore the growing share of the working-aged population in the 1990s with impairment or activity limitations who are, based on their self-reports, considered outside of the labor market.

Our findings are relevant to researchers and policymakers interested in understanding the changing employment outcomes of people with disabilities during the past two decades. We provide a user's guide to the underlying data and assumptions made by researchers attempting to measure the size and employment success of working-aged men and women with disabilities. We offer no firm conclusion about the impact of the ADA or other disability policy changes (e.g., changes in Social Security disability program policy) on employment. However, we strongly argue that when theoretically appropriate populations with disabilities are followed, and appropriate measures of their employment success are used, the employment of people with disabilities fell in the 1990s.

DATA DESCRIPTION

The three data sources for our analysis all include a nationally representative sample of the population, along with some information on activity limitations and health status. The NHIS is an annual cross-sectional survey of approximately 100,000 noninstitutionalized civilians conducted by the U.S. Centers for Disease Control and Prevention. A major advantage of the NHIS is that it includes detailed health and impairment information, as well as general questions about limitations found in other national surveys. Of particular importance here, each year, one-sixth of NHIS respondents are directly asked about their impairments (e.g., "deaf in both ears," "blind in both eyes," etc.) via a checklist without first going through a screener question. Thus, persons with impairments are identified regardless of whether they report an activity limitation or a doctor visit or a number of other positive screener responses. This allows researchers to capture a random sample of the population with this set of impairments.

Unfortunately, not all impairments are included in the checklist. The most serious omissions are mental impairments other than mental retardation. Although information about mental illness can be obtained from the NHIS, it comes only from those who first answer yes to a screener question (e.g., do you have an activity limitation, have you been to a doctor recently, etc.). A sample of those with a mental illness drawn in this way will miss persons with mental illness who do not have such limitations or health care access (see Houtenville 2002 for a more detailed discussion of this problem in using NHIS data). For this reason, it is difficult to disentangle yearly changes in the prevalence of a condition from changes in access to a doctor or other environmental changes that affect one's likelihood of being asked the condition question in the first place. With regard to mental health conditions, Kaye (2002 and Chapter 6) uses information on health conditions and impairments that is obtained from screener questions and, as he recognizes, runs the risks associated with this decision.

In general, comparable questions are available in the NHIS starting in 1983, although the survey changed substantially in 1997. A drawback of the NHIS is that it includes relatively limited information on employment and program participation. Burkhauser et al. (2002), Kaye (2002 and Chapter 6), Hill, Livermore, and Houtenville (Chapter 5), and Trupin et al. (1997) have used the NHIS to examine employment outcomes of people with disabilities.

The CPS is an annual cross-sectional survey of approximately 150,000 noninstitutionalized civilians collected by the U.S. Census Bureau and the Bureau of Labor Statistics. It is the main source of official employment and income statistics in the United States. The major advantage of the CPS is that its design and size allow for state-level estimates and that its work-limitation question has been consistently asked since 1981. A major drawback, however, is that it includes very limited health information. Acemoglu and Angrist (2001), Bound and Waidmann (2002), Burkhauser, Daly, and Houtenville (2001), and Burkhauser et al. (2002) have each used the CPS to examine employment outcomes of people with disabilities. Almost all the chapters in this book rely on CPS data in part or in whole to trace the employment of working-aged people with disabilities.

The SIPP is a longitudinal survey collected by the Census Bureau and the Bureau of Labor Statistics that includes several panels of varying sample size, ranging from approximately 40,000 noninstitutionalized persons (1991 panel) to 95,000 noninstitutionalized persons (1996 panel). We use data from the 1990, 1991, 1992, 1993, and 1996 SIPP panels to capture disability prevalence and employment rates for the months of January in 1990, 1991, 1992, 1993, and 1997, respectively.[2] The SIPP gathers basic information about work limitations in the core of each panel. In addition, during its special topical module interviews, it gathers more general information on other activity limitations.[3] Burkhauser and Wittenburg (1996), DeLeire (2000), Kruse and Schur (Chapter 8), McNeil (2000), and Maag and Wittenburg (2002) have used these data to examine employment outcomes of people with disabilities.

Each of these data sources has advantages and disadvantages for examining trends in the employment of people with disabilities. The

NHIS includes several years of consistent and comprehensive information on health, including a series of questions regarding specific impairments, but it has relatively limited information on employment and program participation outcomes. The CPS includes 20 years of detailed data on employment and program participation, but only includes a few questions on general health and work limitations. Finally, the SIPP includes detailed employment and program participation information, as well as some information on limitations in specific activities, but only a few SIPP panels are available for the analysis.

A major issue in measuring trends using these data sets is that some of the disability or outcome measures may change over time in each survey. These changes may, in turn, bias some of the observed trends. For example, McNeil (2000) raises several questions regarding the comparability of disability measures across SIPP panels because of inconsistencies in measured disability prevalence in these panels from 1990 through 1996.[4] We rely on disability questions in the NHIS, CPS, or SIPP, which have been consistently asked across all years.[5] Table 2.1 summarizes the definitions we use for disability populations in each of our data sources.[6]

Our analysis in the ensuing sections focuses on working-aged men and women aged 25–61. This limited age range avoids confusing reductions in work associated with disability with reductions or declines associated with retirement at older ages or initial transitions into the labor force related to education or job shopping at younger ages.

CONCEPTUALIZING DISABILITY

To measure the employment of the working-aged population with disabilities, it is first necessary to define that population. Unfortunately, unlike age or gender, disability is a far more controversial concept to define and measure. There is no universal agreement on the most appropriate definition of the population with disabilities. For example, Mashaw and Reno (1996) argue that the appropriateness of any definition of disability depends on the purpose for which it is used. They document more than 20 definitions of disability used for pur-

Table 2.1 Summary of Disability in the NHIS, CPS, and SIPP

Measure	Definition	Conceptualization level
NHIS		
Impairment	Respondents are asked if they have any of the following impairments: "blindness in both eyes, other visual impairments, deafness in both ears, other hearing impairments, stammering and stuttering, other speech impairments, mental retardation, absence of both arms/hands, one arm/hand, fingers, one or both legs, feet/toes, kidney, breast, muscle of extremity, tips of fingers, and/or toes, complete paralysis of entire body, one side of body, both legs, other extremity, cerebral palsy, partial paralysis one side of body, legs, other extremity, other complete or partial paralysis, curvature or other deformity of back or spine, orthopedic impairment of the back, spina bifida, deformity/orthopedic impairment of hand, fingers, shoulder(s), other upper extremity, flatfeet, clubfoot, other deformity/orthopedic impairment, and cleft palate." Respondents receive one of six condition lists that ask them if they have a specific condition (we focus on conditions in list #2). This method yields a random sample because being asked about a condition is not dependent on one's response to another question. This method captures those with specific conditions but who may or may not report health or functioning difficulties. Only one-sixth of the sample is directly asked about a specific condition.	Impairment
Work limitation	"Does any impairment or health problem NOW keep [person] from working at a job or business? Is [person] limited in the kind OR amount of work [person] can do because of any impairment?"	Activity
CPS		
Work limitation	"Does anyone in this household have a health problem or disability which prevents them from working or which limits the kind or amount of work they can do? [If so,] who is that? (Anyone else?)"	Activity

(continued)

Table 2.1 (continued)

Measure	Definition	Conceptualization level
One year limitation	Any person who reports that he or she has a work limitation in two consecutive CPS interviews one year apart	Longer-term activity
SIPP		
Work limitation	"Does __ have a physical, mental or other health condition which limits the kind or amount of work __ can do?"	Activity
Housework limitation	"Does __ have a physical, mental or other health condition which limits the kind or amount of work __ can do around the house?"	Activity
Limitations in other activities	"Because of a physical or mental health condition, does __ have difficulty doing any of the following by himself/herself (exclude the effects of temporary conditions): Does __ have any difficulty getting around inside the home? Does __ have any difficulty getting around outside the home, for example to shop or visit a doctor's office? Does __ have any difficulty getting into and out of bed or a chair? Does __ have any difficulty taking a bath or a shower? Does __ have any difficulty getting dressed? Does __ have any difficulty eating? Does __ have any difficulty using the toilet, including getting to the toilet? Does __ have any difficulty keeping track of money and bills? Does __ have any difficulty preparing meals? Does __ have any difficulty doing light housework, such as washing dishes or sweeping a floor?"	Activity

SOURCE: Derived from various documentation of the National Health Interview Survey (NHIS) 1983–1996, various panels of the Survey of Income and Program Participation (SIPP), and the Current Population Survey (CPS) (1981–2000). See Appendix 2A for details.

poses of entitlement to public or private income transfers, government services, or statistical analysis. Unfortunately, no existing, large, general employment-based data set provides sufficient information on the pathologies, impairments, functional limitations, environmental surroundings, and employment outcomes of a representative sample of the U.S. population to fully capture all these potential definitions.

Most of the new work on the employment of people with disabilities comes from the economics literature, where researchers' definitions of disability frequently are functions of already available nationally representative data rather than original data collection or clinical experience. In most surveys of employment and household income, the data on health come from a small set of questions that elicit self-reported responses on whether a person's health limits the kind or amount of work he or she can perform. Caution must be exercised in using global self-reported health measures because they are subjective and can vary from individual to individual. More important, health responses may not be independent of the economic variables being examined (Bound and Burkhauser 1999).

Hale (2001) criticizes the new literature on the employment of working-aged people with disabilities because its findings come from a work-limitation population in the CPS and SIPP. He claims that these results are not representative of the fuller population with disabilities. However, he fails to present an alternative conceptual or operational disability population definition. Rather, he suggests that as yet unspecified health questions be added to the CPS that would better capture this population.

Although no survey questions on disability are ever likely to perfectly capture the true population with disabilities (if one even exists), self-reported answers to questions on currently fielded national surveys have been used to capture representative samples and subsamples of this population. In fact, numerous researchers have shown that self-reported measures of work limitations are highly correlated with both objective assessments of health and clinical measures of disability (see Bound and Burkhauser 1999 for a review of this literature). Nonetheless, any self-reported disability questions must be used with caution, particularly if the answers are sensitive to the respondent's socioeconomic environment.

In Figure 2.1 we place the available empirical evidence based on disability questions from the NHIS, CPS, and SIPP into a framework based on two prominent conceptualizations of disability. The square represents the entire working-aged population, and each of the circles represents a particular population with disabilities.

The largest circle ("Impairment") within the square represents those who report having an impairment. By impairment, we mean a physical or mental loss or abnormality that limits a person's capacity to function. This population could be considered to represent the potential population that many of the supporters of the ADA intended to protect.

Figure 2.1 Disability Conceptualizations

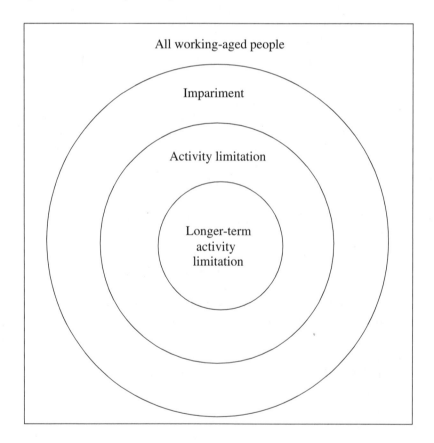

Under the ADA conceptualization, disability is broadly defined as "a physical or mental impairment that substantially limits one or more major life activities, a record of such an impairment, or being regarded as having such an impairment." (See Gordon and Groves 2000 for a broader discussion of the definition of disability in the context of the "protected class" under the ADA and how the courts have narrowed the boundaries of that protected class over time.) This population includes those who are working despite their impairments, and who may not even report a work limitation, as well as those whose impairments, together with their social environment, lead them to report a work limitation. We empirically define this population using the NHIS impairment definition, which includes the largest set of working-aged people with disabilities captured in any of our data sources.

The next circle ("Activity Limitations") represents a subsample of people with impairments who report some type of activity limitation, most closely representing the disability conceptualization by Nagi (1965, 1991) and the World Health Organization.[7] Nagi's conceptualization includes three components. The first, pathology, is the presence of a physical or mental condition that interrupts the physical or mental process of the human body. An example is deafness. This leads to the second component, impairment, which Nagi defines as a physical, anatomical, or mental loss or abnormality that limits a person's capacity to function. For example, deafness limits the ability to interpret sound. The final component, disability, is an inability to perform or a limitation in performing roles and tasks that are socially expected. For example, a person with deafness is unable to use an ordinary telephone.

Nagi's definition is controversial because of the relative importance it places on the socioeconomic environment in determining how pathology results in impairment that leads to disability. Less controversial is his recognition that disability is a dynamic process in which an individual's impairment interacts with the social environment.

Using Nagi's concept, those with a pathology that causes a physical or mental impairment that subsequently limits one or more life activities such as work but who, nevertheless, work would not be considered to have a work limitation. (This would be the case whether work was possible through changes in the work environment, access to rehabilitation, or individual adaptability.) For example, a person with deafness who is accommodated at the workplace with a TTY machine that permits him or her to use the telephone would not be considered work-limited despite his or her impairment.

Hence, the activity-limited population in the Nagi conceptualization is a subcomponent of the impaired population and is one whose boundary is much more likely to be affected by the social environment. The most commonly used activity-limited definition disability includes those who report a work limitation, which is available in the NHIS, CPS, and SIPP. The population with a given activity limitation will change with the specific activity and the corresponding social environment. We also test whether our findings are sensitive to other measures of activity limitations available in the SIPP, including limitations in housework and limitations in a variety of other activities (see Table 2.1 for a list).[8]

The final and smallest circle in Figure 2.1 ("Longer-Term Activity Limitation") represents persons with the most severe and long-term limitations. This population is the most likely to be eligible for Social Security Disability Insurance (SSDI) or Supplemental Security Income (SSI) benefits based on their inability to perform any gainful employment. We define this circle as people who report a work limitation in both the CPS and in the CPS follow-up survey one year later.

Our conceptual model does not attempt to categorize all of the potential disability definitions that exist in the literature. For example, we do not identify a disability population based on participation in a disability program, such as SSDI or SSI. Nor do we attempt to capture a population who need personal assistance (e.g., cane, wheelchair, etc.). Although individuals in these populations would presumably fall within our impairment population (and many would also fall within our other two circles), these populations represent specific subpopulations with disabilities whose boundaries are even more likely to be influenced by their social environment than the three populations we have conceptualized.

EMPIRICAL ANALYSIS

Disability Prevalence

In Figure 2.2, we present estimates of the size of the populations defined under our various disability definitions from the most recent comparable year (1996) available in each of our data sources.[9] The all

Figure 2.2 Disability Prevalence Rates in 1996 Using Alternative Disability Definitions from the NHIS, CPS, and SIPP

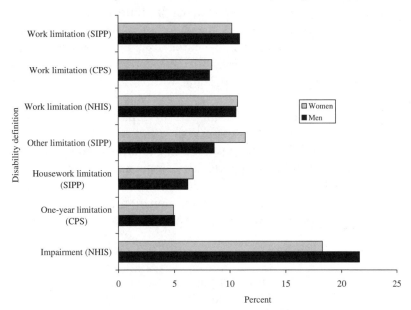

NOTE: The value for the CPS one-year limitation is for the year 1997 because changes in the entire sampling frame in 1996 prohibit the creation of a one-year value for 1996.
SOURCE: Authors' calculations based on data from the 1996 NHIS, 1996 and 1997 CPS, and the 1996 SIPP.

women, captures the largest pool of people with disabilities.[11] The activity-limitation populations, which include the work-limitation populations from the NHIS, CPS, and SIPP, the housework-limitation population from the SIPP, and the other activities-limitation definition from the SIPP, each represent substantially lower prevalence rates of the total population.[12] For men, the various current activity-limitation prevalence rates range from a low of 6.2 percent (SIPP: housework limitations) to a high of 10.9 percent (SIPP: work limitations). For women, the corresponding prevalence rates range from a low of 6.7 percent (SIPP: housework limitations) to a high of 11.4 percent (SIPP: work limitations). Although most of the prevalence rates are similar for men and women, women are more likely to report a higher prevalence of other activities limitations and housework limitations. Finally, as expected, the full-year CPS work-limitation measure captures the smallest population (5 percent of men and 4.9 percent of women).[13]

These findings are consistent with our disability conceptualizations and their orderings in Figure 2.1 and suggest that relying on a current work-limitation question to define the true disability population misses those with impairments who are sufficiently integrated into the workforce so that they do not report being work limited.[14] Although the severity of the impairment undoubtedly explains much of the difference in magnitude between the impairment population and the other disability populations, it does not explain all of it. This suggests that, for instance, a work limitation response can be influenced by the work environment, rehabilitation opportunities, or the inner capacity of individuals to overcome both their impairments and the barriers to work they face. Alternatively, a current work-limitation question overstates the size of the population with longer-term work limitations.

Employment Outcomes

Using the different disability populations we have collected from the NHIS, CPS, and SIPP, we now focus on a major current policy issue: Did the employment rate of working-aged men and women with disabilities fall in the 1990s?

We use a broad measure of employment—employment rate—to examine employment outcomes of each of these populations. In the CPS and SIPP, we consider as employed an individual who reports more than 52 hours of paid employment over the entire year (i.e., one hour per week) from his or her primary and/or secondary job (including self-employment).[15] The NHIS does not contain information on hours of paid employment. Hence, in the NHIS data, we consider individuals to be employed if they report being in a job in the previous two weeks, including those on layoff (see Appendix Table 2A.1 for details).

Figure 2.3 shows differences in employment rates across each of our disability populations using the most recent comparable year (1996). The employment rate of the impairment population is higher than any other group for both men and women. For example, men with impairments have an employment rate of 77.3 percent, whereas the highest employment rate among men in one of the activity-limitation populations is 50.1 percent (SIPP: other activity limitations). Men who

Current Statistics on the Employment of People with Disabilities 37

Figure 2.3 Employment Rates in 1996 of Alternatively Defined Disability Populations from the NHIS, CPS, and SIPP

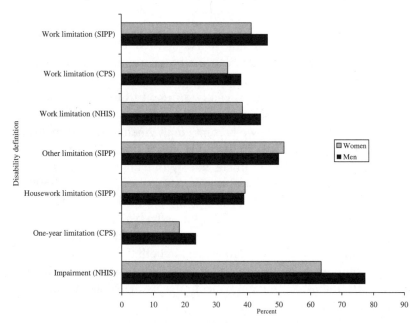

NOTE: The value for the CPS one-year limitation is for the year 1997 because changes in the entire sampling frame in 1996 prohibit the creation of a one-year value for 1996.
SOURCE: Authors' calculations based on data from the 1996 NHIS, 1996 and 1997 CPS, and the 1996 SIPP.

reported longer-term work limitations (CPS one-year work limitations) had employment rates of only 23.6 percent. This is substantially below the one-period CPS work limitation employment rate of 38.2 percent. Similar patterns exist for women.

These findings offer some support for the criticism of Hale (2001) that CPS work-limitation questions will neither capture the larger population with disabilities (our outermost circle in Figure 2.1) nor provide a representative sample of that population with respect to employment behavior. Our data from the NHIS suggest that a substantial portion of those who report impairments do not report having a work limitation, and that this population is much more likely to be employed.[16] On the other hand, our data from the longitudinal component of the CPS show that current measures of work limitation (CPS: work limitation) in 1996 capture a larger and presumably less-activity-limited population than the subsample of this population that reported a work limitation in both 1996 and 1997 (CPS one-year work limitation).

Nonetheless it is still possible to use a current CPS work-limitation question to estimate trends in both the broader and narrower populations with disabilities that we have conceptualized, if the trends in all these populations are not significantly different from one another over the period of the analysis.[17] It is to this critical issue that we now turn.

In Figures 2.4 and 2.5, we present employment trend estimates for men and women in each of our disability populations. The first panel in each figure tracks long-term trends in employment outcomes based on the NHIS and CPS. The second tracks shorter-term trends in employment based on SIPP definitions. Both figures track trends during the 1990s. (See Appendix Table 2A.3 for the actual values.)

Prior to 1990, the employment rates of working-aged men and women with disabilities were procyclical in both the NHIS and CPS. In general, there was a dip in employment rates during the recession in the early 1980s and a rise in employment rates as the economy started to grow in the later 1980s.[18]

In the 1990s, however, there was a consistent and steady drop in the employment rates of men with disabilities in all of our disability populations. This drop began with the recession of the early 1990s and continued through the economic expansion of the mid to late 1990s. From 1990 to 1996, employment rates fell in all populations of men with disabilities. The percent reduction across all measures was between 8 percent and 16 percent, with the largest reduction occurring for the SIPP housework-limitation population, which fell 14.1 percent (from 45.4 to 39 percent). The employment trends across all measures are roughly similar.

Employment trends increase during the growth years of the 1980s in all the NHIS and CPS female disability populations (Figure 2.5). In the 1990s, employment fell in all of these populations but not as much as in the male disability populations. Most of these employment rates declined by less than 8 percent, although the CPS work-limitation population and SIPP housework-limitation population both experienced more than a 10 percent employment decline. These trends consistently

Current Statistics on the Employment of People with Disabilities   39

Figure 2.4 Yearly Employment Rate Trends of Men with Disabilities in Alternatively Defined Disability Populations from the NHIS, CPS, and SIPP

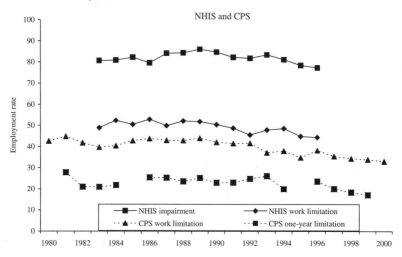

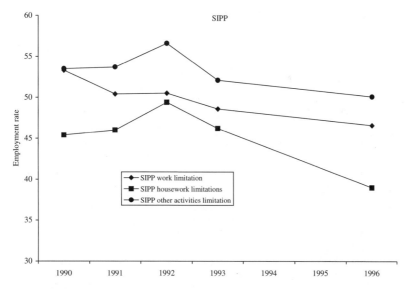

NOTE: Changes in the entire CPS sampling frame in 1986 and 1996 prohibit the creation of one-year limitation values for 1985 and 1995.

SOURCE: Authors' calculations based on data from 1983–1996 NHIS, 1981–2000 CPS, and 1990–1993 and 1996 SIPP.

Figure 2.5 Yearly Employment Rate Trends of Women with Disabilities in Alternatively Defined Disability Populations from the NHIS, CPS, and SIPP

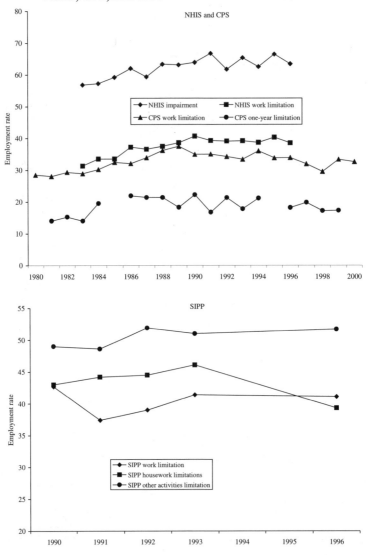

NOTE: Changes in the entire CPS sampling frame in 1986 and 1996 prohibit the creation of one-year limitation values for 1985 and 1995.
SOURCE: Authors' calculations based on data from 1983–1996 NHIS, 1981–2000 CPS, and 1990–1993 and 1996 SIPP/

show that working-aged people with disabilities, particularly men, fared poorly in the labor market in the 1990s.

These findings are all the more troubling because the employment of both men (Figure 2.6) and women (Figure 2.7) without disabilities remained procyclical over both the 1980s and 1990s business cycles (see Appendix Table 2A.4 for the actual values). Thus, in the 1990s the relative employment rates of both men and women with disabilities also declined dramatically compared with men and women without disabilities using data from NHIS, CPS, or SIPP.

EXPLAINING THE DIFFERENCES IN EMPLOYMENT TRENDS IN OTHER STUDIES

Our employment trends appear to be inconsistent with those of Kaye (2002 and Chapter 6), who argues that the employment opportunities for people with disabilities improved significantly during the 1990s, using data from the NHIS and CPS. However, as we show below, the differences in our results are primarily due to the populations on which we focus with our common data rather than with the survey data itself.

Kaye argues that to obtain a population more consistent with the ADA, the population with disabilities must exclude those who either have self-reported "no ability to work" and/or who are not looking for work. Below, we produce trends similar to Kaye, using subsamples of our work-limitation populations in the NHIS, CPS, and SIPP. Having done so, we argue that the disability population Kaye chooses to study excludes a substantial portion of people with disabilities. Specifically, we show that his findings result from limiting the population with disabilities to those who report a work limitation and report that they are either looking for work or are able to do some work. In doing so, he excludes all other working-aged people with a work limitation. Likewise, his focus on the unemployment rate of this exclusive population ignores the growing share of the working-aged population with disabilities in the 1990s who are no longer looking for work. The excluded population no doubt includes many people who could and would work

Figure 2.6 Yearly Employment Rate Trends of Men without disabilities in Alternatively Defined Disability Populations from the NHIS, CPS, and SIPP

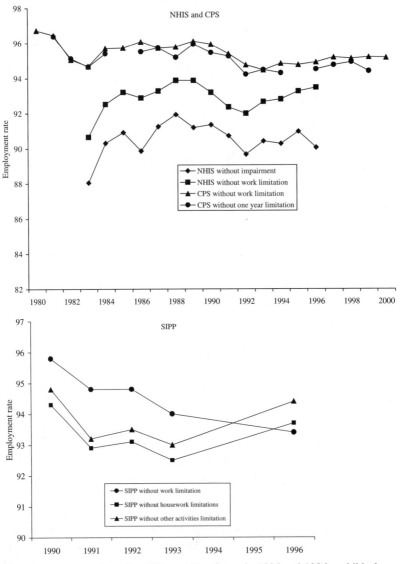

NOTE: Changes in the entire CPS sampling frame in 1986 and 1996 prohibit the creation of one-year limitation values for 1985 and 1995.
SOURCE: Authors' calculations based on data from 1983–1996 NHIS, 1981–2000 CPS, and 1990–1993 and 1996 CPS.

Figure 2.7 Yearly Employment Rate Trends of Women without Disabilities in Alternatively Defined Disability Populations from the NHIS, CPS, and SIPP

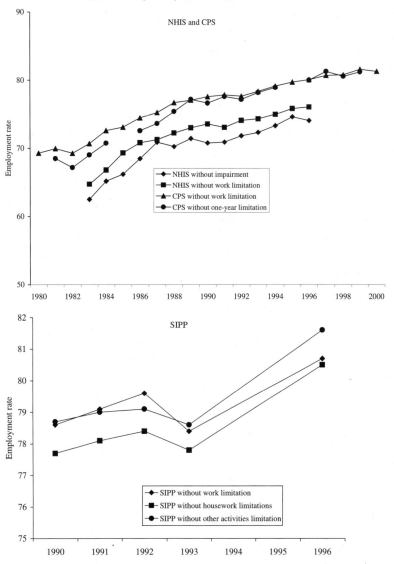

NOTE: Changes in the entire CPS sampling frame in 1986 and 1996 prohibit the creation of one-year limitation values for 1985 and 1995.
SOURCE: Authors' calculations based on data from 1983–1996 NHIS, 1981–2000 CPS, and 1990–1993 and 1996 CPS.

in a different environment, and is therefore of considerable interest for policy purposes.

We now focus on the subcomponent of the working-aged population with work limitations examined by Kaye by creating a subsample of those in our work-limitation population who self-reported being "able to work" or who are looking for work.[19] Focusing on this population has some intuitive appeal because it attempts to measure the employment trends of only those who report being able to participate in the labor force and excludes those who report that they cannot work at all and hence are outside the labor market.

The NHIS, CPS, and SIPP each include questions to identify this population. However, although we still use data from the CPS and SIPP, we now focus on employment in the previous week in the CPS and previous month in the SIPP.[20] Although we report trends for all three surveys, changes in the weekly employment questions in the CPS beginning in 1993 have a major effect on trends in employment for the "able-to-work" population. Consequently, this measure is not as useful for measuring long-term employment trends in this population as the "employment in the previous year" measure (which did not change over the period used) in the broader population considered in Figures 2.4 and 2.5.[21]

In Figure 2.8, we show, similar to Kaye, that the employment rates of men and women with work limitations who say they are able to work are relatively flat during the course of the 1990s in the NHIS and SIPP and increase substantially in the CPS (see Appendix Table 2A.5 for actual values). These post–1990 trends are quite different from those reported for the entire work-limitation populations in Figures 2.4 and 2.5. However, prior to 1990, these trends are similar to those we report for the entire work-limitation population for both men and women in Figures 2.6 and 2.7.

However, in Figure 2.9, we show that the size of the able-to-work subpopulation declined substantially as a share of the entire work-limitation population in the 1990s in all three surveys, particularly in the CPS (see Appendix Table 2A.6 for actual values).[22] Further, in all three surveys, the decline in the overall size of the able-to-work population more than offsets the gain in employment by this group. This explains how the total work-limitation population in both the CPS and NHIS

Current Statistics on the Employment of People with Disabilities 45

Figure 2.8 Employment Rate Trends of the Subsample of the Work-Limitation-Based Disability Population Who Report Being Able to Work from the NHIS, CPS, and SIPP

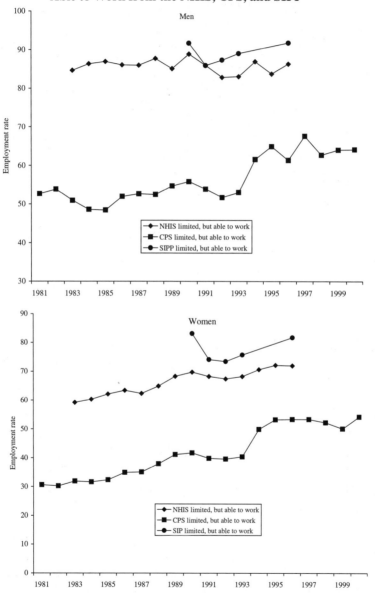

SOURCE: Authors' calculations based on data from 1983–1996 NHIS, 1981–2000 CPS, and 1990–1993 abd 1996 SIPP.

Figure 2.9 Trends in the Proportion of the Work-Limitation-Based Disability Population Who Report Being Able to Work from the NHIS, CPS, and SIPP

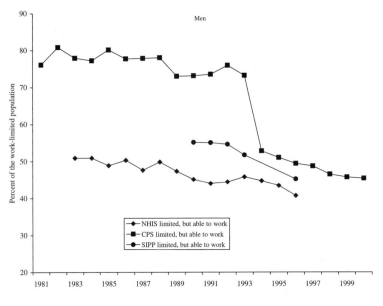
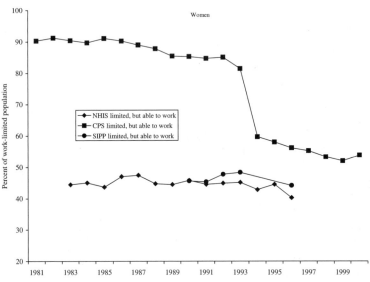

surveys falls during the 1990s, even though the subpopulation that is able to work rises.

Given the substantial decline in the population that both reports a work limitation and being able to work, the critical policy issue is whether this change is from a change in the social environment and/or an increase in the severity of the impairment of those who report a work limitation. Of particular importance is the decline in the work-limitation population who report being able to work in the 1990s. If changes in the size of the able-to-work population are driven by changes in the social environment (e.g., changes in Social Security policy, changes in employers' willingness to employ workers with disabilities) rather than by increases in the severity of their impairments, the increased employment rate is a mixed policy success at best. Furthermore, from a behavioral modeling perspective, unless the change is caused totally by an exogenous increase in severity of impairment, changes in the social environment must be considered.

OTHER LABOR MARKET SUCCESS MEASURES

Unemployment Rate

Another success measure used by Kaye (2002 and Chapter 6) to depict labor market outcomes of people with disabilities is the unemployment rate. The unemployment rate is measured by dividing the unemployed population by the total labor force population.[23] This measure has some intuitive appeal because it measures the average labor force outcomes of those who are participating in the labor market. In addition, it is one of the primary measures used to examine labor market success for the entire working-aged population by the Bureau of Labor Statistics.

In Figure 2.10, similar to Kaye, we show that the unemployment rate of men with work limitations drops significantly following the recession of the early 1990s.[24] The unemployment rates of women with work limitations have a much greater variance but are also generally downward during the 1980s and 1990s. In the CPS, the change in the employment question in 1993 is likely to have influenced the large

Figure 2.10 Unemployment Rate Trends in the Work-Limitation-Based Disability Population from the NHIS, CPS, and SIPP

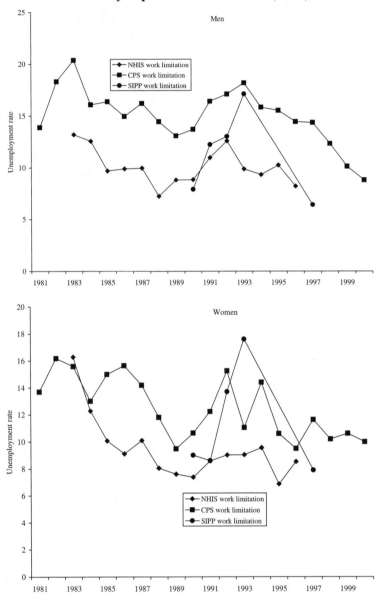

SOURCE: Authors' calculations based on data from 1983–1996 NHIS, 1981–2000 CPS, and 1990–1993 and 1996 SIPP.

drop in the unemployment rate between 1993 and 1994. Despite this measurement issue, the trends for men and, to a lesser extent, women show a decline in the unemployment rate in work-limitation populations during the economic expansion of the 1990s. (See Appendix Table 2A.7 for the actual values in each year.)

In Figure 2.11, however, we show that the drops in the unemployment rates for men and, to a lesser degree, for women with work limitations are accompanied by a drop in their labor force participation rates.[25] The labor force participation rates for men declined significantly from 1990 through 1997, while women experienced a slightly smaller decline. The decline in the labor force participation rate of the work-limitation population raises a question of whether the fall in the unemployment rate seen in Figure 2.10 should be considered a policy success. (See Appendix Table 2A.7 for actual values in each year.)

The primary reason for the decline in the unemployment rate was not a rise in the number of employed people with work limitations. Rather, it fell because the decline in employed people with work limitations was somewhat smaller than the decline in the number of unemployed people with work limitations. To the degree this increase in the population out of the labor force was caused by changes in the social environment, this is a very mixed policy success at best. It is hard to understand how policies that not only lower employment but also induce men and women with work limitations who are not currently employed to stop searching for work could be considered successful in integrating people with disabilities into the labor market, even if those policies lower the unemployment rate of the smaller number of men and women who were still in the labor force. For this reason, in our view the employment rate, not the unemployment rate, is the more appropriate success measure for working-aged people with disabilities.

SSDI and SSI Beneficiaries

The final measure we examine related to labor market integration, and a measure that is often included in studies of the ADA, is receipt of SSDI and SSI benefits. Because the NHIS does not include information on program participation, we limit our analysis to the CPS and SIPP.

In Figure 2.12, we show that in the early 1980s, the percentage of the work-limitation population who received SSDI or SSI benefits

Figure 2.11 Labor Force Participation Rate Trends in the Work-Limitation-Based Disability Population from the NHIS, CPS, and SIPP

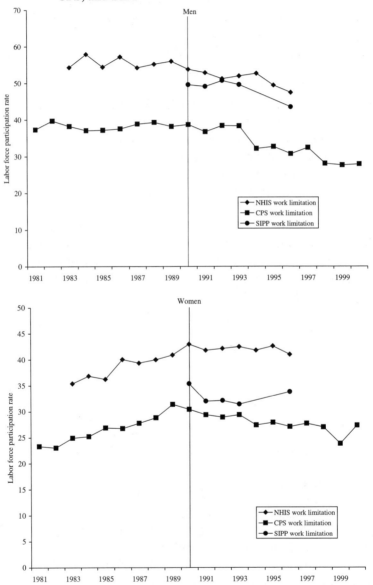

SOURCE: Authors' calculations based on data from 1983–1996 NHIS, 1981–2000 CPS, and 1990–1993 and 1996 SIPP.

Figure 2.12 SSI and SSDI Beneficiary Rate Trends in the Work-Limitation-Based Disability Population from the CPS and SIPP

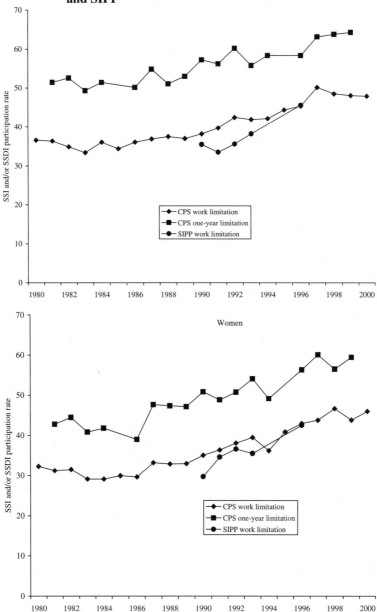

dropped despite the weakening in the economy. During the rest of the decade, despite six years of economic growth, the prevalence of SSDI modestly increased and the prevalence of SSI substantially increased among working-aged men and women with work limitations. This is found in both the CPS and SIPP data. The number of beneficiaries of SSDI and SSI continued to increase among the work-limitation population in the 1990s. By 2000, nearly one-half of men in the work-limitation populations received either SSDI or SSI compared with 36.6 percent in 1981. (See Appendix Table 2A.8 for actual values in each year.)

The share of the longer-term CPS work-limitation population receiving either SSDI or SSI is even greater than in the current work-limitation CPS population. However, the upward trend is less pronounced—from 51.5 percent in 1982 to 64.3 percent in 2000 (Appendix Table 2A.8). However, almost all the growth in benefit prevalence has occurred since 1990. Furthermore, the sharp declines in the employment rates (Figures 2.4 and 2.5) and the rapid rise in the prevalence of disability benefits in this longer-term, work-limitation-based population are consistent with the decline found in our other disability populations. Subsequent chapters of this volume will attempt to determine the causes of the dramatic changes in employment and disability program take-up rates among these populations.

CONCLUSION

In Figure 2.1, we provided a conceptualization of a population with disabilities that operationally placed those who report an activity limitation (as defined by Nagi 1991) within a broader impairment population. Such a placement recognizes that a reported impairment may or may not lead to an activity limitation, such as work.

Using data from the NHIS, we showed that a substantial share of working-aged people who report serious impairments do not report having a work limitation. We further showed that those with impairments who also report having a work limitation are far less likely to be employed than are people with the same reported impairments who do not report a work limitation. This suggests that current work-limitation questions such as those in the CPS are likely to understate the prevalence of disability in the working-aged population based on an impairment-based conceptualization of disability and to understate the share of that population that is employed.

However, we also show that the employment trends in these two distinct conceptualizations of the working-aged population with disabilities are not significantly different from each other. Using the current work-limitation question in the CPS to examine the relative responsiveness of employment of working-aged men and women to business-cycle fluctuations during the past two decades, we find that during the 1980s, employment rates for those with work limitations were procyclical, falling during recession years and rising during expansion. In contrast, the employment rate of working-aged men and women with work limitations fell almost continuously throughout the 1990s.

Recognizing that a current CPS work-limitation population is not the ideal source of information about the broader population with impairments, we checked the robustness of our results using data from the NHIS and SIPP. Although the prevalence of "disability" and the employment of the population with "disabilities" using the current work-limitation question in the CPS as our measure are significantly different from those found in both the work-limitation or impairment questions from the NHIS, there is no significant difference between the employment trends found in these populations. Furthermore, when we examined the employment rates of the working-aged populations with longer-term work limitations using the follow-up CPS data, we once again found significant differences in levels, but not in trends. Hence, we argue that the decline in the employment rate among working-aged men and women with disabilities in the 1990s is not an artifact of the current work-limitation questions in the CPS data, but a real and important phenomenon, which can be demonstrated in the NHIS data and the CPS follow-up data.[26]

This leads us to two sets of conclusions. First, the CPS, SIPP, and NHIS provide valuable data to policymakers and researchers interested in tracing the employment success of working-aged men and women with disabilities. Although the current work-limitation question in the CPS is not perfect, it provides a valid measure of the employment trend in this population and in the broader impairment population captured in the NHIS. Not only would it be unwise to dismiss the power of the current work-limitation question in the CPS to capture long-term employment trends among working people with disabilities, but it would also be unwise to phase out this question, even if additional questions were added that better captured the broader population with disabilities.

Second, the new literature documenting the decline in the relative employment of men with disabilities in the 1990s cannot be dismissed out of hand. We have demonstrated the robustness of this finding in the NHIS, CPS, and SIPP data. Furthermore, when we restrict our CPS population to those who report a work limitation in the CPS follow-up data over one full year, and thus better control for severity, we also find dramatic decreases in their employment rates and dramatic increases in the prevalence of SSDI or SSI beneficiaries. These changes are even greater than those observed in the current CPS work-limitation-based disability population in the 1990s.

These findings appear to be in sharp contrast to those that Kaye (2002 and Chapter 6) finds using similar data. In fact, however, the differences are owing almost entirely to his decision to use the subset of the work-limitation population that reports some ability to work. Although it is true that the employment of this population is rising and its unemployment is falling, Kaye's analysis dismisses the potential importance of the social environment in explaining the sharp decline in the share of the work-limitation population that reports being able to work. Hence, he believes it is appropriate for policy purposes to focus on the subset of the work-limited population that reports being able to work.

This chapter moves the policy debate beyond the question of "did the employment of people with disabilities dramatically fall in the 1990s?" It did. Pinning down the importance of the factors responsible for this drop in employment is the next necessary step to developing policies targeted at reversing this trend.

Notes

This research is funded in part by the United States Department of Education, National Institute on Disability and Rehabilitation Research (NIDRR), cooperative agreement no. 13313980038. It does not necessarily reflect the view of the NIDRR, Cornell University, or the Urban Institute.

1. See Krieger (2000) for a discussion of ADA, its legislative history, and its treatment by the courts.
2. The Census Bureau has collected separate panels of SIPP data in each year from 1984 through 1993 and then again starting in 1996. New SIPP panels were not implemented in 1994 and 1995 for budgetary reasons. We do not use data from pre-1990 SIPP panels for two reasons. First, several of the pre-1990 panels were cut short owing to budgetary considerations. Second, the SIPP gathered very limited disability data in the SIPP panels between 1984 and 1990 (Adler 1991).
3. We only use information from modules that have been consistently collected across all panels. The SIPP includes some information on specific conditions, but only for those who first report a work limitation. Hence, unlike the NHIS, these questions cannot be used to estimate prevalence of impairments in the general population because some people with impairments do not report a work limitation.
4. Maag and Wittenburg (2002) show that changes in the work-limitation question could cause bias in the employment trend of the population with work limitations using these questions. Specifically, they show that most of the problems cited in McNeil (2000) arise because the method of asking the work-limitation question changed in the 1996 panel. In prior SIPP panels, respondents were reminded of their work-limitation responses from previous waves. Starting with the 1996 SIPP, panel respondents were not reminded of their answers in previous waves. This change significantly reduced the prevalence of a work-limitation reported in later periods of the 1996 panel, relative to the pattern found in earlier SIPP panels. The 1996 SIPP panel also allowed people to report a work limitation as a reason for not working, which may increase the prevalence of work limitations in the general population as well as among the unemployed in the 1996 panel. Despite these changes in the 1996 SIPP panel, Maag and Wittenburg (2002) show that it is possible to construct comparable samples of people who report work limitations by using information in the first wave of each panel from 1990 through 1993, together with the various waves of the 1996 panel. Nonetheless, they urge some caution in using the resulting across-panel values because the employment estimates may be biased downward, and they suggest using multiple data sources and disability definitions to examine trends in employment. Importantly, there were no other changes in SIPP questions commonly used in disability research (e.g., housework limitations). Consequently, the comparisons of trends under alternative SIPP disability definitions used in this chapter do not suffer from the same type of potential bias as exists in the work-limitation question.
5. An example is the problematic SIPP two-period work-limitation measure. Because of changes in the 1996 SIPP questionnaire, the prevalence of this measure significantly declines (along with the employment rate for those who report

two consecutive periods of limitations). Therefore, we do not use the measure in our chapter.
6. Appendix Table 2A.1 provides a detailed summary of all variables used in this chapter and the questions on which they are based in the three surveys.
7. See Jette and Bradley (2002) for an excellent comparison of the Nagi and WHO models.
8. Several of these other activities fall under the categories of activities of daily living (ADLs), instrumental activities of daily living (IADL), and other functional limitations. We use other activities as a shorthand to refer to this grouping.
9. The last year that consistent impairment estimates are available in the NHIS is 1996. The one-year disability measure is for the one-year period between the March 1996 and March 1997 CPS surveys.
10. The differences in prevalence rates across definitions are also constant over time (see Appendix Table 2A.1). In general, the relative differences in prevalence rates are approximately the same, although there are some fluctuations in these rates, particularly across the business cycle. As noted above, these fluctuations are consistent with the changing economic conditions noted in Bound and Burkhauser (1999).
11. Here and in all other tables and figures we look at working-aged men and women, aged 25–61.
12. The work-limitation prevalence rates from the NHIS and the SIPP are larger than that from the CPS for both men and women. This difference could arise because of the position and method used to implement the question in the CPS (see Table 2.1 for a description of the questions).
13. Because we do not know when the work limitation began, the actual spell length is at lease one year, assuming that we are not capturing two different spells.
14. These findings are consistent with those of Burkhauser and Houtenville (forthcoming), who illustrate the compositional differences across groups captured under different disability definitions. They show that even those with quite severe impairments do not all report a work limitation. Similarly, as comparisons of prevalence rates of the CPS work-limitation measure to the one-year CPS work-limitation measure indicate, not all those who currently report a work limitation have a longer-term work limitation.
15. Individuals who work fewer than 52 work hours annually are considered not to be employed. Annual hours in the CPS data are calculated by multiplying the number of weeks worked by average hours worked per week. Although our annual definition of employment is somewhat arbitrary, our results are not sensitive to the hour cutoff we chose. In the SIPP, we calculate annual hours by aggregating total monthly hour measures across all 12 months.
16. Burkhauser et al. (2002) use merged data from 1983–1996 in the NHIS to show that within specific impairment categories (e.g., blind in both eyes, deaf in both ears, etc.), a substantial share of those reporting such severe impairments do not report a work limitation. They further show that the employment rates of this subpopulation of severely impaired persons who report no work limitations are sub-

stantially higher than those with the same impairment but who do report a work limitation.
17. More formally, the criticism raised by Hale (2001) is one of measurement error. That is, will a sample of working-aged people who report a current work limitation accurately measure the true population with a disability? Unfortunately, no consensus exists on the dimensions of the conceptually true population with disability. The only effect of this type of measurement error, however, is to introduce noise into the level of the observed event. A potentially more serious problem is selection bias, i.e., that the work-limitation population may represent a select portion of the population with disabilities and, hence, not adequately reflect outcomes for this true population with disabilities. This is a serious concern given that the NHIS work limitation population underestimates the level of prevalence and the employment rate of the NHIS impairment population. To address this more serious problem, in previous work we show that the employment trends of the work-limitation disability population mirror those of other populations with disabilities, including those with impairments (Burkhauser et al. 2002). Specifically, we show that the employment trends in an impairment-based disability population and a work-limitation-based disability population in the NHIS and in the CPS are not significantly different. The impairment-based disability population is presumably less subject to selection bias and less influenced by the social environment. The findings from Burkhauser et al. (2002) also address other concerns raised by Kirchner (1996) and by Kruse and Schur (Chapter 8) that self-perception may change the way people respond to work-limitation questions. For example, if Kirchner's hypothesis were correct, one would have expected the work-limitation population to fall relative to that of the impairment population and for its employment rate to also fall relative to that of the impairment population. We, in fact, find that the work-limitation population increased relative to the impairment population, while the employment trends of both these populations followed the same downward trend. In sum, it is not the level of employment in the working-aged population but its trend that is critical to the debate in the new literature on the employment of working-aged people with disabilities. Consequently, based on our findings, the trends for the work limitation population are real and have important implications for the broader populations of people with disabilities.
18. These trends are discussed in greater detail in Burkhauser et al. (2002).
19. An ability-to-work subsample of broader activity-limitation populations is also used by Kruse and Schur (Chapter 8). They report employment trends that are similar to Kaye (2002 and Chapter 6).
20. We do so because we want to replicate an unemployment concept similar to Kaye (2002 and Chapter 6).
21. In the NHIS and SIPP data, those who report a work limitation are then asked if they are able to work at all. In the CPS data, this is not the case. Operationally, to estimate this population in the CPS, we looked at the population who reported a work limitation and who were either employed or who were not employed but reported not working for some reason other than being disabled. This variable is

consistently constructed from 1981 through 1993. After 1993, a major change occurred in the second part of this measure, which makes this measure after 1993 inconsistent with the previous years.

22. The decline in the population that reports being able to work as a proportion of those with work limitations roughly matches the decline in the overall size of the population of people who report being able to work, given that the size of the work-limitation population was roughly constant during this period.

23. Specifically, it is the ratio of those not currently employed but seeking employment divided by the employed and the unemployed.

24. The unemployment rates vary somewhat across our work-limitation population because of the timeframe used to measure employment. The CPS measure is based on a weekly employment definition, the NHIS measure is based on a two-week employment definition, and the SIPP measure is based on a monthly employment definition.

25. The labor force participation rate is defined as the total number of people in the labor force (unemployed plus employed) divided by the total population.

26. Burkhauser et al. (2002) show this more formally. Because of the short timespan of the SIPP data, no statistical test of its time trends was made.

Appendix 2A

Table 2A.1 Comparison Data Sets and Variable Definitions

Background	The annual cross-sectional survey of the non-institutionalized civilian population of the United States. The federal government uses data from the NHIS to monitor trends in illness and disability. Researchers use this data to analyze access to health care and health insurance and to evaluate federal health programs.	The CPS is a monthly survey of the non-institutionalized population of the United States. Information is collected on labor force characteristics (e.g., employment, earnings, hours of work). In March of each year, the CPS basic monthly survey is supplemented with the Annual Demographic Survey. This supplement focuses on sources of income, government program participation, previous employment, insurance, and a variety of demographic characteristics. The CPS and the Annual Demographic Survey are used extensively by government agencies, academic researchers, policy makers, journalists, and the general public to evaluate government programs, economic well-being and behavior of individuals, families and households. The CPS follows housing units over a course of 4 months and then returns 8 months later to follow them for another 4 months. This allows for the matching of housing units and multi-period analysis. Although people who move out of the housing unit are not followed.	The SIPP is a longitudinal survey that contains detailed monthly demographic, program, employment, and health characteristics for a nationally representative sample of the non-institutionalized resident population of the United States. The purpose of the SIPP is to provide comprehensive information regarding the income and program characteristics from of a representative sample of United States population. Interviewers collect information from a separate rotation group each month regarding their activity in the previous four months. Each panel includes four "rotation" groups. The design allows SIPP interviewers to remain in the field on a continual basis. Each rotation group represents a random sample of the US population. The SIPP interview includes two types of questions: core and topical module (TM). The core questions are updated each interview and include demographic, program participation, and employment information. TM questions relate to special topics of interest that generally do not change each interview period, such as past program participation, work history, or health.
Agency	Center for Disease Control and Prevention	Conducted by the Bureau of the Census on behalf of the Bureau of Labor Statistics	Conducted by the Bureau of the Census on behalf of the Bureau of Labor Statistics

(continued)

Table 2A.1 (continued)

Survey universe	Resident civilian population of the United States: Those on active duty with the Armed Forces and U.S. citizens living abroad are not surveyed, however, the dependents of those on active duty with the Armed Forces who live in the U.S. are included. Those in long-term care facilities are also excluded.	Resident population of the United States: citizens living abroad are not surveyed. Those in long-term care facilities are excluded.	Nationally representative sample of the non-institutionalized resident population of the United States. This population interview includes persons living in-group quarters, such as dormitories, rooming houses, and religious group dwellings. Persons excluded from the SIPP population include crew members of merchant vessels, Armed Forces personnel living in military barracks, institutionalized persons, such as correctional facility inmates, residents of long-term care facilities, and citizens residing abroad. Foreign visitors who work or attend school in this country and their families are eligible for interviews.
Years available and major revisions	The NHIS began in July 1957. We use 1983–1996 because work limitations and impairment information was consistently collected. Major revisions were made to the survey instrument in 1983 and 1997.	The CPS began in the early 1940s, however, the work limitation variable was not asked until 1981. In 1994, major revisions were made to the Basic Monthly Survey and the labor force questions. The changes to the March Supplement were less substantial and reflect the shift to computer-assisted interviews.	The Census Bureau collects data for each SIPP panel, which are available in each year from 1984 through 1993 and then again starting in 1996. While the interview length varies across SIPP panels, since 1990, each panel includes at least eight "interview waves" over approximately a 2.5-year period. Panels for 1994 and 1995 do not exist, because the Census cancelled these efforts in anticipation of the rollout of the 1996 SIPP "redesign." The next SIPP panel will start in 2000. We use data from the 1990, 1991, 1992, 1993, and 1996 panels.

Number of participants	Approximately 80,000 individuals annually	Approximately 150,000 individuals annually	Sample size varies by panel, 40,000 non-institutionalized persons (1991 panel) to 95,000 non-institutionalized persons (1996 panel).
	Specific Information on Disability Measures		
Work limitation	The NHIS asks "[d]oes any impairment or health problem NOW keep [person] from working at a job or business? Is [person] limited in the kind OR amount of work [person] can do because of any impairment?" Those who answer yes to either question are considered to report a work limitation.	The March Supplement asks "[d]oes anyone in this household have a health problem or disability which prevents them from working or which limits the kind or amount of work they can do? [If so,] who is that? (Anyone else?)" Those who answer yes to this question are considered to report a work limitation.	The first core interview asks "Does — have a physical, mental or other health condition which limits the kind or amount of work — can do?"
Housework limitation	Not applicable	Not applicable	In the functional limitations and disability topical module, respondents are asked: "Does — have a physical, mental or other health condition which limits the kind or amount of work — can do around the house?"

(continued)

Table 2A.1 (continued)

	Not applicable	Not applicable
Limitations in other activities		In the functional limitations and disability topical module, respondents are asked: "Because of a physical or mental health condition, does — have difficulty doing any of the following by himself/herself (exclude the effects of temporary conditions)?" Does — have any difficulty getting around inside the home? Does — have any difficulty getting around outside the home, for example to shop or visit a doctor's office? Does — have any difficulty getting into and out of bed or a chair? Does — have any difficulty taking a bath or a shower? Does — have any difficulty getting dressed? Does — have any difficulty eating? Does — have any difficulty using the toilet, including getting to the toilet? Does — have any difficulty keeping track of money and bills? Does — have any difficulty preparing meals? Does — have any difficulty doing light housework, such as washing dishes or sweeping a floor?

One-year limitation	Not applicable	A portion of the March Supplement participants were asked about work limitation in two consecutive years. Those who report work limitations in two consecutive years (March to March) are considered to report a two period work limitation. The years 1986 and 1996 are not applicable because the Census Bureau changed the sampling frame and the thus housing units were not consecutively interviewed. Also note, the CPS follows housing units not the people in the households, so that matched files do not contain movers.	Not applicable: While it is possible to create a two period work limitation variable, we exclude this information from our analysis of the SIPP because of potential selection bias issues that arise due to changes in the 1996 SIPP questionnaire.

(continued)

Table 2A.1 (continued)

Partial work limitation	Those who answer no to the question "[D]oes any impairment or health problem NOW keep [person] from working at a job or business?" but answer yes to the question "[I]s [person] limited in the kinds or amount of work [person] can do because of any impairment?" are considered to report a partial work limitation. These two questions are asked in succession.	Those who report work limitation and not the inability to work due to own illness or disability are considered to report a partial work limitation. The inability to work is derived from questions in the CPS Basic Monthly Survey. Prior to 1994, people are employed according to responses to the following question, [w]hat was...doing most of LAST WEEK?" Inability to work due to illness or disability was a possible response. For 1994 and thereafter, people report the inability to work if answer yes to the question, "(Last month you were reported to have a disability.) [d]oes your disability continue to prevent you from doing any kind of work for the next 6 months (including work in the family business or farm)?" Note those who indicate disability yet report positive hours work elsewhere in the survey are coded in the survey. The method used in 1994 and thereafter is substantially different than in prior years and highlights the switch to computer assisted surveys that allow the interviewer to cite previous responses.	Those who respond that they have a work limitation are asked in the work disability topical module (second wave of every SIPP panel): Does ...'s health or condition prevent ... from working at a job or business

66

Impairment	Respondents receive one of six condition lists that ask them if they have a specific condition (we focus on conditions in list #2). This method yields a random sample because being asked about a condition is not dependent on one's response to another question. This method captures those with specific conditions but who may or may not report having no health or functioning difficulties. Only one-sixth of the sample is directly asked about a specific condition. The set of impairments used in this paper are blindness in both eyes, other visual impairments, deafness in both ears, other hearing impairments, stammering and stuttering, other speech impairments, mental retardation, absence of both arms/hands, one arm/hand, fingers, one or both legs, feet/toes, kidney, breast, muscle of extremity, tips of fingers, and/or toes, complete paralysis of entire body, one side of body, both legs, other extremity; cerebral palsy, partial paralysis one side of body, legs, other extremity, other complete or partial paralysis, curvature or other deformity of back or spine, orthopedic impairment of the back, spina bifida, deformity/orthopedic impairment of hand, fingers, shoulder(s), other upper extremity, flatfeet, clubfoot, or other deformity/ orthopedic impairment, and cleft palate.	Not applicable	Not applicable

(continued)

Table 2A.1 (continued)

Employment measure	In order to be more consistent with the CPS measure of employment in these tables, people are employed if they had a job in the previous two weeks, which includes those on layoff. This definition is based on the following questions: "[during the previous two weeks], did [person] work at any time at a job or business not counting work around the house? (Include unpaid work in the family farm/business.) Even though [person] did not work during those 2 weeks, did [person] have a job a job or business?" ... "Earlier you said that [person] has a job or business but didn't work last week or the week before. Was [person] ... on layoff from a job."	People are employed if they work 52 hours or more and have positive earnings in the previous year. This reflects attachment to the labor force and the underlying survey questions are more consistently worded over time.	We consider an individual who reports more than 52 hours over the entire year (i.e., one hour per week) from their primary and/or secondary job (including self-employment) as employed Individuals with fewer than 52 work hours annually are considered detached from the labor market. We calculate annual hours by aggregating total monthly hour measures across all 12 months.
"Official" employment rate	People are "officially" employed if they had a job in the previous two weeks, excluding those on layoff. This definition is based on the questions: "[during the previous two weeks], did [person] work at any time at a job or business not counting work around the house? (Include unpaid work in the family farm/business.) Even though [person] did not work during those 2 weeks, did [person] have a job a job or business?" ... "Earlier you said that [person] has a job or business but didn't work last week or the week before. Was [person] ... on layoff from a job."	Prior to 1994, people are "officially" employed according to responses to the following question, [w]hat was...doing most of LAST WEEK?" For 1994 and thereafter, people are "officially" employed if "[L]ast week, did [person] do any work for either pay or profit?" And, "[L]ast week, (in addition to the business,) did you have a job either full or part time? Include any job from which you were temporarily absent."	People are officially employed if they work any week during the previous month. Specifically, if they respond to any of the following categories (1) with a job entire month, worked all weeks, (2) With a job entire month, missed one or more weeks, no time on layoff, (3) With a job entire month, missed one or more weeks, spent time on layoff, (4) With job one or more weeks, no time spent looking or on layoff, or (5) With job one or more weeks, spent one or more weeks looking or on layoff.

"Official" labor force participation rate	People are "officially" in the labor force if they are "officially" employed (see above), on layoff or actively looking for work, based on the responses to the following questions: "Earlier you said that [person] has a job or business but did not work last week or the week before. Was [person] looking for work or on layoff from a job during those 2 weeks?"	Prior to 1994, people are "officially" in the labor force if they are "officially" employed (see above), on layoff or actively looking for work, based on the responses to the following question, "[w]hat was...doing most of LAST WEEK?" For 1994 and thereafter, people are in the labor force if they were "officially" employed (see above) on layoff or actively looking for work, based on the responses to the following questions: "[l]ast week, were you on layoff from a job? Have you been doing anything to find work during the last 4 weeks?"	People are in the labor force if they are employed during any week in the month (see above), or are on layoff, or are actively looking for work. Specifically, if they respond to any of the five categories mentioned above or if they respond (6) No job during month, spent entire month looking or on layoff, or (7) No job during month, spent one or more weeks looking or on layoff
"Official" unemployment rate	People are "officially" unemployed if they are "officially" in the labor force (see above) but not "officially" employed (see above).	People are "officially" unemployed if they are "officially" in the labor force (see above) but not "officially" employed (see above).	People are "officially" unemployed if they are "officially" in the labor force (see above) but not "officially" employed (see above).
Receipt of SSDI/SSI participation	Not Applicable	Those who report receiving income from the Social Security Disability Insurance and Supplemental Security Income (SSI) programs in the previous year are considered. It is possible that some SSI recipients are reporting their children's SSI benefits.	Those who report receiving income from the Social Security Disability Insurance (DI) and Supplemental Security Income (SSI) programs in the previous year are considered. It is possible that some SSI recipients are reporting their children's SSI benefits. For DI, we include respondents under age 65 who reported receipt of Social Security benefits and either categorized their main reason for receiving benefits as "disabled" or stated that they also received Medicare.

SOURCE: Derived from various documentation of the National Health Interview Survey (NHIS) 1983–1996, various panels of the Survey of Income and Program Participation (SIPP), and the Current Population Survey (1981–2000).

Table 2A.2 Disability Prevalence Rates Using Alternative Disability Definitions from the NHIS, CPS, and SIPP, by Gender

Year	NHIS Impairment	NHIS Work limitation	CPS Work limitation	CPS One-year limitation	SIPP Work limitation	SIPP Housework limitation	SIPP Other limitation
			Men				
1981	na	na	8.2	na	na	na	na
1982	na	na	8.2	5.0	na	na	na
1983	23.3	10.9	7.8	5.2	na	na	na
1984	24.2	10.2	8.0	4.8	na	na	na
1985	26.1	10.2	8.2	4.9	na	na	na
1986	25.0	10.2	8.3	na	na	na	na
1987	23.9	9.1	8.2	5.3	na	na	na
1988	24.4	9.7	7.7	4.7	na	na	na
1989	22.8	9.9	7.6	4.6	na	na	na
1990	23.7	9.6	7.9	4.7	9.8	5.6	7.7
1991	23.5	9.9	7.7	5.0	9.9	6.2	8.1
1992	26.1	10.9	8.1	4.5	10.2	6.3	8.5
1993	24.5	11.4	8.4	5.3	10.4	6.4	8.6
1994	24.2	10.7	8.8	5.4	na	na	na
1995	22.9	10.9	8.5	5.3	na	na	na
1996	21.6	10.6	8.2	na	10.9	6.2	8.6
1997	na	na	8.3	5.0	na	na	na
1998	na	na	7.8	5.5	na	na	na
1999	na	na	8.0	5.2	na	na	na
2000	na	na	8.0	5.4	na	na	na

	Women				
1981	na	na	7.6	na	na
1982	na	na	7.6	4.0	na	na
1983	16.9	10.7	7.2	3.9	na	na
1984	18.3	10.7	7.2	3.8	na	na
1985	18.9	10.4	7.5	4.0	na	na
1986	17.6	10.0	7.2	na	na	na
1987	18.2	9.7	7.2	4.2	na	na
1988	17.9	9.6	6.7	3.8	na	na
1989	18.0	10.3	6.8	3.3	na	na
1990	18.3	9.6	7.0	3.9	9.3	6.8	11.2
1991	19.2	10.0	7.2	3.5	9.1	7.2	11.0
1992	19.4	10.7	7.2	4.2	10.1	8.1	11.9
1993	19.5	11.4	7.2	4.1	10.1	8.0	12.2
1994	19.6	11.4	8.0	4.4	na	na	na
1995	18.7	10.9	8.2	4.5	na	na	na
1996	18.3	10.7	8.4	na	10.2	6.7	11.4
1997	na	na	8.3	4.9	na	na	na
1998	na	na	8.3	5.1	na	na	na
1999	na	na	7.9	5.2	na	na	na
2000	na	na	7.9	4.8	na	na	na

SOURCE: Authors' calculations using the National Health Interview Survey (NHIS), Current Population Survey (CPS), and the Survey of Income and Program Participation (SIPP). See Appendix Table 2A.1 for details.

Table 2A.3 Yearly Employment Rate Trends of Those with Disabilities in Alternatively Defined Disability Populations from the NHIS, CPS, and SIPP, by Gender

	NHIS		CPS		SIPP			
Year	Impairment	Work limitation	Work limitation	One-year limitation	Work limitation	Housework limitation	Other limitation
			Men				
1980	na	na	42.6	na	na	na	na
1981	na	na	44.8	27.8	na	na	na
1982	na	na	41.8	21.0	na	na	na
1983	80.6	48.9	39.7	20.9	na	na	na
1984	80.9	52.4	40.4	21.8	na	na	na
1985	82.2	50.5	42.8	na	na	na	na
1986	79.6	52.9	43.8	25.5	na	na	na
1987	84.1	49.9	43.0	25.3	na	na	na
1988	84.4	52.1	42.9	23.6	na	na	na
1989	86.1	51.8	44.0	25.2	na	na	na
1990	84.7	50.4	42.1	23.0	53.3	45.4	53.5
1991	82.3	48.7	41.5	23.1	50.4	46.0	53.7
1992	81.8	45.6	41.6	24.9	50.5	49.4	56.6
1993	83.4	47.9	37.2	26.1	48.6	46.2	52.1
1994	81.1	48.6	38.0	20.0	na	na	na
1995	78.5	44.9	34.9	na	na	na	na
1996	77.3	44.4	38.2	23.6	46.6	39.0	50.1
1997	na	na	35.5	20.1	na	na	na
1998	na	na	34.4	18.4	na	na	na

				Women			
1999	na	na	na	34.0	17.1	na	na	na
2000	na	na	na	33.1	na	na	na	na
1980	na	na	na	28.5	na	na	na	na
1981	na	na	na	28.1	14.0	na	na	na
1982	na	na	na	29.3	15.3	na	na	na
1983	56.8	31.3	na	28.9	14.0	na	na	na
1984	57.2	33.5	na	30.2	19.5	na	na	na
1985	59.2	33.5	na	32.4	na	na	na	na
1986	62.0	37.2	na	32.1	21.9	1986	na	na
1987	59.3	36.6	na	33.9	21.4	na	na	na
1988	63.3	37.5	na	36.2	21.4	na	na	na
1989	63.1	38.6	na	37.5	18.3	na	na	na
1990	63.9	40.7	na	34.9	22.2	43.0	42.7	49.0
1991	66.7	39.3	na	35.0	16.7	44.2	37.4	48.6
1992	61.7	39.1	na	34.3	21.3	44.5	39.0	51.9
1993	65.3	39.2	na	33.4	17.8	46.1	41.4	51.0
1994	62.5	38.7	na	36.0	21.1	na	na	na
1995	66.5	40.3	na	33.9	na	na	na	na
1996	63.4	38.5	na	33.9	18.2	39.3	41.4	51.7
1997	na	na	na	31.9	19.8	na	na	na
1998	na	na	na	29.5	17.2	na	na	na
1999	na	na	na	33.4	17.3	na	na	na
2000	na	na	na	32.6	na	na	na	na

SOURCE: Authors' calculations using the National Health Interview Survey (NHIS), Current Population Survey (CPS), and the Survey of Income and Program Participation (SIPP). See Appendix Table 2A.1 for details.

Table 2A.4 Yearly Employment Rate Trends of Those without Disabilities in Alternatively Defined Disability Populations from the NHIS, CPS, and SIPP, by Gender

Year	NHIS Impairment	NHIS Work limitation	CPS Work limitation	CPS One-year limitation	SIPP Work limitation	SIPP Housework limitation	SIPP Other limitation
				Men			
1980	na	na	96.7	na	na	na	na
1981	na	na	96.4	96.4	na	na	na
1982	na	na	95.1	95.1	na	na	na
1983	88.1	90.6	94.7	94.7	na	na	na
1984	90.3	92.5	95.7	95.4	na	na	na
1985	90.9	93.2	95.7	na	na	na	na
1986	89.9	92.9	96.1	95.5	na	na	na
1987	91.2	93.3	95.7	95.7	na	na	na
1988	91.9	93.9	95.8	95.2	na	na	na
1989	91.2	93.9	96.1	95.9	na	na	na
1990	91.3	93.2	95.9	95.5	95.8	94.3	94.8
1991	90.7	92.4	95.4	95.3	94.8	92.9	93.2
1992	89.7	92.0	94.8	94.2	94.8	93.1	93.5
1993	90.4	92.7	94.5	94.5	94.0	92.5	93.0
1994	90.3	92.8	94.8	94.3	na	na	na
1995	91.0	93.3	94.8	na	na	na	na
1996	90.0	93.5	94.9	94.5	93.4	93.7	94.4
1997	na	na	95.2	94.7	na	na	na
1998	na	na	95.1	94.9	na	na	na
1999	na	na	95.2	94.4	na	na	na
2000	na	na	95.2	na	na	na	na

	Women						
1980	na	na	69.3	na	na	na	na
1981	na	na	69.9	68.5	na	na	na
1982	na	na	69.3	67.2	na	na	na
1983	62.5	64.7	70.7	69.0	na	na	na
1984	65.2	66.8	72.6	70.7	na	na	na
1985	66.2	69.3	73.1	na	na	na	na
1986	68.5	70.8	74.4	72.5	na	na	na
1987	70.9	71.3	75.2	73.6	na	na	na
1988	70.2	72.2	76.7	75.4	na	na	na
1989	71.4	73.0	77.0	77.2	na	na	na
1990	70.8	73.5	77.6	76.6	78.6	77.7	78.7
1991	70.9	73.0	77.8	77.6	79.1	78.1	79.0
1992	71.8	74.1	77.6	77.2	79.6	78.4	79.1
1993	72.3	74.3	78.3	78.2	78.4	77.8	78.6
1994	73.3	75.0	79.1	789	na	na	na
1995	74.6	75.8	79.7	na	na	na	na
1996	74.0	76.1	80.1	80.0	80.7	80.5	81.6
1997	na	na	80.7	81.3	na	na	na
1998	na	na	80.8	80.6	na	na	na
1999	na	na	81.6	81.2	na	na	na
2000	na	na	81.3	na	na	na	na

SOURCE: Authors' calculations using the National Health Interview Survey (NHIS), Current Population Survey (CPS), and the Survey of Income and Program Participation (SIPP). See Appendix Table 2A.1 for details.

Table 2A.5 Employment Rate Trends of the Subsample of the Work-Limitation-Based Disability Population Who Report Being "Able to Work" from the NHIS, CPS, and SIPP, by Gender

	Men			Women		
Year	NHIS	CPS	SIPP	NHIS	CPS	SIPP
1981	na	52.7	na	na	30.6	na
1982	na	53.9	na	na	30.2	na
1983	84.7	50.9	na	59.2	31.9	na
1984	86.3	48.6	na	60.3	31.6	na
1985	86.9	48.4	na	62.1	32.4	na
1986	86.0	52.0	na	63.4	34.9	na
1987	86.0	52.7	na	62.4	35.1	na
1988	87.7	52.5	na	64.9	38.0	na
1989	85.1	54.7	na	68.3	41.2	na
1990	88.9	55.8	91.7	69.7	41.7	83.1
1991	85.9	53.9	85.9	68.2	39.8	74.1
1992	82.8	51.7	87.3	67.4	39.6	73.4
1993	83.0	53.0	89.0	68.2	40.4	75.7
1994	86.9	61.6	na	70.7	49.9	na
1995	83.7	64.9	na	72.2	53.2	na
1996	86.3	61.4	91.8	72.0	53.3	81.7
1997	na	67.6	na	na	53.4	na
1998	na	62.7	na	na	52.3	na
1999	na	64.1	na	na	50.1	na
2000	na	64.2	na	na	54.2	na

SOURCE: Authors' calculations using the National Health Interview Survey (NHIS), Current Population Survey (CPS), and the Survey of Income and Program Participation (SIPP). See Appendix Table 2A.1 for details.

Table 2A.6 Trends in the Proportion of the Work-Limitation-Based Disability Population Who Report Being "Able to Work" from the NHIS, CPS, and SIPP, by Gender

	Men			Women		
Year	NHIS	CPS	SIPP	NHIS	CPS	SIPP
1981	na	76.1	na	na	90.3	na
1982	na	80.8	na	na	91.2	na
1983	50.9	77.9	na	44.4	90.4	na
1984	50.9	77.2	na	45.0	89.7	na
1985	48.9	80.1	na	43.7	91.0	na
1986	50.3	77.7	na	47.0	90.2	na
1987	47.6	77.8	na	47.4	89.0	na
1988	49.8	78.0	na	44.7	87.8	na
1989	47.3	73.0	na	44.5	85.4	na
1990	45.1	73.1	55.1	45.8	85.3	45.6
1991	44.0	73.5	55.0	44.5	84.7	45.3
1992	44.4	75.9	54.6	44.9	85.0	47.7
1993	45.8	73.2	51.7	45.1	81.4	48.3
1994	44.7	52.8	na	42.8	59.7	na
1995	43.4	51.0	na	44.5	58.0	na
1996	40.7	49.4	45.2	40.2	56.1	44.1
1997	na	48.7	na	na	55.2	na
1998	na	46.5	na	na	53.2	na
1999	na	45.7	na	na	51.9	na
2000	na	45.4	na	na	53.8	na

SOURCE: Authors' calculations using the National Health Interview Survey (NHIS), Current Population Survey (CPS), and the Survey of Income and Program Participation (SIPP). See Appendix Table 2A.1 for details.

Table 2A.7 Unemployment Rate and Labor Force Participation Trends of Those in the Work-Limitation-Based Disability Population from the NHIS, CPS, and SIPP, by Gender

Year	NHIS Unemployment	NHIS Labor force participation	CPS Unemployment	CPS Labor force participation	SIPP Unemployment	SIPP Labor force participation
			Men			
1981	na	na	13.9	37.3	na	na
1982	na	na	18.3	39.7	na	na
1983	13.2	54.3	20.4	38.2	na	na
1984	12.5	57.9	16.1	37.1	na	na
1985	9.7	54.4	16.4	37.2	na	na
1986	9.9	57.2	14.9	37.5	na	na
1987	9.9	54.2	16.2	38.9	na	na
1988	7.2	55.2	14.4	39.3	na	na
1989	8.8	55.9	13.0	38.2	na	na
1990	8.8	53.8	13.7	38.7	7.9	49.6
1991	11.0	52.9	16.4	36.7	12.2	49.1
1992	12.6	51.2	17.1	38.4	13.0	50.7
1993	9.9	51.9	18.2	38.3	17.1	49.6
1994	9.3	52.6	15.8	32.2	na	na
1995	10.2	49.4	15.5	32.7	na	na
1996	8.2	47.4	14.4	30.7	43.5	43.5
1997	na	na	14.3	32.4	na	na
1998	na	na	12.3	28.1	na	na
1999	na	na	10.1	27.7	na	na
2000	na	na	8.8	27.9	na	na

79

			Women		
1981	na	na	13.7	23.3	na
1982	na	na	16.2	23.1	na
1983	16.3	35.4	15.6	24.9	na
1984	12.3	36.9	13.0	25.2	na
1985	10.1	36.2	15.0	26.9	na
1986	9.1	40.1	15.6	26.8	na
1987	10.1	39.4	14.2	27.8	na
1988	8.0	40.0	11.8	28.8	na
1989	7.6	40.9	9.5	31.4	na
1990	7.4	43.0	10.6	30.4	9.0	35.4
1991	8.6	41.8	12.2	29.4	8.6	32.0
1992	9.0	42.1	15.3	28.9	13.7	32.1
1993	9.0	42.5	11.0	29.4	17.6	31.4
1994	9.6	41.8	14.4	27.4	na	na
1995	6.9	42.6	10.6	27.9	na	na
1996	8.5	41.0	9.5	27.1	7.9	33.8
1997	na	na	11.6	27.7	na	na
1998	na	na	10.2	27.0	na	na
1999	na	na	10.6	23.8	na	na
2000	na	na	10.0	27.3	na	na

SOURCE: Authors' calculations using the National Health Interview Survey (NHIS), Current Population Survey (CPS), and the Survey of Income and Program Participation (SIPP). See Appendix Table 2A.1 for details.

Table 2A.8 SSI and SSDI Beneficiary Rate Trends in the Work-Limitation-Based Disability Population from the CPS and SIPP, by Gender

	Men			Women		
	CPS			CPS		
Year	Work limitation	One-year limitation	SIPP	Work limitation	One-year limitation	SIPP
1980	36.6	na	na	32.3	na	na
1981	36.4	51.5	na	31.2	42.8	na
1982	34.9	52.6	na	31.5	44.5	na
1983	33.4	49.3	na	29.1	40.8	na
1984	36.1	51.4	na	29.1	41.8	na
1985	34.4	na	na	29.9	na	na
1986	36.1	50.1	na	29.6	39.0	na
1987	36.9	54.8	na	33.2	47.6	na
1988	37.5	51.0	na	32.9	47.3	na
1989	37.0	53.0	na	33.0	47.1	na
1990	38.2	57.2	35.5	35.0	50.9	29.7
1991	39.7	56.2	33.5	36.3	48.8	34.6
1992	42.4	60.2	35.6	38.1	50.8	36.6
1993	41.9	55.8	38.2	39.5	54.1	35.5
1994	42.2	58.3	na	36.2	49.2	na
1995	44.4	na	na	40.8	na	na
1996	45.3	58.3	45.6	43.0	56.3	42.5
1997	50.1	63.2	na	43.7	60.1	na
1998	48.5	63.8	na	46.6	56.5	na
1999	48.1	64.3	na	43.8	59.4	na
2000	47.9	na	na	46.0	na	na

SOURCE: Authors' calculations using the National Health Interview Survey (NHIS), Current Population Survey (CPS), and the Survey of Income and Program Participation (SIPP). See Appendix Table 2A.1 for details.

Figure 2A.1 Annual Disability Prevalence Rates of Men in Alternatively Defined Disability Populations from the NHIS, CPS, and SIPP

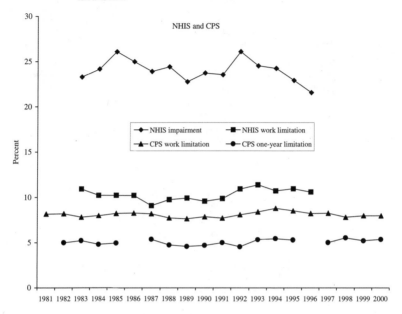

NOTE: Changes in the entire CPS sampling frame in 1986 and 1996 prohibit the creation of one-year limitation values for these years.

SOURCE: Authors' calculations based on data from 1983–1996 NHIS, 1981–2000 CPS, and 1990–1993 and 1996 SIPP.

Figure 2A.1 (continued)

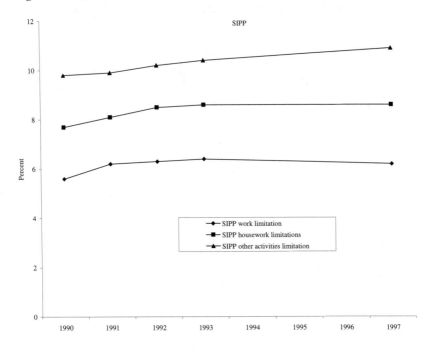

NOTE: Changes in the entire CPS sampling frame in 1986 and 1996 prohibit the creation of one-year limitation values for these years.
SOURCE: Authors' calculations based on data from 1983–1996 NHIS, 1981–2000 CPS, and 1990–1993 and 1996 SIPP.

Figure 2A.2 Annual Disability Prevalence Rates of Women in Alternatively Defined Disability Populations from the NHIS, CPS, and SIPP

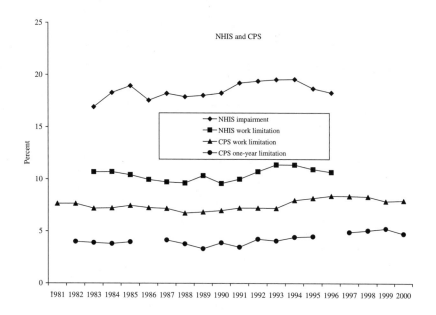

Figure 2A.2 (continued)

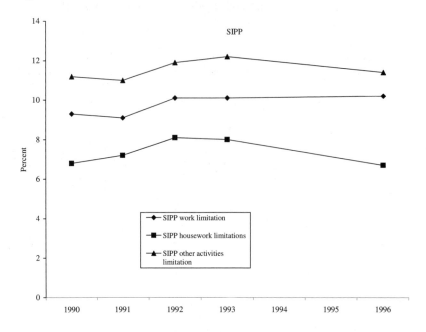

NOTE: Changes in the entire CPS sampling frame in 1986 and 1996 prohibit the creation of one-year limitation values for these years.
SOURCE: Authors' calculations based on data from 1983–1996 NHIS, 1981–2000 CPS, and 1990–1993 and 1996 SIPP.

References

Acemoglu, Daron, and Joshua Angrist. 2001. "Consequences of Employment Protection? The Case of the Americans with Disabilities Act." *Journal of Political Economy* 109 (5): 915–957.

Adler, Michelle. 1991. "The Future of SIPP for Analyzing Disability and Health." Washington, DC: U.S. Department of Health and Human Services, Office of Disability, Aging and Long-Term Care Policy. Available at: <http://aspe.hhs.gov/search/daltcp/Reports/SIPP.HTM>. (Accessed: August 15, 2001.)

Bound, John, and Richard V. Burkhauser. 1999. "Economic Analysis of Transfer Programs Targeted on People with Disabilities." In *Handbook of Labor Economics*, Vol. 3, Orley Ashenfelter and David Card, eds. New York, Amsterdam: Elsevier Science, pp. 3417–3528.

Bound, John, and Timothy Waidmann. 2002. "Accounting for Recent Declines in Employment Rates among the Working-Aged Disabled." *Journal of Human Resources*. 37(2): 231–250.

Burkhauser, Richard V., Mary C. Daly, and Andrew Houtenville. 2001. "How Working Age People with Disabilities Fared over the 1990s Business Cycle." In *Ensuring Health and Income Security for an Aging Workforce*, P. Budetti, R.V. Burkhauser, J. Gregory, and H.A. Hunt, eds. Kalamazoo, MI: W.E. Upjohn Institute for Employment Research, pp. 291–346.

Burkhauser, Richard V., Mary C. Daly, Andrew J. Houtenville, and Nigar Nargis. 2002. "Self-Reported Work Limitation Data: What They Can and Cannot Tell Us." *Demography* 39(3): 541–555.

Burkhauser, Richard V., and Andrew J. Houtenville. Forthcoming. "Employment among Working-Age People with Disabilities: What Current Data Can Tell Us." In *Work and Disability: Issues and Strategies for Career Development and Job Placement*, 2d ed., Edna Mora Szymanski and Randall M. Parker eds. Austin, TX: Pro-Ed, Inc.

Burkhauser, Richard V., and David C. Wittenburg. 1996. "How Current Disability Transfer Policies Discourage Work: Analysis from the 1990 SIPP." *Journal of Vocational Rehabilitation* 7(½): 9–27.

DeLeire, Thomas. 2000. "The Wage and Employment Effects of the Americans with Disabilities Act." *Journal of Human Resources* 35(4): 693–715.

Gordon, Kate, and Catherine Grove, eds. 2000. ADA Symposium Issue. *Berkeley Journal of Employment and Labor Law* 21(1).

Hale, Thomas. 2001. "Lack of a Disability Measure in Today's Current Population Survey." *Monthly Labor Review* 124(6): 38–40.

Houtenville, Andrew J. 2002. "Employment and Economic Consequences of Visual Impairments." In *Visual Impairments: Determining Eligibility for Social Security Benefits,* Peter Lennie and Susan B.Van Hemel, eds. Washington, DC: National Academy Press, pp. 275–321.

Jette, Alan, and Elizabeth Bradley. 2002. "Conceptual Issues in the Measurement of Work Disability." In *The Dynamics of Disability: Measuring and Monitoring Disability for Social Security Programs*, Gooloo Wonderlich, Dorothy P. Rice, and Nicole L. Amado, eds. Washington, DC: National Academy Press, pp. 183–210.

Kaye, H. Stephen. 2002. "Improved Employment Opportunities for People with Disabilities." Disability statistics report no. 17. Washington, DC: U.S. Department of Education, National Institute on Disability and Rehabilitation Research.

Kirchner, Corinne. 1996. "Looking Under the Street Lamp: Inappropriate Uses of Measures Just Because They are There." *Journal of Disability Policy Studies* 7(1): 77–90.

Krieger, Linda H. 2000. "Forward-Backlash against the ADA: Interdisciplinary Perspectives and Implications for Social Justice Strategies." *Berkeley Journal of Employment and Labor Law* 21(1): 1–8.

Maag, Elaine, and David Wittenburg. 2002. "Trends in Disability Prevalence and Employment from the Survey of Income and Program Participation." Washington, DC: The Urban Institute.

Mashaw, Jerry, and Virginia Reno. 1996. "Balancing Security and Opportunity: The Challenge of Disability Income Policy." Report of the Disability Policy Panel, National Academy of Social Insurance, Washington, DC.

McNeil, John. 2000. "Employment, Earnings, and Disability." Paper presented July 3, 2000 at the annual meeting of the Western Economic Association International.

Nagi, Saad. 1965. "Some Conceptual Issues in Disability and Rehabilitation." In *Sociology and Rehabilitation,* M.B. Sussman, ed. Washington, DC: American Sociological Association, pp. 100–113.

———. 1991. "Disability Concepts Revisited: Implications to Prevention." In *Disability in America: Toward a National Agenda for Prevention*, A.M. Pope and A.R. Tarlove, eds. Washington, DC: National Academy Press, pp. 309–327.

Trupin, Laura, Douglas S. Sebesta, Edward Yelin, and Michell P. LaPlante. 1997. "Trends in Labor Force Participation among Persons with Disabilities." Disability statistics report, no. 10. Washington, DC: National Institute on Disability and Rehabilitation Research.

3
Employment Declines among People with Disabilities

Population Movements, Isolated Experience, or Broad Policy Concern?

Andrew J. Houtenville
Cornell University

Mary C. Daly
Federal Reserve Bank of San Francisco

Chapter 2 showed that the decline in employment rates among working-aged men and women with disabilities during the 1990s was not an artifact of measurement choices or research design, but robust across definitions of disability and data sources. Although this overall trend is disturbing, a greater understanding of what underlies it is needed before an appropriate policy response can be crafted. Specifically, policymakers need to know whether the recent employment decline was broad-based or concentrated among a few subgroups of the population, whether it reflects changes in the characteristics of the population with disabilities or changes in their behavior or labor market opportunities, and finally, whether it was associated with exogenous changes in health or changes in environmental factors.

With these questions in mind, we look beyond the overall decline in employment among people with disabilities to track the importance of three factors on the observed changes: 1) trends among key subgroups, especially those with employment-risk factors other than disability; 2) population shifts toward subgroups with lower than average employment rates; and 3) changes in self-reported health status. Our analysis is based on the same cross-sectional data from the Current Population Survey (CPS) discussed in Chapter 2. Throughout the analyses we rely on descriptive analyses and more formal decomposition methods to evaluate the contribution of each of these three factors to the average employment decline described in Chapter 2.

Our results suggest that the decline in employment among those with disabilities was broad-based, present in a wide range of demographic and educational subgroups. In terms of population shifts, we find no evidence that compositional changes in the population with disabilities during the 1990s account for the average employment decline during the period. In contrast, we find that compositional changes were important to the increase in employment among those with disabilities during the 1980s. Finally, we show that self-reported health among those with disabilities remained relatively stable in the latter half of the 1990s, making changes in health status an unlikely cause of declining employment rates.

DATA AND MEASUREMENT

We base our analyses on data from the March CPS discussed in Chapter 2. We focus on working-aged men and women, aged 25–61, who self-report a work-limitation-based disability (defined below).[1] To avoid attributing cyclical fluctuations to secular trends, we make comparisons of employment rates at similar points in the business cycle (see Burkhauser et al. 2002 for a complete description of the relationship between employment rates and business cycles for those with disabilities).

Defining Disability

We use the same conceptualization of disability discussed in Chapter 2.[2] We operationalize this concept using the work-limitation-based definition of disability in the CPS.[3] Although not an ideal measure of disability, the work-limitation-based question in the CPS has been shown to provide a consistent measure of trends in the employment status of people with disabilities.[4] Important for our purpose, the sample size in the CPS is large enough to allow us to focus on the employment of key subgroups within the working-aged population with disabilities and to do so over a long period of time. The CPS question we use is "[D]oes anyone in this household have a health problem or disability which prevents them from working or which limits the kind or amount of work they can do? [If so,] Who is that? (Anyone else?)"

Defining Employment

For consistency, we define employment as in Chapter 2. People are classified as employed if they worked 52 hours or more in the previous year.[5] The use of last year's employment introduces minor time inconsistencies, given that our disability and population characteristics data are for the "current" or survey year. To reduce confusion, we use the employment year to anchor our analysis. We choose the employment year as our point of reference, rather than the survey year, to better control for business cycle effects.

Defining Key Subpopulations

Throughout the analyses we divide the population with disabilities into broad, and frequently overlapping, subgroups based on gender, age, race, and education. Specifically, we compare employment and disability patterns for men, women, whites, nonwhites, individuals aged 25–34, 35–44, 45–54, and 55–61, and individuals with less than high school, high school degree, some college, and college or more. Small sample sizes prohibit us from making more detailed comparisons.

Individuals are classified into as many of these groups as they fit based on responses to survey questions. The CPS questions regarding age and gender are straightforward. Race information comes from the question, "What is [person's] race? Probe: [Is person] White, Black, American Indian, Aleut or Eskimo, Asian or Pacific Islander or something else?" We divide individuals into whites and all others. Education information is derived from two different questions. Prior to 1992, the CPS asked, "[W]hat is the highest grade or year of regular school [person] has ever attended? Did [person] complete that grade (year)?" In 1992, the CPS switched from a "grade/years attended" characterization of education to a "credential" characterization of education: "[W]hat is the highest level of school [person] has completed or the highest degree [person] has received?" To provide continuity, we converted these credentials to years completed using standard assumptions.

Measuring Health

In 1996, the CPS began to include questions regarding self-reported health status. The health question we use is: "Would you say (name's/your) health in general is excellent, very good, good, fair, poor?" Although the short history of this question limits its usefulness in our analyses, we incorporate it as a first indication of the role that health plays in the employment decline among those with disabilities.

SHIFTS IN POPULATION COMPOSITION

As in the U.S. population as a whole, employment rates for those with disabilities vary greatly across key subgroups. Figure 3.1 shows

Figure 3.1 Employment Rates in 2000 of Those Reporting Work Limitations, by Gender, Age, Race, and Education (percentages)

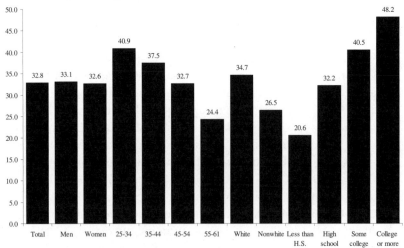

SOURCE: Authors' calculations using the March Current Population Survey, 2001.

employment rates in 2000 of those reporting work limitations, by gender, age, race, and educational attainment. As the figure indicates, among working-aged adults reporting work limitations, employment rates were lower for women than for men, for older than younger workers, and for nonwhites relative to whites. Employment rates also were strongly correlated with educational attainment, being more than twice as high for someone with a college education or more as for someone with less than a high school education.

Although this pattern is not surprising and follows general population trends fairly closely, the different patterns of employment across groups opens the possibility that changes in population shares among those reporting work limitations may be driving the overall decline in the employment of working-aged people with disabilities documented in Chapter 2. This concern is especially salient when one recognizes that these same correlates also are good predictors of disability, as shown in Figure 3.2.[6] For example, the prevalence of disability among those with less than a high school education is six times that of someone with a college education or more.

Figures 3.3–3.6 provide a first look at the role that population shifts may have played in the decline in employment among those with disabilities.[7] The figures display changes in population characteristics (gender, age, race, and education) among those with disabilities from 1980 through 2000. As the figures indicate, there have been some movements in the composition of the population with disabilities during the past two decades. As in the U.S. population more generally, the largest movements have occurred in the age (Figure 3.4) and education (Figure 3.6) distributions. Shifts in the gender (Figure 3.3) and race (Figure 3.5) composition have been substantially smaller. For example, between 1989 and 2000, the share of women in the population with disabilities rose from 48.3 percent to 52.2 percent, an increase of 3.9 percentage points. In the prior decade, the share of women fell slightly, from 50.1 percent in 1980 to 48.3 percent in 1989. Shifts in the racial composition of those with disabilities also have been small. Between 1989 the share of nonwhites increased just slightly, from 19.7 percent in 1980 to 19.8 percent in 1989. Movements in the 1990s also were modest, with the share of nonwhites rising to 22.3 percent by 2000, an increase of 2.5 percentage points from 1989.

Figure 3.2 Prevalence of Work Limitations in Employment in 2000, by Gender, Age, Race, and Education (percentages)

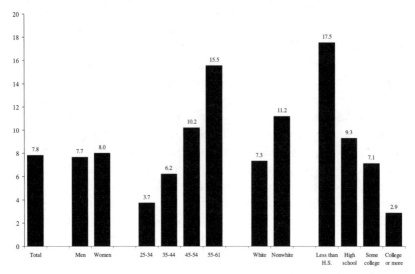

SOURCE: Authors' calculations using the March Current Population Survey, 2001.

Shifts in the distribution of age and education among those with disabilities were far more dramatic. For example, the share of the population with disabilities aged 25–34 fell from 20.3 percent in 1989 to 12.8 percent in 2000, a drop of 7.5 percentage points. In the previous decade, the share of 25–34-year-olds rose slightly. The share of 55–61-year-olds also declined, although the drop was substantially smaller, 2.2 percentage points between 1989 and 2000. The decline in the share of 55–61-year-olds represented a continuation of a trend begun in the 1980s. The population share of the remaining two age groups—35–44 and 45–54—increased during the 1990s. As a result of these shifts, in 2000, 61.5 percent of the population with disabilities was between the ages of 35 and 54, a 10 percentage point increase from 1989.

In considering whether shifts in the age distribution of those with disabilities can explain the relative decline in employment (compared with those without disabilities and over time) two things emerge from these figures. First, although large, movements in the distribution of age among those with disabilities largely mirror shifts in the rest of the

Figure 3.3 Yearly Trends (1980–2000) of Those Reporting Work Limitations, by Gender

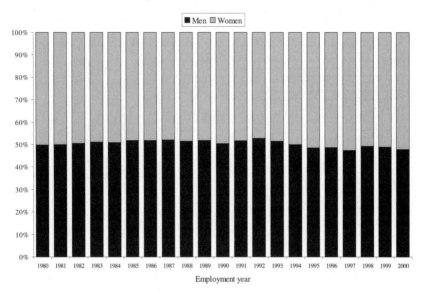

SOURCE: Authors' calculations using the March Current Population Survey, 1981–2001.

population.[8] In 2000, for example, 59.9 percent of the working-aged population without disabilities was between the ages of 35 and 54; in 1989, 51.9 percent of those without disabilities fell within this age range. Thus, differing shifts in age are unlikely to account for the divergent employment experiences of those with disabilities during the 1990s. Second, the effect of shifts in the population with disabilities on the time series of employment trends for those with disabilities is more complicated. The decline in the share of younger adults (aged 25–34) with disabilities should pull down the overall employment rate while the decline in the share of older adults (aged 55–61) should boost it. More formal decomposition analysis, presented later in this chapter, is necessary to quantify the net results of these joint movements.

Turning to education (Figure 3.6), the link between population shifts and employment patterns is clearer. As in the population as a whole, educational attainment among those with disabilities surged during the past two decades. Between 1989 and 2000, the share of the

Figure 3.4 Yearly Trends (1980–2000) of Those Reporting Work Limitations, by Age

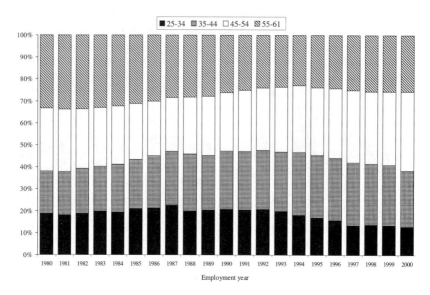

SOURCE: Authors' calculations using the March Current Population Survey, 1981–2001.

population with disabilities and less than a high school education fell by more than 10 percentage points, about the same decline recorded during the 1980s. The share of those with a high school degree also fell, although by a much smaller amount. By 2000, 35.5 percent of the population with disabilities had at least some college; in 1989, only 22.8 percent had some college, and in 1980, about 18 percent had any college.[9] Again, these shifts in educational attainment mirror those for the population without disabilities. More important, given the relationship between education and employment documented in Figure 3.1, the movement toward higher educational attainment should have boosted, rather than pushed down, the population employment rate for those with disabilities. This will be formally examined in the section, "Decomposition of Employment Decline."

Figure 3.5 Yearly Trends (1980–2000) of Those Reporting Work Limitations, by Race (percentages)

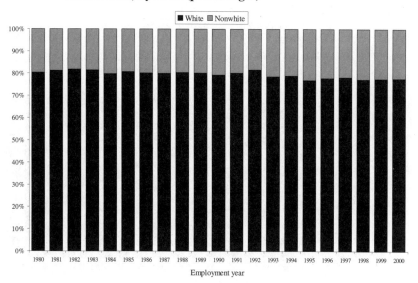

SOURCE: Authors' calculations using the March Current Population Survey, 1981–2001.

ISOLATED OCCURRENCE OR WIDESPREAD DECLINE?

The prior section showed that shifts in population shares toward those with lower than average employment rates is not likely to explain much of the overall decline in employment among working-aged adults with disabilities observed during the 1990s. Nevertheless, this leaves the possibility that decline for one or more subgroups is driving the overall decline, and that this decline is not representative of the experience of all, or even most, subgroups of the population with disabilities. Given the different employment experiences in the cross-section shown in Figure 3.1, such an outcome certainly is plausible.

To examine whether the recent decline in employment rates, as well as the increases during the 1980s, were broad-based across the population with disabilities, Figures 3.7–3.10 show employment rate trends (1980 through 2000) by gender, age group, race, and educational

Figure 3.6 Yearly Trends (1980–2000) of Those Reporting Work Limitations, by Education

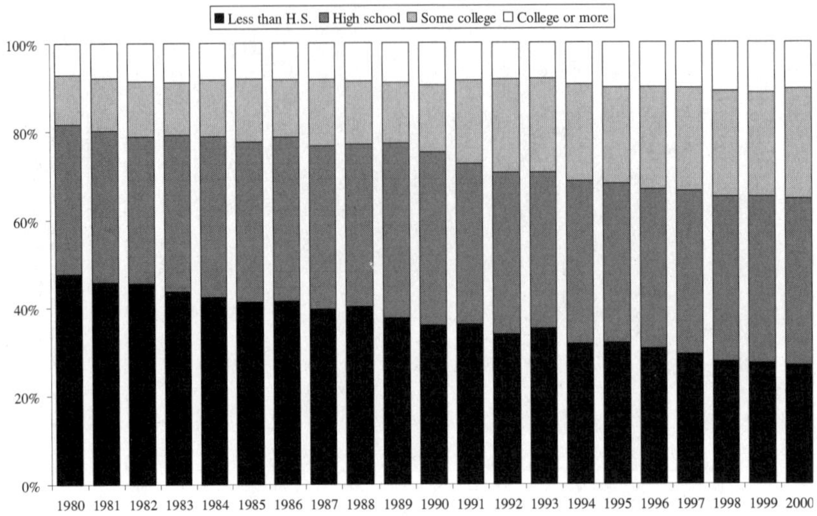

[Stacked bar chart, 1980–2000, with categories: Less than H.S., High school, Some college, College or more]

SOURCE: Authors' calculations using the March Current Population Survey, 1981–2001.

attainment.[10] Similar to Chapter 2, Figure 3.7 points to a substantial decline in employment among both men and women with disabilities during the 1990s. Between 1989 and 2000, the employment rate of men with disabilities declined more than 10 percentage points, from 44.0 percent in 1989 to 33.1 percent in 2000. The decline for women was about half as large, five percentage points, but still sizeable. These declines contrast sharply with the patterns observed for those without disabilities as well as the patterns observed in the previous decade. Over the same period, the employment rate of men without disabilities fell one percentage point, while the employment rate for women without disabilities rose by 4.3 percentage points.[11] Between 1980 and 1989, employment rates for men and women with disabilities rose 1.4 and 9.0 percentage points, respectively.

Figure 3.8 displays employment rates for those with disabilities by four major age groups. As the figure indicates, no age group was immune to the 1990s trend toward lower employment rates. Younger men and women with disabilities aged 25–34 and 35–44 experienced

Figure 3.7 Yearly Employment Rate Trends (1980–2000) of Those Reporting Work Limitations, Total and by Gender (percentages)

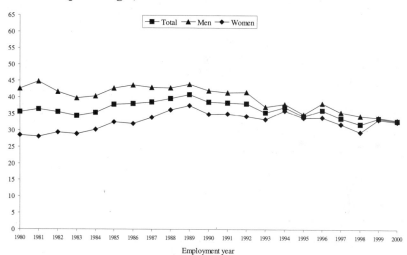

SOURCE: Authors' calculations using the March Current Population Survey, 1981–2001.

the largest declines. Between 1989 and 2000, the employment rate of those with disabilities aged 25–34 fell from 57.5 percent to 40.9 percent, a drop of more than 16 percentage points. The employment rate for those aged 35–44 also fell precipitously, dropping by nearly 11 percentage points over the period. Employment rates of individuals in these age groups without disabilities rose slightly between 1989 and 2000. The 1990s decline in employment among younger adults with disabilities contrasts sharply with the previous decade, when employment rates for 25–34-year-olds with disabilities rose 9 percentage points and employment rates for 35–44-year-olds with disabilities rose 5.3 percentage points.

Declines in employment rates of older men and women with disabilities (aged 45–54 and 55–61) were more modest than those of younger adults during the 1990s. Employment rates dropped 3.8 percentage points for those aged 45–54 and 1.8 percentage points for those aged 55–61. This trend contrasts with the previous decade, when employment rates rose for both age groups with disabilities. It also

Figure 3.8 Yearly Employment Rate Trends (1980–2000) of Those Reporting Work Limitations, by Age (percentages)

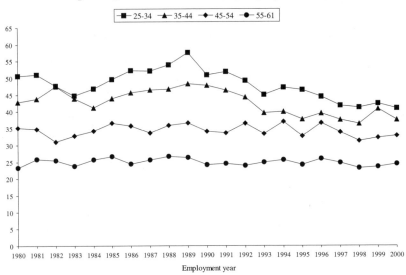

SOURCE: Authors' calculations using the March Current Population Survey, 1981–2001.

contrasts with the trend among same-aged individuals without disabilities during the 1990s, who experienced rising employment rates.

Employment trends by race reveal similar patterns, with employment rates of both whites and nonwhites with disabilities falling during the 1990s (Figure 3.9). The largest declines occurred for whites, with employment falling 9.1 percentage points (from 43.8 to 34.7 percent) between 1989 and 2000. Employment rates for nonwhites fell 2.3 percentage points (from 28.8 to 26.5 percent) over the period. During the previous decade employment rates for whites with disabilities rose 5.7 percentage points, while employment rates for nonwhites increased 3.6 percentage points. Again, the reversal of fortune in employment between the 1980s and 1990s was limited to those with disabilities, with employment rates for whites and nonwhites without disabilities rising between 1989 and 2000.

Figures 3.7–3.9 showed that the decline in employment among working-aged adults with disabilities documented in Chapter 2 was broad-based across gender, age, and racial subgroups. As Figure 3.10

Employment Declines among People with Disabilities 99

Figure 3.9 Yearly Employment Rate Trends (1980–2000) of Those Reporting Work Limitations, by Race (percentages)

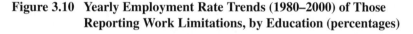

SOURCE: Authors' calculations using the March Current Population Survey, 1981–2001.

Figure 3.10 Yearly Employment Rate Trends (1980–2000) of Those Reporting Work Limitations, by Education (percentages)

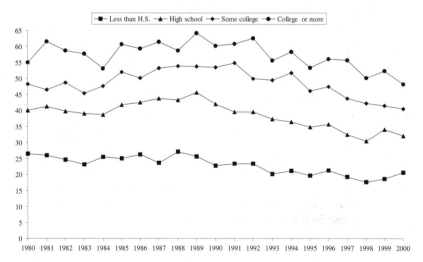

SOURCE: Authors' calculations using the March Current Population Survey, 1981–2001.

shows, the employment decline also was broad-based across subpopulations characterized by different levels of educational attainment. Employment rates of those with disabilities and less than a high school education fell 4.9 percentage points between 1989 and 2000. For similarly educated adults without disabilities, employment rose during the period, hitting a two-decade high in 2000. In contrast to other groups with disabilities, the 1990s decline in employment among those with less than high school represented an acceleration in a downward trend that extended back to 1980; the employment rate for adults with disabilities and less than a high school education fell 0.9 percentage points between 1980 and 1989.

The remaining graphs in Figure 3.10 display the familiar pattern of solid employment gains among those with disabilities during the 1980s followed by substantial employment losses during the 1990s. Employment rates for adults with disabilities and a high school degree or some college fell 13.4 and 13.0 percentage points, respectively, between 1989 and 2000. During the prior decade, employment rates for both groups increased by 5.6 percentage points. The most pronounced declines occurred among college-educated adults with disabilities. Between 1989 and 2000, the employment rate of those with at least a college degree fell 16 percentage points, from 64.2 percent to 48.2 percent. Like most other subpopulations examined, employment rates among college-educated adults with disabilities rose during the previous decade. With the exception of those with college or more, employment rates for comparable educational groups without disabilities increased during the 1990s.

Figures 3.7–3.10 and Appendix Tables 3A.4 and 3A.5 show that the decline in employment among those with disabilities during the 1990s expansion was broad-based, occurring in all major subgroups of the population. The results also indicate that in nearly every case, the 1990s decline represented a significant reversal in the positive employment trends recorded during the 1980s expansion. Finally, the figures highlight the divergence of employment trends for those with disabilities from those in the rest of the population.

DECOMPOSITION OF EMPLOYMENT DECLINE

As shown in Figure 3.7, the overall employment rate of those reporting work limitations declined from 40.8 percent in 1989 (the peak of the 1980s business cycle) to 32.8 percent by 2000 (the peak of the 1990s business cycle). This 8.0 percentage point decline in employment may be due to a change in the characteristics of the population, changes in the employment rates of various subgroups within the population, or to some combination of both factors. The evidence reported above in "Shifts in Population Composition" suggests that the characteristics of the population with disabilities changed substantially during the past two decades. Still, the evidence presented in the prior section indicates that all subgroups experienced declining employment rates during this period, implying that the employment rate of those with disabilities would have declined absent compositional changes. Hence, it is likely that some combination of compositional shifts and subgroup-specific employment rate changes affected the overall decline in employment observed in the data.

To quantify the relative influence of compositional changes and subgroup-specific declines in employment, we rely on a decomposition technique that breaks the 8.0 percentage point employment decline into two components: 1) the change in the composition of the population, and 2) the change in subgroup employment rates. The overall employment rate in any given year (E^t) is the sum of subgroup employment rates (E_g^t) weighted by subgroup population shares (S_g^t) over all subgroups ($g = 1, 2, ... G$). This calculation requires mutually exclusive subgroups. The change in overall employment rates from one year (t) to another year (t') is

$$(1) \quad E^{t'} - E^t = \sum_{g=1}^{G}\left(E_g^{t'} S_g^{t'}\right) - \sum_{g=1}^{G}\left(E_g^t S_g^t\right).$$

To facilitate decomposition, this change can be rewritten as

$$(2) \quad E^{t'} - E^t = \sum_{g=1}^{G}\left(\left(S_g^{t'} - S_g^t\right)\left(E_g^t - E^t\right)\right) + \sum_{g=1}^{G}\left(\left(E_g^{t'} - E_g^t\right)S_g^{t'}\right)$$

$$= \sum_{g=1}^{G}\left(\Delta S_g e_g^t\right) + \sum_{g=1}^{G}\left(\Delta E_g S_g^{t'}\right).$$

In other words, the impact of the change in subgroup composition (the first term) is the weighted sum of changes in subgroup population shares (ΔS_g) over all subgroups, where each subgroup is weighted by the deviation of its initial employment rate from the initial overall employment rate (e_g^t). A rise in a population share of a subgroup with a below-average employment rate will reduce the overall employment rate. The change owing to changes in subgroup employment rates (the second term) is the weighted sum of changes in subgroup employment rates (ΔE_g) over all subgroups, where each subgroup is weighted by its population share in the second year (S_g^t). A rise in the employment rate of any subgroup will increase the overall employment rate.

To perform the decomposition, we divide the population with disabilities into 16 mutually exclusive subgroups based on male, female, white, nonwhite, aged 25–44, aged 45–61, high school or less, and more than high school.[12] Table 3.1 reports the population shares and employment rates for the 16 mutually exclusive subgroups used in the decomposition as well as how they changed between 1980 and 2000 (in percentage point terms).[13] Looking first at changes in population shares, Table 3.1 points to a shift in the population with disabilities towards greater educational attainment. With the exception of white men aged 25–44, educational attainment among all subgroups increased between 1989 and 2000. In most cases, this continued a pattern of improvement begun in the 1980s.

As the last five columns of Table 3.1 show, the patterns for employment rates were much different. Of the 16 subgroups displayed, 5 experienced employment declines between 1980 and 1989, and 13 experienced declines between 1989 and 2000. During the 1990s, the most notable declines in employment were among white men and women aged 25–44 with more than a high school education—27.6 and 20.0 percentage points, respectively. The smallest declines were among white and nonwhite women aged 45–61 with high school or less; employment among white women declined 4.1 percentage points, while nonwhite women in this group experienced a 3.2 percentage point decline in employment between 1989 and 2000. Only nonwhite men aged 45–61 and nonwhite women aged 45–61 with more than high school saw substantial increases in their employment rates over the 1990s. In contrast, during the previous decade employment rates rose for all groups except certain nonwhites and white men with high

Table 3.1 Population Shares and Employment Rates of Those Reporting Work Limitation, by Gender, Age, Race, and Education (16 mutually exclusive groups) (percentages and percentage point changes)

Group	Population shares					Employment rate				
	Employment year			Change		Employment year			Change	
	1980	1989	2000	1980–1989	1989–2000	1980	1989	2000	1980–1989	1989–2000
Total population	100.0	100.0	100.0	0.0	0.0	35.5	40.8	32.8	5.3	-8.0
Men, 25–44, white, HS or less	11.3	14.7	9.9	3.4	-4.8	53.9	50.9	37.6	-3.0	-13.3
Men, 25–44, white, more than HS	4.2	5.2	4.4	1.0	-0.8	70.0	74.4	46.8	4.4	-27.6
Men, 25–44, nonwhite, HS or less	3.4	3.4	3.5	0.0	0.1	24.3	34.2	27.3	9.9	-6.9
Men, 25–44, nonwhite, more than HS	0.8	1.1	1.3	0.3	0.2	54.6	47.4	39.1	-7.2	-8.3
Men, 45–61, white, HS or less	20.3	17.0	14.6	-3.3	-2.4	36.5	34.4	26.5	-2.1	-7.9
Men, 45–61, white, more than HS	4.5	5.2	8.9	0.7	3.7	48.6	53.0	38.1	4.4	-14.9
Men, 45–61, nonwhite, HS or less	4.6	4.4	3.9	-0.2	-0.5	23.4	21.1	21.2	-2.3	0.1
Men, 45–61, nonwhite, more than HS	0.6	0.9	1.4	0.3	0.5	36.0	27.1	36.0	-8.9	8.9
Women, 25–44, white, HS or less	10.8	11.5	8.9	0.7	-2.6	40.3	47.4	34.6	7.1	-12.8
Women, 25–44, white, more than HS	3.4	5.1	5.7	1.7	0.6	55.8	71.2	51.2	15.4	-20.0
Women, 25–44, nonwhite, HS or less	3.2	3.2	3.1	0.0	-0.1	26.4	33.6	28.5	7.2	-5.1
Women, 25–44, nonwhite, more than HS	0.8	0.9	1.8	0.1	0.9	40.0	49.3	43.0	9.3	-6.3
Women, 45–61, white, HS or less	22.1	17.9	15.9	-4.2	-2.0	20.0	26.2	22.1	6.2	-4.1
Women, 45–61, white, more than HS	3.6	3.7	9.4	0.1	5.7	34.0	39.0	46.3	5.0	7.3
Women, 45–61, nonwhite, HS or less	5.7	5.2	4.8	-0.5	-0.4	19.3	20.1	16.9	0.8	-3.2
Women, 45–61, nonwhite, more than HS	0.4	0.7	2.6	0.3	1.9	25.5	38.4	26.0	12.9	-12.4

SOURCE: Authors' calculations using the March Current Population Survey, 1981, 1990, and 2001.

school or less. These simple descriptive statistics point to a broad-based decline in employment among those with disabilities, a decline not fully accounted for by employment reductions among high-risk groups such as nonwhites, older workers, and individuals with below-average educational attainment.

Table 3.2 reports the results of the decompositions. For comparison purposes, we perform the decompositions for both business cycle periods in our sample, 1980–1989 and 1989–2000.[14] The first row of Table 3.2 shows that between 1989 and 2000, changes in employment rates, rather than changes in population shares, account for the 8.0 percentage point decline in overall employment among those with disabilities. Indeed, changes in subgroup population shares contributed positively, albeit modestly, to changes in the overall employment rate during the period, boosting it by 0.2 percentage points. Changes in subgroup employment rates contributed negatively to changes in the overall employment rate, reducing it 8.2 percentage points. This experience contrasts with that of the previous decade, when movements in population shares and changes in subgroup employment rates moved together to boost employment among those with disabilities. Between 1980 and 1989, employment among working-aged adults increased 5.3 percentage points; changes in population shares accounted for 2.2 percentage points while changes in employment rates contributed 3.1 percentage points.[15]

The remaining rows of Table 3.2 display the patterns for each of the 16 subgroups; the third and sixth columns ("Total") show the contribution of each subgroup to the change in the overall employment rate over the period. For example, white men aged 25–44 with more than a high school education contributed negatively to the employment rate of those with disabilities between 1989 and 2000, lowering it 1.5 percentage points. Measured this way, white men aged 25–44 at all levels of education and white women aged 25–44 with high school or less contributed the most to the overall decline in employment, accounting for 4.6 percentage points of the 8.0 percentage point decline. Only three groups contributed positively to the overall employment rate: nonwhite men aged 45–61 in either education group (a total of 0.1 percentage points) and white women aged 45–61 with more than a high school education (0.6 percentage points).

Table 3.2 Decomposition of the Percentage Point Change in the Employment Rate of Those Reporting Work Limitation, by Changes in Population Shares and Employment Rates and by Gender, Age, Race, and Education

	Contribution to change in the overall employment rate							
	1980–1989				1989–2000			
	Percentage point				Percentage point			
Group	Population share	Employment rate	Total	Percent of total[a]	Population share	Employment rate	Total	Percent of total[a]
Total population	2.2	3.1	5.3	100.0	0.2	−8.2	−8.0	100.0
Men, 25–44, white, HS or less	0.6	−0.4	0.2	3.2	−0.5	−1.3	−1.8	−22.4
Men, 25–44, white, more than HS	0.3	0.2	0.6	10.6	−0.3	−1.2	−1.5	−18.4
Men, 25–44, nonwhite, HS or less	0.0	0.3	0.3	6.4	0.0	−0.2	−0.2	−3.0
Men, 25–44, nonwhite, more than HS	0.1	−0.1	0.0	−0.4	0.0	−0.1	−0.1	−1.1
Men, 45–61, white, HS or less	0.0	−0.4	−0.4	−7.4	0.2	−1.1	−1.0	−12.4
Men, 45–61, white, more than HS	0.1	0.2	0.3	5.9	0.5	−1.3	−0.9	−10.9
Men, 45–61, nonwhite, HS or less	0.0	−0.1	−0.1	−1.3	0.1	0.0	0.1	1.1
Men, 45–61, nonwhite, more than HS	0.0	−0.1	−0.1	−1.5	−0.1	0.1	0.1	0.6
Women, 25–44, white, HS or less	0.0	0.8	0.8	15.9	−0.2	−1.1	−1.3	−16.3
Women, 25–44, white, more than HS	0.4	0.8	1.2	21.7	0.2	−1.1	−1.0	−12.1
Women, 25–44, nonwhite, HS or less	0.0	0.2	0.2	4.4	0.0	−0.2	−0.2	−1.9
Women, 25–44, nonwhite, more than HS	0.0	0.1	0.1	1.1	0.1	−0.1	0.0	−0.5
Women, 45–61, white, HS or less	0.7	1.1	1.8	33.3	0.3	−0.6	−0.4	−4.5
Women, 45–61, white, more than HS	0.0	0.2	0.2	3.4	−0.1	0.7	0.6	7.4

Women, 45–61, nonwhite, HS or less	0.1	0.0	0.1	2.5	0.1	-0.2	-0.1	-1.0
Women, 45–61, nonwhite, more than HS	0.0	0.1	0.1	1.1	0.0	-0.3	-0.4	-4.6

[a] Percent of total is calculated as the total percentage point contribution for each subgroup, divided by the total percentage point change in employment.

SOURCE: Authors' calculations using the March Current Population Survey, 1981, 1990, and 2001.

Another useful way to think about the relative contributions of each subgroup to the total decline is to compare their percent of total contributions to the overall employment decline (columns 4 and 8 of Table 3.2) with their population shares (columns 1–3 of Table 3.1). This comparison shows that white men and women of all educational levels contributed disproportionately to the overall decline in employment among those with disabilities during the 1990s. For example, white men with high school or less made up about 12 percent of the population over the 1989–2000 period, but accounted for 22.4 percent of the employment decline among those with disabilities. The relative contribution of white men with more than high school was even larger. Based on their population shares, they should have accounted for about 5 percent of the overall employment decline between 1989 and 2000. Instead, they accounted for 18.4 percent of the decline, roughly four times their population share. The patterns for white women are similar. Overall, this comparison indicates that although nonwhites with lower than average educational attainment make up a disproportionate share of the population with disabilities (15.3 percent in 2000), they accounted for just 4 percent (0.4 percentage points) of the total decline in employment rates among those with disabilities. Taken together, these results support the earlier descriptive evidence that population shifts or narrowly focused employment declines cannot account for the sharp decline in employment among working-aged adults with disabilities during the 1990s.

Finally, some simple counterfactual exercises illustrate these findings. If population shares did not change over this period, and the change in the employment rate for each group were the same, the decline in the employment rate would have been larger, assuming no behavioral or policy responses. Instead of the 8.0 percentage point decline, there would have been an 8.2 percentage point decline. Conversely, if the employment rate within each group did not change over this period, and the population share changes were the same, the employment rate would have increased by 0.2 percentage points.

The results of the decompositions underscore the descriptive analyses in prior sections, pointing to broad-based reductions in employment rates among nearly every subgroup. More important, the results suggest that the largest relative declines in employment were among those groups best prepared to take advantage of the economic expansion of the 1990s (i.e., individuals with more than a high school education). The groups traditionally least attached to the labor market—nonwhites with high school or less—experienced the smallest relative declines in employment. These patterns contrast sharply with those of the 1980s, when large shifts in educational attainment and demographic characteristics helped boost employment rates for those with disabilities.

WITHIN-GROUP CHANGES IN HEALTH

The analyses in the previous sections rule out the possibility that simple shifts in population shares or employment declines among narrowly defined groups explain the aggregate employment trends for the population with disabilities during the 1990s business cycle. The final element of change we consider is the extent to which the population with disabilities is becoming less healthy. The use of self-reported health is not without its problems. However, unlike measures such as the ability to work, it is not directly tied to the employment variable we are tracking in our analysis. Thus, it provides one method of checking whether changes in health, unrelated to changes in labor markets, may be driving the employment declines observed in the 1990s.

Figure 3.11 shows the share of the population with disabilities reporting poor, fair, good, very good, and excellent health. The data are for 1995–2000, the only years these questions appear in the CPS.[16] Although the time series is too short to draw many conclusions about changes in self-reported health, we see no indication of shifts in this variable. There is no visible consistent upward or downward trend. Figure 3.12 considers employment trends among those with disabilities by self-reported health status, once again asking whether the overall decline in employment can be traced to pronounced reductions among one group, such as those with poor health. As the figure shows, there is little evidence that one subgroup accounts for the decline. Rather, the reductions in employment appear broad-based, or evenly slightly weighted toward those with better health.

Figure 3.11 Yearly Trends of Those Reporting Work Limitations, by Self-Reported Health Status (percentages)

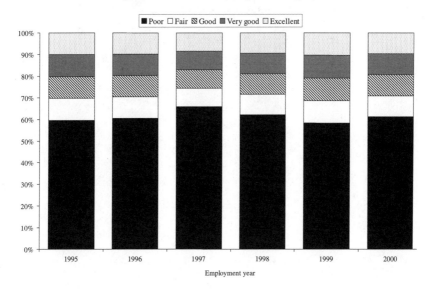

SOURCE: Authors' calculations using the March Current Population Survey, 1996–2001.

Figure 3.12 Yearly Employment Rate Trends (1980–2000) of Those Reporting Work Limitations, by Self-Reported Health Status (percentages)

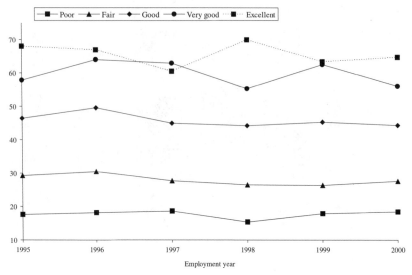

SOURCE: Authors' calculations using the March Current Population Survey, 1996–2001.

CONCLUSION

We began this chapter by asking whether the decline in employment among those with disabilities documented in Chapter 2 was broad-based or narrowly focused, explained by population shifts or changes in behavior or opportunities among those with disabilities, or simply reflective of exogenous deteriorations in health, relatively immune from policy corrections. Our findings point strongly to changes in behavior or opportunities as the key to understanding the recent decline. We show that employment declines were very broad-based across key population subgroups, that the largest contributions to the decline were among subgroups most connected to the labor market, and that shifts in population shares actually contributed positively, rather than negatively, to employment among those with disabilities during the 1990s. These findings tell us that there are no simple answers to the disturbing trend in employment. Instead, the decline appears due to a complex combination of behavioral and policy changes that came together to dramatically alter the connection of people with disabilities to the labor market during the 1990s.

Notes

This research is funded in part by the United States Department of Education, National Institute on Disability and Rehabilitation Research, cooperative agreement No. 13313980038. It does not reflect the view of the National Institute on Disability and Rehabilitation Research or the Federal Reserve Bank of San Francisco.

1. Using this age range avoids confusing reductions in work or economic well-being associated with disabilities, with reductions or declines associated with retirement at older ages, and initial transitions into the labor force related to job shopping at younger ages.
2. Nagi (1991) and the recently developed International Classification of Functioning, Disability, and Health (ICF) provide similar frameworks to conceptualize the definition of disability within the context of social roles and environmental influences.
3. The CPS is a monthly survey of the noninstitutionalized population of the United States. Information is collected on labor force characteristics (e.g., employment, earnings, hours of work). In March of each year, the CPS basic monthly survey is supplemented with the Annual Demographic Survey. This supplement focuses on sources of income, government program participation, annual employment, insurance, and a variety of demographic characteristics. In 1981, the March supplement was expanded to include several questions about disability and income derived from disability programs and insurance. The CPS and the Annual Demographic Survey are used extensively by government agencies, academic researchers, policymakers, journalists, and the general public to evaluate government programs, economic well-being, and behavior or individuals, families, and households.
4. See Burkhauser et al. (2002).
5. Although the CPS obtains information on current employment, the question changed notably in 1994, limiting its usefulness for time series analysis.
6. Appendix Table 3A.1 provides disability prevalence rates by population subgroup from 1980 through 2000. The data show that the patterns described in Figure 3.2 persist across time.
7. The data for Figures 3.3–3.6 are provided in Appendix Table 3A.2. Data for those without disabilities are provided in Appendix Table 3A.3.
8. Although volatile from year to year, the prevalence of disability by age group was largely the same in 2000 as in 1980. The largest changes were for individuals

aged 35–44 and 45–54, for whom prevalence increased in the late 1980s and early 1990s.
9. Decomposing the shift into that associated with general population trends versus that associated with changes in prevalence indicates that for those with high school or some college, the prevalence of work limitation rose substantially in the 1990s (especially for the high school group). This change in prevalence of self-reported work limitation is consistent with the story of Autor and Duggan (2003) which states that replacement rates on earnings for those with relatively low levels of education (i.e., high school only) have risen, inducing more to apply for benefits.
10. The underlying numbers for these figures, referred to in the text, are provided in Appendix Table 3A.4.
11. The figures reported for those without disabilities can be found in Appendix Table 3A.5.
12. Limited sample sizes prohibit us from splitting the population into mutually exclusive subgroups based on the full set of subgroups in the previous sections.
13. Appendix Table 3A.6 provides the data for the population without disabilities.
14. Decomposition results for those without disabilities are provided in Appendix Table 3A.7.
15. To check the robustness of our findings, we pooled the data into three-year periods 1987–1989 and 1998–2000. The results were very similar. We also tried different education subcategories (less than high school and high school or more), and again the results were very similar. These results are available upon request.
16. Appendix Table 3A.8 provides similar information for those without disabilities.

Appendix 3A

Supplementary Tables

Table 3A.1 Prevalence of Work Limitation, by Gender, Age, Race, and Education (percentages)

Employ-ment year	Gender			Age				Race		Education			
	Total	Men	Women	25–34	35–44	45–54	55–61	White	Nonwhite	Less than H.S.	High school	Some college	College or more
1980	7.9	8.2	7.6	4.0	5.9	10.3	16.8	7.3	12.9	16.3	6.6	5.3	2.9
1981	7.9	8.2	7.6	3.9	5.9	10.4	17.4	7.4	12.2	16.5	6.7	5.6	3.1
1982	7.5	7.8	7.2	3.8	5.7	9.7	16.7	7.1	11.1	16.2	6.2	5.4	3.0
1983	7.6	8.0	7.2	4.1	5.6	9.8	17.1	7.1	11.2	16.6	6.6	5.2	3.1
1984	7.8	8.2	7.5	4.1	6.0	10.2	17.5	7.2	12.4	17.3	7.0	5.6	2.9
1985	7.7	8.3	7.2	4.4	6.0	9.8	17.2	7.2	11.5	17.2	6.9	5.9	2.8
1986	7.7	8.2	7.2	4.4	6.2	9.5	17.0	7.2	11.6	17.7	7.0	5.3	2.8
1987	7.2	7.7	6.7	4.4	5.9	8.6	15.6	6.7	11.0	16.1	6.6	5.8	2.6
1988	7.2	7.6	6.8	4.0	6.3	9.0	16.0	6.8	10.4	16.9	6.7	5.5	2.6
1989	7.4	7.9	7.0	4.2	6.0	9.5	16.6	7.0	10.9	17.0	7.3	5.1	2.8
1990	7.5	7.7	7.2	4.4	6.3	9.4	15.8	6.9	11.1	16.8	7.4	5.6	3.0
1991	7.6	8.1	7.2	4.6	6.4	9.7	15.9	7.2	10.6	18.1	7.6	6.0	2.7
1992	7.8	8.4	7.2	4.8	6.5	9.7	15.6	7.5	10.0	18.2	8.0	6.5	2.6
1993	8.4	8.8	8.0	5.1	7.0	10.7	17.1	7.8	12.5	20.6	8.6	6.7	2.7
1994	8.3	8.5	8.2	4.7	7.3	10.6	16.7	7.8	12.5	19.3	9.1	6.9	3.0
1995	8.3	8.2	8.4	4.5	7.3	10.5	16.8	7.6	12.6	19.0	8.9	6.9	3.2
1996	8.3	8.3	8.3	4.3	7.1	10.6	16.9	7.7	12.2	18.7	8.9	7.3	3.2
1997	8.1	7.8	8.3	3.6	7.0	10.5	16.5	7.6	11.2	18.1	8.9	7.0	3.1
1998	7.9	8.0	7.9	3.8	6.7	10.0	16.2	7.3	11.8	17.3	9.0	7.1	3.1
1999	7.9	8.0	7.9	3.8	6.7	9.8	16.1	7.4	11.7	17.9	9.2	6.9	3.2
2000	7.8	7.7	8.0	3.7	6.2	10.2	15.5	7.3	11.2	17.5	9.3	7.1	2.9

SOURCE: Authors' calculations using the March Current Population Survey, 1981–2001.

Table 3A.2 Share Composition of Those Reporting Work Limitation, by Gender, Age, Race, and Education (percentages)

Employ- ment year	Gender		Age					Race		Education			
	Men	Women	25–34	35–44	45–54	55–61		White	Nonwhite	Less than H.S.	High school	Some college	College or more
1980	49.9	50.1	18.8	19.2	28.8	33.2		80.3	19.7	47.7	33.9	11.2	7.2
1981	50.0	50.0	18.2	19.7	28.4	33.8		81.4	18.6	45.8	34.4	12.0	7.8
1982	50.5	49.5	18.8	20.5	27.2	33.5		81.8	18.2	45.5	33.3	12.6	8.6
1983	51.0	49.0	19.8	20.4	26.8	33.1		81.4	18.6	43.8	35.4	12.1	8.8
1984	50.9	49.1	19.3	21.8	26.6	32.2		79.8	20.2	42.5	36.3	12.9	8.3
1985	51.9	48.1	20.8	22.4	25.5	31.2		80.7	19.3	41.4	36.2	14.3	8.2
1986	51.9	48.1	21.3	23.7	24.9	30.2		80.3	19.7	41.5	37.2	13.0	8.3
1987	52.1	47.9	22.6	24.5	24.5	28.5		80.0	20.0	39.8	36.9	15.1	8.3
1988	51.4	48.6	19.9	26.1	25.8	28.2		80.5	19.5	40.2	36.8	14.5	8.6
1989	51.7	48.3	20.3	24.9	27.0	27.8		80.2	19.8	37.7	39.5	13.8	9.0
1990	50.4	49.6	20.6	26.6	26.5	26.3		79.4	20.6	36.0	39.2	15.3	9.5
1991	51.6	48.4	20.5	26.5	27.9	25.1		80.2	19.8	36.3	36.3	18.9	8.5
1992	52.8	47.2	20.6	26.9	28.4	24.0		81.6	18.4	33.9	36.6	21.2	8.3
1993	51.5	48.5	19.8	27.0	29.5	23.7		78.6	21.4	35.3	35.2	21.4	8.1
1994	50.0	50.0	17.9	28.8	30.4	22.9		78.9	21.1	31.8	36.8	22.1	9.3
1995	48.5	51.5	16.7	28.7	30.7	23.9		77.0	23.0	31.9	36.0	22.0	10.0
1996	48.8	51.2	15.7	28.4	31.7	24.2		77.8	22.2	30.7	36.0	23.3	10.1
1997	47.5	52.5	13.2	28.8	33.0	25.0		78.3	21.7	29.5	36.9	23.3	10.3
1998	49.2	50.8	13.6	27.9	32.8	25.6		77.2	22.8	27.7	37.3	23.9	11.0
1999	48.9	51.1	13.3	27.7	33.3	25.7		77.5	22.5	27.4	37.7	23.6	11.3
2000	47.8	52.2	12.8	25.6	35.9	25.6		77.7	22.3	26.8	37.7	25.0	10.5

SOURCE: Authors' calculations using the March Current Population Survey, 1981–2001.

Table 3A.3 Share Composition of Those Reporting No Work Limitation, by Gender, Age, Race, and Education (percentages)

Employ-ment year	Gender		Age					Race		Education			
	Men	Women	25–34	35–44	45–54	55–61		White	Nonwhite	Less than H.S.	High school	Some college	College or more
1980	48.1	51.9	38.4	26.1	21.5	14.0		87.8	12.2	20.9	41.3	17.3	20.5
1981	48.2	51.8	38.6	26.8	20.9	13.7		87.6	12.4	19.9	41.4	17.5	21.3
1982	48.2	51.8	38.4	27.6	20.5	13.5		87.1	12.9	19.1	40.8	17.7	22.3
1983	48.2	51.8	38.4	28.4	20.1	13.1		87.1	12.9	18.1	41.1	18.0	22.8
1984	48.2	51.8	38.4	28.9	19.9	12.9		86.9	13.1	17.3	40.8	18.6	23.3
1985	48.3	51.7	38.4	29.3	19.7	12.6		86.7	13.3	16.7	40.8	19.1	23.3
1986	48.3	51.7	38.3	29.7	19.7	12.2		86.4	13.6	16.0	40.9	19.4	23.7
1987	48.4	51.6	37.8	30.1	20.2	11.9		86.3	13.7	16.1	40.6	19.2	24.1
1988	48.5	51.5	37.5	30.5	20.4	11.6		86.0	14.0	15.4	40.1	19.4	25.1
1989	48.5	51.5	36.9	31.3	20.6	11.2		85.8	14.2	14.8	39.9	20.3	25.1
1990	48.7	51.3	36.1	32.0	20.6	11.3		85.8	14.2	14.4	39.8	20.7	25.2
1991	48.6	51.4	35.3	32.3	21.4	11.0		85.4	14.6	13.6	36.4	24.8	25.3
1992	48.6	51.4	34.2	32.5	22.3	11.0		85.2	14.8	12.8	35.4	25.8	25.9
1993	48.8	51.2	33.9	33.0	22.6	10.5		85.1	14.9	12.4	34.3	27.0	26.3
1994	48.9	51.1	33.2	33.1	23.3	10.4		85.3	14.7	12.0	33.6	27.3	27.1
1995	49.0	51.0	32.4	33.2	23.6	10.7		84.5	15.5	12.3	33.2	27.0	27.5
1996	49.1	50.9	31.5	33.5	24.3	10.7		84.2	15.8	12.1	33.3	26.9	27.7
1997	49.1	50.9	30.6	33.5	24.8	11.1		83.9	16.1	11.7	33.0	27.0	28.3
1998	48.8	51.2	29.6	33.4	25.5	11.4		83.9	16.1	11.4	32.4	26.9	29.2
1999	48.8	51.2	28.8	33.2	26.4	11.6		83.8	16.2	10.8	32.0	27.5	29.6
2000	48.9	51.1	28.3	33.0	26.9	11.9		83.4	16.6	10.7	31.4	27.7	30.2

SOURCE: Authors' calculations using the March Current Population Survey, 1981–2001.

Table 3A.4 Employment Rates of Those Reporting Work Limitations, by Gender, Age, Race, and Education (percentages)

Employ-ment year	Total	Gender		Age					Race		Education			
		Men	Women	25–34	35–44	45–54	55–61		White	Nonwhite	Less than H.S.	High school	Some college	College or more
1980	35.5	42.6	28.5	50.6	42.9	35.1	23.2		38.1	25.2	26.4	40.0	48.2	55.0
1981	36.5	44.8	28.1	51.0	43.7	34.7	25.8		39.0	25.3	26.0	41.2	46.5	61.5
1982	35.6	41.8	29.3	47.6	47.4	31.0	25.4		37.7	26.4	24.6	39.8	48.7	58.7
1983	34.4	39.7	28.9	44.8	43.9	32.7	23.8		37.1	22.6	23.1	39.0	45.4	57.7
1984	35.4	40.4	30.2	46.8	41.2	34.1	25.7		38.2	24.3	25.5	38.7	47.6	53.1
1985	37.8	42.8	32.4	49.5	43.9	36.6	26.7		40.0	28.6	25.0	41.8	52.0	60.7
1986	38.1	43.8	32.1	52.2	45.6	35.7	24.4		40.1	30.2	26.2	42.5	50.2	59.3
1987	38.6	43.0	33.9	52.1	46.5	33.6	25.6		41.6	26.7	23.6	43.8	53.3	61.5
1988	39.6	42.9	36.2	53.8	46.6	35.8	26.6		42.4	28.0	27.1	43.2	53.9	58.7
1989	40.8	44.0	37.5	57.5	48.2	36.5	26.2		43.8	28.8	25.5	45.6	53.8	64.2
1990	38.5	42.1	34.9	50.9	47.8	34.1	24.1		41.7	26.3	22.8	42.0	53.5	60.2
1991	38.4	41.5	35.0	51.8	46.3	33.6	24.5		41.2	27.0	23.4	39.5	54.9	60.9
1992	38.2	41.6	34.3	49.2	44.2	36.5	23.9		41.1	25.1	23.4	39.5	50.0	62.5
1993	35.3	37.2	33.4	45.0	39.6	33.4	24.8		37.5	27.4	20.2	37.3	49.5	55.6
1994	37.0	38.0	36.0	47.1	39.9	36.9	25.6		40.6	23.7	21.1	36.5	51.8	58.4
1995	34.3	34.9	33.9	46.4	37.7	32.6	24.1		37.7	23.1	19.7	34.8	46.1	53.3
1996	36.0	38.2	33.9	44.3	39.5	36.6	25.9		38.8	26.5	21.2	35.7	47.4	56.1
1997	33.6	35.5	31.9	41.8	37.5	33.8	24.7		35.8	25.8	19.3	32.5	43.8	55.7
1998	31.9	34.4	29.5	41.1	36.4	31.2	23.2		34.3	24.0	17.7	30.6	42.2	50.1
1999	33.7	34.0	33.4	42.3	40.8	32.2	23.6		35.6	27.0	18.7	34.1	41.5	52.3
2000	32.8	33.1	32.6	40.9	37.5	32.7	24.4		34.7	26.5	20.6	32.2	40.5	48.2

SOURCE: Authors' calculations using the March Current Population Survey, 1981–2001.

Table 3A.5 Employment Rates of Those Reporting No Work Limitation, by Gender, Age, Race, and Education (percentages)

Employ-ment year	Total	Gender		Age				Race		Education			
		Men	Women	25–34	35–44	45–54	55–61	White	Non-white	Less than H.S.	High school	Some college	College or more
1980	82.5	96.7	69.3	84.4	84.2	82.7	73.8	82.8	80.6	74.2	81.3	85.6	90.8
1981	82.7	96.4	69.9	84.3	85.1	82.6	73.9	83.0	81.0	74.2	81.3	85.9	90.8
1982	81.7	95.1	69.3	83.4	84.3	81.3	72.2	82.2	78.2	71.2	80.0	85.3	90.9
1983	82.2	94.7	70.7	83.5	84.9	82.4	72.7	82.8	78.6	71.4	80.6	85.6	91.1
1984	83.7	95.7	72.6	85.5	85.9	83.9	73.4	84.1	81.1	72.7	82.6	87.4	91.1
1985	84.0	95.7	73.1	85.4	86.7	84.7	72.7	84.4	81.9	73.2	82.9	86.9	91.5
1986	84.9	96.1	74.4	85.9	87.9	85.5	73.4	85.2	82.7	74.1	83.5	87.9	92.1
1987	85.2	95.7	75.2	86.5	88.0	85.5	73.2	85.7	82.0	73.6	84.1	88.5	91.9
1988	85.9	95.8	76.7	86.7	88.9	86.3	75.0	86.5	82.5	73.7	85.0	89.4	92.3
1989	86.3	96.1	77.0	87.3	88.8	87.0	74.8	86.8	83.3	74.5	85.6	88.7	92.3
1990	86.5	95.9	77.6	87.1	89.0	87.4	75.9	87.1	82.9	75.1	85.6	88.9	92.4
1991	86.4	95.4	77.8	86.7	88.7	87.8	75.5	87.1	82.3	73.5	85.5	88.9	92.1
1992	86.0	94.8	77.6	86.4	88.1	87.3	75.6	86.8	81.3	72.4	84.7	88.7	91.7
1993	86.2	94.5	78.3	86.4	88.0	88.0	76.2	87.0	81.9	73.7	84.8	88.5	91.6
1994	86.8	94.8	79.1	86.6	88.5	88.8	77.6	87.3	83.6	74.2	85.5	89.0	91.8
1995	87.1	94.8	79.7	86.8	89.0	88.9	77.9	87.7	83.5	74.5	85.9	89.7	91.6
1996	87.3	94.9	80.1	87.3	88.7	89.4	78.6	88.0	84.0	74.7	86.6	89.4	91.8
1997	87.8	95.2	80.7	88.2	88.9	89.8	78.9	88.2	85.6	77.1	86.6	89.6	92.0
1998	87.8	95.1	80.8	87.9	89.3	89.6	79.0	88.2	85.8	76.5	86.9	89.6	91.5
1999	88.2	95.2	81.6	88.5	89.7	90.3	78.6	88.4	87.4	77.3	87.2	89.9	91.7
2000	88.1	95.2	81.3	88.4	89.7	90.1	78.3	88.3	86.9	77.7	87.5	89.7	90.8

SOURCE: Authors' calculations using the March Current Population Survey, 1981–2001.

Table 3A.6 Population Shares and Employment Rates of Those Reporting No Work Limitations, by Gender, Age, Race, and Education (16 mutually exclusive groups) (percentages and percentage point changes)

Group	Population shares					Employment rate				
	Employment year			Change		Employment year			Change	
	1980	1989	2000	1980–1989	1989–2000	1980	1989	2000	1980–1989	1989–2000
Total population	100.0	100.0	100.0	0.0	0.0	82.5	86.3	88.1	3.8	1.8
Men, 25–44, white, HS or less	14.2	14.2	11.1	0.0	-3.1	98.1	97.3	96.5	-0.8	-0.8
Men, 25–44, white, more than HS	13.3	14.5	13.9	1.2	-0.6	98.2	98.2	97.6	0.0	-0.6
Men, 25–44, nonwhite, HS or less	2.3	2.5	2.3	0.2	-0.2	90.5	88.6	89.7	-1.9	1.1
Men, 25–44, nonwhite, more than HS	1.5	2.0	2.8	0.5	0.8	91.7	95.1	94.3	3.4	-0.8
Men, 45–61, white, HS or less	9.8	7.4	6.3	-2.4	-1.1	95.2	93.6	92.6	-1.6	-1.0
Men, 45–61, white, more than HS	5.4	6.1	10.0	0.7	3.9	97.6	96.1	94.7	-1.5	-1.4
Men, 45–61, nonwhite, HS or less	1.3	1.2	1.2	-0.1	0.0	92.2	89.8	86.1	-2.4	-3.7
Men, 45–61, nonwhite, more than HS	0.4	0.6	1.4	0.2	0.8	92.6	94.9	93.5	2.3	-1.4
Women, 25–44, white, HS or less	17.3	15.3	9.9	-2.0	-5.4	67.5	75.0	76.5	7.5	1.5
Women, 25–44, white, more than HS	11.2	14.0	15.3	2.8	1.3	79.0	85.0	85.0	6.0	0.0
Women, 25–44, nonwhite, HS or less	3.1	3.2	2.5	0.1	-0.7	66.7	71.3	82.2	4.6	10.9
Women, 25–44, nonwhite, more than HS	1.6	2.4	3.5	0.8	1.1	83.5	86.2	85.7	2.7	-0.5
Women, 45–61, white, HS or less	12.5	9.3	7.4	-3.2	-1.9	61.2	67.7	74.2	6.5	6.5
Women, 45–61, white, more than HS	4.1	5.0	9.5	0.9	4.5	70.6	78.9	84.3	8.3	5.4
Women, 45–61, nonwhite, HS or less	1.7	1.5	1.5	-0.2	0.0	67.2	69.2	74.0	2.0	4.8
Women, 45–61, nonwhite, more than HS	0.4	0.7	1.5	0.3	0.8	86.2	85.1	86.3	-1.1	1.2

SOURCE: Authors' calculations using the March Current Population Survey, 1981, 1990, and 2001.

Table 3A.7 Decomposition of the 1.8 Percentage Point Increase in the Employment Rate of Those Reporting No Work Limitations, by Changes in Population Shares and Employment Rates and by Gender, Age, Race, and Education

	Contribution to change in the overall employment rate							
	1980–1989				1989–2000			
	Percentage point				Percentage point			
Group	Population share	Employment rate	Total	Percent of total[a]	Population share	Employment rate	Total	Percent of total[a]
Total population	0.9	2.9	3.8	100.0	0.7	1.0	1.8	100.0
Men, 25–44, white, HS or less	0.0	-0.1	-0.1	-2.9	-0.3	-0.1	-0.4	-24.1
Men, 25–44, white, more than HS	0.2	0.0	0.2	5.0	-0.1	-0.1	-0.2	-9.0
Men, 25–44, nonwhite, HS or less	0.0	0.0	0.0	-0.8	0.0	0.0	0.0	1.1
Men, 25–44, nonwhite, more than HS	0.1	0.1	0.1	3.2	0.1	0.0	0.0	2.2
Men, 45–61, white, HS or less	-0.3	-0.1	-0.4	-11.1	-0.1	-0.1	-0.1	-7.8
Men, 45–61, white, more than HS	0.1	-0.1	0.0	0.0	0.4	-0.1	0.3	14.0
Men, 45–61, nonwhite, HS or less	0.0	0.0	0.0	-1.1	0.0	0.0	0.0	-2.2
Men, 45–61, nonwhite, more than HS	0.0	0.0	0.0	1.1	0.1	0.0	0.1	2.8
Women, 25–44, white, HS or less	0.3	1.1	1.4	38.0	0.6	0.1	0.8	42.6
Women, 25–44, white, more than HS	-0.1	0.9	0.8	19.8	0.0	0.0	0.0	-1.7
Women, 25–44, nonwhite, HS or less	0.0	0.1	0.1	3.7	0.1	0.3	0.4	21.3
Women, 25–44, nonwhite, more than HS	0.0	0.1	0.1	1.8	0.0	0.0	0.0	-1.1
Women, 45–61, white, HS or less	0.7	0.6	1.3	34.0	0.4	0.5	0.8	46.5
Women, 45–61, white, more than HS	-0.1	0.4	0.3	8.2	-0.3	0.5	0.2	10.1
Women, 45–61, nonwhite, HS or less	0.0	0.0	0.1	1.3	0.0	0.1	0.1	3.9
Women, 45–61, nonwhite, more than HS	0.0	0.0	0.0	0.0	0.0	0.0	0.0	0.6

[a] Percent of total is calculated as the total percentage point contribution for each subgroup, divided by the total percentage point change in employment.

SOURCE: Authors' calculations using the March Current Population survey, 1981, 1990, and 2001.

Table 3A.8 Population Shares and Employment Rates of Those Reporting No Work Limitations, by Self-Reported Health (percentages)

Year	Population share Self-reported health status				
	Poor	Fair	Good	Very good	Excellent
1995	30.3	32.9	21.6	10.1	5.1
1996	30.8	32.2	22.6	9.4	5.0
1997	30.2	33.0	23.5	9.4	3.9
1998	29.6	34.0	22.2	9.7	4.5
1999	29.5	32.5	23.4	9.3	5.3
2000	30.6	33.9	21.4	9.3	4.8
	Employment rate				
1995	17.6	29.3	46.4	57.8	68.0
1996	18.2	30.5	49.6	64.0	67.0
1997	18.7	27.7	45.0	63.0	60.5
1998	15.4	26.5	44.3	55.3	69.9
1999	18.0	26.4	45.3	62.6	63.5
2000	18.4	27.6	44.4	56.1	64.7

NOTE: Survey years 1998–2001.
SOURCE: Authors' calculations using the March Current Population Survey, 1996–2001.

References

Autor, David and Mark Duggan. 2003. "The Rise in Disability Recipiency and the Decline in Unemployment." *Quarterly Journal of Economics* 118(1): 157–205.

Burkhauser, Richard V., Mary C. Daly, Andrew J.Houtenville, and Nigar Nargis. 2002. "Self-Reported Work Limitation Data: What They Can and Cannot Tell Us." *Demography* 39 (3): 541–555.

Nagi, Saad. 1991. "Disability Concepts Revisited: Implications for Prevention." In *Disability in America: Toward a National Agenda for Prevention*. A.M. Pope and A.R. Tarlove, eds. Washington DC: National Academy Press, pp. 309–327.

4
Have Changes in the Nature of Work or the Labor Market Reduced Employment Prospects of Workers with Disabilities?

David C. Stapleton
Nanette Goodman
Andrew J. Houtenville
Cornell University

According to conventional wisdom, the world of work has changed dramatically in response to globalization and technological change. Companies are restructuring, reorganizing, reinventing, and demanding different skills from their workers. At the same time, the conventional wisdom tells us that the long-term relationship between employer and employee is dead and that we should expect to change professions three times, and jobs six times, over our working lives. Although the conventional wisdom may be overstated, the nature of work is clearly changing, and the labor market is in constant flux. Some allege that recent changes have made it more difficult for people with disabilities to compete for jobs, while others claim the opposite. Because people with disabilities are widely diverse, both could be right.

Beginning in 1990, the employment rate of men and women with disabilities fell relative to that of the rest of the working-aged population (see Chapter 2). In this chapter, we look at this decline from a somewhat different perspective. We consider the decline in the percentage of jobs filled by workers who report work limitations and how that might be related to changes in the nature of those jobs.

The trend in the percentage of jobs filled by workers with limitations reflects the trend in the employment rate for people with disabilities, although there are important qualitative differences (Figure 4.1).[1] After hovering at just above 2.8 percent from 1985 to 1995, the three-

Figure 4.1 Three-Year Moving Average of Percentage of Jobs Filled by Workers with Work Limitations

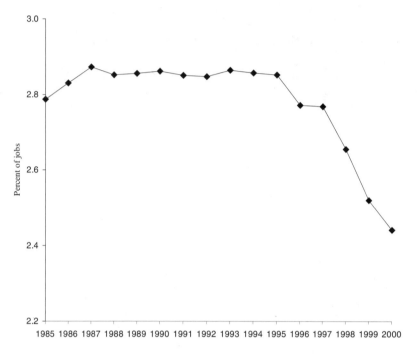

SOURCE: Authors' calculations based on the 1991 *Dictionary of Occupational Titles* job characteristics merged with CPS March Supplement 1985–2000.

year moving average started to fall. By comparison, the decline in the employment rate of people with disabilities starts in 1990. The fall in the percentage of jobs filled by workers with limitations is especially precipitous from 1998 to 2000, and by 2000, the percentage was below 2.5 percent.[2] This decline coincided with an economic expansion, but a similar decline did not occur during the expansion of 1985–1989.

This chapter considers whether changes in the nature of work might account for the decline. On the one hand, it seems that the increasing technical skills demanded by employers would disadvantage people with disabilities who, on average, attain substantially less schooling. It also is widely believed that work is becoming more stressful, requiring greater adaptability on the part of the employee, again to the disadvantage of people with disabilities. On the other hand, the physical demands of work have declined, and information and other technologies might have made it easier for people with disabilities to compete.

We distinguish between two aspects of work. The first is the "static" aspect. This refers to what we would see workers doing, what qualifications they would have, and what their work environment would look like if we took a snapshot of them at a point in time. Clearly, a snapshot taken today would show a much different set of activities, qualifications, and environments than a snapshot taken 20, or even 10, years ago.[3] We can then ask if, relative to workers without disabilities, workers with disabilities are more or less qualified to perform the activities seen in today's snapshot than in snapshots taken one or two decades ago.

The second is the "dynamic" aspect of work. This refers to the features of change itself as work moves from what we see in one snapshot to what we see in a later one—that is, what we would see in the motion picture besides just a series of snapshots. To what extent do workers need to perform new activities to be successful? Do they need to retrain often? How often do they need to change employers? Frequent or unpredictable changes such as these might disadvantage most workers with disabilities relative to workers without disabilities because of the role that the environment plays in determining whether a physical or mental condition is accompanied by a work limitation. Even when the final result of the change is a very positive one for the person with a disability (e.g., a better job), the process of change itself (e.g., finding the new job and adapting to it) might be very difficult.[4]

Clearly, it is critical to recognize the diversity of people with disabilities when considering this issue—diversity in age of onset, education, work experience, family supports, as well as diversity in physical or mental conditions. Our limited task, however, is to assess the extent to which changes in the characteristics of work might have contributed to the overall decline in the employment rate. Future work that focuses on specific subgroups could be of substantial value.

In the next section, we present empirical evidence on how static job characteristics have changed, the relationship between those characteristics and the percentage of workers with limitations in an occupation, and the effects of changes in job characteristics on the overall percentage of workers with limitations. We follow with what we know about how the dynamic aspects of work have changed, and discuss possible implications.

THE STATIC ASPECTS OF WORK

There can be little doubt that static job characteristics have changed substantially in the last two decades because of both compositional shifts (the creation or elimination of jobs in specific occupations and the distribution of people among occupations) and changes in the content of work within occupations. Compositional shifts occur, in part, because of industry shifts. One of the most dramatic shifts is from manufacturing to a service economy (Figure 4.2). The percentage of jobs in manufacturing declined steadily over four and one-half decades, from 33 percent in 1954 to 14 percent in 2000, accompanied by a comparable increase in the percentage of service jobs, from 12 percent to 31 percent.

Figure 4.2 Distribution of Employment by Industry, 1954–2000

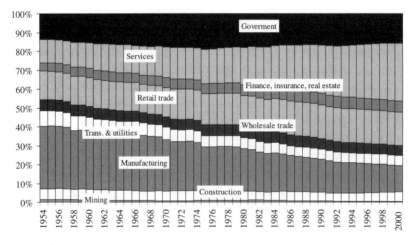

SOURCE: Council of Economic Advisors (2000).

Compositional changes also occur within industries. Many of the changes in occupations within an industry are designed to take advantage of new information technologies and changes in management techniques. For example, more reliance on automated technologies in the goods-producing sector has increased the number of jobs that require abstract reasoning ability and decreased the number of jobs that require physical strength. In the service sector, changes in management techniques have resulted in an increase in both high-skilled, high-wage jobs and low-skilled, low-wage jobs, with a decline in medium-skilled, medium-wage jobs (Howell and Wolff 1991; Gittleman and Howell 1995).

Although changes in the composition of occupations are quantifiable, changes in job characteristics that have occurred within occupations are difficult to measure, and may vary dramatically across occupations and for different definitions of skill.

We consider six dimensions of job characteristics (Table 4.1).[5] For each characteristic, we discuss evidence about how the mean characteristic has changed for all jobs, the relationship between the characteristic and whether a specific job is filled by a worker with a limitation at a point in time, and evidence that change in the mean characteristics affects the percentage of all jobs filled by workers with limitations. To conduct this analysis, we developed a database using the Current Population Survey (CPS) for 1983 through 2000, the 1991 *Dictionary of Occupational Titles* (DOT), and other sources. We view each observation of an employed person in the CPS as an observation of a job. Because the survey is designed as a nationally representative sample of the population, it also provides a nationally representative sample of jobs. We matched the CPS respondent's occupation with job characteristics from DOT, educational requirements from the Bureau of Labor Statistics, and job mobility classifications developed by Kusmin and Gibbs (2000). Additional job characteristics were constructed using data from the CPS. (See Appendix 4A for details of the database.)

We report on 11 of the 93 characteristics developed for the analysis here (column 3 of Table 4.1), selected on the basis of three criteria. First, we computed simple correlations between the characteristic and an indicator for whether the job was held by a worker with a work limitation. We focused on measures that had significant correlations in pooled samples for at least two of the following three-year periods:

Table 4.1 Summary of Findings for Six Dimensions of Static Job Characteristics

Dimension	Definition	Operational measures[a]	Sign of change in measure's mean[b]	Relation to % of workers with limits[c]	Evidence of effect on % of workers with limits[d]
Substantive complexity	Level of cognitive skills required	GED language score	+	–	–
		Specific vocational preparation	+	–	–
		Repetitive tasks	–	+	none
Relational or interactive	Extent to which interactions with other workers and customers is critical to performance	Direct/control plan activities of others	+	–	none
Autonomy/control	Worker control of content, manner, and speed with which a task is done	None available	na	na	na
Task scope	Range or breadth of tasks	Bachelor's degree	+	–	none
		Dead end	–	+	none
Physical demands	Physical and manipulative skills required; environmental conditions	Strength score	–	+	none
Terms of employment	Benefits, hours worked, schedule flexibility, place of work, etc.	Full-year/full-time	+	–	none
		Employer-subsidized health insurance	–	–	mixed
		# of employees:			
		1,000+	+	?	mixed
		1–24	–	+	mixed

[a] Selected from database of 93 characteristics, based on the CPS, the DOT, Kusmin and Gibbs (2000), and BLS educational requirements.
[b] Plus sign (+) indicates that three-year moving average of mean increased from 1990 to 2000, and minus sign (−) indicates it declined.
[c] Sign indicated is the sign of the simple correlation between the measure and whether or not a job is held by a worker with a limitation, in each of three pooled CPS samples, covering three years each: 1983–1985, 1988–1990, 1998–2000; question mark (?) indicates variation in sign across samples. With two exceptions, the sign is the same in all three pooled samples and statistically significant at the 0.05 level in at least two of the three. The two exceptions are the employer size variables, which are only available in the 1988–1990 sample. The correlation for 1,000+ employees is negative and significant in the 1988–1990 sample, but positive and not significant in the 1998–2000 sample. The correlation for 1–24 employees is positive in both samples, significant at the 0.01 level in 1988–1990, but only at the 0.10 level in 1998–2000.
[d] Indicates our assessment of the evidence concerning the contribution of the change in the mean of the variable to the percentage of jobs filled by workers with limitations from 1990–2000. See text for the assessment.

1983–1985, 1988–1990, and 1999–2000. Second, we looked for characteristics that were conceptually different from each other, as it would be problematic to distinguish between the effects of characteristics that are conceptually very similar. Third, we looked for job characteristics for which the means have changed over time. (See Appendix 4A for a more detailed description of the process of selecting variables.)

An important limitation to this approach is that it captures changes in job characteristics caused only by changes in the composition of jobs; it does not capture any within-occupation changes in requirements over the period.

In the next section, we present trends in means for the selected characteristics in the context of broader discussions of each of the dimensions of job characteristics listed above. We also consider how these measures are related to whether a job is filled by a worker with a limitation at a point in time (i.e., in the cross-section). At the end of the section, we present an empirical assessment of the extent to which these characteristics are related to whether a job is filled by a worker with a limitation, as well as the extent to which the trend in the characteristic's mean could explain the decline in percentage of workers with limitations. Although it first appears that trends in several static characteristics might have played a role in the decline, based on trends in the mean characteristics and the simple correlations, more careful analysis suggests that most have not, and where we find effects, they appear to be small. We also discover some interesting changes in the relationships between whether a job is filled by a worker with a limitation and a few job characteristics, after controlling for others.

Changes in Static Job Characteristics

In this section, we describe what is known about changes in job characteristics within each of the six conceptual categories described above, what we found about changes in these characteristics from our analysis, and how changes might have affected employment opportunities of people with disabilities.

Substantive complexity

An increase in the demand for more-skilled versus less-skilled workers, at least in certain sectors of the economy, is well established

(U.S. Department of Labor 1999b). The cause of the change is a subject of debate.[6] Two principal causes are cited in the literature: advances in technology; and globalization and international trade, spurred by the North American Free Trade Agreement (NAFTA) and the creation of the World Trade Organization (WTO), and resulting in greater competition from less-skilled labor in other countries (Deardorff 1998).

Technology substantially affects the way we work, but the impact varies dramatically by industry, job, and type of technology. Hence, it is unclear whether technology has, in the aggregate, increased or decreased necessary skills. Technology is best suited to replacing repetitive manual and cognitive tasks and for complementing tasks requiring nonroutine problem-solving. Accordingly, computers substitute for information processing, communication, and coordinating functions performed by clerks, cashiers, telephone operators, bank tellers, bookkeepers, and others who handle repetitive information (Autor, Levy, and Murname 2001). For example, highly automated checkout machines have reduced the math and language skills required by cashiers, while computer-aided design has changed the types of skills required in the drafting trade. Disagreement exists about the overall effect of technology on skill requirements, but most agree that there are offsetting trends.[7] Technology can replace low-skilled workers performing repetitive tasks, but it can also create opportunities for all workers to be more productive.[8] Although some new opportunities might require little skill, many of these opportunities do require skill.

Ultimately, the effects of technology on job skill requirements also depend on consumer demand for goods or services. How much more do consumers demand as technology reduces prices and improves quality? To what extent does consumer demand for other goods and services change as a result, and what are the skill requirements in the production of those items?

We have selected three measures of substantive complexity from the DOT: 1) *GED-Language*, the aptitude required to perform adequately on the job as measured by scores on the language section of the General Aptitude Test Battery[9]; 2) *Specific Vocational Preparation*, the amount of vocational training time needed to learn how to perform a specific job; and 3) *Repeat*, a yes or no measure of whether the worker performs repetitive or short-cycle work.

The average GED-language score and the average amount of specific vocational preparation required increased gradually between 1983 and 2000 (Figures 4.3 and 4.4). This finding is consistent with earlier findings reported by Spenner (1995). We also find that fewer jobs required very limited substantive complexity, as defined by the *repeat* measure (Figure 4.5).

It is likely that increased substantive complexity makes it more difficult for workers with disabilities to compete with others, on average, due to relatively low levels of education (see below) and mental conditions that limit learning. Of course, this does not apply to all people with disabilities, many of whom have the mental ability to perform highly complex tasks. Krueger, Drastal, and Kruse (1995) found that computer skills facilitate return to work for people who have suffered spinal cord injuries, but that many of those injured had no prior experi-

Figure 4.3 Mean of GED-Language, 1985–2000.

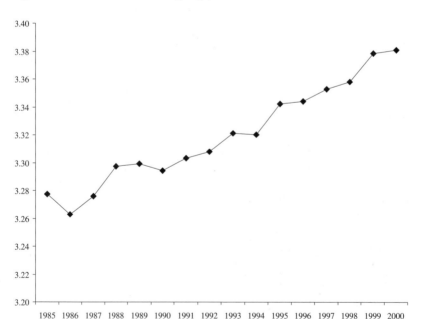

SOURCE: Authors' calculations based on 1991 *Dictionary of Occupational Titles* job characteristics merged with CPS March Supplement 1985–2000.

Figure 4.4 Mean of Specific Vocational Preparation

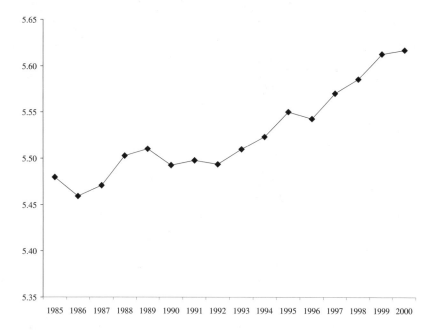

SOURCE: Authors' calculations based on 1991 *Dictionary of Occupational Titles* job characteristics merged with CPS March Supplement 1985–2000.

ence using computers. Kaye (2000) found a "digital divide," with just under one-quarter of people with disabilities having a computer at home in 1998 compared with more than half of people without disabilities.

Relational/interactive

The interactive dimension of work has become more important as firms move toward more collaborative organizational forms. A number of studies have focused on the increased importance of interactive skills on both blue-collar and professional jobs, as team-based work structures become more common.[10] In addition, the shift to service work, where interaction with customers is often fundamental to the job, has clearly increased the need for relational or interactive skills. We found that the percentage of jobs in which the worker "directs, controls

Figure 4.5 Percent of Jobs that Require Repetitive Tasks, 1985–2000

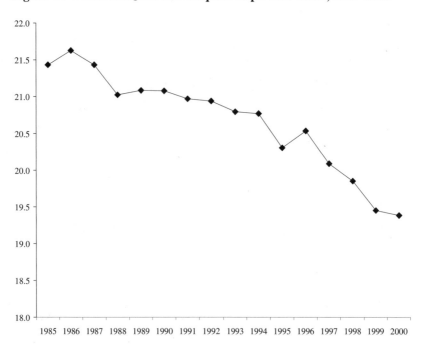

SOURCE: Authors' calculations based on 1991 *Dictionary of Occupational Titles* job characteristics merged with CPS March Supplement 1985–2000.

and/or plans the activities of others" has increased from 29 percent to nearly 34 percent between 1983 and 2000 (Figure 4.6).

Although little research is available on communication limitations for people with disabilities, it is likely that this particular skill requirement challenges not just those whose disability includes a language disorder or limitations in interpersonal skills, but the much broader disability community. Communication relies on understanding, acceptance, and mutual respect among team members. There is substantial evidence that the public continues to have negative attitudes toward people with disabilities (Loo 2001).

Figure 4.6 Percent of Jobs that Require Employee to Direct the Actions of Others, 1985–2000

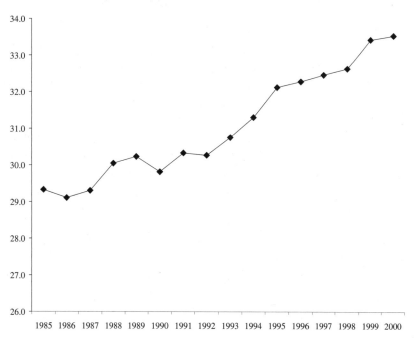

SOURCE: Authors' calculations based on 1991 *Dictionary of Occupational Titles* job characteristics merged with CPS March Supplement 1985–2000.

Autonomy and control

Researchers disagree on whether there have been increases or decreases in workers' autonomy and control over their own work. On the one hand, workers who now participate in team decision-making have more autonomy and control than previously. On the other hand, technology has made many processes more routine, and in many instances allows management to better monitor and control the pace and quality of work.[11] Clearly, the level of autonomy varies greatly not only by occupation but also by organizational structure.[12]

The autonomy/control dimension of jobs is often overlooked in analyses of job characteristics (Spenner 1995), perhaps because it is difficult to measure. In fact, we were unable to find a measure of autonomy/control for inclusion in our job characteristics database. Nonetheless, it might be a particularly important dimension for workers with disabilities.

The level of discretion and leeway that a job offers is likely to affect both the chance that an individual will develop a stress-related disability and the chance that an individual with a disability will be able to work. For example, Karasek and Theorell (1992) found that the greatest risk to physical and mental health from stress occurs when workers face high psychological workload demands or pressures combined with low control or decision latitude in meeting those demands. Yelin (1997) found that people who have discretion over their work activities are less likely to stop working when faced with the onset or exacerbation of a disability. However, the causal relationship in this finding is unclear. Workers in jobs with more discretion may have other characteristics that are related to their continued working. Further, changes that result in increased discretion, such as the flattening of organizational hierarchies and increase in team-based work, do not necessarily ameliorate stress or allow individuals to more effectively accommodate their limitations.

Task scope

The skills required for a job are not necessarily limited to specific tasks, but might include the ability to operate effectively in a wide range of mental, interpersonal, and manipulative tasks across a range of situations. Although task scope is related to substantive complexity, it is distinguished by a type of flexibility that may pose particular obstacles for workers with disabilities.

Many jobs require a nonspecialized degree, such as a high school diploma or a bachelor's degree. Unlike specific vocational preparation, which teaches the worker a particular skill, a general education requirement is often used to ensure that the worker can perform a wider scope of work.[13] Education serves as a screening device (i.e., someone with a college degree is more likely to be able to pick up new skills needed as the breadth of the job expands) as well as providing general skills needed to perform jobs that have a wide task scope. It is clear that educational attainment has become more important in the workforce. The share of hours worked by those without a high school diploma has been declining for the past two decades, from 23 percent for men in 1978 to

12 percent in 1997, and from 20 percent to 9 percent for women (U.S. Department of Labor 1999). The value of education is reflected in increases in educational attainment. Over the same period, the percentage of men aged 25–54 with less than a high school diploma has decreased from 22 percent to 14 percent; the same percentage for women declined from 25 percent to 12 percent.[14] Based on changes in the distribution of jobs (ignoring changes in educational requirements within a job category), we find that jobs requiring a bachelor's degree or higher increased from 28 percent in 1983 to 33 percent in 2000 (Figure 4.7).

Increases in general degree requirements likely disadvantage workers with disabilities as a group, because of their relatively low levels of education. Statistics on the differences in educational attainment depend on how disability is defined, but are always large. For instance,

Figure 4.7 Percent of Jobs that Require Bachelor's Degree or Higher

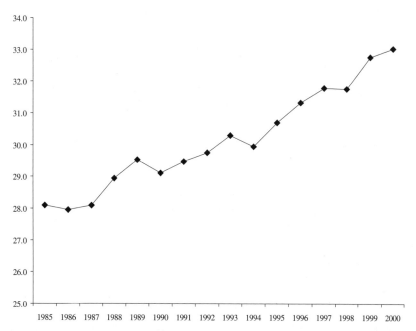

SOURCE: Authors' calculations based on 1991 *Dictionary of Occupational Titles* job characteristics merged with CPS March Supplement 1985–2000.

Kruse (1998) reports that 29 percent of working-aged people with disabilities have less than a high school degree, compared with 13 percent of those without a disability.

Task scope can also be measured by where along the career path a particular job falls. For example, some entry-level jobs are "starter jobs" that often lead to employment in better paying jobs. These are likely to encompass a larger task scope than "dead-end" jobs that are unlikely to lead to better employment. Based on the career paths of workers with low educational levels, Kusmin and Gibbs (2000) identify 27 dead-end jobs from the 482 occupations in the CPS. We find that, from 1985–2000, jobs that fall into this group declined from 24 percent to 20 percent (Figure 4.8).

Figure 4.8 Percent of Jobs that Are Dead-End

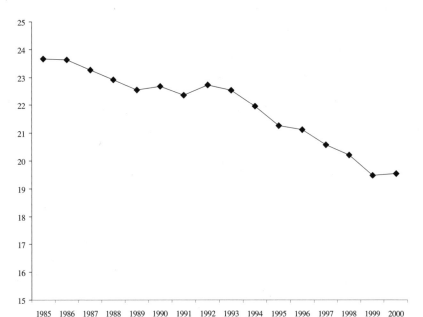

SOURCE: Authors' calculations based on 1991 *Dictionary of Occupational Titles* job characteristics merged with CPS March Supplement 1985–2000.

Physical demands

As "shop floors" have become more automated, the need for strength and manual dexterity has declined. At the same time, shifts in occupation and industry employment decreased the number of people working on shop floors and increased the number of people in less physically demanding jobs (Howell and Wolff 1991).

Based on the CPS data, a changing mix of jobs accounted for a slow, steady decrease of the average "strength" needed for a job. As measured on a scale of 1–5, where 1 is sedentary and 5 is very heavy work, the average strength score declined from 1.10 to 1.06 between 1983 and 2000 (Figure 4.9). This trend reflects only changes in the distribution of occupations; it misses within-occupation changes, which might be substantial.[15]

Figure 4.9 Mean Value of Strength Score

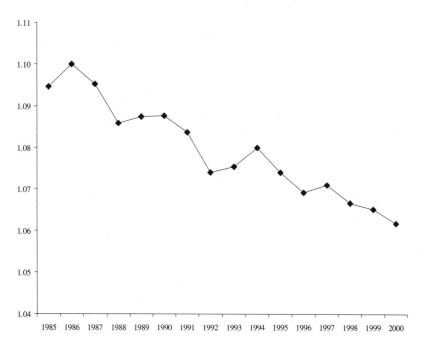

SOURCE: Authors' calculations based on 1991 *Dictionary of Occupational Titles* job characteristics merged with CPS March Supplement 1985–2000. The strength score is scaled 1–5 from sedentary to very heavy work.

If people with disabilities, on average, are at a disadvantage in performing jobs that require physical strength, one might expect relatively few workers with limitations to hold physically strenuous jobs. Findings from the literature are ambiguous, however, and our analysis of the CPS found the opposite relationship, especially in the first half of our sample period. There are at least three possible reasons for this counterintuitive result. First, those with disabilities who have mental limitations might have a comparative advantage in jobs that are physically strenuous. Second, workers in physically strenuous jobs might be more likely to report that a given physical condition is limiting than those in less physically strenuous jobs. Third, physically strenuous jobs are more likely to cause a disabling condition, and in many instances the condition will not result in immediate termination (Loprest, Rupp, and Sandell 1995).

These findings have no clear implications for the likely effect of decreases in strength requirements on employment outcomes for people with disabilities relative to others. They simply show how workers are sorted into jobs with varying strength requirements as the result of a complex, dynamic process. Studies that look at how the relationship between the physical demands of a job and the effect of disability onset on return-to-work might be more informative, but such studies are rare. One study did find that persons employed in white-collar jobs and jobs that were not physically demanding were more likely to return to work in the first three months after a lower extremity injury than others (MacKenzie et al. 1998). Results such as this would suggest that declines in the physical demands of work would reduce labor force exit after disability onset.

Like physical demands, adverse environmental conditions may affect the chance that a job is held by a worker with a disability in opposite ways. First, the difficult conditions make it less likely that workers with certain disabilities could perform the tasks, and second, the hazardous conditions might contribute to disabilities. The net result is that, although the DOT provides data on 14 adverse environmental conditions, none was consistently correlated with the job being filled by a worker with a disability. For this reason, we did not include any of them in our empirical analysis.

Terms of employment

The terms of employment offered by an employer might affect the ability of a person with a disability to compete for a job. Here we consider the possible effects of several nonstandard work arrangements, as well as the role of employee benefits. We also consider employer size. Although employer size is not a term of employment per se, the terms of employment for one who works for a large corporation are likely to be much different from those encountered in a medium-sized or small business.

Nonstandard work arrangements. Conventional wisdom points to a dramatic increase in "nonstandard" work arrangements including part-time employment, working for temporary help agencies, contract or on-call work, day labor, and independent contracting. Although there have been increases in some types of alternative work arrangements, the suggestion that these changes have radically changed the workforce is exaggerated.

Overall, the percentage of the workforce that is working part-time has not grown appreciably since 1983, after growing substantially in the 1970s from 16 percent to 18 percent (U.S. Department of Labor 1999). The percentage of workers who are part-time varies considerably by sector. Although 40 percent of retail and 30 percent of service workers are part-time, only 11 percent of manufacturing employees are part-time. The conventional wisdom is fueled by the correct perception that the faster-growing sectors of the economy are employing more part-time workers (Fallick 1999). Also fueling the concern is a shift in part-time employment from voluntary to involuntary (three-quarters of the part-time workforce would rather be working full-time) and an increase in workers with multiple part-time jobs (Tilly 1991).

Based on analysis of our job characteristics database, the percentage of jobs that are both full-time and full-year (FTFY) has been increasing during most of the last two decades (Figure 4.10). From 1989 to 2000, the share increased from almost 73 percent to just over 77 percent. This finding seems inconsistent with the notion that nonstandard work is increasing, but a closer look reconciles the two.

Many types of jobs considered to be nonstandard are, in fact, FTFY jobs. One such position is temporary help. Employment in temporary help agencies has been growing at an average rate of 11 percent

Figure 4.10 Percent of Jobs that Are Full-Time/Full-Year

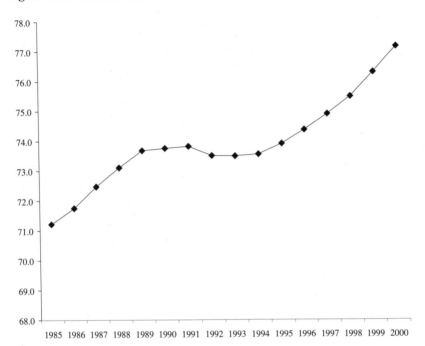

SOURCE: Authors' calculation of three-year moving average of full-time/full-year occupations based on CPS March Supplement 1983–2000. See note 2.

per year since 1972, although it still only accounts for about 3 percent of the labor force (Segal and Sullivan 1996). Employees of a temporary help agency are often employed FTFY.

Another type of nonstandard work is contract work. Although contract work may represent an important change for an organization, it may not represent a decline of standard work for employees. Consider, for example, a corporation that contracts out tasks previously performed by permanent employees. If the work goes to an organization with its own permanent employees, it may represent no net change in the percentage of standard jobs in the economy, even though it does represent a decline in job security of its current workers.

Flextime, compressed work weeks, and telecommuting are other forms of nonstandard work that include many FTFY positions. These job features have increased dramatically in recent years. By 1997, 27 percent of full-time wage and salary workers had some flexibility in scheduling their work day, more than twice the rate in 1985. Needless to say, the level of flexibility offered to full-time workers varies dramatically by industry and occupation. For many occupations, flexibility is available only to part-time workers (Golden 2001).

Growth in nonstandard work relationships could be very important for people with disabilities, in a variety of ways. On the positive side, part-time arrangements might be favorable for those whose impairments make it difficult to work full-time. Such arrangements might also allow some to work while maintaining public income and medical benefits. Schedule flexibility can help those who have difficulty keeping a regular schedule because of an impairment or health condition. Job flexibility has been shown to be important in forestalling retirement (Hurd and McGarry 1993). Telecommuting would be especially advantageous for those facing difficult transportation challenges because of their impairment or where they happen to live.

Employment in nonstandard jobs is likely to be associated with lower compensation (wages and benefits) for people with given qualifications, including those with disabilities. Some features that might make these jobs attractive to people with disabilities might also impose costs on employers. Many people with disabilities might, however, find that the lower compensation is more than made up for by job features such as flextime, telecommuting, and less than full-time work.[16]

Benefits. Among the variety of benefits offered to different workers, health and disability insurance are the ones most likely to affect the employment of people with disabilities. As Hill, Livermore, and Houtenville discuss in Chapter 5, some workers with disabilities might choose to stay out of the labor force to obtain the insurance benefits that come with Social Security Disability Insurance (SSDI) and Supplemental Security Income (SSI), owing to problems with private health insurance.

Our analysis shows a decline from 1985 through 1993 of about 6 percentage points in workers who have employer-subsidized health insurance but after that, the percentage stabilized, increasing only slightly by 2000 (Figure 4.11). As Hill and colleagues (Chapter 5) discuss, the decline in coverage appears to be due more to a decline in

Figure 4.11 Percent of Jobs with Employer-Subsidized Health Insurance

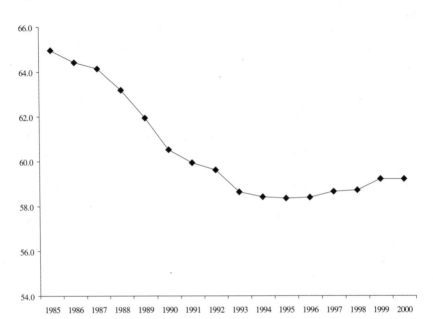

SOURCE: Authors' calculations based on 1991 *Dictionary of Occupational Titles* job characteristics merged with CPS March Supplement 1985–2000.

employee take-up of employer-offered coverage than a decline in offered coverage, perhaps because of rapidly growing employee premiums and growth in coverage restrictions.

Another benefit of considerable relevance is disability insurance, which might affect the probability that a worker will remain on a job after the onset of a disability, in potentially conflicting ways. On the one hand, the income provided to a worker with a successful claim might encourage the worker to leave the labor force. On the other hand, disability managers affiliated with disability insurance programs often encourage and help potential claimants to go back to work, and encourage employers to make needed accommodations.

Long-term disability insurance, which generally replaces 60 percent of the worker's wage, is available to about 25 percent of employees.[17] This benefit, like health insurance, varies dramatically by size of firm, union status, and wage.[18] It is impossible to gauge the impact of long-term disability insurance on the employment rate of workers with disabilities because there is a lack of information on whether there have been any significant changes in the number of workers covered.

Employer size. Firm size may influence the employment relationship through several avenues. First, the "traditional" lifetime commitment model, where the employer provides training, internal development, and job ladders, makes most sense in relatively large firms (more than 500 employees) (Cappelli 1999). Although large firms have most dramatically changed the employment relationship in the past decade, they continue to have lower turnover rates.

For people with disabilities, firm size has several other effects. First, large firms may enable workers who experience onset of a disability to remain with the company in a different position. A large firm is also more likely to offer a range of benefits, including health and disability insurance,[19] and, as discussed above, these might affect the chance that a worker with a disability will continue working after onset.

In addition, if the enactment of the Americans with Disabilities Act (ADA) had a negative effect on the employment of people with disabilities, it should be most apparent in medium-sized firms (Acemoglu and Angrist 2000). Small firms (fewer than 25 employees) are exempt from the ADA, and large firms should find it less expensive to comply with ADA requirements.

The CPS did not ask workers about the size of their firm before 1988. Since then, there has been a slight growth in the percentage of workers employed in firms of 1,000 or more employees, and a slight decline in the percentage employed in firms with 25 or fewer employees (Figure 4.12). We found a negative, significant correlation between whether the job is at a firm with 1,000+ employees and whether the job is filled by a worker with a limitation in the 1988–1990 sample, but the correlation was positive and insignificant in the 1998–2000 sample. The correlation between whether a firm has 1–24 employees and whether a job is filled by a worker with a limitation is positive and at least marginally significant in the samples for both periods.

Figure 4.12 Employer Size

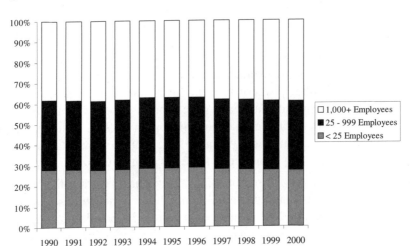

SOURCE: Authors' calculation of three-year moving average of employer size based on CPS March Supplement 1983–2000. See note 2.

Effect on the Employment Rate of People with Disabilities

The discussion above indicates that people with disabilities, on average, are better able to compete for jobs with certain static characteristics relative to others. Whether people with work limitations end up in jobs that have relevant characteristics depends on a complex "sorting" process, through which workers and jobs are matched—namely, the labor market. This includes what economists call internal labor markets (the process through which workers are assigned to jobs within firms) as well as the more commonly recognized external labor market, through which people move between employers. The observed result of the sorting process, how it has changed over time, and trends in mean job characteristics might provide clues about factors that are influencing trends in the employment of people with disabilities.

We use our database to examine the relationship between the percentage of workers with limitations and each of the 11 static job characteristics we selected, holding each of the other 10 characteristics constant. We use linear regression to go beyond the simple correlations reported earlier and determine what relationship remains after controlling for the other characteristics. We also take a closer look at the stability of the remaining relationship over the period from 1990 to 2000.

We estimated the relationship between the percentage of workers with limitations and job characteristics in every year for each year from 1990 through 2000.[20] Although all of the characteristics were correlated to the percentage of workers with limitations when considered individually, for several characteristics, the relationship became statistically insignificant after controlling for the other characteristics. We also found that some characteristics were statistically significant predictors of the percentage of workers with limitations in some years, but not in others. For some characteristics, there is intriguing evidence of a shift in the relationship.

As documented in the previous section, the means of several of the characteristics revealed substantial trends during the last two decades. For each characteristic, we use the results of the analysis described in the previous paragraph along with the trend in the mean characteristic to assess the extent to which the characteristic might have contributed to the decline in the percentage of all workers with limitations from 1990 through 2000. Mechanically, this analysis proceeds as follows. Say we find that the percentage of workers with limitations is higher by amount A (the "coefficient") if the job has characteristic X than if it does not (holding other characteristics constant), and the percentage of jobs with characteristic X changes by P percentage points from 1990 to 2000. We infer that the change in the percentage of jobs with characteristic X might have changed the percentage of all workers with limitations by $A \times P$.

A key assumption in this analysis is that the observed relationship between characteristics and the percentage of workers with limitations in any given year is a causal one reflecting how an exogenous change in a job characteristic will affect the percentage of workers with limitations.[21] As indicated above, however, the observed relationship is the outcome of a complex sorting process, and might not reflect a causal relationship. Hence, for each variable, we must consider whether the estimated effect for each variable (i.e., the coefficient) really represents an effect. The possibility also exists that the relationship between a characteristic and the percentage of workers with limitations changes over time (i.e., A is not constant). In that case, it is important to understand the reason for the change and its implication for the interpretation of the findings. We discuss the results for individual characteristics below, in diminishing order of the approximate strength of the finding.

Employer-subsidized health insurance

The relationship between employer subsidized health insurance and the percentage of workers with limitations, holding other characteristics constant, was the most statistically significant of all the characteristics considered, over the entire period. The average estimate, over all years, implies that, holding other job characteristics constant, the percentage of workers with limitations in an occupation is almost five points higher if no workers in that occupation receive employer-subsidized insurance than if they all do.[22] This is a very large difference, considering that the percentage of all workers with limitations was only 2.5 in 2000. Although there is some variability in the results from year to year, there is no apparent trend in the strength of the relationship.

Three hypotheses possibly explain this finding. First, it might be that employers who provide subsidized health insurance are less likely to employ people with disabilities because of their relatively high health care costs. Second, people with disabilities might be less likely to have the skills and productivity necessary to qualify for the types of high-paying jobs that typically include health insurance as part of compensation. Third, people with work limitations might be less willing than others to take the type of job that offers insurance, perhaps for health reasons (e.g., because they are unable to work as many hours, or as intensely, as the job requires) or because they do not want to lose eligibility for public income and health benefits. We have tried to limit the extent to which the latter two explanations could influence the finding by controlling for other characteristics, but those characteristics probably only partially capture the effects of these factors.

As discussed earlier, the percentage of workers who are covered by employer-subsidized health insurance has declined significantly. Our finding that employer-subsidized health insurance is negatively related to the percentage of workers with limitations would seem to imply that the decline in employer coverage has had a substantial, favorable impact on the overall percentage of workers with limitations. Mechanical application of the methodology described above leads to the conclusion that the decline in employer coverage, alone, increased the percentage of workers with limitations by about 2 percent (compared with an actual decline of about 13 percent).

This conclusion might be correct if the main reason for the observed relationship between employer coverage and the percentage of workers with limitations is the relatively high health care costs of such workers. If an employer stops offering coverage, imposes restrictions on coverage, or requires larger employee premiums or co-payments, health care costs for workers with limitations become less of an issue for the employer.

If, instead, the primary reason for the negative relationship is that workers with limitations are less likely to have the skills and productivity necessary to obtain such jobs, or are less likely to want them for other reasons related to their condition, then the decline in employer coverage might have little effect. Instead, it might simply be that many good jobs are increasingly less likely to provide health insurance benefits that are attractive to workers with limitations because the employer's cost for such benefits has increased relative to the cost of other forms of compensation (e.g., wages and retirement benefits). Further, if individuals with limitations are unwilling to take jobs for health or public benefit reasons, the decline in employer coverage for some jobs is likely, if anything, to increase that reluctance.

Hence, although there is a strong negative relationship between employer-subsidized health insurance and the percentage of workers with limitations, it seems premature to conclude that the decline in employer-subsidized health insurance has had a favorable impact on job opportunities for people with disabilities. At the same time, it seems plausible that tightening of employer-subsidized benefits has reduced the cost to employers of hiring workers with disabilities who might require substantial health care relative to others. For further analysis of the relationship between employment of people with disabilities and the growth of health care costs, see Hill and colleagues (Chapter 5).

Educational and training requirements

Three of the included characteristics are measures of educational and training requirements. We expected each to have a negative relationship with the percentage of workers with limitations, but only two of the three did:

- The more *specific vocational preparation* a job requires, the lower the percentage of workers with limitations, after controlling for the other characteristics. The average estimate of 0.20 indicates that if the level of specific vocational preparation for a job increased from a short demonstration to more than 10 years (the maximum possible increase), the percentage of such jobs filled by a worker with a limitation would decline by 1.8 points.
- Jobs with low *GED language* requirements have a higher percentage of workers with limitations than others, after controlling for other characteristics. The relationship is statistically significant in most years. Although the magnitude of the estimated relationship varies substantially from year to year, there is no evidence of a trend in its strength. The average estimate, of 0.30, implies that for each additional level of competency (i.e., moving from an elementary level of competency successively to, middle, early high school, late high school, and college), the percentage of workers with limitations declines 0.3 percentage points.
- We did not find consistent evidence of a positive relationship between whether the job required a *bachelor's or higher degree* and the percentage of workers with limitations, after controlling for the other characteristics, although we did find positive significant relationships in 3 of the 11 years.

In the previous section, we presented evidence of positive trends in the education and training requirements for the average job, although the most notable trend was in degree requirements—the variable that has the weakest relationship with the percentage of workers with limitations. If we assume that the observed relationship between these characteristics and the percentage of workers with limitations reflects the effect of these requirements on employment of people with work limitations, then we infer that increases in mean requirements for these variables have reduced the percentage of all workers with limitations by about 1.5 percent from 1990 to 2000 (compared with the actual decline of about 13 percent).

Employer size

We included two employer size variables—an indicator for small firms (fewer than 25 employees) and one for large firms (1,000 or more employees). The implicit comparison group is medium-sized firms (25–999 employees).[23] The estimated relationship between the percentage of workers with limitations and our employer size variables changed over the period from 1990 to 2000.

Before 1995, there was no statistically significant difference between the percentage of workers with limitations in large and medium firms, after controlling for other variables. From 1995 on, however, the percentage for large firms was significantly higher, holding the other characteristics constant. The average estimate for 1995 through 2000 indicates that the percentage of workers with limitations is about three points (0.03) higher if the job is in a large firm than if it is in a medium-sized firm, holding other job characteristics constant. The evidence also suggests that in the early 1990s, jobs in small firms were slightly less likely than those in medium-sized firms to be filled by a person with a work limitation, but slightly more likely in the late 1990s, holding other characteristics constant. The timing of the change in coefficients approximately coincides with the beginning of the sharp decline in the percentage of all workers with limitations.

In some ways, this finding is consistent with the hypotheses and evidence discussed by DeLeire (Chapter 7), concerning the potential effects of the ADA on employment of people with disabilities. The ADA does not apply to small employers, and medium firms are more likely than large firms to find that costs prohibit compliance. The theoretical expectation is that the ADA will reduce employment of people with disabilities in medium-sized firms relative to employment in small and large firms. Our finding for large firms relative to medium firms is particularly striking. Note, however, that the findings by themselves do not indicate whether the ADA had a positive or negative effect on employment of people with work limitations overall; they only suggest effects that vary by firm size in a manner that is consistent with theoretical predictions. Although they could be consistent with an overall negative impact of the ADA on the percentage of workers with limitations, they are equally consistent with a scenario under which the ADA increases the percentage of workers with limitations in firms of all sizes, but by more in small and large firms than in medium firms.[24] Note also that the change in the relationship appears to occur in 1995, five years after the ADA's passage and three years after initial implementation. Of course, it might have taken several years for any substantial effect to materialize, but much of the other evidence concerning the ADA finds effects that begin several years earlier.[25]

As the distribution of jobs by employer size changed little during the last two decades, change in firm size itself cannot be a major source of change in employment of people with disabilities. It appears, instead, that factors that influence the employment of people with disabilities within firms of any given size are responsible for the trends, and the effects of at least some of these factors vary with the size of the employer.

Dead-end jobs

In 9 of the 11 years, we found that jobs classified as dead-end have a lower percentage of workers with limitations than others, holding other characteristics constant, but the relationship was only statistically significant in four of these years, and there is no apparent trend.

Strength

For 1990 and 1991, we found a strong, positive relationship between a job's strength requirement and the percentage of workers with limitations, holding other characteristics constant, but this relationship disappeared in later years. To assess whether the early relationship reflects the recession or some other temporary phenomenon, we replicated the analysis extending back to 1985, excluding the employer size variables, which were unavailable in earlier years. We found a positive relationship in each of the five additional years, although it was only significant in three.[26] From 1985 through 1991, a one-step increase in strength demand led to a 0.26 percentage point increase in the percentage of workers with limitations. We also found that simple correlations between other measures of physical job requirements and whether a job is filled by a worker with a limitation were significant in the early years of our data, but not in the later years.[27] What is notable is not that the percentage of jobs that require physical strength and dexterity has decreased (a well documented fact), but rather that this job characteristic exerts progressively less influence on whether a job is held by a worker with a disability. We have no solid explanation for the finding, but there are at least two possibilities. People in jobs that require strength might leave the jobs sooner after the onset of a disability than they once did, or maybe highly physical jobs cause fewer or less severe disabilities than in previous years.

Other variables. After controlling for the other variables, we found no consistent, statistically significant relationship between each of the following characteristics and the percentage of workers with limitations:

- full-year/full-time;[28]
- job requires the holder to direct, control or plan the activities of others; and
- job requires largely repetitive tasks.

Although each of these three characteristics has a significant simple correlation with whether a job is filled by a person with a work limitation, each relationship disappears after controlling for other factors. Thus, we do not find any link between changes in these job characteristics and trends in the employment of people with disabilities.[29]

Combined effects of changes in static job characteristics

To summarize, the empirical analysis does not identify any single static job characteristic that could account for a large share of the decline in the percentage of workers with limitations. It does not, however, rule out the possibility that a wide variety of changes in job characteristics, each small, and some too small to measure, might account for the decline. To assess this possibility further, we conducted an analysis that separates the decline in the percentage of workers with limitations between two three-year periods a decade apart, 1988–1990 and 1998–2000,[30] into two components: 1) change owing to change in the distribution of occupations, holding the percentage of workers with limitations within each occupation constant ("composition effect"), and 2) change owing to within-occupation change in the percentage of workers with limitations. The composition effect indicates the maximum extent to which change in the mean characteristics of occupations owing to changes in the distribution of occupations could account for the decline in the percentage of workers with limitations. The within-occupation component captures all changes associated with changes in the percentage of workers with limitations within individual occupations, including changes that might stem from changes in the characteristics of individual occupations.[31]

The percentage of workers with limitations declines from 2.90 percent in 1988–1990 to 2.51 percent in 1998–2000 (Figure 4.1), a decline of 13.4 percent, or 0.39 percentage points. The decomposition attributes just 0.04 percentage points of the decline to the compositional effect, or just 10 percent of the total decline. The remainder is owing to within-occupation declines.

Within-occupation decline in the percentage of workers with limitations could stem from within-occupation changes in job characteristics. It seems unlikely that this effect would be substantial, however, unless there was also a substantial decline owing to change in the distribution of occupations. Another feature of the evidence that makes us skeptical about the possibility that within-occupation changes in job characteristics can explain much of the decline is that characteristics for which we can observe within-occupation changes (e.g., employer size, employer-subsidized health insurance, and full-time, full-year) have been changing slowly during the last two decades, while the decline in the percentage of workers with limitations occurred in the last one-third of that period. We have not found quantitative or qualitative evidence of a comparable pattern of change in any static characteristic.

THE DYNAMIC ASPECTS OF WORK

Job change of any type, and under any circumstances (voluntary or involuntary; same employer or new employer), likely disadvantages many workers with disabilities relative to workers without disabilities. Change can be difficult for anyone,[32] but the process of identifying another appropriate job or occupation, retraining, applying for a new job, convincing a prospective employer that you are able to perform the needed tasks, getting the job, and adapting to the new job (including determining and obtaining needed accommodations) can all be more difficult because of a disability. Job change resulting from involuntary job loss is likely to be the most challenging type of change for any worker, and especially for a worker with a disability. Under this circumstance, it is likely that reemployment must be with a new employer, in a new industry, in a new occupation, or in a new area. Between 1983 and 1988, one in six displaced workers moved to another city or county to find work (Herz 1990). Finding suitable housing, arranging for transportation to work, and other aspects of moving generally require more effort for people with disabilities.

The dynamic nature of the labor market is also a significant challenge to the programs that provide support for people with disabilities, and has additional adverse consequences for the people they serve. The most obvious example is vocational rehabilitation, which must take into account how the labor market is changing and how the abilities of their clients affect their ever-changing opportunities. Unemployment insurance might provide an adequate safety net for workers without disabilities, but many with disabilities might find it inadequate and turn to the SSDI program for support, even though this program is intended to provide long-term assistance to those who cannot work and is ill-equipped to provide temporary support. Similar issues arise with health insurance. The ultimate result might be permanent labor force exit of many people with disabilities who really are capable of work (see Goodman and Waidmann, Chapter 10), as well as denial of benefits to some who are not, and prolonged hardship from joblessness for many others.

Evidence provided by Yelin (1992) illustrates the greater difficulty that workers with disabilities have adjusting to a changing labor market. He found that workers with disabilities experienced a disproportionate amount of displacement from declining sectors and a less than proportionate increase in expanding ones.

Of course, jobs have always had some level of insecurity, and presumably insecurity has always disadvantaged workers with disabilities relative to others. The difficult question to address is whether jobs became substantially less secure in the 1990s—sufficiently so to account for a substantial share of the decline in the employment rate for people with disabilities.

At least two reasons may explain why jobs might have become less secure. The first is increased competitiveness, owing to reduction in trade barriers, industry deregulation, and the Internet. The second is the more direct impact of information technology on how goods and services are produced, which has made some jobs obsolete even as it has generated many new ones. Unfortunately, the evidence on the extent of decline in job security is poor. People who study large corporations tend to find revolutionary changes in the employment relationship, but labor economists who study the aggregate labor market argue that the change is modest, at best.

Ryan (1995) finds a general perception that the life-long job with a big company is a thing of the past, and that we should all expect to change jobs six times, and careers three times, over the course of our work life. Capelli (1999, pp. 2–3) writes, "If the traditional, lifetime employment relationship was like a marriage, then the new employment relationship is like a lifetime of divorces and remarriages." He describes a sweeping change from corporations that provide a lifetime of job security, internal job development, training, job ladders, good benefits, and pensions in exchange for loyalty, hard work, and a stable workforce to a free agency workforce, where workers go to the highest bidder, and employers churn the workforce, downsizing, contracting, and outsourcing in an effort to gain a competitive edge.

A number of studies by economists find evidence of increased involuntary job loss offset by a decrease in voluntary resignations.[33] Official employment statistics show a substantial, positive, long-term trend in the percentage of unemployed persons who have experienced involuntary job loss, as can be seen by comparing figures from the strong economy of the late 1960s to the strong economy of the late 1980s (Figure 4.13). During the strong economy of the late 1990s, however, the percentage of unemployed workers who had experienced involuntary job loss was actually lower than in the late 1980s.

Another aspect of job security is job tenure. Unfortunately, survey data on tenure are known to be poor.[34] A number of studies conducted in the mid 1990s found little evidence of a decline in job tenure.

In summary, although the perception of a decline in job stability might have some basis in evidence over three and one-half decades, available evidence does not suggest a change in the last decade that could explain the employment rate decline for people with disabilities.

These statistics consider the entire labor force, and might hide trends that are more specific to people with disabilities. In fact, Farber (1995) reports that there is evidence that job tenure has declined for men with less than a high school degree, although this study does not extend to the period of most interest to us. It seems likely that increased

Figure 4.13 Involuntary Job Loss as a Percent of Total Unemployment

SOURCE: Council of Economic Advisors (2003).

international competition and changes caused by advances in information technology have reduced job security for those with fewer skills and less education, especially. Hence, it is possible that a decline in job security could help explain why the employment rate for people with disabilities who also have limited education has declined more sharply than for those with higher levels of education. It might also be, however, that the decline in job duration for this group reflects an increase in labor force exits for those who have disabilities. More research on this issue would be necessary to assess the direction of causality.

The statistics on job loss and job tenure do not necessarily reflect all labor force trends that might be reducing job security. Earlier, we discussed the rise in nonstandard work arrangements. Among others, these include contingent workers—workers who are brought in on a part-time or temporary basis when needed and are quickly let go when the need subsides. There are a variety of arrangements that enable firms to maintain an elastic workforce, including subcontracting or outsourcing parts of the business, hiring through a temporary employment agency, hiring on-call workers, or hiring workers as consultants. On the one hand, these arrangements seem to offer flexibility, but on the other hand, they offer limited security.

Contingent work was first identified as a phenomenon in 1985 (Hipple 2001). Unemployment statistics might not reflect a rise in contingent workers, who likely report themselves as employed. The same is true for job tenure statistics, because contingent workers might view themselves as working for a single employer over a long period of time. Unfortunately, no reliable data are available on contingent workers before 1995. The Bureau of Labor Statistics estimates that 4.9 percent of workers were contingent workers in 1995, by the agency's broadest definition, and that the figure declined to 4.3 percent by 1999. Although it could be that contingent work is especially problematic for workers with disabilities, the phenomenon does not seem large enough to explain the decline in the employment rate, especially given that the phenomenon was already large enough to be widely recognized by the late 1980s.

In summary, there are many reasons to think that involuntary job loss disadvantages workers with disabilities relative to otherwise comparable workers, and some evidence also suggests a long-term decline in job security. What is missing is evidence of a sudden, widespread decline in job security during the 1990s. It seems unlikely, therefore, that a decline in job security could explain a significant share of the decline in the employment rate. If declines in job security played any role in the decline of the employment rate, it most likely was for those with low levels of education only.

CONCLUSION

The world of work is always changing, and there is no doubt that many changes affect the ability of people with disabilities to compete in the labor market. Can recent changes, however, explain the decline in the percentage of workers with limitations that occurred in the 1990s? Although the evidence is imperfect, we conclude that changes in the nature of work and the labor market cannot account for much of the decline. The analysis shows that any substantial effects owing to changes in job characteristics must be from changes within occupations, not changes in the distribution of occupations. We doubt that within-occupation change in characteristics could explain much of the decline, either, because trends in the static characteristics we observe within occupations are gradual and long-term. In contrast, the percentage of workers with limitations displayed no trend from the mid 1980s through the mid 1990s, then began a sharp decline.

The one trend in the static characteristic of jobs for which there is reasonably convincing evidence of a depressing effect on employment for people with disabilities is growth in skill requirements, but it appears that this is a slow, long-term trend, rather than a sudden, recent change.

The dynamic characteristics of work are also changing. Most important, a decline in job security could potentially contribute to the employment rate decline because workers with disabilities likely find it significantly more challenging to change jobs than workers without disabilities who are otherwise similar. Although it is a common perception that job security has declined markedly in recent years, data on historical trends are limited. There is a long-term trend toward more involuntary separations, but this trend is strongest before the 1990s. No clear evidence indicates a decline in job tenure, either, although some evidence suggests a decline for workers with limited education. No departure from long-term trends is apparent that could explain why the percentage of workers with limitations was quite stable before the early 1990s, then started to decline fairly sharply.

Overall, available evidence does not implicate changes in the nature of work or the labor market as the cause of the decline in the percentage of workers with limitations or, therefore, the decline in the employment rate for people with disabilities. The possibility remains, of course, that this overlooks some very substantial effects for subgroups of people with disabilities. We would expect, however, that changes in job characteristics would affect employment of subgroups gradually and over a long period, rather than precipitously.

Notes

1. The measure of work limitation we use is the same CPS measure used by Burkhauser, Houtenville, and Wittenburg in Chapter 2, as well as by many other researchers. As others have pointed out (see, especially, Hale 2001), this measure is highly imperfect. We will not address these issues here, except to say that we

think the CPS measure is useful for measuring long-term trends in the employment of people with disabilities, based on the evidence presented in Chapter 2 and in Burkhauser et al. (2001).
2. Visual inspection of the figure indicates the decline started in 1996, but recall that the series is a three-year moving average. The 1996 figure represents the means of the three values for 1994 through 1996.
3. In fact, today we would be more likely to call it a motionless digital image rather than a snapshot.
4. While conceptually different, the static and dynamic aspects of work are related because the activities that workers participate in are influenced by the dynamics of work. For instance, in a rapidly changing work environment, communication is likely to be a more frequent and important activity than it would be in a slowly changing one. Hence, changes in the dynamic aspects of work can also affect the ability of workers to compete through their impact on static aspects of work. But these changes might or might not be advantageous for a person with a disability, depending on the person's characteristics.
5. The categories are based on work by Spenner (1995), Howell and Wolff (1991), Commission on Behavioral and Social Sciences (1999), and our own analysis of correlations between job characteristics and employment of workers with disabilities.
6. See Deardorff (1998) for a review of the literature.
7. See Spenner (1995) for a review of the literature.
8. This is the standard economic argument of substitutes and complements.
9. The levels correspond to the curricula taught in primary and secondary schools and colleges. A code of 1 indicates that the individual needs the language competency taught in elementary school; 5 indicates a college level of competency is needed.
10. See Commission on Behavioral and Social Sciences (1999) for a review of the literature.
11. For example, the scripted, closely monitored activities of telephone operators.
12. See Commission on Behavioral and Social Sciences (1999) for a review of the literature.
13. There are several studies that show that more educated workers are better able to adapt to technological change (see Spenner 1995 for a review).
14. Computed from Census Historical Table A-1, "Years of School Completed by People 25 Years Old and Over, by Age and Sex: Selected Years 1940 to 2000." Available at: <http://www.census.gov/population/socdemo/education/tableA-1.txt>. (Accessed: July 3, 2002.)
15. The Social Security Administration uses the same strength score in the disability determination process for the Social Security Disability Insurance and Supplemental Security Income programs.
16. Loss of job security owing to some nonstandard work arrangements (e.g., temporary work or contract work) might be especially problematic for people with disabilities. See the discussion on the dynamics of the labor market.

17. Bureau of Labor Statistics, Employee Benefits Survey. Available at <:http://www.bls.gov/data/home.htm >. (Accessed: June 27, 2002.)
18. Short-term disability insurance is available to 36 percent of workers but is less likely to have an impact on a worker's permanent withdrawal from the labor force.
19. In firms with more than 100 employees, 65 percent had employer-sponsored health insurance and 36 percent had long-term disability insurance compared with 36 percent and 17 percent, respectively, in firms with 1–99 employees (Disability insurance statistics: U.S. Department of Labor 1999a; Health insurance statistics: U.S. Census Bureau 2002, Own employment coverage, 1998).
20. 1990 is the first year because the CPS did not collect information on firm size before 1988 and because we found it necessary for sample size reasons to use three-year moving averages for some characteristics. We conducted additional analysis using all predictor variables other than firm size for 1985 through 2000.
21. Those trained in econometrics and statistics recognize that we are using relationships estimated from cross-section samples to interpret time-series changes. The problem we face is that the cross-section relationships and the time-series relationships might be quite different.
22. The data do not allow us to distinguish between workers who do not have the option of buying health insurance that is subsidized by the employer from those who have the option but do not purchase it. Our measure of health insurance for each occupation is based on reported enrollment in employer plans for all CPS respondents during the last three years who are in that occupation and who do not report a work limitation.
23. Preliminary analysis revealed no significant distinction in employment of people with work limitations between employers of varying sizes within the intermediate category.
24. Additional assumptions are needed to make inferences about the total effect on the percentage of all workers with limitations. To illustrate, if we assume that the ADA is the only factor that has varying effects on the percentage of workers with limitations by firm size (holding other characteristics constant), that the ADA had no effect in small firms, and that the changes in the average coefficients for the firm size variables from before 1996 to 1996 and later reflect the effects of such factors, then we infer that such factors *increased* the percentage of workers with limitations from 1990 to 2000, by about three-tenths of a point (0.003). See Appendix 4A for details on this calculation.
25. See DeLeire (Chapter 7), Kruse and Schur (Chapter 8), and Blanck, Schwochau, and Song (Chapter 9).
26. To confirm that the earlier results were not owing to omission of the employer size variables, we repeated the analysis for 1990 and later years without the employer size variables.
27. Including the following physical demands: stooping, reaching, talking, hearing, near acuity, field of vision, and mobility.

28. In an earlier version of this chapter, we reported significant results for full-year full-time. This result disappeared when we added the firm-size variables to the analysis.
29. Although the coefficient for the repetitive task variable is not significant in most years, we did find that the change in the coefficient from 1990 to 2000 was statistically significant, and positive. Thus, there is some indication that the relationship between repetitive tasks and whether a job is filled by a person with a limitation, holding other characteristics constant, has gone from a weak negative one to a weak positive one.
30. We pooled three years of data for each period to increase samples sizes for individual occupations.
31. The methodology is the same as that used by Houtenville and Daly (Chapter 3). Our CPS samples include observations for 440 distinct occupations. Of these, four had no observations in the first of the two periods, and nine had none in the second. For this analysis we combined each of these 13 occupations with similar occupations, to reduce the total number to 427. Because the number of observations for each occupation is small, we cannot produce reliable statistics on the change in the percentage of workers with limitations within each occupation. The two terms in our decomposition are, however, estimated quite precisely.
32. For example, although 75 percent of long-tenured workers who lost full-time wage and salary jobs in 1991 or 1992 were reemployed by February 1994, 8 percent were in part-time jobs, 8 percent were self-employed, 28 percent were in full-time jobs with lower earnings, and 32 percent were employed in full-time jobs with the same or higher earnings (Gardner 1995).
33. See Commission on Behavioral and Social Sciences (1999) for review of the evidence.
34. The discussion in this paragraph is based on Nardone, Veum, and Yates (1997).

Appendix 4A
Data and Methodology

DATA

The data we use for the analyses described in this chapter are files that have been constructed by merging the March Supplement of the Current Population Survey (CPS) data to several sources of information on job requirements, namely:

- 1991 *Dictionary of Occupational Titles* (DOT91);
- Department of Labor, Bureau of Labor Statistics (BLS) education and training categories; and
- Job mobility classifications developed by Kusmin and Gibbs (2000).

The CPS is a monthly survey of approximately 50,000 people that provides a range of data on employment, including occupation, hours worked, earnings, size of employer, and so forth. The March Supplement provides data on whether the respondent has a disability that limits the type or amount of work he or she can do, as well as health insurance status.

Because the CPS provides data on occupations for respondents who report that they are in the labor force, we were able to match the occupation with job characteristics from the three other sources.[1] Additional job characteristics were computed using data from the CPS.[2] We matched job characteristics to an average of 47,247 respondents who were assigned occupation codes in each of the years 1983–2000.

Rather than using the standard approach of viewing each observation as a person, we view each observation of an employed person in the CPS as an observation of a job. Because the survey is designed as a nationally representative sample of the population, it also provides a nationally representative sample of jobs held.[3] For each year from 1983 to 1999, we have created a large, nationally representative database of observations on jobs and job requirements.

One important limitation of this approach is that the job requirement measures from non-CPS sources do not capture any within-occupation changes in requirements during the period. This is a significant weakness of the data because we assume there have been significant changes in requirements within occupations during the 18 years spanned by the data. As a result, changes in mean occupational requirements during the period reflect only changes owing to changes in the distribution of occupations, and miss changes owing to within-occupation changes in job requirements.

Sources of Data on Job Characteristics

We developed job characteristics variables based on data from the DOT91, BLS education groups, Kusmin and Gibbs mobility groups, and the CPS. DOT91 has been used for many years by the Social Security Administration in assessing the residual functional capacity of applicants to its disability programs. It is also used by vocational counselors and others to help counselors guide clients to appropriate occupations.[4] The job requirements in DOT91 fall into six categories: 1) relationship to data, people, and things; 2) general education and training; 3) general aptitude; 4) temperaments; 5) physical demands; and 6) environmental conditions (see Table 4A.1).

The BLS Office of Employment Projections classifies occupations into one of 11 categories based on an analysis of education or on-the-job training needed to become fully qualified for the job.[5] BLS uses the classifications for a variety of statistical purposes.

Table 4A.1 Job Requirements in the 1991 *Dictionary of Occupational Titles*

Data/people/things			
DATA	Synthesizing, coordinating, analyzing, compiling, computing, copying, comparing		
PEOPLE	Mentoring, negotiating, instructing, supervising, diverting, persuading, speaking-signaling, serving, taking instruction		
THINGS	Setting up, precision working, operating-controlling, driving-operating, manipulating, tending, feeding-offbearing, handling		
Education and training			
GEDR	General educational development reasoning score		
GEDM	General educational development math score		
GEDL	General educational development language score		
SVP	Specific vocational preparation: length of time needed in various vocational activities		
Aptitudes			
APTITUDG	General learning ability	APTITUDK	Motor coordination
APTITUDV	Verbal	APTITUDF	Finger dexterity
APTITUDN	Numerical	APTITUDM	Manual dexterity
APTITUDS	Spatial	APTITUDE	Eye-hand-foot coordination
APTITUDP	Form Perception	APTITUDC	Color discrimination
APTITUDQ	Clerical		
Temperaments			
TEMPA	Working alone or apart in physical isolation from others	TEMPR	Performing repetitive and/or continuous short-cycle work
TEMPD	Directing, controlling, and/or planning activities of others	TEMPS	Performing effectively under stress

TEMPE	Expressing personal feelings	TEMPT	Attaining precise set limits, tolerances, and standards
TEMPI	Influencing people in their opinions, attitudes and judgments	TEMPU	Working under specific instructions
TEMPJ	Making judgments and decisions	TEMPV	Performing a variety of duties
TEMPP	Dealing with people		

Physical demands

STRENGTH	Strength score: sedentary, light work, medium work, heavy work, very heavy work		
PHYDMD02	Climbing	PHYDMD12	Talking
PHYDMD03	Balancing	PHYDMD13	Hearing
PHYDMD04	Stooping	PHYDMD14	Tasting/smelling
PHYDMD05	Kneeling	PHYDMD15	Near acuity
PHYDMD06	Crouching	PHYDMD16	Far acuity
PHYDMD07	Crawling	PHYDMD17	Depth perception
PHYDMD08	Reaching	PHYDMD18	Accommodation
PHYDMD09	Handling	PHYDMD19	Color vision
PHYDMD10	Fingering	PHYDMD20	Field of vision
PHYDMD11	Feeling		

Environmental conditions

ENVCON01	Exposure to weather	ENVCON08	Proximity to moving mechanical parts
ENVCON02	Extreme cold	ENVCON09	Exposure to electrical shock
ENVCON03	Extreme heat	ENVCON10	Working in high exposed places
ENVCON04	Wet and/or humid	ENVCON11	Exposure to radiant energy
ENVCON05	Noise	ENVCON12	Working with explosives
ENVCON06	Vibration	ENVCON13	Exposure to toxic or caustic chemicals
ENVCON07	Atmospheric conditions	ENVCON14	Other hazards

In a study of occupational opportunities for less-educated workers, Kusmin and Gibbs (2000) divided the CPS occupations into starter, dead-end, goal, other low-mobility occupations, and other high-mobility occupations. Goal jobs are defined as having wages in the top one-third of jobs that are available to people with a high school education or less. They defined *starter* and *dead-end* jobs based on the probability that the worker moved to a goal job, using data from the October 1996 Occupational Mobility Supplement to the CPS. Dead-end jobs have average or below-average wages and near-average or below-average prospects for moving into a better paying job, while starter jobs are defined by a higher than average probability that the worker moved into a goal job. Other low-mobility and high-mobility occupations are defined as such because of the inaccuracy of estimates based on small numbers of low-educated workers in the occupation.

The CPS provides data on health insurance status, hours worked (full-time or part-time, full-year or part-year), number of employees in company (fewer than 25, 25–999, more than 1,000), sex, age, and union status. Because we wanted to assign a value to these variables based on the norm for the occupation, rather than the actual job for the individual, we pooled for each year the current and two prior year samples and computed the mean value of the variable for each occupation, based on workers without limitations only, and assigned that value to each occurrence of the occupation in the current year. Thus, the value of this characteristic that is attached to a record is the moving average for that occupation among sampled workers without disabilities in that occupation during the last three years.

Selection of Analysis Variables

Because of the large number of job characteristics in our database, and the likelihood that many were highly correlated with one another, we developed a systematic method for selecting a much smaller number for the analysis. As a first step in the process, we pooled the data into three time periods (1983–1985, 1988–1990, and 1998–2000) and examined the simple correlations between the characteristics and the limitation. We found that 26 characteristics were significantly correlated with the work limitation variable in all three of the time periods, and an additional 30 were significantly correlated in two of the time periods. Second, focusing on characteristics that had significant correlations in at least two time periods, we looked for job characteristics that were conceptually different from one another to minimize the correlation between the selected characteristics. Third, we looked for job characteristics that have changed over time.

Table 4A.2 describes the variables used in the final analyses presented in this chapter.

METHODOLOGY

Approach

The first step in the analysis is to examine the relationship between job requirements and whether the job is filled by a person with a "work limitation." Work limitation is the measure of work disability that the CPS has used consistently throughout this period, and is defined as a health problem or disability that prevents the respondent from working or that limits the kind or amount of

Table 4A.2 **Job Characteristics Used in the Analysis**

Name	Description	Source	Values
GED: Language	GED, language score	DOT91	1–5 corresponding to the curricula taught in primary and secondary schools and colleges. 1 indicates the level of competency normally taught in elementary school; 5 indicates a required college-level competency.
DIRECT	Directing, controlling, or planning the activities of others	DOT91	1 if skill is required; 0 otherwise.
SVP	Specific vocational preparation	DOT91	1: short demonstration 2: up to 1 month 3: 1–3 months 4: 3–6 months 5: 6 months to one year 6: 1–2 years 7: 2–4 years 8: 4–10 years 9: 10+ years
REPEAT	Performing repetitive or continuous short-cycle work	DOT 91	1 if skill is required; 0 otherwise.
STRENGTH	Strength score	DOT91	1: sedentary 2: light work 3: medium work 4: heavy work 5: very heavy work
BA-Plus	Job requires bachelor's degree or higher	BLS	1 if bachelor's degree required; 0 otherwise.

(continued)

Table 4A.2 (continued)

Name	Description	Source	Values
Dead-end	Job is unlikely to lead to better employment	Kusmin & Gibbs (2000)	1 if job is dead-end; 0 otherwise.
FTFY	Full-time/full-year	CPS	1 if job is full-time/full year.
Health Ins	Employer-subsidized health insurance	CPS	1 if employer offers subsidized health insurance, otherwise 0.
Small employer	Employer size: < 25 employees	CPS	1 if employer size is < 25; 0 otherwise.
Large employer	Employer size: > 1,000 employees	CPS	1 if employer size is > 1,000; 0 otherwise.

work he or she can do. For each year, we estimate a multiple regression model for work limitation, including selected job requirements and other job descriptors as explanatory variables (Table 4A.3).[6]

Analysis of Trends

The next step uses the regression results to examine the extent to which trends in the proportion of workers with limitations can be accounted for by changes in the coefficients from the regression and changes in the means of the occupational characteristics. The analysis is based on the following decomposition identity

$$(1) \quad y_1 - y_0 = a_1 - a_0 + \Sigma_k (a_{k1} - a_{k0})(x_{k0} + x_{k1})/2 + \Sigma_k (x_{k1} - x_{k0})(a_{k0} + a_{k1})/2$$

where: 0 and 1 are used to index two comparison years; y_j is the proportion of workers with limitations in year j; x_{kj} is the mean of characteristic k in year j; a_j is the intercept in year j; and a_{kj} is the regression coefficient of characteristic k in year j. The second term on the right-hand side is the difference owing to differences in the estimated coefficients, and the third term is the change owing to differences in the means.

It is important to recognize that the decomposition identity is just an identity. We cannot interpret the various components of change on the right-hand-side of Equation 1 as the causes of the change in y. Hence, in the text, we focus on whether the estimated coefficients can be interpreted in a causal fashion; examination of coefficients that change significantly over the period considered $(a_{k1} - a_{k0})$, and, for coefficients that are statistically significant and do not change significantly, the extent to which the trend in the variable's mean can account for the change in the proportion with limitations: $[(x_{k1} - x_{k0})(a_{k0} + a_{k1})/2]$.

In Table 4A.4, we show the estimated components of the change in the proportion of workers with limitations from 1990 to 2000. The estimates are based on the regression coefficients for those two years, as reported in Table 4A.3. In general, the discussion in the text is restricted to coefficient changes that were statistically significant. In assessing the significance of changes in coefficients, however, we also considered whether the change from 1990 to 2000 was consistent with a trend for the entire period, rather than just the result of random annual variability. For some coefficients, annual variability is quite high, and changes in coefficients from 1990 to 2000 that appear to be large are within the range of that variation. There is much less annual variability in the means of the characteristics, as evidenced from the graphics that appear in the text. Changes from 1990 to 2000 are all statistically significant, even though some are small from a substantive perspective. This is because sample sizes are large, on the order of 50,000 observations on jobs in each year.

Table 4A.3 Regression Coefficients, 1990–2000, Dependent Variable: Presence of a Work Limitation

	1990	1991	1992	1993	1994	1995	1996	1997	1998	1999	2000
Intercept	0.076***	0.060***	0.080***	0.086***	0.086***	0.061***	0.076***	0.082***	0.077***	0.044***	0.067***
FTFY	−0.001	0.002	0.013	0.004	0.006	0.018*	−0.025**	0.003	−0.010	−0.013	−0.009
GED-language	−0.003**	0.001	−0.006***	−0.003**	−0.001	−0.002	−0.005***	−0.001	−0.004**	−0.002	−0.003*
SVP	−0.003***	−0.002*	−0.002	−0.002	−0.003***	−0.002**	−0.003**	−0.004***	−0.002	−0.003***	−0.001
Health ins.	−0.035***	−0.045***	−0.044***	−0.047***	−0.065***	−0.060***	−0.018	−0.052***	−0.054***	−0.025**	−0.057***
BA-plus	0.005*	−0.003	0.003	0.000	0.003	−0.004	−0.001	0.001	0.006***	0.004*	0.001
Dead-end	−0.003	−0.006***	−0.008***	−0.007***	−0.002	0.000	−0.005**	−0.003	0.003	0.002	−0.001
Direct	0.005*	−0.001	0.000	−0.001	−0.001	0.000	0.005*	0.001	0.004	−0.001	0.004*
Repeat	−0.005	0.004	−0.003	0.001	−0.001	0.003	−0.002	−0.001	0.004	0.000	0.010**
Strength	0.004***	0.004***	0.002	0.000	0.001	0.000	−0.002	−0.001	−0.001	0.001	0.000
Small emp.	−0.007	−0.009	−0.021**	−0.026**	−0.024**	−0.005	0.019*	−0.014	−0.008	0.027***	−0.004
Large emp.	0.004	0.004	−0.005	−0.007	0.006	0.028***	0.031***	0.013	0.022**	0.049***	0.033***

*p ≤ 0.10; **p ≤ 0.05; ***p ≤ 1.01.

Table 4A.4 Estimated Components of Change in the Proportion of Workers with Limitations, 1990–2000

Variable	Change in Coefficient	Change in Mean	Change accounted for by change in[a] Coefficient	Change accounted for by change in[a] Characteristic
% limited	–	–0.389	–	–
Intercept	–0.0086	–	–0.86	
FTFY	–0.0080	0.0341*	–0.60	–0.02
GED-language	0.0004	0.0866*	0.12	–0.03
SVP	0.0023	0.1244*	1.26	–0.03
Health ins.	–0.0224	–0.0131*	–1.34	0.06
BA-plus	–0.0033	0.0392*	–0.10	0.01
Dead-end	0.0019	–0.0314*	0.04	0.01
Direct	–0.0004	0.0372*	–0.01	0.02
Repeat	0.0145*	–0.0169*	0.29	0.00
Strength	–0.0039*	–0.0257*	–0.42	0.00
Small employer	0.0026	–0.0063*	0.07	0.00
Large employer	0.0293*	0.0101*	1.14	0.02
Total			–0.42	0.03

[a] Based on decomposition analysis of CPS. See equation 1.
*Statistically significant change.

Appendix Notes

1. Merging the CPS to the DOT was a complicated task. Census uses 535 unique occupations in the more recent CPS files (530 prior to 1992) compared with the DOT, which uses 12,741 codes. The number of DOT91 codes per Census code varies substantially across occupations. For instance, 72 of the Cen90 codes (the codes used by Census from 1992 on) had unique DOT91 matches, while three Cen90 codes were each matched to more than 500 DOT91 codes. To produce job requirements for each Census code, we computed the mean of the job requirements over all corresponding DOT91 codes. We have not conducted a full analysis of how much detail on job requirements is obscured by this method. It appears from inspection that variation in job requirements within DOT91 codes corresponding to a common Census code is small relative to total variation in job requirements. Nonetheless, we expect that the aggregation of job requirements in

this manner is likely, if anything, to obscure the relationship between job requirements and work limitations.
2. Full-time/full-year, employer-paid health insurance, and firm size were computed by pooling years and computing the mean value of the variable for each occupation, based on workers without limitations only, and assigning that value to each occurrence of the occupation. For each year, we pooled data from the current year and the previous two years to compute these means. Thus, the value of this characteristic that is attached to a record is not the actual characteristic of that worker's job, but the mean for that occupation among sampled workers without disabilities in that occupation over the last three years.
3. We apply the population weights to get a representative sample of jobs.
4. The Department of Labor has recently replaced the DOT with a new system, O*NET, which provides data on a wider array of job characteristics. The DOT has some significant limitations. For example, its job characteristics are not consistently updated, and it differentiates between blue-collar jobs more accurately than white-collar. Nevertheless, the DOT is more relevant for the time period of interest to this study.
5. The 11 categories are 1) first professional degree, 2) doctoral degree, 3) master's degree, 4) work experience plus bachelor's or higher degree, 5) bachelor's degree, 6) associate's degree, 7) postsecondary vocational training, 8) work experience in related occupation, 9) long-term on-the-job training, 10) moderate-term on-the-job training, and 11) short-term on-the-job training. Postsecondary awards, if generally needed for entry into the occupation, take precedence over work-related training.
6. The table is based on the analysis of the period from 1990 through 2000. We have estimated other models using data for 1985 through 1989. We restrict our attention to the years indicated because the firm-size variables could not be constructed for earlier years. Earlier year models without firm-size variables are generally consistent with the later models, except that the full-year/full-time variable has a larger coefficient and is more significant.

References

Acemoglu, Daron, and Joshua Angrist. 2000. "Consequences of Employment Protection: The Case of the Americans with Disabilities Act." NBER working paper no. 6670. Cambridge, MA: National Bureau of Economic Research.

Autor, David H., Frank Levy, and Richard J. Murname. 2001. "The Skill Content of Recent Technological Change: An Empirical Explanation." NBER working paper no. 8337. Cambridge, MA: National Bureau of Economic Research.

Burkhauser, Richard V., Mary C. Daly, Andrew J. Houtenville, and Nigar Nargis. 2001. "Employment of Working-Age People with Disabilities in the 1980s and 1990s: What Current Data Can and Cannot Tell Us." Working paper. Ithaca, NY: Cornell Rehabilitation Research and Training Center.

Cappelli, Peter. 1999. *The New Deal at Work: Managing the Market Driven Workforce*. Boston: Harvard Business School Press.

Commission on Behavioral and Social Sciences, National Research Council. 1999. *The Changing Nature of Work: Implications for Occupational Analysis*. Washington, DC: National Academy Press.

Council of Economic Advisors. 2000. *Economic Report of the President*, Table B-46, "Employees on Nonagricultural Payrolls, by Major Industry, 1954–2001." Available at: <http://w3.access.gpo.gov/usbudget/fy2001/sheets/b46.xls>. Accessed: 9/15/02.

———. 2003. *Economic Report of the President*, Table B-44, "Unemployment by Duration and Reason, 1955–2001." Available at: <http://w3access.gpo.gov/usbudget/fy2003/sheets/b44.xls>. Accessed: 9/15/2002.

Deardorff, Alan V. 1998. "Technology, Trade, and Increasing Inequality: Does the Cause Matter for the Cure?" *Journal of International Economic Law* 1(3): 353–376.

Fallick, Bruce C. 1999. "Part-Time Work and Industry Growth." *Monthly Labor Review* 122(3): 22–29.

Farber, Henry S. 1995. *Are Lifetime Jobs Disappearing? Job Duration in the United States: 1973–1993*. NBER working paper no. 5014. Cambridge, MA: National Bureau of Economic Research.

Gardner, Jennifer M. 1995. "Worker Displacement: A Decade of Change." *Monthly Labor Review* 118(4): 45–57.

Gittleman, Maury B., and David R. Howell. 1995. "Changes in the Structure and Quality of Jobs in the United States: Effects by Race and Gender, 1973–1990." *Industrial and Labor Relations Review* 48(3): 420–440.

Golden, Lonnie. 2001. "Flexible Work Schedules: What Are We Trading Off to Get Them?" *Monthly Labor Review* 124(3): 50–67.

Hale, Thomas. 2001. "Lack of a Disability Measure in Today's Current Population Survey." *Monthly Labor Review* 124(6): 38–40.

Herz, Diane E. 1990. "Worker Displacement in a Period of Rapid Job Expansion, 1983–1987." *Monthly Labor Review* 113(5): 21–33.

Hipple, Steven. 2001. "Contingent Work in the Late 1990s." *Monthly Labor Review* 124(3): 3–27.

Howell, David R., and Edward N. Wolff. 1991. "Trends in the Growth and Distribution of Skills in the U.S. Workplace, 1960–1985." *Industrial and Labor Relations Review* 44(3): 486–502.

Hurd, Michael, and Kathleen McGarry. 1993. "The Relationship between Job Characteristics and Retirement." NBER working paper no. 4558. Cambridge, MA: National Bureau of Economic Research.

Karasek, Robert A., and Tores Theorell. 1992. *Healthy Work: Stress, Productivity, and the Reconstruction of Working Life.* New York: Basic Books.

Kaye, H. Stephen. 2000. Disability and the Digital Divide. *Disability Statistics Report no. 22.* San Francisco: University of California, Disability Statistics Center.

Krueger, Alan, Susan Drastal, and Douglas Kruse. 1995. "Labor Market Effects of Spinal Cord Injuries in the Dawn of the Computer Age." NBER working paper no. 5302. Cambridge, MA: National Bureau of Economic Research.

Kruse, Douglas L. 1998. "Persons with Disabilities: Demographic, Income and Health Care Characteristics, 1993." *Monthly Labor Review* 121(9): 13–22.

Kusmin, Lorin D., and Robert M. Gibbs. 2000. "Less Educated Workers Face Limited Opportunities to Move Up to Good Jobs." *Rural America* 15(2): 32–42.

Loo, Robert. 2001. "Attitudes of Management Undergraduates toward Persons with Disabilities: A Need for Change." *Rehabilitation Psychology* 46(3): 285–295.

Loprest, Pamela, Kalman Rupp, and Steven H. Sandell. 1995. "Gender, Disabilities, and Employment in the Health and Retirement Study." *Journal of Human Resources* 30 (Suppl. 1995): S293–318.

MacKenzie, Ellen, John A. Morris, G.J. Jurkovich, Y. Yasui, B.M. Cushing, A.R. Burgess, B.J. DeLateur, M.P. McAndrew, and M.F. Swiontkowski. 1998. "Return to Work Following Injury: The Role of Economic, Social, and Job-Related Factors." *American Journal of Public Health* 88(11): 1630–1637.

Nardone, Thomas, Jonathan Veum, and Julie Yates. 1997. "Measuring Job Security." *Monthly Labor Review* 120(6): 26–33.

Ryan, Carole P. 1995. "Work Isn't What It Used To Be: Implications, Recommendations, and Strategies for Vocational Rehabilitation." *Journal of Rehabilitation* 61(4): 8–15.

Segal, Lewis, and Daniel Sullivan. 1996. "The Growth of Temporary Services Work." Working Paper series, macroeconomic issues 96–26. Chicago: Federal Reserve Bank of Chicago.

Spenner, Kenneth I. 1995. "Technological Change, Skill Requirements, and Education: The Case for Uncertainty." In *The New Modern Times: Factors Reshaping the World of Work.* Series in the Sociology of Work, David B. Bills, ed. Albany: State University of New York Press, pp. 81–137.

Tilly, Chris. 1991. "Reasons for the Continuing Growth of Part-time Employment." *Monthly Labor Review* 114(3): 10–18.

U.S. Census Bureau. 2002. *Health Insurance Coverage: 1998.* Washington, DC: U.S. Census Bureau. Available at <http://www.census.gov/hhes/hlthin/hlthin98.html>. (Accessed: June 27, 2002.)

U.S. Department of Labor. 1999. *Employee Benefits Survey.* Washington, DC: Bureau of Labor Statistics. Available at <http://www.bls.gov/data/home.htm>. (Accessed: June 27, 2002.)

———. 1999b. *Report on the American Workforce.* Washington, DC: U.S. Department of Labor.

Yelin, Edward H.. 1992. *Disability and the Displaced Worker.* New Brunswick, NJ: Rutgers University Press.

———. 1997. "The Employment of People with and without Disabilities in an Age of Insecurity." *Annals of the American Academy of Political and Social Science* 549: 117–128.

5
Rising Health Care Expenditures and the Employment of People with High-Cost Chronic Conditions

Steven C. Hill
Agency for Healthcare Research and Quality

Gina A. Livermore
Cornell University

Andrew J. Houtenville
Cornell University

The cost of health care substantially increased during the 1990s, and this, coupled with how health care is financed in this country, may have decreased employment among people with disabilities. Nonelderly Americans finance health care primarily through private health insurance, and employment-related health insurance is the most important source of private insurance. Many people with disabilities have another option for financing health care, however; they can obtain Medicare or Medicaid coverage via the Social Security Disability Insurance (SSDI) or Supplemental Security Income (SSI) program, although to do so they must have severely limited earnings. Access to private and public insurance may be especially important for people with disabilities because many have special health care needs, such as ongoing needs for specialized care, and, as a group, they have substantially greater health care costs than those without disabilities (Alecxih, Corea, and Kennell 1995; DeJong et al. 2002; Rice and LaPlante 1992).

Rapid growth in the costs of health care, and concomitant changes in health care financing, may have decreased employment among people with disabilities by:

- increasing employee contributions to employment-related health insurance and thus decreasing the appeal of seeking insurance through employment;
- prompting commercial insurers to adopt managed care strategies to constrain costs, possibly reducing the adequacy of employer-sponsored coverage for people with disabilities, and making such insurance less attractive than public health insurance, where managed care is growing at a slower pace (Regenstein and Schroer 1998); and
- increasing the cost of employing people with disabilities relative to others, and thus reducing job opportunities when employers who provide insurance have a growing incentive to encourage people with disabilities to leave their jobs, or not hire them in the first place.

Our analyses focus on working-aged persons with high-cost chronic health conditions. We focus on these individuals primarily because, although people with disabilities as a group have higher than average health care needs and expenditures, not all persons with disabilities experience a large and sustained demand for health care. For example, a person who loses a limb because of an accident may experience high demand for health care and high expenditures in the short-term, but once the condition has stabilized, no longer has an exceptional need for services, assuming no secondary conditions. In contrast, end-stage renal disease, multiple sclerosis, severe mental disorders, and muscular dystrophy require intensive, ongoing care. Our hypothesis about the effect of changes in health care financing on employment is most pertinent to persons with ongoing, high expenditures.

We use data from three surveys to study people with high-cost chronic conditions. Using the 1987 National Medical Expenditure Survey (NMES) and the 1996 and 1997 Medical Expenditure Panel Survey (MEPS), we chart the rising prevalence of (treated) chronic conditions[1] and compare expenditures and health insurance coverage of people with chronic health conditions in 1987 and 1996–1997. These data, while rich in expenditure information, have a limited number of observations of people with both disabilities and high-cost chronic conditions. In addition, the disability measures differ between the NMES and MEPS, which affects our ability to make inferences about the effect of changes in health insurance on employment over time. For these reasons, we also use data from the 1984–1996 National Health Interview Survey (NHIS). The NHIS data were collected in a consistent fashion over a long period, annually. We pool data from multiple years to increase sample sizes for more precise estimates. With the NHIS data, we measure the rising prevalence of high-cost chronic conditions and compare trends in employment between people with work limitations and high-cost chronic conditions, and other people with work limitations. If changes in health care finance are a factor, then we expect a more negative employment trend among those with high-cost chronic conditions.

In the next section, we provide background on the relationship between health insurance and the employment of people with disabilities, rising health expenditures and employee contributions, and managed care. We follow with a description of our empirical strategy, which focuses on people with work limitations and high-cost chronic conditions; the data; and define high-cost chronic conditions.

In the "Findings" section, we present descriptive information about the rising prevalence of high-cost chronic conditions, rising health expenditures, changes in health insurance coverage, and changes in employment of people with high-cost chronic conditions relative to those without such conditions. We also present findings that suggest that the rising prevalence of high-cost chronic conditions, and the decline in the employment rate of people with disabilities who have such conditions, had a small, but nontrivial depressing effect on the overall employment rate for people with work limitations.

BACKGROUND

Sources of Health Insurance for People with Disabilities

Private insurance

Private health insurance is the primary source of health insurance for nonelderly Americans, and employment-related health insurance is the most important source of private insurance. People with disabilities who obtain private insurance may face substantial restrictions in coverage (Friedland and Evans 1996). A 1998 survey that included 1,000 Americans with disabilities aged 16 and older found that although 90 percent of those with disabilities reported being covered by health insurance, 32 percent of those said that a special need related to their disability (for example, therapies, equipment, or medicine) was not covered by their insurance. Moreover, 20 percent reported being unable to obtain needed medical care on at least one occasion during the previous year, compared with 11 percent of those surveyed without disabilities (Louis Harris and Associates 1998).

People with chronic health conditions and disabilities may be unable to purchase private insurance outside of work because of high premiums and underwriting restrictions. Premiums for individual insurance policies are generally higher than those for employment-related policies and also vary depending on how tightly a state regulates its insurance market. A recent study of the accessibility of individual insurance policies to people with health problems reports that the average premium offered to hypothetical single individuals with a variety of health conditions in eight less-regulated markets was $333 per month (Pollitz, Sorian, and Thomas 2001). The highest *monthly* premium quoted among the policies studied was $2,504, for an overweight smoker with high blood pressure. Individuals with chronic health conditions may be unable to purchase a private individual health insurance policy at any price. According to Pollitz, Sorian, and Thomas, conditions commonly considered "uninsurable" by insurers in the individual insurance market include AIDS/HIV, brain or spinal cord injury, cystic fibrosis, diabetes, epilepsy, hemophilia, hepatitis C, kidney disease, lupus, multiple sclerosis, muscular dystrophy, organ transplant, osteoporosis, paraplegia or quadriplegia, Parkinson's disease, and stroke.

Public insurance

People with disabilities are much more likely than those without disabilities to rely on public health insurance, namely, Medicare and Medicaid. Working-aged people with disabilities are eligible for these programs when they qualify for SSDI or SSI, which means they must initially leave the labor force to qualify for Medicare and Medicaid.[2] Data from the 1994 NHIS show that nearly 60 percent of people with disabilities who are unemployed rely on public health insurance compared with 17 percent of unemployed individuals without disabilities. Among employed persons, roughly 9 percent of those with disabilities rely on public health insurance compared with less than 2 percent of those without disabilities (Stapleton et al. 1998).

Policies to improve access to public insurance were implemented early in our study period, and then again after the study period. Beginning in 1986, former SSDI beneficiaries can keep Medicare benefits for up to four years after returning to work. Former SSI beneficiaries can keep Medicaid benefits if their employment income is insufficient to pay for the equivalent of the Medicaid and SSI benefits they formerly received. The 1999 Ticket to Work and Work Incentives Improvement Act (TWWIIA) extended the period of Medicare coverage for SSDI beneficiaries who leave the rolls because of work, and expanded options for states to provide Medicaid coverage to people with disabilities. The goal of these policies is to enable people with disabilities to return to work without fear of being unable to pay for health care.

Rising expenditures and employee contributions

From 1987 to 1996, per capita health care expenditures rose 14 percent above the inflation rate for noninstitutionalized persons (Zuvekas and Cohen 2002). Rising health care costs and improved medical technologies may have increased the importance of health insurance for people with disabilities, but it also may have increased the importance of health insurance for employers. Evidence suggests that employers who offer insurance avoid hiring people with poor health (Buchmueller 1995). As expenditures rise, employers may be even less likely to hire people with disabilities.

Employee contributions for employment-related insurance rose considerably between 1988 and 1996; in large firms, they tripled for single coverage and quadrupled for family coverage. Employee contributions in small firms rose by even larger factors (Gabel, Ginsburg, and Hunt 1997). Increasing employee contributions are the primary reason for the decline in private insurance coverage (Cutler 2002). They also decrease the attractiveness of employment-related insurance for people with disabilities.[3]

Managed care and private insurance benefits

Differences in the prevalence of managed care in private and public health insurance may affect employment because some people with disabilities have poor experiences with managed care. Enrollment in managed care has grown most significantly in employment-related insurance. By 1996, 73 percent of those enrolled in employer-sponsored plans participated in a managed care plan (Levitt, Lundy, and Srinivasan 1998). Managed care is less pervasive in public insurance, and people with disabilities were less likely to be enrolled in Medicaid managed care than other Medicaid enrollees. In 1998, a quarter of nonelderly Medicaid enrollees with disabilities were in managed care, and two-thirds of those in managed care were in capitated arrangements (Regenstein and Schroer 1998). The greater prevalence of managed care in the private sector may have made private insurance less attractive. Several studies of people with disabilities and those with chronic conditions in managed care plans have generally found good access to primary care; problems accessing more specialized care; less satisfaction, relative to fee-for-service; and no differences in quality of care, health status, or functioning (Abt Associates 2000; Clement et al. 1992; Gold et al. 1997; Hawkinson and Frates 2000; Hill and Wooldridge 2003; McCall 1989; Miller and Luft 1997; Retchin et al. 1992; Safran, Tarlow, and Rogers 1994).

On the other hand, employment-related insurance became more generous because more people were enrolled in HMOs, which have less cost-sharing, and because other plans added benefits. Employees in medium and large firms were increasingly enrolled in plans that were much more likely to cover hospice, hearing exams, physical exams, and preventive care, such as immunizations (U.S. Department of Labor 1989, 1999a). Employees were also able to lower their out-of-pocket expenditures because HMOs tend to have fixed copayments rather than coinsurance and deductibles. In addition, the proportion of employees in non-HMO plans that did not have deductibles increased.

The Link Between Health Insurance and Employment

Because of the importance of health insurance, access to insurance coverage is likely to figure heavily in the employment decisions of people with disabilities. Employment-related health insurance has the potential to serve as an incentive to enter the labor market, as it may induce people with disabilities to seek employment to access employment-based health insurance. Public health insurance, however, may be a disincentive to employment. Because SSI and SSDI eligibility requires a participant's earnings to be below a certain threshold, employment can mean the potential loss of health benefits for many working-aged people with disabilities covered by Medicare or Medicaid.

Much anecdotal evidence from surveys and other sources suggests that health insurance is important in the employment decisions of people with disabilities. A survey of 1,200 leaders of major disability constituencies conducted by the President's Committee on Employment of People with Disabilities (1994) identified the fear of losing Medicaid or Medicare as the greatest barrier to the employment of people on SSI and SSDI. A survey of Alaska residents with disabilities found that 51 percent of respondents reported not having affordable health insurance as a major barrier to work. Similar surveys conducted in Oregon, Vermont, and Wisconsin found that a large proportion of respondents with psychiatric disabilities and those with multiple impairments report that, unless a job offered prescription drug coverage, they could not afford to work (Hanes 2000).

Economic studies of the effects of health insurance on employment or program participation have attempted to assess the effects of insurance, controlling for other factors. Using the Health and Retirement Survey, Kreider and Riphahn (2000) found that adults aged 50–61 who had health insurance through their most recent employer were less likely to apply for SSDI, presumably because those with employment-related health insurance would be less likely to quit their jobs and become uninsured. Their results may, however, overstate the effects of employment-related health insurance because this benefit may be correlated with other unmeasured job characteristics that would encourage continued employment (Gruber and Madrian 2002).

Stapleton et al. (1998) examined whether some SSI recipients constrain their earnings to stay below the eligibility threshold for receipt of Medicaid. Section 1619 of the Social Security Act allows SSI recipients who work and whose monthly earnings exceed the substantial gainful activity (SGA) level to receive Medicaid benefits if their income, after certain deductions, remains below the 1619(b) eligibility threshold.[4] Controlling for other factors, these authors find strong evidence that some employed SSI recipients substantially increase their earnings as the eligibility threshold increases. This suggests that they, in fact, keep earnings at or below the Medicaid eligibility level. This group, however, is a small proportion of SSI beneficiaries.

Two other studies focused on Medicaid benefit generosity. Yelowitz (1998) examined the effect of Medicaid benefit generosity on SSI participation among those most likely eligible for Medicaid because of a disability, that is, men aged 40–64 and women aged 44–64, who are high school dropouts and who are not single parents with children under 18. Using instrumental variable analysis to account for potential spurious correlation between employment and expenditures, Yelowitz estimated that the effect of increases in Medicaid expenditures on this subpopulation explains 20 percent of the growth in SSI rolls over time. Stapleton et al. (1995) studied the number of applicants for SSI, which should be more sensitive than the SSI participation rates used by Yelowitz. Yet Stapleton found that Medicaid had no effect. Both studies had difficulty in detecting effects, perhaps because studies using mean expenditures as a measure of benefit generosity are biased toward finding no effect (Gruber and Madrian 2002). A factor that may explain the difference in significant levels between these two studies is that Stapleton controlled for changes in general assistance programs, and these changes are associated with changes in SSI participation rates, while Yelowitz did not control for changes in such programs.

In summary, although three of the four economic studies suggest that health insurance affects the employment or program participation of people with disabilities, questions remain because of methodological limitations that bias estimates, similar studies yield conflicting results, and the subpopulation found to be affected is quite small.

DATA AND METHODS

Empirical Strategy

We take a different approach from prior studies on health insurance and employment among people with disabilities by focusing on the considerable variation in health care needs among people with disabilities. For example, some people with disabilities have cancer, and, hence, considerable health care needs, while others have visual impairments, which generally have fewer associated health care needs. Thus, people with disabilities are heterogeneous in the value they place on insurance. Our approach is especially advantageous when studying all sources of insurance (Medicaid, Medicare, and private insurance) because variation in individuals' valuation of Medicare is the only source of variation for that program, as eligibility has not changed and benefits have changed minimally over time.

Measures of health status have been used in many studies of health insurance and employment. We attempt to overcome the two primary limitations of prior studies using health status (Gruber and Madrian 2002). First, most population survey data have small samples of people with poor health, so even large effects can be difficult to detect. We pool multiple years of NHIS data to improve the precision of our estimates. Second, in prior studies, it was difficult to completely separate the effects of insurance from other factors related to health. Specifically, poor health and chronic conditions can affect employment directly, through disability, as well as indirectly, through health insurance. In our analysis of the NHIS, we attempt to control for the direct effects of disability by focusing on people with work limitations and comparing changes over time in the employment between those with and without high-cost chronic conditions.

NMES, MEPS, and NHIS

We used data from three national surveys of the civilian noninstitutionalized population to study people with high-cost chronic conditions because each survey provides additional information. We used the NMES and the MEPS to estimate the prevalence of chronic conditions, health care expenditures for people with those conditions, their health insurance status, and their employment status during a year. The NMES is a stand-alone survey that was conducted in 1987. The MEPS is a panel survey, conducted by the Agency for Healthcare Research and Quality every year beginning in 1996. We used data from the first year of the first panel (1996) and the first year of the second panel (1997), which oversampled people with activity limitations. Estimates from the MEPS are weighted to represent the population in 1996 and 1997. The NMES Household Component was conducted in four rounds over the course of 1987. The MEPS Household Component interviewed respondents twice per year over two and one-half years. Both surveys also have a Medical Provider Component, in which a sample of the medical providers identified in the Household Component surveys was interviewed to supplement household-reported health care expenditure and source of payment information. These data, while rich in expenditures and service use information, have a limited number of observations of working-age (aged 25–61) people with both disabilities and high-cost chronic conditions. In addition, the disability measures differ between the NMES and MEPS, which affects our ability to make inferences about the effect of changes in health insurance on employment over time.

We also used the 1984–1996 NHIS, an ongoing household survey, to estimate the prevalence of high-cost chronic conditions among people with work limitations and changes in their employment over time. The NHIS has larger sample sizes, and we pool data from two, four-year periods of economic expansion to increase sample sizes and improve the precision of our estimates of working-aged people with reported work limitations. Both periods start a year after an economic trough and end in the middle of a business cycle expansion. From 1984 to 1987, the sample consists of 18,503 adults with work limitations, and from 1993 through 1996, the sample consists of 21,417 such observations. The NHIS collects information on illness, disability, chronic impairments, and employment during the two weeks prior to the survey interview, but it does not collect health expenditure data. All statistical tests take into account the complex sample designs of the three surveys. Below, we describe how we created the key variables used in our analysis.

Chronic Health Conditions

We created indicators for the presence of high-cost chronic health conditions based on disease classification schemes developed by Hwang et al. (2001) and Kronick et al. (2000). From all three surveys, we used conditions reported by the household respondents, which professional coders classified into the three-digit *International Classifica-*

tion of Disease, ninth edition (ICD-9) codes. The surveys differ in the context and frequency with which conditions were collected.

NMES and MEPS condition data

In the NMES and MEPS, the household respondent reported health conditions associated with service use and disability days during the year.[5] To remove differences in how the surveys collected data on conditions and allow comparisons between the MEPS and NMES, we used data on conditions associated with service use only and excluded conditions reported elsewhere in either survey (Table 5.1). NMES asks about the conditions associated with each disability day, but MEPS asks about the conditions associated with all disability days, which may reduce the number of conditions collected. Using only conditions associated with health care service use may cause the number of people with conditions to increase over time, as more people visit doctors and receive diagnoses for their health problems.

NHIS condition data

The NHIS collects condition data in a consistent manner from 1984 to 1996, but there are differences between the NHIS and the NMES and MEPS (Table 5.1). The NHIS collects condition information related to current limitations in major activities, all hospital stays in the prior 12 months, and all physician visits and disability days in the last two weeks.[6] Because of the generally shorter time frame used in asking about conditions, fewer conditions are reported in the NHIS than in the NMES and MEPS. With the NHIS, however, we focused on people with work limitations who report conditions associated with their limitations and use more services—a population with more complete condition data. Also, unlike the analysis using the MEPS and NMES data, we used conditions reported for any reason in the NHIS, including diagnoses associated with disability and disability days.

Classifying conditions by chronicity and costliness

Hwang et al. (2001) developed a system to differentiate between individuals with and without chronic conditions using data from the MEPS. Five internists reviewed the ICD-9 codes of all conditions reported by adults in the MEPS, and used a consistent definition to judge whether the conditions were chronic.[7] The internists identified

Table 5.1 Condition Data Collection in Three Surveys

	NHIS	NMES	MEPS
Services	Inpatient Hospital outpatient and emergency room Office-based	Inpatient Hospital outpatient and emergency room Office-based Home health Prescription drug	Inpatient Hospital outpatient and emergency room Office-based Home health Prescription drug Alternative care [a]
Time period	The two full weeks prior to the interview date	Calendar year	Calendar year [b]
Disability days			
Types of disability days	Lost work days Lost days of usual activity Bed days	Lost work days [a] Lost days of usual activity [a] Bed days [a]	Lost work days [a] Bed days [a]
Asks about conditions associated with	Total disability days in the last two weeks	Each period of disability days since last interview	Total disability days since last interview
Time period	The two full weeks prior to the interview date	Calendar year	More than one year, varies with date of third interview
Activity limitations			
Activities	Work Housework Any activities	—	—
Time period	Now	—	—

NOTE: All three surveys also asked about lost school days, but only for persons younger than are in our sample. During the time period of our study, NHIS also asked questions about four lists of specific conditions, but each respondent was asked about only one list. NMES and MEPS also ask about conditions associated with dental visits, but our analysis focuses on medical conditions. MEPS also asks about conditions that may not be associated with service use or disability days, including conditions associated with a variety of disability measures, but these are excluded from the analysis to increase comparability with the NMES. NHIS = National Health Interview Survey. NMES = National Medical Expenditure Survey. MEPS = Medical Expenditure Panel Survey.

[a]Conditions collected solely because they were associated with disability days were not used in analysis of NMES and MEPS to increase comparability between NMES and MEPS.

[b]MEPS collects conditions associated with service use over a two-year period, and our analysis is limited to conditions associated with service use in the first calendar year.

177 chronic conditions for adults. To distinguish between separate chronic conditions and a single condition associated with multiple ICD-9 codes, Hwang used the Clinical Classification Software (CCS) developed by Elixhauser et al. (1998). The CCS aggregates ICD-9 codes into distinct and mutually exclusive categories.

Kronick et al. (2000) developed the Chronic Illness and Disability Payment System (CDPS) to provide state Medicaid programs a system for adjusting capitation rates based on the health status of the population enrolled. The authors used regression analysis to identify three- to five-digit ICD-9 codes reported in claims data that were associated with elevated Medicaid expenditures in the following year. Within each of 19 major body systems, they ranked conditions as very high cost, high cost, medium cost, low cost, very low cost, and extra low cost, as well as another group of conditions that are very prevalent with even lower costs. In addition, they identified conditions that are not well defined or that they otherwise excluded from the CDPS.

Table 5.2 summarizes the four chronic condition cost categories we use in our analyses. The categories are based on the ICD-9 codes associated with chronic conditions as identified by Hwang et al. (2001), classified using the Kronick et al. (2000) expenditure groups, with four modifications:[8]

1) We aggregated the 56 expenditure groups in the CDPS into four groups (high, medium, low, and very low), because the size of the NMES and MEPS samples are relatively small compared with the population of an entire Medicaid program, and because the most expensive conditions are very rare. We aggregated the groups based on mean Medicaid expenditures for the 56 groups reported in Kronick.[9]

2) The three-digit ICD-9 codes for chronic conditions in Table 5.2 do not exactly match Hwang. Because the NHIS did not code ICD-9 codes for family history of illness, aftercare, and other factors that are not illness or injury specific ("V codes"), we excluded these codes from the NMES and MEPS analysis as well.[10] In addition, some codes not found in the 1996 MEPS were in the 1997 MEPS; hence, Hwang did not assess their chronicity.[11] Most of these "new" ICD-9 codes were clearly acute condi-

Table 5.2 Summary of Chronic Condition Categories

Type of chronic condition	Three-digit ICD-9 codes	Sample diagnoses	Kronick et al.'s categories
High cost	038, 042, 155, 156, 157, 183, 203, 204, 205, 208, 252, 253, 255, 263, 268, 277, 279, 282, 284, 295, 335, 337, 340, 359, 425, 428, 494, 507, 512, 555, 556, 567, 571, 572, 579, 582, 584, 585, 586	Human immonodeficiency virus, malignant neoplasm of the liver, multiple myeloma, leukemia, parathyroid disorders, schizophrenia, multiple sclerosis, muscular dystrophy, cardiomyopathy, heart failure, chronic liver disorder, chronic nephritis, renal failure	Very high, high, medium (except medium cancer)
Medium cost	140–154, 159–161, 164–170, 172–175, 179, 182, 184–187, 189, 191–196, 199–202, 234, 250, 286, 288, 290, 296–299, 304, 305, 310, 314, 315, 317, 319, 331–334, 336, 343–347, 353, 355–358, 363, 394, 397, 398, 410, 411, 413, 414, 416, 423, 424, 426, 427, 430–434, 436, 437, 441, 443, 444, 446, 453, 491, 492, 493, 496, 515, 534, 552, 562, 581, 583, 596, 707, 710, 712, 714, 730, 741, 742, 745–747, 751, 758, 797, 952	Most other cancers, diabetes, affective psychoses, mental retardation, ischemic heart disease, emphysema, asthma	Low, medium cancers
Low cost	270, 274, 291, 303, 365, 366, 370, 401, 600, 617, 618, 628, 715, 717, 720, 721, 722, 731, 743	Hypertension, osteoarthritis, spondylosis, intervertebral disc disorder	Very low, extra low

(continued)

Table 5.2 (continued)

Type of chronic condition	Three-digit ICD-9 codes	Sample diagnoses	Kronick et al.'s categories
Very low cost	135, 138, 235–239, 242–245, 251, 256, 257, 259, 271–273, 275, 278, 294, 300–302, 306, 307, 311–313, 348, 354, 360, 362, 369, 377, 379, 389, 412, 429, 435, 438, 440, 447, 455, 457, 473, 474, 477, 500, 501, 505, 557, 573, 576, 587, 588, 607, 626, 627, 691, 696, 716, 725, 732, 750, 984, 985	Hypothyroidism, neurotic disorders, atherosclerosis, impaired renal function, allergic rhinitis, menopausal disorders, atopic dermatitis	Prevalent and even less costly

NOTE: For our study, we aggregated the Kronick very high, high, and medium conditions into one "high-cost" group. However, we grouped their medium cancer group, which had lower mean Medicaid expenditures than the other medium-cost groups, with their low-cost groups (which we call "medium cost"), because the average costs of the medium cancer and the Kronick et al. low-cost groups were similar.
SOURCE: Categories are based on Hwang et al. (2001) and Kronick et al. (2000).

tions. We classified 79 of them as chronic, consulting a nurse when the chronicity of the condition was not apparent.

3) Some of the conditions classified as chronic by Hwang were classified as not well defined or otherwise excluded by Kronick. We put these in the lowest cost group because no other information was available, and the lowest cost group is the largest.

4) Although Kronick generally relied on three-digit ICD-9 codes, in some cases he used more detailed ICD-9 codes. Generally, we classified these conditions using an unweighted average of the costliness of the conditions within the three-digit category.[12]

Focus on people with work limitations and high-cost chronic conditions in the NHIS

We applied the chronic condition classification to all three surveys. In all three surveys, we found that somewhat similar proportions of the population had high-cost chronic conditions and similar trends: in the

NMES, 1.1 percent; in the MEPS, 1.6 percent; in the NHIS, 0.8 percent in 1984–1987 and 1.1 percent in 1993–1997. In the NHIS, however, we found that the reported prevalence of medium-, low-, and very low-cost chronic conditions to be considerably lower than in the NMES and MEPS. This is likely because the NHIS uses fewer measures of service use over shorter time frames to collect conditions. For this reason, our analysis of the NHIS focuses on people with high-cost chronic conditions relative to people without those conditions. Even the prevalence of high-cost chronic conditions is lower in the NHIS; therefore, we further focus on people with work limitations who had an opportunity to report a condition associated with their limitation, and hence are likely to have more complete condition data. In any case, the data are collected in a consistent manner over time in the NHIS.

Other Variables

Health expenditures

Both the NMES and the MEPS combined data were collected from health care providers and from households to create measures of health care costs.[13] The two surveys differ somewhat in the measure of costs publicly released, with the NMES releasing charges and the MEPS releasing payments. To compare expenditures across the two surveys, we use the adjustment method described in Zuvekas and Cohen (2002) to convert charge amounts from the NMES to payment amounts. We also adjusted all expenditure variables from the 1987 NMES and from the first panel of the MEPS (1996) to 1997 dollars using the Consumer Price Index for all items. To compare expenditures over time, we conducted one-tailed tests because the overwhelming trend in health expenditures is upward. We used two-tailed tests to compare rates of increase among groups. We bootstrapped standard errors to compare medians and to compare rates of increase.

Health insurance coverage

We examined insurance coverage over the year of the NMES and the first year of the MEPS using overlapping categories.[14] Insurance coverage was divided into four major categories: private (which includes CHAMPUS and CHAMPVA coverage), Medicare, Medicaid, and other sources of public insurance. If participants had coverage from any of these types of insurance during any month of the year, they were considered to be covered by that type of insurance. The insurance categories are not mutually exclusive; individuals could be covered by more than one type of insurance, either simultaneously or during different periods of the year. We also examined whether the sample member was uninsured for any month of the year.

Employment

The measures of employment differ between the surveys. The NMES and MEPS have information on employment throughout the year, and we use this richer information to measure whether a sample member was employed at any time during the year of the NMES or the first year of the MEPS. In contrast, the NHIS asks whether the person was employed in the two weeks before the interview.

Work limitation

For the NHIS sample, we defined people with work limitations as those answering yes to either: "Does any impairment or health problem NOW keep [person] from working at a job or business?" or "Is [person] limited in the kind or amount of work [person] can do because of any impairment?" This is identical to the definition used in Burkhauser, Houtenville, and Wittenburg (Chapter 2). The NMES, however, does not ask the same questions about work limitations as the MEPS; thus, we cannot compare people with work limitations using those two data sets.

FINDINGS

Rising Prevalence of Chronic Conditions

Table 5.3 shows the change in the percent of the population aged 25–61 in each of the chronic condition categories, based on analysis of the NMES and MEPS. The percent with high-cost chronic conditions rose by nearly half, from 1.1 percent in 1987 to 1.6 percent in 1996–1997. The percent of people in the medium and very low-cost chronic condition categories also increased, and the percent with low-cost chronic conditions and no chronic conditions declined.

Analysis of the NHIS shows that, among people with work limitations, the percentage with high-cost chronic conditions increased from 5.4 percent in the 1984–1987 period to 7.0 percent in the 1993–1996 period (Table 5.4). The increase is apparent for both men and women and is statistically significant for both groups.

Table 5.3 Reported Prevalence of Chronic Conditions, by Costliness, Persons Aged 25–61

Type of chronic condition	1987 NMES		1996–1997 MEPS		Pct. pt. change
	N	%	N	%	
All	16,441	100.0	16,153	100.0	
High cost	167	1.1	288	1.6	0.5***
Medium cost	1,729	11.5	2,432	14.0	2.5***
Low cost	1,560	10.3	1,347	8.2	−2.1*
Very low cost	1,797	12.8	2,581	17.0	4.2***
None	11,188	64.3	9,505	59.3	−5.0***

NOTE: The chronic condition categories are based on all conditions associated with service use and are mutually exclusive and hierarchical, so that a person is in the highest cost category found among his or her diagnoses. For example, the category medium-cost chronic conditions excludes persons who also have high-cost chronic conditions. Categories are based on Hwang et al. (2001) and Kronick et al. (2000) (see Table 5.2).
*** $p \leq 0.01$ level, two-tailed test; * $p \leq 0.10$ level, two-tailed test.
SOURCE: Authors' calculations from the National Medical Expenditures Survey (NMES) and the Medical Expenditures Panel Survey (MEPS), first years of panel 1 (1996) and panel 2 (1997); noninstitutionalized civilians.

Table 5.4 Reported Prevalence of High-Cost Chronic Conditions among People with Work Limitations, Aged 25–61

	1984–87		1993–96		Percentage point change
	N	Percent	N	Percent	
All	18,503	5.4	21,417	7.0	1.6***
Men	8,602	5.5	10,068	7.1	1.5***
Women	9,901	5.2	11.349	7.0	1.7***

NOTE: High-cost chronic conditions associated with service use or disability are based on Hwang et al. (2001) and Kronick et al. (2000) (see Table 5.2). ***1993–1996 statistically different from 1984–1987 at the 0.01 level, two-tailed test.
SOURCE: Authors' calculations from the National Health Interview Survey (NHIS). Noninstitutionalized civilians.

Thus, using both the NHIS and the NMES/MEPS data we find an increase in the percentage of persons reporting high-cost chronic conditions. This suggests that the prevalence of high-cost chronic conditions has increased over time.

Rising Health Care Expenditures

The data from the NMES and MEPS show that the chronic condition cost categories are, in fact, highly correlated with expenditures in the general working-aged population (Table 5.5). We present both medians and means because health care expenditures are highly skewed. People in all the high-, medium-, low-, and very low-cost chronic condition groups experienced increases in mean or median expenditures. Those with no chronic conditions experienced no increase in expenditures. The mean expenditure increase for people with high-cost chronic conditions is large (37 percent), statistically significant, and larger than the corresponding increases for any other group. Median expenditures for people with high-cost chronic conditions did not increase by a statistically significant amount, perhaps owing to sample size or other factors.

The findings suggest that cost increases were greatest for those who have the highest costs within the high-cost group. A limitation of the findings is that the trends are based on conditions associated with service use. For persons with the more severe conditions, however, it is unlikely that many went without care in either time period. In addition, expenditures might have risen more rapidly for people with high-cost chronic conditions if this population had not experienced a large decline in private coverage and an increase in Medicaid coverage, described in the next section. Medicaid generally pays less for care than private insurance (Norton and Zuckerman 2000).

Changes in Health Insurance Coverage

Data from the NMES and MEPS show that, between 1987 and 1996/97, private coverage decreased, while Medicare and Medicaid coverage increased, but on net the likelihood of not being covered by any type of insurance increased among persons aged 25–61 (Table 5.6). For people with high-cost chronic conditions, the changes were

Table 5.5 Annual Expenditures per Person, Aged 25–61, by Costliness of Chronic Conditions

Type of chronic condition	1987 NMES			1996–1997 MEPS			Pct. change	
	N	Median ($)	Mean ($)	N	Median ($)	Mean ($)	Median	Mean
All	16,441	280	1,519	16,153	337	1,670	20***	10**
High cost	167	3,307	8,665	288	3,692	11,879	12	37**
Medium cost	1,729	1,271	4,720	2,432	1,720	4,287	35***	–9
Low cost	1,560	747	2,220	1,347	1,025	2,334	37***	5
Very low cost	1,797	616	1,748	2m581	671	1,783	9*	2
None	11,188	103	668	9,505	102	660	–1	–1
Difference-in-difference (pct. pt change from cost category below)								
High cost							–23	46+
Medium cost							2	–14
Low cost							28+++	3
Very low cost							10	3
None							na	na

NOTE: The chronic condition categories are based on all conditions associated with service use and are mutually exclusive and hierarchical so that a person is in the highest cost category found among his or her diagnoses. For example, the category medium-cost chronic conditions excludes persons who also have high-cost chronic conditions. Categories are based on Hwang et al. (2001) and Kronick et al. (2000) (see Table 5.2). All expenditures are in 1997 dollars.

***$p \leq 0.01$, one-tailed test; **$p \leq 0.05$, one-tailed test; *$p \leq 0.10$, one-tailed test.

+++ change from category below significant at 0.01 level, two-tailed test; + change from category below significant at 0.10 level, two-tailed test.

SOURCE: Authors' calculations from the National Medical Expenditures Survey (NMES) and the Medical Expenditures Panel Survey (MEPS), first years of panel 1 (1996) and panel 2 (1997); noninstitutionalized civilians.

Table 5.6 Health Insurance by Costliness of Chronic Conditions for Persons Aged 25–61

Type of chronic condition	Insurance coverage at any time during the year (%)				Ever uninsured (%)
	Private	Medicare	Medicaid	Other public	
1987 NMES					
All	84.0	1.9	5.7	1.8	20.3
High cost	73.2	19.0	15.9	3.9	13.1
Medium cost	82.2	6.5	11.5	4.1	14.4
Low cosst	85.9	2.6	5.7	2.4	15.6
Very low cost	87.9	2.0	5.8	1.6	15.1
None	83.5	0.7	4.5	1.4	23.3
1996–1997 MEPS					
All	78.6	2.3	7.3	1.1	25.3
High cost	63.1	22.6	25.6	1.8	17.3
Medium cost	74.6	6.9	14.9	1.6	21.1
Low cost	84.7	3.2	6.0	1.8	16.9
Very low cost	87.6	1.9	5.6	0.8	15.2
None	76.6	0.7	5.8	0.9	30.6
Pct. pt. change					
All	−5.4***	0.4**	1.7***	−0.8***	5.0***
High cost	10.1**	3.6	9.8**	−2.1	4.2
Medium cost	−7.7***	0.4	3.4***	−2.5***	6.6***
Low cost	−1.2	0.6	0.3	−0.6	1.4
Very low cost	−0.3	−0.1	−0.1	−0.8**	0.1
None	−6.8***	0.0	1.3***	−0.5**	7.3***

NOTE: The chronic condition categories are based on all conditions associated with service use and are mutually exclusive and hierarchical so that a person is in the highest-cost category found among his or her diagnoses. For example, the category medium-cost chronic conditions excludes persons who also have high-cost chronic conditions. Categories are based on Hwang et al. (2001) and Kronick et al. (2000) (see Table 5.2). Insurance coverage is at any time during the calendar year; thus the categories are not mutually exclusive.

***$p \leq 0.01$, two-tailed test; **$p \leq 0.05$, two tailed test.

SOURCE: Authors' calculations from the National Medical Expenditures Survey (NMES) and the Medical Expenditures Panel Survey (MEOS), first years of panel 1 (1996) and panel 2 (1997); noninstitutionalized civilians.

larger: the 10.1 percentage point decline in private coverage (from 73 percent to 63 percent) and 9.8 percentage point increase in Medicaid coverage (from 16 percent to 26 percent) were statistically significant, but other changes were not. Among people with medium-cost chronic conditions and no chronic conditions, private insurance also fell, but the likelihood of being uninsured rose much more than Medicaid coverage.

The switch from private to public insurance among people with high-cost chronic conditions parallels the growth in the SSDI and SSI programs, reported elsewhere in this volume, because eligibility for Medicare and Medicaid are tied to eligibility for SSDI and SSI. This change in type of health insurance coverage by itself, however, does not imply that changes in health care costs caused the decline in employment among people with high-cost chronic conditions.

Changes in employment

Employment rates. Data from the NMES and MEPS show that the chronic condition cost categories are correlated with employment (Table 5.7). Within each year, the percent employed was lowest among those with high-cost chronic conditions, and greatest among those without chronic conditions. These comparisons do not control for the direct effects of disability on employment; they are for the population as a whole, not just those who have a work limitation. Comparisons of changes in employment from 1987 to 1996–1997 are of greater interest. The overall percent employed at any time during the calendar year increased by 4 percentage points (from 82 percent to 86 percent). Employment increased for people in three of the four chronic condition cost groups. Employment declined by 3.4 percentage points among those with high-cost chronic conditions, but the decline is not statistically significant, nor is it statistically significantly different from the increase among those without high-cost chronic conditions, owing to the small sample size.

To control for the direct effects of disability, we turn to the NHIS data, which have larger sample sizes and a consistent definition of work limitation across time. Among people with work limitations in the NHIS, those with high-cost chronic conditions were less likely to be employed than others with work limitations (Table 5.8). The

Table 5.7 Percent of Persons Aged 25–61 Employed Any Time During the Year, by Costliness of Chronic Conditions

Type of chronic condition	1987 NMES		1996–1997 MEPS		Pct. pt. change
	N	%	N	%	
All	16,441	82.4	16,153	86.4	4.0**
High cost	167	59.8	288	56.4	−3.4
Medium cost	1,729	67.6	2,432	74.2	6.6***
Low cost	1,560	76.5	1,347	83.1	6.6***
Very low cost	1,797	80.0	2,581	87.2	7.2***
None	11,188	86.9	9,505	90.3	3.4***

NOTE: The chronic condition categories are based on all conditions associated with service use and are mutually exclusive and hierarchical such that a person is in the highest-cost category found among his or her diagnoses. For example, the category medium-cost chronic conditions excludes persons who also have high-cost chronic conditions. Categories are based on Hwang et al. (2001) and Kronick et al. (2000) (see Table 5.2).
***$p \leq 0.01$, two-tailed test; **$p \leq 0.05$, two tailed test.
SOURCE: Authors' calculations from the National Medical Expenditures Survey (NMES) and the Medical Expenditures Panel Survey (MEPS), first years of panel 1 (1996) and panel 2 (1997); noninstitutionalized civilians.

employment rate was only somewhat higher for men with high-cost chronic conditions than women with these conditions. On the other hand, the employment rate was consistently higher for men without these conditions than for women without these conditions, although the gap narrowed between the two periods. Thus, it is important to control for gender in the analysis.

Between the 1984–1987 and the 1993–1996 periods, employment among people with work limitations and high-cost chronic conditions was persistently low. About 24 percent of women were employed in both periods. Among men, employment fell 3.2 percentage points (from 28.7 percent to 25.5 percent), but the change is not statistically significant. At the same time, employment among men with work limitations but no high-cost chronic conditions fell 4.9 percentage points (from 52.7 percent to 47.9 percent), and this change is statistically significant. Thus, employment fell 1.7 percentage points more among men without high-cost chronic conditions than for those with high-cost conditions, suggesting that changes in health care financing were not a factor in the changing employment among men with work limitations.

Table 5.8 People with Work Limitations, Aged 25–61, Employed in the Past Two Weeks

Type of chronic condition	1984–1987 N	1984–1987 %	1993–1996 N	1993–1996 %	Pct. pt. change
All	18,503	42.9	21,417	42.6	–0.4
Men	8,602	51.4	10,068	46.3	–5.1***
Women	9,901	35.2	11,349	39.1	3.9***
High-cost chronic conditions	992	26.7	1,478	24.6	–2.0
Men	476	28.7	7.4	25.5	–3.2
Women	516	24.7	774	23.8	–0.8
No high-cost chronic conditions	17,500	43.9	19,939	43.9	0.1
Men	8,126	52.7	9,364	47.9	–4.9***
Women	9,385	35.7	10,575	40.2	4.5***
Difference-in-difference: Change in high cost minus change in not high cost					
All					–2.1
Men					4.6
Women					–5.3++

***1993–1996 statistically different from 1984–1987 at the 0.01 level, two-tailed test.
++Significant at the 0.05 level, one-tailed test.
SOURCE: Authors' calculations from the National Health Interview Survey (NHIS); noninstitutionalized civilians. High-cost chronic conditions associated with service use or disability are based on Hwang et al. (2001) and Kronick et al. (2000) (see Table 5.2).

Among women with work limitations and no high-cost chronic conditions, employment rose 4.5 percentage points (from 35.7 percent to 40.2 percent).[15] Employment for women with limitations and high-cost conditions remained fairly constant. The difference in the change in employment between the two groups of women (5.3 percentage points) is statistically significant. The pattern of stagnant employment among women with limitations and high-cost conditions, and rising employment for others, suggests that changes in health care financing might have had a negative effect on the employment of women with high-cost chronic conditions. The different patterns for men and women suggest, however, that the effects of changes in health care financing are not robust across gender.

Decomposing the changes in employment. We decomposed the changes in employment rates for those with work limitations into the relative roles of the rising prevalence of more expensive chronic conditions and the changes in employment rates among people within chronic condition categories. The decomposition method used is the same as that described in Houtenville and Daly (Chapter 3). This technique breaks down the change in the employment rate for the group as a whole to changes owing to: change in the share of the group in each subgroup (high-cost condition versus other), and change in the employment rate within each subgroup. The share components can be added across subgroups to find the total change from changes in shares and the total change from within-group changes in the employment rate. We perform the decomposition by sex because of the differences in the changes of male and female employment rates over this period.

Our results (Table 5.9) indicate that only 11 percent of the 5.1 percentage point decline in the employment rate for men with work limitations between the two pooled sample periods is because of either the growth in the prevalence of high-cost chronic conditions (–0.3 percentage points) or the decline in their employment rate (–0.2 percentage points). The growth in the prevalence of high-cost chronic conditions among women also made a small negative contribution to the change in the employment rate for women with work limitations (–0.2 percentage points), as did the change in the employment rate for women with work limitations who also have high-cost chronic conditions (–0.1 percentage points). Put differently, had the share of women with work limitations who have high-cost conditions and their employment rate remained constant, the 3.9 percentage point growth in the employment rate for women with work limitations would have been just 6 percent higher.

In sum, the growth in the share of workers with limitations who have high-cost chronic conditions and the decline in their employment rate both had a depressing effect on the employment rates for men and women, but the decomposition analysis shows that the contribution of these two factors to the changes in the employment rates for men and women with work limitations over this period is small relative to the size of those changes.

Table 5.9 Decomposition of Change in Employment Rate for People with Work Limitations, Aged 25–61

	Sample size		Population share (%)			Employment rate (%)			Contrib. to chng. in overall employ. rate		
	1984–87	1993–96	1984–87	1993–96	Change	1984–87	1993–96	Change	Pop. share	Employ. rate	Sum
All people with work limitations	18,503	21,417	100.0	100.0	0.0	42.9	42.6	-0.4	-0.3	-0.1	-0.4
With high-cost chronic conds.	992	1,478	5.4	7.0	1.6	26.7	24.6	-2.0	-0.3	-0.1	-0.4
Without high-cost chronic conds.	17,511	19,939	94.6	93.0	-1.6	43.9	43.9	0.1	-0.1	0.1	0.0
Men with work limitation	8,602	10,068	100.0	100.0	0.0	51.4	46.3	-5.1	-0.4	-4.7	-5.1
With high-cost chronic conds.	476	704	5.5	7.1	1.5	28.7	25.5	-3.2	-0.3	-0.2	-0.6
Without high-cost chronic conds.	8,126	9,364	94.5	92.9	-1.5	52.7	47.9	-4.9	0.0	-4.5	-4.5
Women with work limitations	9,901	11,349	100.0	100.0	0.0	35.2	39.1	3.9	-0.1	4.0	3.9
With high-cost chronic conds.	516	774	5.2	7.0	1.7	24.7	43.8	-0.8	-0.2	-0.1	-0.2
Without high-cost chronic conds.	9,385	10,575	94.8	93.0	-1.7	35.7	40.2	4.5	0.1	4.1	4.1

NOTE: High-cost chronic conditions associated with service use or disability are based on Hwang et al. (2001) and Kronick et al. (2000) (see Table 5.2).
SOURCE: Authors' calculations from the National Health Interview Survey (NHIS); noninstitutionalized civilians.

DISCUSSION

Limitations

There are several limitations to the findings that should be noted. First, the sample sizes of people with high-cost chronic conditions are small, making it difficult to measure changes with precision. Second, our hypothesis is quite general—that growth in health care costs had an adverse impact on employment of those with work limitations—and competing factors may have counteracted each other. Third, our analysis of employment includes all people with reported work limitations. This population may vary in the extent of work limitations, and our measure of high-cost chronic conditions may reflect unmeasured severity of work limitation as well as sensitivity to health care costs. Greater severity of work limitations may explain the consistently low employment among people with high-cost chronic conditions.[16]

In addition, our measure of high-cost chronic conditions has limitations. There is considerable heterogeneity in chronic conditions among those with and without high-cost chronic conditions. Our measure relies on a point-in-time classification of the costliness of treating specific conditions relative to other conditions, but new technologies likely changed the costliness of treating specific conditions over time. The measure from the NHIS includes only those conditions associated with a disability, a hospital stay in the past year, or a physician visit in the past two weeks.

Finally, other subgroups of people with disabilities may be even more sensitive to health insurance than the population on which we focused. Specifically, people who use personal assistance services or assistive technology must rely on Medicaid or pay out-of-pocket for these services because they are not covered by private insurance. A study focusing on this population might find different results. For instance, a study could use variation across states in the implementation dates of Medicaid buy-in programs to evaluate the effects of Medicaid on employment by comparing employment among those using personal assistance or assistive technology with other people with disabilities.

SUMMARY OF FINDINGS

The rising costs of health care will affect all consumers of these services. Because their health care needs are likely to be much greater than those of other groups, it is possible that the rising costs of health care may have had a disproportional effect on working-aged people with disabilities and, given the way that health care is financed in this country, could explain part of the decline in their employment during the 1990s. We tested this hypothesis in this chapter.

We focused on those with high-cost chronic conditions because they are most likely to be affected by increases in health care costs. Significantly, we found that this was not only a small subpopulation of the working-aged population, but it was also a small part of the working-aged population with work limitations. Although people with work limitations have higher than average health care needs and expenditures, most do not experience exceptionally large and sustained health care costs. We found that fewer than 2 percent of those aged 25–61 had high-cost chronic conditions, and only 7 percent of those in this age group with work limitations had high-cost chronic conditions.

The proportion of people with high-cost chronic conditions has, however, increased over time in both the general working-aged population and among those with disabilities. Hence, this increase could explain some of the decline in the employment rate of working-aged people with disabilities, both because this population grew over time and because it experienced a decline in employment rates owing to increased health care costs. The mechanism that results in lower employment could be a declining willingness of these workers to seek employment because growing costs and restrictions on private coverage have reduced the attractiveness of financing health care services through work versus Medicare or Medicaid. It could also be that higher costs reduce employer willingness to hire them, or it could be because of both reasons.

Using data from the NMES and the MEPS, we showed that mean and median health care costs significantly increased between 1987 and 1996–1997 for all working-aged people, but did so disproportionately for those with high-cost chronic conditions. We also found that the share of this population who had private insurance coverage fell, while their Medicare and Medicaid coverage increased over the period. These outcomes are consistent with the hypothesis that increases in health care costs weighed more heavily on those with high-cost chronic conditions, causing them to purchase less of it in the private market, and turn more to the public sector. Furthermore, we found that the employment rate of those with high-cost chronic conditions (including those without disabilities) fell by 3.4 percent over the period (although this decline was not significant at the 0.10 percent level), while the employment rate of all other health care cost groups significantly increased.

Given this information, we then focused on the population with disabilities who also had high-cost chronic health conditions to determine whether changes in the population size and employment rate over the period could explain the overall decline in the employment rate of the working-aged population with work limitations, as reported in the other chapters. When we used data from the NHIS and restricted our sample to those men with work limitations, we found that the employment rate of those with high-cost chronic conditions was below that of those with no high-cost chronic conditions in 1984–1987, and that employment rates for both groups were lower in 1993–1996 than in the earlier period. Somewhat surprisingly, however, the decline in the employment of men with work limitations and high-cost chronic conditions was actually smaller than for men with no high-cost chronic conditions. For women, we obtained a result that was more in line with our expectations: the employment rate for women with work limitations and high-cost chronic conditions fell slightly, while the employment rate for other women with work limitations increased substantially. If the results for women are because of growth in health care costs, it is hard to understand why we do not find similar results for men.

When we performed a formal decomposition of the changes in the employment rates for men and women with work limitations over the period examined, we found that increases in the shares with high-cost chronic conditions and declines in the employment rates of those with these conditions had a negative influence, but the size of this influence was small, although not trivial—on the order of 10 percent of the change in each group's employment rate for the period.

Notes

The work of Houtenville and Livermore on this chapter was supported by the National Institute on Disability and Rehabilitation Research (NIDRR) through the Cornell Rehabilitation Research and Training Center for Economic Research on Employment Policy for Persons with Disabilities, cooperative agreement No. 13313980038. Jennifer Duffy provided excellent programming and other support. The views expressed are those of the authors, and no official endorsement by the U.S. Agency for Healthcare Research and Quality, the U.S. Department of Health and Human Services, NIDRR, or Cornell University is intended or should be inferred.

1. For reasons to be discussed, throughout the chapter we focus on the prevalence of conditions for which survey respondents report receipt of treatment. Hence, unless otherwise indicated, prevalence estimates are for treated conditions only.
2. SSDI beneficiaries do not become eligible for Medicare coverage until 24 months after qualifying for SSDI.
3. For some workers, increasing contributions were partially offset by changes in tax treatment, because more workers pay their employee contributions from pre-tax dollars. In 1997, about a quarter of employees of medium and large private establishments paid their contributions with pre-tax dollars, but this is less prevalent in smaller establishments (about one in ten employees in 1996) (U.S. Department of Labor 1999a,b).
4. To be eligible for either SSI or SSDI, earnings must be below the SGA level. As of January 2003, the SGA level for non-blind individuals is equal to $800 monthly. The SGA level for people who are blind is $1,330 monthly. It is adjusted annually based on changes in the national average wage index.
5. MEPS respondents also reported conditions that bothered them, but to maximize comparability with the NMES, we did not use these.
6. In addition, subsamples of respondents are asked about subsets of specific conditions, regardless of whether they have indicated a limitation, but few of these conditions are high-cost chronic conditions, so these are not included in our analysis.
7. Hwang et al. (2001) define chronic as a "condition [that] had lasted or was expected to last twelve or more months and resulted in functional limitations and/ or the need for ongoing medical care."
8. Although the MEPS data include the CCS codes for each expenditure record, the NMES data do not. The CCS scheme could not be retroactively applied to the NMES data because the NMES ICD-9 codes include only three digits, and the CCS is based on a five-digit ICD-9 coding system.
9. For our study, we aggregated the CDPS very high, high, and medium conditions into one "high-cost" group. However, we grouped the CDPS medium cancer group, which had lower mean Medicaid expenditures than the other medium cost groups, with the CDPS low-cost groups, which we call "medium cost" because the average costs of medium cancer and the CDPS low-cost groups were similar.

10. For high-cost chronic conditions, this mainly affected people with heart devices, including pacemakers, but at the three-digit level, the code also includes orthodontic devices, hearing aids, and contact lenses and glasses; therefore, this V-code would not necessarily reflect high-cost cases anyway.
11. New condition codes appeared because the 1997 sample was larger and because less collapsing was necessary to maintain respondent confidentiality in the publicly released data.
12. In a few cases, additional detail about the prevalence of the four- or five-digit ICD9 codes was available from the MEPS, and we used this information instead of the unweighted average.
13. Data on health care expenditures are not collected for the NHIS.
14. The NMES and MEPS have information on insurance status over the entire year, while the NHIS has insurance status only at a point in time.
15. Among women without work limitations, employment rose by a similar amount, 6.4 percentage points, from 68.6 to 75 percent.
16. On the other hand, changes over time in willingness to report work limitations are likely not a limitation in the analysis because as Burkhauser, Houtenville and Wittenburg (Chapter 2) found, trends in employment among people reporting work limitations are similar to trends found using other definitions of disability.

References

Abt Associates. 2000. *Evaluation of the District of Columbia's Demonstration Program, "Managed Care System for Disabled and Special Needs Children": Final Report Summary.* Boston: Abt Associates. Sponsored by the U.S. Department of Health and Human Services. Available at: <http://aspe.hhs.gov/daltcp/reports/dc-frs.htm>. (Accessed: December 16, 2002.)

Alecxih, Lisa Marie B., John Corea, and David L. Kennell. 1995. "Implications of Health Care Financing, Delivery, and Benefit Design for People with Disabilities." In *People with Disabilities: Issues in Health Care Financing and Service Delivery*, Joshua Wiener, Steven Clauser, and David Kennell, eds. Washington, DC: The Brookings Institution, pp. 95–116.

Buchmueller, Thomas C. 1995. "Health Risk and Access to Employer Provided Health Insurance." *Inquiry* 32(1): 75–86.

Clement, Dolores G., Sheldon M. Retchin, MeriBeth H. Stegall, and Randall S. Brown. 1992. "Evaluation of Access and Satisfaction with Care in the TEFRA Program." Princeton, NJ: Mathematica Policy Research, Inc.

Cutler, David M. 2002. "Employee Costs and the Decline in Health Insurance Coverage." NBER working paper no. W9036. Cambridge, MA: National Bureau of Economic Research.

DeJong, Gerben, Susan E. Palsbo, Phillip W. Beatty, Gwyn C. Jones, Thilo Kroll, and Melinda T. Neri. 2002. "The Organization and Financing of Health Services for Persons with Disabilities." *Milbank Quarterly* 80(2): 261–301.

Elixhauser, Anne, Claudia A. Steiner, C.A. Whittington, and E. McCarthy. 1998. *Clinical Classifications for Health Policy Research: Hospital Inpatient Statistics, 1995.* Healthcare Cost and Utilization Project, HCUP-3 research note. Rockville, MD: Agency for Health Care Policy and Research.

Friedland, Robert B., and Alison Evans. 1996. "People with Disabilities: Access to Health Care and Related Benefits." In *Disability Work and Case Benefits,* Jerry L. Mashaw, Virginia P. Reno, Richard V. Burkhauser et al., eds. Kalamazoo, MI: W.E. Upjohn Institute for Employment Research, pp. 357–388.

Gabel, Jon R., Paul B. Ginsburg, and Kelly A. Hunt. 1997. "Small Employers and Their Health Benefits, 1988-1996: An Awkward Adolescence." *Health Affairs* 16(5): 103–110.

Gold, Marsha, Lyle Nelson, Randall Brown, A. Ciemnecki, A. Aizer, and E. Docteur. 1997. "Disabled Medicare Beneficiaries in HMOs: New Research." *Health Affairs* 16(5): 149–162.

Gruber, Jonathan, and Bridgitte C. Madrian. 2002. "Health Insurance, Labor Supply, and Job Mobility: A Critical Review of the Literature." NBER working paper no. 8817. Cambridge, MA: National Bureau of Economic Research.

Hanes, Pamela. 2000. "Testimony Presented at the House Ways and Means Subcommittee on Social Security Hearing on Work Incentives for Blind and Disabled Social Security Beneficiaries." Available at: <http://waysandmeans.house.gov/socsec/106cong/3-23-00/3-3hane.htm>. (Accessed: December 16, 2002.)

Hawkinson, Zeina C., Janice E. Frates. 2000. "Mandated Managed Care for Blind and Disabled Medicaid Beneficiaries in a County-Organized Health System: Implementation Challenges and Access Issues." *American Journal of Managed Care* 6(7): 829–836.

Hill, Steven C., and Judith Wooldridge. 2003. "SSI Enrollees Health Care in TennCare." *Journal of Health Care for the Poor and Underserved* 14(2): 229–243.

Hwang, Wenke, Wendy Weller, Henry Ireys, and Gerard Anderson. 2001. "Out-of-Pocket Medical Spending for Care of Chronic Conditions." *Health Affairs* 20(6): 267–278.

Kreider, Brent, and Regina T. Riphahn. 2000. "Explaining Applications to the U.S. Disability System: A Semiparametric Approach." *Journal of Human Resources* 35(1): 82–115.

Kronick, Richard, Todd Gilmer, Tony Dreyfus, and Lora Lee. 2000. "Improving Health-Based Payment for Medicaid Beneficiaries: CDPS." *Health Care Financing Review* 21(3): 29–63.

Levitt, Larry, Janet Lundy, and Srija Srinivasan. 1998. *Trends and Indicators in the Changing Health Care Marketplace Chartbook.* Menlo Park, CA: The Kaiser Family Foundation. Available at: <http://www.kff.org/content/archive/1429/trends.pdf>. (Accessed: December 16, 2002.)

Louis Harris and Associates Inc. 1998. *1998 National Organization on Disability/Harris Survey of Americans with Disabilities.* New York: National Organization on Disability.

McCall, Nelda. 1989. "Evaluation of the Arizona Health Care Cost Containment System: Final Report." Menlo Park, CA: SRI International.

Miller, Robert H., and Harold S. Luft. 1997. "Does Managed Care Lead to Better or Worse Quality of Care?" *Health Affairs* 16(5): 7–25.

Norton, Stephen, and Stephen Zuckerman. 2000. "Trends in Medicaid Physician Fees, 1993-1998." *Health Affairs* 19(4): 222–232.

Pollitz, Karen, Richard Sorian, and Kathy Thomas. 2001. *How Accessible Is Individual Health Insurance for Consumers in Less-than-Perfect Health?* Menlo Park, CA: The Kaiser Family Foundation. Available at: <http://www.kff.org/content/2001/ 20010620a/report.pdf>. (Accessed: December 16, 2002.)

President's Committee on Employment of People with Disabilities. 1994. *Operation People First: Toward a National Disability Policy, A Report of the President's Committee on Employment of People With Disabilities 1993 Teleconference Project.* Washington, DC: President's Committee on Employment of People with Disabilities.

Regenstein, Marsha, and Christy Schroer. 1998. "Medicaid Managed Care for People with Disabilities." Washington, DC: Henry J. Kaiser Family Foundation.

Retchin, Sheldon M., Randall Brown, Rhoda Cohen, Dolores Gurnick, Meri-Beth Stegall, and Barbara Abujaber. 1992. "The Quality of Care in TEFRA HMOs/CMPs: Final Version." Princeton, NJ: Mathematica Policy Research, Inc.

Rice, Dorothy P. and Mitchell P. LaPlante 1992. "Medical Expenditures for Disability and Disabling Comorbidity." *American Journal of Public Health* 82(5): 739–741.

Safran, Dana G., Alvin R. Tarlow, and William H. Rogers. 1994. "Primary Care Performance in Fee-for-Service and Prepaid Health Care Systems: Results from the Medical Outcomes Study." *JAMA: The Journal of the American Medical Association* 271(20): 1579–1586.

Stapleton, David, Kimberly Dietrich, Jeffrey Furman, and Gilbert Lo. 1995. "Longer Term Factors Affecting Disability Program Applications and Awards." Washington, DC: Lewin-VHI.

Stapleton, David, Gina Livermore, Scott Scrivner, and Adam Tucker. 1998. "Exploratory Study of Health Care Coverage and Employment of People with Disabilities: Final Report." Final Report to the Office of the Assistant Secretary for Planning and Evaluation, U.S. Department of Health and Human Services. Washington, DC: The Lewin Group.

U.S. Department of Labor. 1989. "Employee Benefits in Medium and Large Firms, 1988." Bulletin no. 2336. Washington, D.C.: Bureau of Labor Statistics.

———. 1999a. "Employee Benefits in Medium and Large Private Establishments, 1997." Bulletin no. 2517. Washington, DC: Bureau of Labor Statistics.

———. 1999b. "Employee Benefits in Small Private Establishments, 1996." Bulletin no. 2507. Washington, DC: Bureau of Labor Statistics.

Yelowitz, Aaron S. 1998. "Why Did the SSI-Disabled Program Grow So Much? Disentangling the Effect of Medicaid." *Journal of Health Economics* 17(3): 321–349.

Zuvekas, Samuel, and Joel Cohen. 2002. "A Guide to Comparing Health Care Expenditures in the 1996 MEPS to the 1987 NMES." *Inquiry* 39(1): 76–86.

6
Employment and the Changing Disability Population

H. Stephen Kaye
University of California, San Francisco

Although the overall employment rate of working-age adults with disabilities has not improved since the passage of the Americans with Disabilities Act (ADA), a closer look at employment data from two national surveys hints that there may still be room for some measure of optimism. Perhaps the ADA has, after all, expanded employment opportunities for people with disabilities, or at least for a segment of the disability population. And perhaps confounding factors, such as the changing size and composition of the disability population, have hidden those improvements from view.

An examination of employment measures, as presented in this chapter, does suggest that the overall rate of employment may not be the best measure of job opportunities because it includes many people unlikely to acquire jobs regardless of any improvement in employer attitudes or workplace accessibility. Many working-age adults with disabilities are not oriented toward participation in the labor force, either because they consider themselves unable to work or because they are engaged in other activities. When we leave this group out of our statistics, that is, when we consider only those with disabilities who are able and available to work, we obtain what we believe to be a truer indication of changes in employer practices with regard to workers and job applicants with disabilities. Among the segment of the disability population most likely to take advantage of job opportunities, there was a significant increase in employment levels during the 1990s.

Is it reasonable to measure employment exclusive of people who say they cannot work? Work limitation measures are highly subjective and controversial; perceptions of inability to work may be heavily influenced by factors unrelated to functional ability and health. This chapter examines the validity of these measures and considers whether the disadvantages of relying on self-reports of inability to work (for example, in excluding from the analysis some people who truly could work if offered appropriate supports) are outweighed by the advantage of focusing on the segment of the disability population most likely to respond to employment opportunities when they are offered.

The proportion of people with disabilities who consider themselves able to work has declined over the years. The overall disability rate among working-age adults rose dramatically during the early 1990s, with a disproportionate share of that increase occurring among people reporting inability to work. This disturbing and unanticipated change in the composition of the disability population accounts for the difference between the bleak employment picture evident when everyone is included and the far brighter outlook when the analysis is limited to those oriented toward working. In other words, the stagnation in overall employment rates among people with disabilities is due, in part, to a broadening of the population classified as limited in activity, accompanied by a shift toward the most severe level of limitation—inability to work.

What caused the sudden rise in both the overall disability rate and the rate of inability to work, as reported in surveys? It would be plausible to attribute the increase to changes in societal attitudes toward disability brought about by the gains achieved by the independent living movement, in particular the passage of the ADA in 1990. With disability much more prominent as a political and social issue, and with the stigma associated with having a disability consequently lessened, people with disabilities would presumably become more candid in mentioning their limitations to survey takers.

Another explanation attributes the increases to economic factors. Perhaps people with chronic health conditions or impairments who lost their jobs during the 1990–1991 recession chose to emphasize their limitations and label themselves as unable to work in order to obtain benefits. The Social Security disability benefit rolls expanded quite rapidly during the same period (Social Security Administration 2001), and this increase has been blamed on a liberalization in the eligibility criteria for disability benefits, coupled with high unemployment rates during the first few years of the decade (Autor and Duggan 2003).

In this chapter, I propose a third hypothesis, one more straightforward than either of the above: that the rise in disability rates was brought about not primarily by economic or social causes, but instead most directly by epidemiologic factors. More people are reported in surveys as having disabilities, this hypothesis holds, because the underlying health conditions and impairments that cause disability have increased in prevalence, in particular those more severe conditions associated with inability to work.

I explore this hypothesis using nine years of nationally representative survey data on health conditions and impairments affecting working-age adults overall and on those conditions that cause limitations in activity. The results point to widespread increases in the prevalence of chronic conditions among the working-age population, as well as striking similarities between trends in disability rates—both limitations in any activity and inability to work—and trends in the underlying causes of disability. I then examine two of the risk factors that might be responsible for these broadly based increases: rising rates of obesity among the working-age population and the impact of recession on mental and physical health.

EMPLOYMENT MEASURES FOR THE DISABILITY POPULATION

Employment Rates from the National Health Interview Survey

When analyzing data from the National Health Interview Survey (NHIS), we use a relatively broad definition of disability that includes limitations in work and any other activities the person might engage in. In the questionnaire used before a major revision in 1997, working-age adults were asked about their ability to work: "Does any impairment or health problem [NOW] keep____ from working at a job or business?" If the answer was no, they were next asked whether they are otherwise limited in work: "Is ____ limited in the kind OR amount of work ____ can do because of any impairment or health problem?" If the answer was still no, then they were asked about limitations in other activities: "Is ____ limited in ANY WAY in any activities because of an impairment or health problem?" Respondents who identified their "major activity" as housework were also asked about that activity: "Does any impairment or health problem NOW keep ____ from doing any housework at all?" and, for those answering no, "Is ____ limited in the kind OR amount of housework ____ can do because of any impairment or health problem?"

A person answering yes to any of the activity limitation questions is classified as having a disability. Because of substantial changes to the survey, data prior to 1997 are not directly comparable to data from later years; I have, therefore, limited the analysis to the nine-year period between 1988 (two years prior to the enactment of the ADA) and 1996.

The employment rate for the working-age (18–64) population with disabilities is shown in Figure 6.1. The proportion of working-age adults with disabilities who had jobs declined from a high of 49.0 per-

Figure 6.1 NHIS Employment Rates among Working-Age Adults with Disabilities, 1988–1996

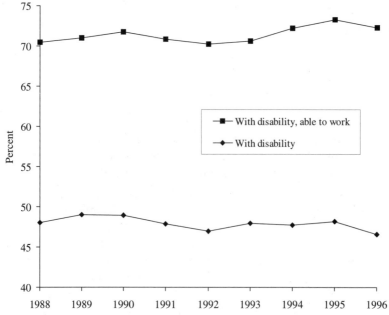

SOURCE: National Health Interview Survey.

cent in 1989 and 1990 to a low of 47.0 percent in 1992, immediately following the 1990–1991 recession. Although there appears to have been an increase in subsequent years, there is no statistically significant trend, and, even at its highest post-recession value (48.2 percent in 1995), the employment rate had not managed to regain its pre-recession level.

The figure also shows a second employment rate, for working-age adults with disabilities answering no to the first question about work limitation, that is, for people with disabilities who say they are able to work. Among this population, there is evidence of substantial improvement following the recession. From a 1992 low of 70.2 percent employed, the rate climbed to a high of 73.3 percent by 1995 (dropping slightly, but not significantly, to 72.3 percent in 1996). The upward trend is statistically significant and is comparable to the gains experienced by people without disabilities during the same period (not shown in the figure).

Employment Rates from the CPS

In contrast to the somewhat elaborate set of questions in the NHIS, the Annual Demographic Supplement to the Current Population Survey (CPS) provides only a single question that we can use to identify respondents as having disabilities: "Does anyone in this household have a health problem or disability which prevents them from working or which limits the kind or amount of work they can do?" Thus, rather than defining disability broadly in terms of limitations in any activities, as in the NHIS data, we are forced to narrow the definition to work limitation.

The CPS also provides a way of separating the disability population into two groups based on the ability to work, but again, the approach is different from that available in the NHIS data. When asked in the basic monthly survey whether they worked during the prior week, respondents often volunteer that they are retired, "disabled," or "unable to work." When they specify either of the last two, they are asked whether they have a disability that prevents them "from accepting any kind of work during the next six months." Presumably, only people with quite severe limitations in their ability to work would answer affirmatively to such a question. Because an extensively revised basic questionnaire was introduced in 1994, I limit the analysis to that and subsequent years.

Employment rates for the total working-age population with disabilities, and for the subset who consider themselves able to work, are shown in Figure 6.2. Because of the much narrower definition of disability, rates from the CPS are much lower than those from the NHIS. Nevertheless, the same pattern emerges. There is no statistically significant trend in the overall employment rate, with the 2000 value of 24.5 percent about the same as the 1994 value of 24.0 percent. Among people with disabilities who are able to work, however, there is an 8.3 percentage point increase between 1994, when the employment rate was 50.4 percent, and 2000, when it had risen to 58.7 percent. Again, the upward trend is highly statistically significant.

Figure 6.2 CPS Emplyment Rates among Working-Age Adults with Disabilities, 1994–2000

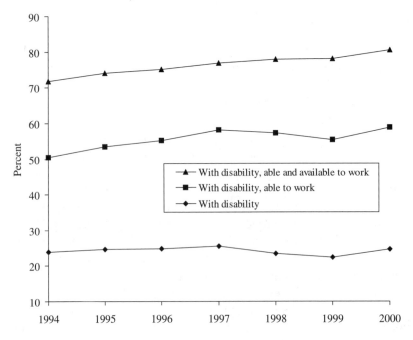

SOURCE: Current Population Survey.

A third employment rate is also shown in the figure, that for people with disabilities who are able and available to work. This group includes people who are either labor force participants (working, on layoff, or actively looking for work) or are nonparticipants who consider themselves able to work and answer yes or maybe when asked whether they would like to have a job. The increasing trend in employment is even more striking for this group: from a 71.9 percent rate in 1994 to a 80.5 percent—fully four-fifths of this population—in 2000. This 8.6 percentage point increase is more than twice that for working-age adults without disabilities who are available to work (not shown in the figure), which was 3.6 percentage points.

Which Employment Measure Is More Appropriate?

In both surveys, employment rates that include the entire working-age population with disabilities present a bleak picture of stagnation, while employment rates that include only those people with disabilities who consider themselves able to work (and, in particular, those who are available to work) indicate that substantial progress has been made. Further analysis of these data (Kaye 2003a) hints that some share of these gains might be attributed specifically to the ADA, and not merely to rapid economic growth during the latter part of the decade.

Which measure more accurately reflects the labor market experiences of people with disabilities? By including in its denominator people who see themselves as unable to work or who prefer not to work, the overall employment rate may be too broad. The ADA talks about "equality of opportunity," not about coercing people to take jobs when they do not feel they are able; no one suggests that "full participation" is about forcing people to participate when they do not so choose. When low employment rates for people with disabilities are reported in the media, the implication is that there is a vast pool—even a majority—of working-age adults with disabilities who would take jobs if only employers would hire them. This sets up unrealistic expectations that, once employer attitudes change and accommodations become available, the employment rate will climb steadily from 25 or 45 percent to nearly 100 percent. Although there is certainly room for improvement, it is unreasonable to hope for anything like the two- to fourfold increase that a naive observer might have expected.

Furthermore, the inclusion of so many labor force nonparticipants in the employment rate's denominator makes that measure very sensitive to the size of that population. As discussed in the next section, any increase in the proportion of the disability population who are unavailable to work could easily mask any gains made in employment opportunities for those who are available to work.

If the goal is to measure improvements in the level of *employment opportunity* for people with disabilities, as the ADA's goal statement suggests, one should use a measure that includes those people who are likely to take advantage of such opportunities and leaves out everyone else. Thus, a more limited employment measure—one including only those able and available to work—might better serve as a barometer of improvements in employer practices in hiring and retaining workers with disabilities. It has the disadvantage, however, of excluding some people who truly could work—if offered good jobs with appropriate accommodations and training—but who do not consider themselves able to do so.

THE CHANGING SIZE AND COMPOSITION OF THE DISABILITY POPULATION

As Figure 6.3 shows, there was a large and rapid increase in the size of the population with disabilities during the early 1990s. According to data from the NHIS, the overall disability rate (any limitation in activity) rose from 12.8 percent of working-age adults in 1990 to 14.6 percent in 1993. The rate fell somewhat during subsequent years, declining to just under 14 percent by 1996. Much of that increase is among people with disabilities reporting inability to work; that rate increased from 5.2 percent of working-age adults in 1990 to 6.0 percent in 1993 and then remained steady at about that level.

According to the CPS, there was a further decline in the disability rate (defined in this case as any degree of work limitation) during the late 1990s, from a fairly steady 7.8 percent between 1994 and 1997 to 7.5 percent in 2000 (Figure 6.4). However, there was no corresponding decline in the rate of inability to work, which actually increased from a 1994 value of 3.3 percent of working-age adults to 3.6 percent in 2000.

Figure 6.3 NHIS Disability Rate and Rate of Inability to Work among Working-Age Adults, 1988–1996

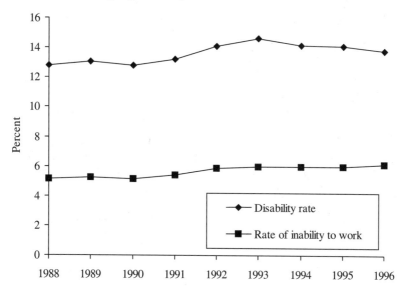

SOURCE: National Health Interview Survey.

As mentioned above, these rates are all considerably lower than those from the NHIS because of the different measures used.

Because the rate of inability to work continued to increase even after the overall disability rate had begun to decline, the proportion of people with disabilities reported as unable to work rose steadily during the latter part of the decade (Figure 6.5). After hovering around 41 percent up until 1993, the NHIS proportion unable to work climbed to 44.6 percent in 1996. In the CPS, the proportion rose steadily from 41.5 percent in 1994 to 49.0 percent in 1999 (and then declined slightly to 47.8 percent in 2000).

The different trends in overall disability and inability to work are responsible for the different behaviors of the two employment measures discussed above—the overall employment rate and the employment rate for those able to work. The former includes an increasing proportion of people who consider themselves unable to work; the stagnation in this measure can be seen as a consequence of this change

Figure 6.4 Disability Rate and Rate of Inability to Work among Working-Age Adults, 1994–2000

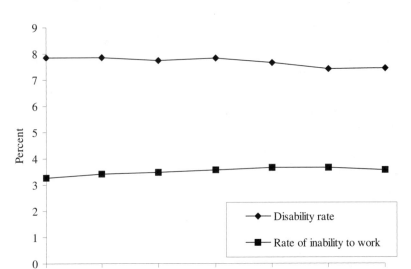

SOURCE: Current Population Survey.

in the composition of the disability population. The latter measure, which excludes those reporting inability to work, shows an increasing likelihood of employment, but only for the shrinking proportion of the overall disability population included in the denominator.

Can We Accept Self-Reports of Inability to Work?

A person's self-assessment of his or her ability to work may be influenced by many considerations besides health and impairment, including environmental factors such as negative employer attitudes and workplace barriers. When influenced by motivational factors, when unaware of the progress that has been made in workplace accessibility, or when defeated by past rejection, someone who might perform well in a sufficiently accommodating work environment might instead report being unable to work. Another person with a greater impairment or in worse health, but perhaps with an unrealistic attitude about his or her own capabilities, might report no work limitation at all.

Figure 6.5 Proportion of Working-Age Adults with Disabilities Reported as Unable to Work, 1988–2000

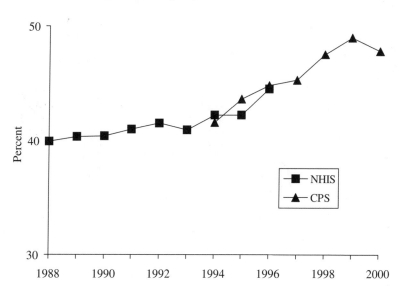

SOURCE: National Health Interview Survey and Current Population Survey.

As a result, perceived ability or inability to work may not be a perfectly accurate reflection of a person's true potential. Nevertheless, based on various measures contained in the surveys, it is apparent that people reporting inability to work are in much worse health and have much more severe functional limitations than people with disabilities who consider themselves able to work.

As shown in Figure 6.6, people who report inability to work are much more likely than other people with disabilities to say that they are in poor or fair health. In the NHIS data, nearly two-thirds (64.4 percent) of people unable to work are in either fair or poor health compared with only about one-quarter (26.3 percent) of people with disabilities who are able to work and only 4.5 percent of people without disabilities. The proportion of people unable to work who are in poor health, 31.4 percent, is about six times that of those with disabilities who can work, 5.4 percent. In the CPS data, we find an even higher proportion, 77.4 percent, of those unable to work in either fair or poor health compared with 44.5 percent of those with disabilities who are

Figure 6.6 Proportion of Working-Age Adults Reporting Poor or Fair Health, by Disability Status, 1988–1996 (NHIS) and 1996–2000 (CPS)

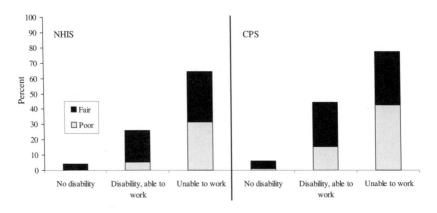

SOURCE: National Health Interview Surlvey and Current Population Survey.

able to work. Once again, the poor health statistics show an even more striking difference between the groups: 42.7 percent of the unable-to-work group versus 15.4 percent of the others with disabilities.

The NHIS also includes quantitative measures that reflect a mixture of health status and functional limitation. In a measure of restricted activity, respondents are asked whether they missed work or school, or cut down on their other usual activities, during the prior two weeks due to illness or injury; if so, they are asked the number of days during which more than half the day's activities were missed. Working-age adults who report inability to work have 4.0 mean restricted activity days during the prior two weeks compared with 1.2 for people with disabilities who are able to work and only 0.3 for people with no disabilities.

In a second measure of restrictions in activity, respondents are asked whether they stayed in bed during the prior two weeks because of illness or injury, and, if so, how many days they spent more than half the day in bed. People without disabilities have an average of only 0.1 bed days; people with disabilities who are able to work have four times as many, 0.4; people with disabilities reporting inability to work have a further 4 times as many bed days, 1.7 per two-week period.

Another measure from the NHIS core also shows a dramatic difference according to ability to work: the need for personal assistance in the activities of daily living (ADLs, such as "eating, bathing, dressing, or getting around the house") and instrumental activities of daily living (IADLs, such as "everyday household chores, doing necessary business, shopping, or getting around for other purposes"). As Figure 6.7 shows, people unable to work are almost 10 times as likely as the rest of the disability population to need assistance in ADLs—10.1 percent versus 1.1 percent. And they are 5 times as likely to need help in either ADLs or IADLs—32.0 percent versus 6.5 percent.

Also useful is a comparison of functional ability between those who say they can and cannot work. Using measures from the National Health Interview Survey on Disability, we can construct a functional limitation severity scale, combining information on limitations in mobility, vision, hearing, communication, cognition, and mental health.[1] As shown in Figure 6.8, more than two-thirds (68.2 percent) of working-age adults reported as unable to work are identified as having either moderate or severe limitations in physical, cognitive, or emotional functioning compared with only 29.6 percent of those who are limited in activity but able to work. The unable-to-work group is more than four times as likely to have severe functional limitations: 34.7 percent versus 8.0 percent.

Health Has Worsened and Disability Severity Has Increased Over Time

During the same period that the proportion reporting inability to work increased, other measures also revealed a worsening of health status or disability severity. For example, the proportion of working-age adults reporting either poor or fair health increased from about 41 percent in 1988–1990 to about 43 percent by 1995–1996.

Levels of what might be termed severe disability—measured apart from any reference to ability to work—increased markedly during the period. As shown in Figure 6.9, there were large increases in the proportion of the population needing personal assistance, both with self-care (ADL) and home-management (IADL) activities. Only 4.0 percent of working-age adults needed help with ADLs in 1988, but that proportion had risen to 5.2 percent by 1996. An additional 11.4 percent

Figure 6.7 Need for Personal Assistance among Working-Age Adults with Disabilities, by Ability to Work, 1988–1996

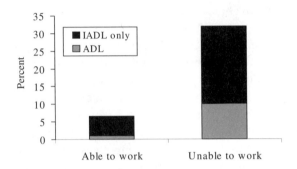

SOURCE: National Health Interview Survey.

Figure 6.8 Functional Limitations among Working-Age Adults with Disabilities, by Ability to Work, 1994–1995

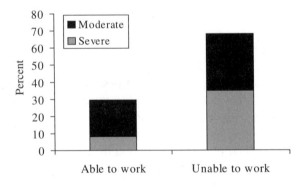

SOURCE: National Health Interview Survey on Disability.

Figure 6.9 Proportion of Working-Age Adults Needing Personal Assistance in Self-Care and Home-Management Activities, 1988–1996

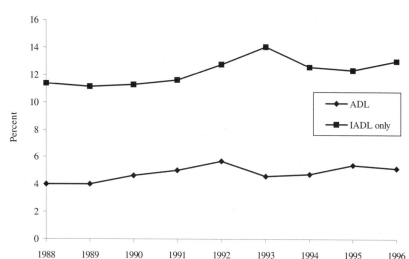

SOURCE: National Health Interview Survey.

needed help with IADLs in 1988; this figure increased to 13.0 percent in 1996.

These indications of worsening health and greater levels of need for personal assistance suggest that the increases in reported levels of inability to work might reflect real increases in disability severity. What caused these changes? Some of the primary health conditions and impairments that cause disability are examined in the next section.

Contributions to the Rising Disability Rates

Using data from the NHIS on the health condition or impairment identified as the main cause of disability, we can classify the population with disabilities according to the body system that is primarily affected. Shown in Figure 6.10 are prevalence rates for the five leading body system causes of disability. Musculoskeletal conditions are by far the leading source of disability among working-age adults, affecting 5.6 percent of working-age adults in 1988 and rising rapidly beginning

Figure 6.10 Leading Body System Sources of Disability among Working-Age Adults, 1988–1996

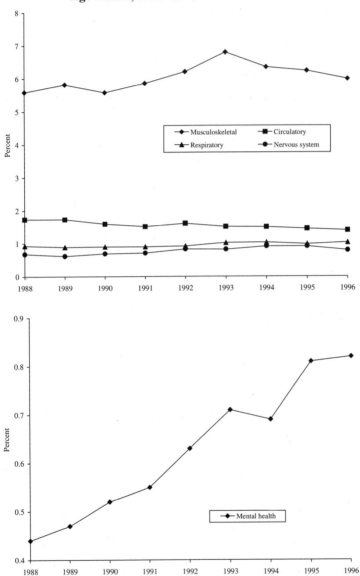

SOURCE: National Health Interview Survey.

in 1990 to a high of 6.8 percent in 1993. By 1996, the prevalence had dropped somewhat, down to 6.0 percent.

Back problems (mostly coded either as orthopedic impairments of the back or neck or as intervertebral disk disorders) dominate this category of disabling conditions, along with various forms of arthritis and orthopedic impairments of the lower extremity (leg, foot, knee, etc.). Note that the 1.2 percentage point increase in musculoskeletal system conditions between 1990 and 1993 accounts for about two-thirds of the 1.8 percentage point increase in overall disability during the same three-year period. As for the longer-term rise of 1 percentage point in the disability rate between 1988 and 1996, musculoskeletal conditions account for less than half of that increase.

Circulatory system conditions fall a distant second in their contribution to the disability rate, causing disability among 1.7 percent of working-age adults in 1988. That figure began to decline in 1990, and had fallen more or less steadily to 1.4 percent by 1996. This decline mirrors long-observed reductions in mortality rates due to cardiovascular conditions, which have dropped by 60 percent since 1950, when adjusted for age (National Center for Disease Prevention and Health Promotion 1999). Reductions in risk factors, such as smoking and high blood pressure, along with improved diagnosis and treatment, are credited with this dramatic improvement.

Respiratory conditions are next in prevalence as a main cause of disability. Respiratory disability affected 0.9 percent of working-age adults in 1988, remaining at about that level before rising slightly to 1.0 percent in 1993 and holding steady through 1996. The increase is statistically significant, and is largely attributable to a rise in asthma, which dominates this category.

Nervous system conditions, the largest components of which are epilepsy, carpal tunnel, multiple sclerosis, and migraine, follow. The prevalence of nervous system disability rose substantially during the period, from 0.7 percent of working-age adults in 1989–1991 to as high as 0.9 percent in 1994–95 (and then dropping to 0.8 percent in 1996, but the decline is not statistically significant). The prevalence of disability due to carpal tunnel syndrome tripled during the period, and an increase in epilepsy is also apparent.

Finally, we see the most dramatic increase of any body system in the prevalence of mental health disability, which nearly doubled during the period, climbing steadily from just over 0.4 percent of working-age adults in 1988 to 0.8 percent in 1996. The most common conditions in this category are schizophrenia, depression, and bipolar disorder. Depression, bipolar disorder, and anxiety disorder all roughly tripled in prevalence as causes of disability during the period; a substantial increase in schizophrenia is also apparent.

There are no trends worth noting among the remaining body systems, which are not shown in the figure. The few observable changes in the prevalence of disability due to these systems are, at best, of marginal statistical significance.

INCREASED PREVALENCE OF CHRONIC CONDITIONS AND IMPAIRMENTS

Did rates of disability due to musculoskeletal, respiratory, nervous system, and mental health causes increase because of increases in the underlying prevalence of these conditions? In other words, is the increase in back problems as a cause of disability simply the result of a broad increase in back problems overall?

Two distinct sources of data from the NHIS core can be used to shed light on the prevalence of the health conditions and impairments that are potential causes of disability: conditions reported in response to a checklist and conditions reported as the reason for a physician contact. In contrast to the subjectivity inherent in measuring the prevalence of conditions causing activity limitation, these sources of condition data are likely to be far more objective.

Each household is randomly assigned one of six condition checklists: musculoskeletal and skin conditions; impairments; digestive system conditions; glandular, blood, nervous system, and genitourinary conditions; circulatory system conditions; and respiratory conditions. Respondents are asked whether they have each of the conditions on the assigned checklist at the time of the interview (or ever had the condition, or had it within the past year, depending on the condition). Subjectivity would presumably enter into the answer when conditions are asked about that are not currently causing bothersome symptoms, especially when the respondent is uncertain whether the condition persists or has been cured or gone into remission. For highly stigmatized conditions, additional subjectivity arises when the respondent must decide whether to reveal the condition to the interviewer.

Even more objectivity is likely in the reporting of conditions discussed with a physician during a two-week reference period prior to the interview. Respondents would presumably have little trouble recalling so recent a doctor visit or naming the condition or conditions that motivated it. Despite the subjectivity inherent in a person's decision to see or not see a doctor for a particular severity of a particular condition, the reporting of the actual visit would seem quite straightforward. Again, a subjective element enters into the picture when the respondent must decide whether to name a highly stigmatized condition.

Back Problems

As mentioned above, back problems dominate the category of musculoskeletal conditions; they are also the largest single cause of disability among working-age adults. When comparing the prevalence of disabling back problems (by which we mean back problems identified as the primary cause of a person's limitation in activity) with overall back problems (any back problem reported on the checklist of musculoskeletal conditions), the trends are quite similar. As shown in Figure 6.11, the overall reported prevalence of back problems rose sharply, from 8.6 percent of working-age adults in 1988 to as high as 10.8 percent in 1992 and 1993, before declining gradually to 9.6 percent in 1996. Over the same period, the prevalence of back problems reported as the main cause of disability increased from 2.6 percent of working-age adults in 1988 to a high of 3.4 percent in 1993, before falling back to 2.9 percent by 1996. Similarly, as the main cause of inability to work, back problems increased from 0.9 percent of working-age adults in 1988–1990 to as high as 1.1 percent beginning in 1993.

Note that during the entire period, about one-third of overall back problems cause disability and about one-tenth cause inability to work. Put another way, about nine times as many people report back problems that do not prevent them from working as report back problems that do prevent them from working, and twice as many people report back problems that do not limit activity as those that do limit activity;

Figure 6.11 Prevalence of Back Problems, Overall and as a Cause of Disability or Inability to Work, Ages 18–64, 1988–1996

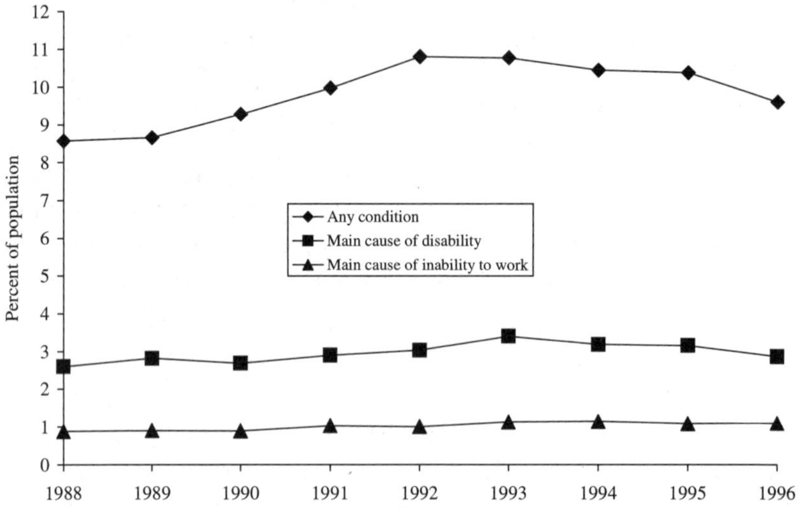

SOURCE: National Health Interview Survey.

across the board, there are similar prevalence increases of approximately 30 percent between 1988 and 1993. Thus, it would appear that back problems increased as a cause of both disability and inability to work because they became more widespread overall, rather than because of any worsening in the severity or impact of the impairment or any change in the motivation of people to report disability due to this condition.

Depression and Bipolar Disorder

As a second example, we turn to mental health disability, whose dramatic increase as a cause of disability was shown in Figure 6.10. Because mental health conditions are not included in the checklists, we cannot make comparisons to the overall prevalence of these conditions. Instead, in Figure 6.12, we present trends in physician contacts as a rough proxy. Because the doctor visit question contains a parenthetical specifying both psychiatrists and general practitioners as types of "medical doctors," respondents would be expected to include psycho-

Figure 6.12 Rates of Disability, Inability to Work, and Physician Contact Due to Depression or Bipolar Disorder, ages 18–64, 1988–1996

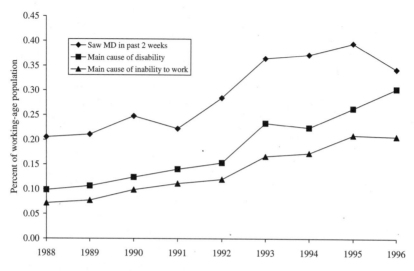

SOURCE: National Health Interview Survey.

therapy visits, visits to general practitioners or specialists to obtain medication for a mental health condition, or phone calls or visits to renew such prescriptions. Those obtaining therapy (and, in some states, medication) from someone other than an M.D. would presumably not be counted, along with those using non-medical community supports or not currently receiving treatment at all.

Shown in Figure 6.12 are the rates of physician contacts, disability, and inability to work due to either depression or bipolar disorder. All three increased dramatically over the eight-year period. The proportion of working-age adults who saw a doctor for depression or bipolar disorder doubled, from 0.21 percent in 1988 to as high as 0.40 percent in 1995 (the subsequent decline to 0.34 percent in 1996 is not statistically significant). Disability due to these conditions tripled in prevalence, increasing from 0.10 percent of the working-age population in 1988 to 0.30 percent in 1996. Inability to work due to these conditions also tripled, from 0.07 percent to 0.21 percent.

It is unlikely that the true prevalence of these mental health conditions doubled or tripled over an eight-year period, but it is possible that the number of diagnosed conditions really did increase so markedly. One explanation for the upsurge both in physician contacts and disability relates to the availability of new, effective medications. Prozac became available for prescription in the United States right at the start of the period, in January 1988, and gained popularity soon thereafter. Once viable treatments become available for any condition, that condition gains visibility and legitimacy, especially a formerly dubious and highly stigmatized condition such as depression; people then become less reluctant to seek diagnosis and treatment and to acknowledge the condition, to themselves and others, as a source of activity limitation.

The Condition-Specific Disability Rate

For back problems and depression, changes in the prevalence of disability due to the condition appear to track changes in the overall reported prevalence of the condition. Is this true for other conditions? We can explore this hypothesis by calculating the condition-specific disability rate, namely, the ratio of the number of people with disability due to a particular condition divided by the total number of people affected by the condition.

Figure 6.13 shows the condition-specific disability rates for some of the leading causes of disability. Although there is substantial variation in the disability rate across conditions, all of the condition-specific rates remain basically flat during the nine years of interest. In other words, the disability rate due to the condition closely matches the overall prevalence of the condition. Of the conditions shown, back problems are the most disabling, with about 30 percent of working-age adults with back problems reporting limitations in activity. Next is diabetes, which causes disability in about 17 percent of those who have it. Asthma causes disability in about 15 percent of those reporting the condition overall, and arthritis and heart disease (including hypertension) are disabling for about 10 percent of those who have them.

It is important to emphasize that, for these and most other conditions that cause disability, the vast majority of people reporting the condition give no indication that they are limited in activity, and an even larger majority report that they are able to work. By and large,

Figure 6.13 Condition-Specific Disability Rates for Selected Conditions among Working-Age Adults, 1988–1996

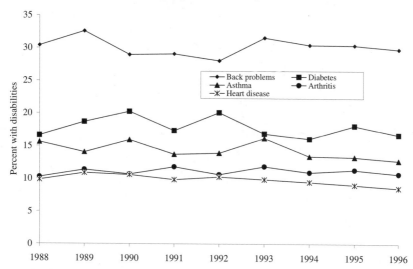

SOURCE: National Health Interview Survey.

whenever there is an increase in the prevalence of a condition, most of that increase occurred among people without disabilities.

Widespread Increases in Chronic Condition Prevalence

Adding up the prevalence estimates of the various conditions captured on the checklists produces an estimate of the total prevalence of chronic conditions among working-age adults. These are increases in chronic condition prevalence among people with and without disabilities, among both conditions that cause disability (either as a primary or secondary cause) and those that do not. As shown in Figure 6.14, prevalence rates for chronic conditions causing and not causing disability both increased sharply during the early 1990s. The former increased in prevalence by 1.8 conditions per hundred population, from 12.5 conditions in 1990 to a high of 14.3 in 1992. During the same period, the prevalence of conditions not identified as causing disability increased by 8.4 conditions per hundred population, from 127.5 in 1990 to 135.9 in 1992.

Figure 6.14 Prevalence of Disabling and Nondisabling Chronic Conditions among Working-Age Adults, 1988–1996

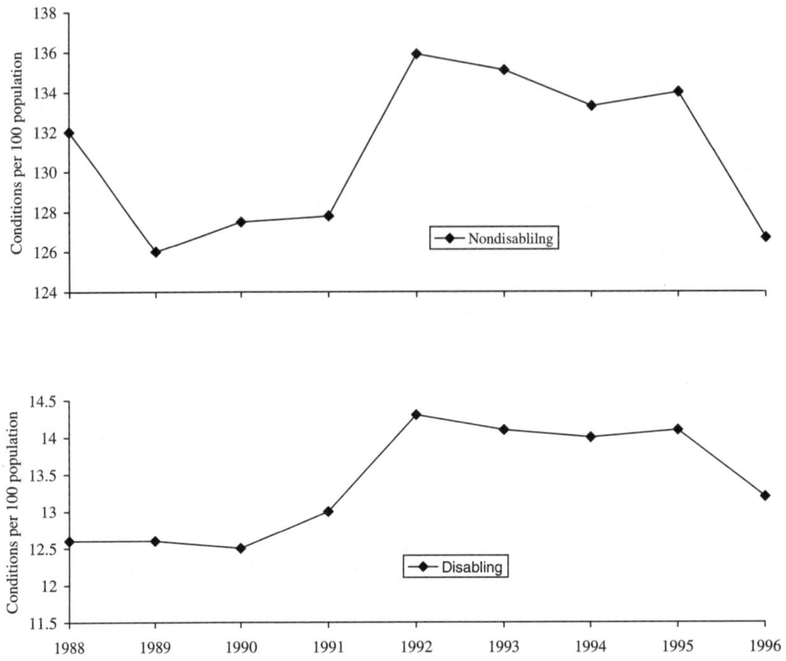

SOURCE: National Health Interview Survey.

Thus, more than 80 percent of the total increase in chronic condition prevalence occurred among conditions that do not cause disability. Only a tiny fraction (7.6 percent) of the 1990–1992 increase is attributable to conditions that cause inability to work (not shown in the figure). This widespread increase in chronic condition prevalence, occurring mainly among conditions causing neither inability to work nor any other activity limitation, cannot be attributed to causes related to a person's self-attribution of disability status, such as a desire for disability benefits or legal protections or an increased awareness of disability.

Do Increases in Chronic Conditions Predict Rising Disability?

Because the conditions-specific disability rates are stable over time, the checklist data can be used to model trends in the disability rate based on changes in the prevalence of the conditions that can lead to disability. Do increases in the overall prevalence of health conditions and impairments account for the rising disability rates?

To answer that question, I gather condition data across the six checklists and classify the conditions into 52 categories according to the body system affected. For each category, I average the condition-specific disability rate over the nine years to obtain a measure of the likelihood that a person having that condition in any year will have a disability (or, analogously, be unable to work) due to that condition. I use this factor to rescale the overall prevalence of each of the 52 condition categories in each year to estimate the expected contribution of that condition to the disability rate. Adding up those expected contributions results in a prediction for the overall disability rate (or the rate of inability to work) in a given year, due to conditions that are included on the checklists.

Figure 6.15 shows the actual rates of disability and inability to work, excluding conditions not on the checklists, as well as the rates expected from this model. For both rates, there is remarkable agreement between the expected and actual trends. Most notably, the expected trends mirror the actual in showing sharp increases between 1990 and 1993 and then leveling off.

The presumably more straightforward and objective condition data gathered with the checklists has proved entirely consistent with the more complex and subjective self-assessments of limitations in activity and ability or inability to work. For the conditions that are included on the checklists (all of the principal causes of disability except mental health conditions and learning disabilities), changes in the overall prevalence of the underlying health conditions and impairments that result in disability appear to fully explain the large and rapid increases in the disability and inability-to-work rates that occurred during the early 1990s.

Figure 6.15 Actual and Predicted Rates of Disability and Inability to Work from Chronic Condition Prevalence, Ages 18–64, 1988–1996

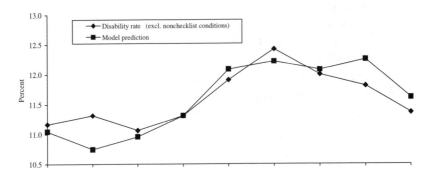

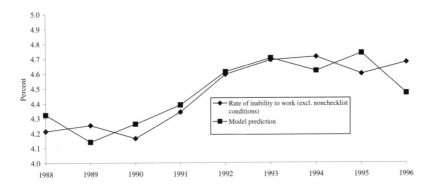

SOURCE: National Health Interview Survey.

WHAT RISK FACTORS MIGHT HAVE LED TO THESE INCREASES?

If the rising rates of disability are truly attributable to epidemiologic factors—affecting a much broader spectrum of the working-age population than the approximately 14 percent reporting limitations in activity—then the next step is to explore some of the risk factors that might have led to increases in the prevalence of chronic conditions. In this section, I examine two such risk factors, both of which can be analyzed to some extent using the NHIS data: increasing prevalence of obesity among the working-age population and the physical and psychological effects of economic recession. See Kaye (2003b) for a discussion of a third risk factor, the loss of health insurance coverage and a consequent reduction in access to health care.

Based as it is on a series of cross-sections of the population rather than a panel interviewed over time, these analyses lack the longitudinal perspective that would help to distinguish cause and effect and rule out simultaneous, coincidental changes. Although I can only make plausibility arguments for the risk facts examined, the speculative nature of this discussion should not detract from the validity of the conclusions drawn in the previous sections.

Rising Levels of Overweight and Obesity

As shown in Figure 6.16, the proportion of the working-age population classified as either overweight or obese has grown considerably.

Figure 6.16 Proportion of Working-Age Adults Considered Overweight or Obese, 1988–1996

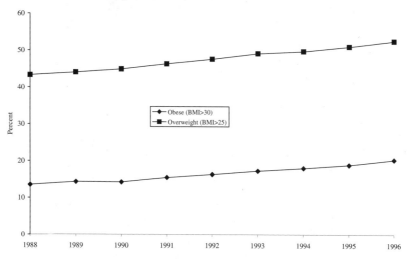

SOURCE: National Health Interview Survey.

Self-reported height and weight data from the NHIS core show a 50 percent increase in obesity among working-age adults during the period, from 13.5 percent of that population in 1988 to 20.3 percent in 1996. The proportion classified as overweight, a broader category including everyone above the normal range, grew steadily from 43.3 percent in 1988 to 52.5 percent—a majority—in 1996.

These estimates are based on government guidelines published in 1998 (National Institutes of Health 1998), which rely on body mass index (BMI), calculated by dividing the weight (in kilograms) by the square of the height (in meters). A BMI between about 18 and 25 is considered normal, while those with a BMI above 25 are classified as overweight, and those with BMI above 30 are considered obese.

Obesity is a risk factor for a variety of health conditions, and even people considered merely overweight have higher rates of some conditions than those in the normal range. As shown in Figure 6.17, the rate of musculoskeletal disability more than triples with increasing BMI, steadily increasing from a minimum of 3.8 percent at the low end of the

Figure 6.17 Prevalence of Disability among Working-Age Adults, by Body System and Body Mass Index, 1988–1996

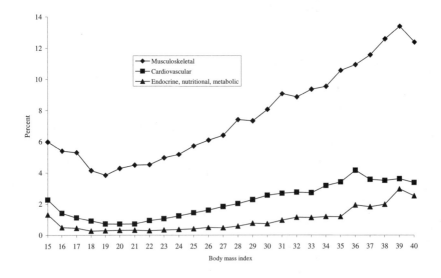

SOURCE: National Health Interview Survey.

normal range (BMI of 19) to a high above 12 percent for those with BMI of 38 or higher. Cardiovascular disability increases from a low of 0.7 percent (at BMI around 20) to more than three times that level for those in the obese range (2.6 percent) and to about five times that level (about 3.5) for those with the highest values of BMI. The risk of endocrine, nutritional, and metabolic disability is quite small for those in the normal range (0.3 percent), but it increases almost an order of magnitude at the high end of the spectrum (to 2.9 at BMI of 39); diabetes is the principal contributor to this category.

It seems reasonable to suggest that rising rates of overweight and obesity have resulted in increases in the prevalence of certain chronic conditions and impairments, thus contributing to the increases in disability rates. A simple model of the effect of increases in BMI on disability risk[2] can explain the observed increases in disability due to some conditions but not others (Figure 6.18); the rising trend in observed disability due to diabetes is well matched by the prediction from the model. For back problems, however, the model predicts only a steady, modest increase, while the actual data show a sharp rise in back problems as a cause of disability between 1991 and 1993. By 1996, however, the rate drops to about the level predicted by the model; perhaps BMI considerations can explain only the long-term growth but not the short-term.

Overall, the model suggests that rising overweight and obesity among working-age adults might have led to a steady 5 percent increase in the disability rate over eight years. Clearly, however, we must look to other factors to explain the more rapid increase in disability observed in the first few years of the 1990s.

"Economic Distress"

The recession that began in July 1990 technically ended when the economy began to recover in March 1991 (National Bureau of Economic Research 1992). But unemployment continued to rise, not reaching a peak until June 1992, when 7.8 percent of labor force participants were unemployed. Although the unemployment rate fell more or less steadily after that, it remained above 6 percent through the middle of 1994, finally returning to prerecession levels below 5.5 percent in mid 1996.

Figure 6.18 Rate of Disability Due to Back Problems or Diabetes, Actual and Expected from Body Mass Index Model, 1988–1996

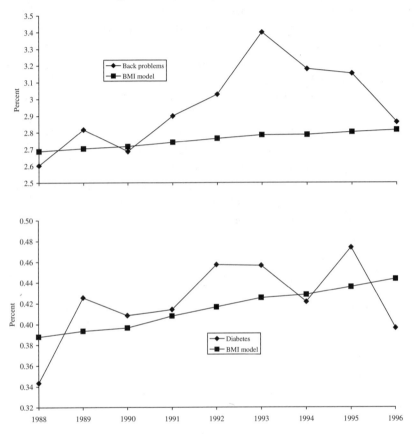

SOURCE: National Health Interview Survey.

The degree of difficulty in finding a job is further illustrated by the duration of unemployment. Figure 6.19 shows the average amount of time an unemployed person had spent looking for work (or on layoff) at the time of the CPS interview. The average was 11.7 weeks just before the recession, increasing by just under a week to 12.6 weeks by the first quarter of 1991 (and the official end of the recession). The average began to increase more rapidly after that, growing most sharply during the last quarter of 1991 and the first two quarters of

Figure 6.19 Averrage Duration of Unemployment at Time of Interview, Seasonally Adjusted, 1988–1996

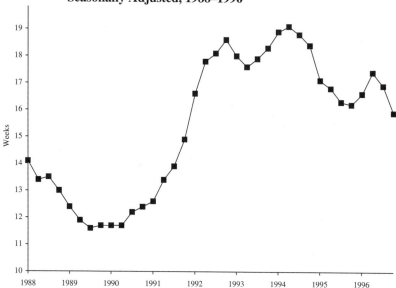

SOURCE: Current Population Survey.

1992, when it rose by 4 weeks, reaching a fairly steady level of about 18 weeks, until rising to its highest level of about 19 weeks in 1994. Even by the end of 1996, the average duration of unemployment had fallen back only to 16 weeks, much higher than the prerecession level.

In other words, from the second quarter of 1992 until the end of 1994, an unemployed person, when interviewed, had been unsuccessfully looking for work for an average of 4 to 5 months; the total duration of the job search would be perhaps twice as long, without any guarantee of eventual success.

The period of rapid increase in the duration of unemployment, when the unemployment rate was climbing to its peak level, corresponds precisely to the period when the prevalence rates of chronic conditions and disability both rose dramatically (Figure 6.20, which presents quarterly estimates, seasonally adjusted,[3] from the NHIS). The disability rate increased by a full percentage point over the nine-month period, from 13.1 percent during the third quarter of 1991 to 14.1 percent during the second quarter of 1992. During the first two quarters of

Figure 6.20 Chronic Conditions and Disability among Working-Age Adults, Seasonally Adjusted, 1988–1996

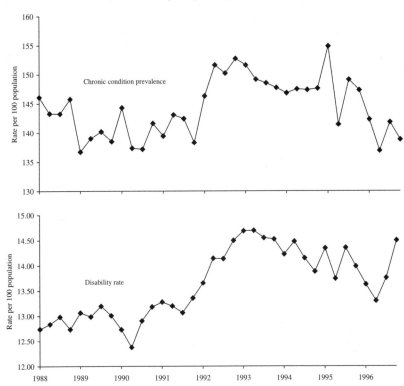

NOTE: Quarterly estimates from NHIS.
SOURCE: National Health Interview Survey.

1992, the prevalence of chronic conditions (as reported on the checklists) rose from 138.3 to 151.6 conditions per hundred working-age adults.

Following the rapid increase, all three measures—unemployment duration, chronic condition prevalence, and disability—continue to exhibit similar behavior. Each reaches and maintains its maximum level during the subsequent three years and then, by the end of the period, begins to decline.

Rates of physician contact for chronic conditions (Figure 6.21) show a similar pattern, with an even more dramatic 9 percent increase in just one quarter. Before 1990, about 7.8 percent of working-age adults reported seeing a doctor about a chronic condition in the prior two-week period. That rate had risen gradually to just under 8.2 percent by the first quarter of 1991, and then jumped to 8.9 percent during the next three months. Only in 1995 did the chronic condition physician contact rate drop back below 8.5 percent.

Does economic recession, along with its aftereffect of increasing long-term unemployment, really cause people's health to worsen, and their degree of impairment and disability to increase? Plausible though it may be to blame the rapid increases in chronic conditions and disability on what might be called "economic distress," this hypothesis cannot be adequately tested with a cross-sectional data set such as the NHIS. The simultaneous rise in unemployment duration and chronic condition rates could be coincidental.

Many studies have addressed the question of whether health is affected by recession or unemployment (for critical reviews of these

Figure 6.21 Proportion of Working-Age Adults Discussing a Chronic Condition with a Physician in Prior Two Weeks, Seasonally Adjusted, 1988–1996

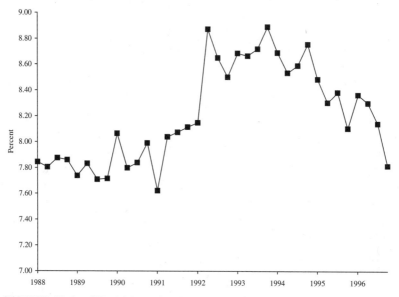

SOURCE: National Health Interview Survey.

studies, see Mathers and Schofield 1998; Goldney 1997; Dooley, Fielding, and Levi 1996; and Jin, Shah, and Svoboda 1995). Most show an association between job loss or job insecurity and poor subsequent health status; however, because they rely on cross-sectional data, many of these cannot actually demonstrate that health worsened following economic distress, as opposed to a competing hypothesis that people already in poor health are at greater risk of losing their jobs during a recessionary period. A few longitudinal studies do follow individuals through periods of economic distress, and some of these show fairly convincing patterns of worsening health following threatened or actual loss of employment (Kraut et al. 2000; Ferrie et al. 1998).

Better established is a causal link between economic distress and worsening mental health (Claussen 1999; Theodossiou 1998; Hamilton, Merrigan, and Dufresne 1997; Hammarstrom and Janlert 1997; Dooley, Catalano, and Wilson 1994). There is a well demonstrated—and far from surprising—association between unemployment and greater levels of stress, anxiety, and depression (Comino et al. 2000; Gien 2000; Viinamaki et al. 1993; Graetz 1993; Linn, Sandifer, and Stein 1985), due to loss of income, status, social contact, and structured activity (Creed and Macintyre 2001).

As Figure 6.22 shows, there was an enormous increase between 1991 and 1993 in the proportion of working-age adults consulting a medical doctor for depression or stress. Until the end of 1991, a fairly steady rate of about 0.35 percent reported discussing one of these mental health conditions with a doctor during the prior two-week period; over the next four quarters, that rate increased to nearly 0.5 percent, continuing to rise to an average of 0.57 percent over the four quarters of 1993. The 1993 rate is a 63 percent increase over the 1991 level.

Could a pronounced increase in mental health conditions have led to greater prevalence of physical conditions? Clinical studies have implicated psychological stress in causing or worsening a variety of musculoskeletal conditions, such as rheumatoid arthritis and back, neck, and shoulder pain (Feyer et al. 2000; Walker et al. 1999; Lundberg et al. 1999); digestive system conditions, such as intestinal inflammation and dyspepsia (Collins 2001; Elenkov and Chrousos 1999; Tryba and Cook 1997; Koch and Stern 1990); respiratory system conditions, such as asthma and allergies (Marshall and Agarwal 2000; Elenkov and Chrousos 1999); nervous system symptoms, such as head-

Figure 6.22 Proportion of Working-Age Adults Seeing Doctor for Depression or Stress in Prior Two Weeks, Seasonally Adjusted, 1988–1996

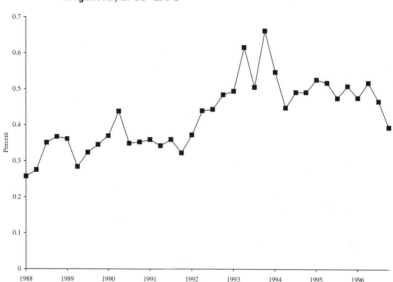

SOURCE: National Health Interview Survey.

ache, dizziness, and epileptic seizures (Andersson and Yardley 2000; Spector, Cull, and Goldstein 2000; Buzzi, Pellegrino, and Bellantonio 1995); and circulatory system conditions, such as hypertension and even heart disease and possibly stroke (Cerrato 2001; Everson et al. 2001; Yudkin et al. 1999; Barnes et al. 1997).

For its part, depression has been implicated in causing or worsening a similar list of conditions (Feyer et al. 2000; Spector, Cull, and Goldstein 2000; Galil 2000; Udell and Weiss 1998; Addolorato et al. 1998; Fifield et al. 1998). In particular, causal relationships have been observed or proposed between depression and coronary artery disease, stroke, hypertension, and other circulatory system conditions (Krishnan 2000; O'Connor, Gurbel, and Serebruany 2000; Lavoie and Fleet 2000; Ferketich et al. 2000; Jonas and Mussolino 2000).

Dividing the checklist chronic condition data by body system (Figure 6.23), most of the 1992 increase occurs among the musculoskeletal, respiratory, digestive, and nervous system conditions—four of the five

Figure 6.23 Chronic Condition Prevalence among Working-Age Adults, by Body System, Seasonally Adjusted, 1988–1996

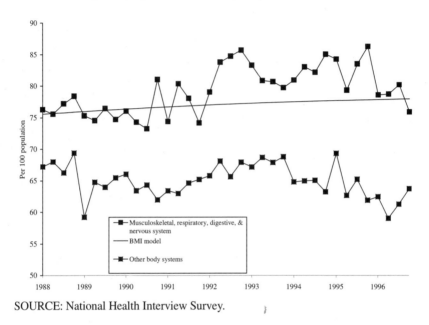

SOURCE: National Health Interview Survey.

body systems most commonly linked to stress and depression in the literature. For these conditions, the prevalence rose sharply during the first half 1992, climbing from a 1991 average of 77 conditions per hundred population to 85 conditions during the second half of 1992, and remaining above 80 for most quarters through the end of 1995. In contrast, the prevalence of conditions involving all other body systems rose only modestly, from a 1991 average of 64 conditions per hundred working-age adults to 67 in 1992, returning to its former level by 1994.

Also shown in the figure is the expected trend for musculoskeletal, respiratory, digestive, and nervous system conditions, obtained using our BMI model. At best, rising rates of overweight and obesity could account for a general upward trend over the period, but do not explain the 1992–1995 increase.

All in all, sharp increases in physician contact rates for both mental and physical health conditions, in prevalence rates for certain types of conditions and impairments, and in disability rates appear to be quite consistent with the hypothesis that the 1990–1991 recession, and in particular the aftereffect of increased long-term unemployment, might well have caused a worsening in the health and disability status of working-age adults.

CONCLUSION

The stagnation in the overall employment rate among people with disabilities can be seen as a consequence of the increasing proportion of the population who consider themselves unable to work. The analysis presented in this chapter suggests that this increase reflects an actual worsening in the extent of work limitation among a changing population with disabilities. Furthermore, employment measures that exclude those reporting inability to work reveal significant progress in employment opportunities for those with disabilities who are able and available to work.

I find that the sharp increases in the reported rates of both overall activity limitation and inability to work during the early 1990s can be fully accounted for by widespread increases in the prevalence of chronic conditions and impairments among working-age adults. The growth in chronic condition prevalence affects a broad spectrum of the working-age population, far broader than just the 14 percent or so reporting limitations in activity. Because most of the increase in chronic condition prevalence is unrelated to disability status, explanations focusing on disability status—involving a greater desire to obtain cash benefits or an increased willingness to be seen as having a disability—cannot account for this change.

What risk factors might have led to the large and widespread increases in both disability and the chronic conditions and impairments that cause disability? A rising trend in the proportion of the population classified as overweight or obese has increased the risk of certain chronic conditions and the ensuing disability; this change probably resulted in a gradual, steady increase in the disability rate over the period. A sharper increase, observed in the data for the early 1990s, is more plausibly explained as a result of the economic recession, which continued to affect the unemployment rate as late as 1994. The psychological distress resulting from job insecurity and job loss might have led to worsening physical health and, in turn, greater disability. A third hypothesis, not addressed here, refers to the increasing economic vulnerability of certain workers, whose access to health insurance and health care has eroded over the years.

Again, when I postulate economic causes as factors in the increasing disability rates, I differ from other authors in proposing that these factors have increased the actual prevalence of the underlying conditions causing disability, rather than simply increasing the likelihood that a person with a given severity of a given condition will regard himself or herself as having a disability.

Notes

1. For details on the functional limitation scale, see Kaye (2003a).
2. Using data from 1988–1990, I calculate a rate of disability caused by each of the conditions modelled in each of 12 BMI bins for each sex (24 BMI-sex cells). I then multiply that rate by the actual population each BMI-sex cell in each year and then sum to obtain the predicted prevalence of disability due to that condition in that year.
3. Adjusted using the Census Bureau's X-11 procedure as implemented in SAS. The NHIS sample is nationally representative in each quarter.

References

Addolorato, G., L. Marsigli, E. Capristo, F. Caputo, C. Dall'Aglio, and P. Baudanza. 1998. "Anxiety and Depression: A Common Feature of Health Care Seeking Patients with Irritable Bowel Syndrome and Food Allergy." *Hepatogastroenterology* 45(23): 1559–1564.

Andersson, G., and L. Yardley. 2000. "Time-Series Analysis of the Relationship between Dizziness and Stress." *Scandinavian Journal of Psychology* 41(1): 49–54.

Autor, David H., and Mark G. Duggan. 2003. "The Rise in Disability Recipiency and the Decline in Unemployment." NBER working paper no. W8336. Cambridge, MA: National Bureau of Economic Research.

Barnes, V., R. Schneider, C. Alexander, and F. Staggers. 1997. "Stress, Stress Reduction, and Hypertension in African Americans: An Updated Review." *Journal of the National Medical Association* 89(7): 464–476.

Buzzi, M.G., M.G. Pellegrino, and P. Bellantonio, 1995. "Causes and Mechanisms of Primary Headaches: Toward a Bio-Behavioral Model. *Italian Journal of Neurological Sciences* 16(8 Suppl): 15–19.

Cerrato, Paul L. 2001. Stress, "Marriage, and Carotid Atherosclerosis." *Contemporary OB/GYN* 46(4): 93.

Claussen, B. 1999. "Health and Re-Employment in a Five-Year Follow-up of Long-Term Unemployed." *Scand J Public Health* 27(2): 94–100.

Collins, S.M. 2001. "Stress and the Gastrointestinal Tract IV. Modulation of Intestinal Inflammation by Stress: Basic Mechanisms and Clinical Relevance." *American Journal of Physiology Gastrointestinal and Liver Physiology* 280(3): G315–318.

Comino, E.J., E. Harris, D. Silove, V. Manicavasagar, and M.F. Harris. 2000. "Prevalence, Detection and Management of Anxiety and Depressive Symptoms in Unemployed Patients Attending General Practitioners." *Australian and New Zealand Journal of Psychiatry* 34(1): 107–113.

Creed, P.A., and S.R. Macintyre. 2001. "The Relative Effects of Deprivation of the Latent and Manifest Benefits of Employment on the Well-Being of Unemployed People." *Journal of Occupational Health Psychology* 6(4): 324–331.

Dooley, D., R. Catalano, and G. Wilson. 1994. "Depression and Unemployment: Panel Findings from the Epidemiologic Catchment Area Study." *American Journal of Community Psychology* 22(6): 745–765.

Dooley, D, J. Fielding, and L. Levi. 1996. "Health and Unemployment." *Annual Review of Public Health* 17: 449–465.

Elenkov, I.J., and G.P. Chrousos. 1999. "Stress, Cytokine Patterns and Susceptibility to Disease." *Baillieres Best Practice and Research Clinical Endocrinology and Metabolism* 13(4): 583–595.

Everson, S.A., J.W. Lynch, G.A. Kaplan, T.A. Lakka, J. Sivenius, and J.T. Salonen. 2001. "Stress-Induced Blood Pressure Reactivity and Incident Stroke in Middle-Aged Men." *Stroke* 32(6): 1263–1270.

Ferketich, A.K., J.A. Schwartzbaum, D.J. Frid, and M.L. Moeschberger. 2000. "Depression as an Antecedent to Heart Disease among Women and Men in the NHANES I Study." *Archives of Internal Medicine* 160(9): 1261–1268.

Ferrie, J.E., M.J. Shipley, M.G. Marmot, S.A. Stansfeld, and G.D. Smith. 1998. "An Uncertain Future: The Health Effects of Threats to Employment Security in White-Collar Men and Women." *American Journal of Public Health* 88(7): 1030–1036.

Feyer, A.M., P. Herbison, A.M. Williamson, I. de Silva, J. Mandryk, L. Hendrie, and M.C. Hely. 2000. "The Role of Physical and Psychological Factors in Occupational Low Back Pain: A Prospective Cohort Study." *Occupational and Environmental Medicine* 57(2): 116–120.

Fifield, J., H. Tennen, S. Reisine, and J. McQuillan. 1998. "Depression and the Long-Term Risk of Pain, Fatigue, and Disability in Patients with Rheumatoid Arthritis." *Arthritis Rheumatism* 41(10): 1851–1857.

Galil, N. 2000. "Depression and Asthma in Children." *Current Opinions in Pediatrics* 12(4): 331–335.

Gien, L.T. 2000. "Land and Sea Connection: The East Coast Fishery Closure, Unemployment and Health." *Canadian Journal of Public Health.* 91(2): 121–124.

Goldney, R.D. 1997. "Unemployment and Health: A Re-Appraisal." *International Archives of Occupational and Environmental Health* 70(3): 145–147.

Graetz, B. 1993. "Health Consequences of Employment and Unemployment: Longitudinal Evidence for Young Men and Women." *Social Science and Medicine* 36(6): 715–724.

Hamilton, V.H., P. Merrigan, and E. Dufresne. 1997. "Down and Out: Estimating the Relationship between Mental Health and Unemployment." *Health Economics* 6(4): 397–406.

Hammarstrom, A., and U. Janlert. 1997. "Nervous and Depressive Symptoms in a Longitudinal Study of Youth Unemployment—Selection or Exposure?" *Journal of Adolescence* 20(3): 293–305.

Jin, R.L., C.P. Shah, and T.J. Svoboda. 1995. "The Impact of Unemployment on Health: A Review of the Evidence." *Canadian Medical Association Journal* 153(5): 529–540.

Jonas, B.S., and M.E. Mussolino. 2000. "Symptoms of Depression as a Prospective Risk Factor for Stroke." *Psychosomatic Medicine* 62(4): 463–471.

Kaye, H. Stephen. 2003a. "Improved Employment Opportunities for People with Disabilities." *Disability Statistics Report* 17. Washington, DC: U.S. Department of Education, National Institute on Disability and Rehabilitation Research.

———. 2003b. "Accounting for the Rising Disability Rates among Working-Age Adults." *Disability Statistics Report* 18. U.S. Department of Education, National Institute on Disability and Rehabilitation Research.

Koch, K.L., and R.M. Stern. 1990. "Functional Disorders of the Stomach." *Seminars in Gastrointestinal Disease* 1(1): 23–36.

Kraut, A., C. Mustard, R. Walld, and R. Tate. 2000. "Unemployment and Health Care Utilization." *Scandinavian Journal of Work, Environment and Health* 26(2): 169–177.

Krishnan, K.R. 2000. "Depression as a Contributing Factor in Cerebrovascular Disease." *American Heart Journal* 140(4 Suppl): 70–76.

Lavoie, K.L., and R.P. Fleet. 2000. "The Impact of Depression on the Course and Outcome of Coronary Artery Disease: Review for Cardiologists." *Canadian Journal of Cardiology* 16(5): 653–662.

Linn, M., R. Sandifer, and S. Stein. 1985. "Effects of Unemployment on Mental and Physical Health." *American Journal of Public Health* 75: 502–506.

Lundberg, U., I.E. Dohns, B. Melin, L. Sandsjo, G. Palmerud, R. Kadefors, M. Ekstrom, and D. Parr. 1999. "Psychophysiological Stress Responses, Muscle Tension, and Neck and Shoulder Pain among Supermarket Cashiers." *Journal of Occupational Health Psychology* 4(3): 245–255.

Marshall, G.D. Jr., and S.K. Agarwal. 2000. "Stress, Immune Regulation, and Immunity: Applications for Asthma." *Allergy and Asthma Proceedings* 21(4): 241–246.

Mathers, C.D., and D.J. Schofield. 1998. "The Health Consequences of Unemployment: The Evidence." *Medical Journal of Australia* 168(4): 178–182.

National Bureau of Economic Research. 1992. "NBER Business Cycle Dating Committee Determines That Recession Ended in March 1991." Press release, October 22. Cambridge, MA: NBER.

National Center for Disease Prevention and Health Promotion. 1999. "Decline in Deaths from Heart Disease and Stroke—United States, 1900–1999." *Morbidity and Mortality Weekly Report* 48(30): 649–656.

National Institutes of Health. 1998. "Clinical Guidelines on the Identification, Evaluation and Treatment of Overweight and Obesity in Adults: The Evidence Report." NIH publication no. 98–4083. Washington, DC: NIH.

O'Connor, C.M., P.A. Gurbel, and V.L. Serebruany. 2000. "Depression and Ischemic Heart Disease. *American Heart Journal* 140(4 Suppl): 63–69.

Social Security Administration. 2001. *Annual Statistical Supplement, 2000. Social Security Bulletin*. Washington, DC: Social Security Administration, Office of Policy. Available at: <http://www.ssa.gov/statistics/Supplement/2000/> (Posted: June 19, 2001. Accessed: December 2002).

Spector, S., C. Cull, and L.H. Goldstein. 2000. "Seizure Precipitants and Perceived Self-Control of Seizures in Adults with Poorly-Controlled Epilepsy." *Epilepsy Research* 38(2-3): 207–216.

Theodossiou, I. 1998. "The Effects of Low-pay and Unemployment on Psychological Well-Being: A Logistic Regression Approach." *Journal of Health Economics* 17(1): 85–104.

Tryba, M., and D. Cook. 1997. "Current Guidelines on Stress Ulcer Prophylaxis." *Drugs* 54(4): 581–596.

Udell, E.T., and K.J. Weiss. 1998. "Anxiety, Depression, and Diseases of the Lower Extremities." *Clinics in Podiatric Medicine and Surgery* 15(4): 619–628.

Viinamaki, H., K. Koskela, L. Niskanen, R. Arnkill, and J. Tikkanen. 1993. "Unemployment and Mental Wellbeing: A Factory Closure Study in Finland." *Acta Psychiatrica Scandinavica* 88(6): 429–433.

Walker, J.G., G.O. Littlejohn, N.E. McMurray, and M. Cutolo. 1999. "Stress System Response and Rheumatoid Arthritis: A Multilevel Approach." *Rheumatology* 38(11): 1050–1057.

Yudkin, J.S., M. Kumari, S.E. Humphries, and V. Mohamed-Ali. 1999. "Inflammation, Obesity, Stress, and Coronary Heart Disease: Is Interleukin-6 the Link?" *Atherosclerosis* 148(2): 209–214.

7
The Americans with Disabilities Act and the Employment of People with Disabilities

Thomas DeLeire
University of Chicago

A major goal of the Americans with Disabilities Act of 1990 (ADA) is to more fully integrate working-aged people with disabilities into the labor force and to increase their employment rate to be more in line with the rest of the population. At the time of its passage, ADA proponents believed that the ADA's antidiscrimination and reasonable accommodation mandates would accomplish this goal and increase both the employment and economic well-being of working-aged people with disabilities. Few would disagree with this ADA goal. In fact, the 1964 Civil Rights Act, despite great controversy at the time of its passage, has been shown to contribute to the achievement of this goal for blacks. In contrast, ADA critics today argue that instead of increasing their employment, the costs associated with these mandates had the unintended consequence of reducing the employment opportunities of those with disabilities.

This chapter summarizes the empirical evidence on the labor market consequences of the ADA. It will show that, to date, the ADA—as well as similar state-level legislation that preceded the ADA—has reduced the employment opportunities of those with disabilities. This evidence is consistent with the argument that accommodation and employment-protection costs can reduce the employment of the individuals these actions are meant to protect. This policy failure, rather than a disagreement on goals, is the basis for the case against the ADA as a vehicle for improving the labor market outcomes for working-aged people with disabilities. The ADA has not only failed to increase employment opportunities for people with disabilities but has actually reduced them. Hence, those interested in more fully integrating working-aged people with disabilities into the workforce and reducing their dependence on government disability-related transfers should reconsider their support of the ADA as the vehicle for achieving that goal and instead focus on alternative policies.

BACKGROUND

Many working-aged Americans are limited in their ability to function as a result of a health-related impairment—in 1993, 16 percent of men aged 18–62 reported a functional limitation, and 11 percent reported a work limitation owing to a health impairment (DeLeire 2001). Moreover, many American workers are at risk of disability as a result of a workplace injury. Reville and Schoeni (2002) find that 34 percent of working-aged adults with disabilities in the Health and Retirement Study say their disability was the result of a work-related injury or from the nature of their work. Social policy in the United States has increasingly focused on integrating working-aged people with disabilities into the labor force and reducing their reliance on disability transfer programs. The most important effort in this regard has been the passage of the ADA. This act, fashioned in large part on the civil rights protection granted to other protected minorities by the Civil Rights Act of 1964, was an attempt through mandates to achieve this goal for working-aged people with disabilities.

The ADA was passed on July 26, 1990, and became effective two years later. Although numerous states had laws providing employment protections for workers with disabilities prior to 1990 (Beegle and Stock 2002), the ADA represents the first federal law providing employment protections for workers with disabilities in the private sector (although the Rehabilitation Act of 1973 applied to federal contractors). There are two components of Title I of the ADA. First, the ADA bans discrimination in wages, hiring, firing, and promotion. Second, employers are required to provide "reasonable" accommodation for their disabled workers. Examples of reasonable accommodation include providing access to work areas, job restructuring, and special equipment or assistive devices.

These two provisions, while protecting individuals' rights, also impose costs on employers. Further, the cost of accommodation is one that is unlike costs that were associated with the civil rights protection under the 1964 Civil Rights Act. Enforced through the Equal Employment Opportunity Commission (EEOC) and through the courts, the ADA imposes litigation costs on firms. For example, firms that have settled with the EEOC have paid an average settlement of $13,137 (U.S. EEOC 2001). Even without a judgment, however, the cost of defending a discrimination suit has been estimated to be as much as $100,000 (Olson 1997).

The evidence on the magnitude of the cost of accommodation to firms is thin. What evidence exists suggests that these costs are small on average (Berkeley Planning Associates 1982; Job Accommodation Network 1999). However, as I have argued elsewhere (DeLeire 2000b), these data seriously underestimate the potential costs of accommodations by including accommodations that would have been granted even in the absence of the law and by counting certain accommodations as zero cost because they do not involve the purchase of equipment. For example, the studies count job restructuring as zero cost despite large costs this accommodation can impose on firms. Despite shortcomings, these studies have found that a potentially important fraction of accommodations are quite expensive. For example, while the Berkeley Planning Associates study found that the average cost of accommodation was small, the study also found that 8 percent of accommodations cost more than $2,000, 4 percent cost more than $5,000, and 2 percent cost more than $20,000 (which in 2001 dollars would be more than $3,700, $9,300, and $37,000, respectively). Moreover, this survey reports only the costs of accommodations made, not the costs of accommodations that were requested and denied. It is reasonable to suspect that the costs of denied accommodations would exceed the costs of those that were granted. Therefore, the average costs of new accommodation requests under the ADA are likely to be much larger than the average costs reported in these surveys.

Defining Disability

The most common image of those targeted for ADA protection is of working-aged people with mobility, vision, or hearing impairments. The ADA, however, covers a much broader set of health impairments. The ADA defines disability as "a physical or mental impairment that substantially limits one or more of the major life activities of . . . [an] individual, a record of such an impairment; or being regarded as having such an impairment" (ADA 1990). Major life activities include walking, lifting, seeing, hearing, breathing, and working. In fact, the set of individuals with mobility, vision, and hearing impairments represent only 17 percent of the population of people with disabilities, according to the Survey of Income and Program Participation (SIPP). The other 83 percent of people with disabilities in the SIPP have back impairments, impairments arising from stroke, heart problems, asthma, diabetes, cancer, high blood pressure, kidney or stomach problems, are HIV positive or have AIDS, have a mental disability, or have a substance abuse problem (based on author's calculations from the SIPP).

Although the ADA potentially covers a much broader set of impairments than is commonly understood, still uncertain is which members of the population with impairments are considered to be part of the class protected by the ADA. The EEOC and the courts have disagreed over how broadly disability is defined under the ADA. For example, in *Toyota v. Williams*, the Supreme Court unanimously ruled that an individual with carpal tunnel syndrome who could still do tasks central to most people's daily lives was not disabled under the ADA. The EEOC had previously taken the position that they were. If the EEOC and the courts have been uncertain over who is protected by the ADA, surely employers have been even more uncertain. For such employers, this uncertainty is likely to have further increased their risks and costs associated with hiring people with disabilities.

Moreover, eligibility to sue under the ADA is determined by the courts on an individual basis. Many individuals who have filed claims against employers through the EEOC or the courts have been found not to be protected by the ADA. The claims and lawsuits filed by these individuals are not costless to employers. Even a successful defense of a claim can cost a firm tens of thousands of dollars. In addition, because there is a lottery aspect to any court proceeding, where judge or jury determines the facts of the case, some individuals will be successful in their claims when identical individuals will be unsuccessful. Therefore, even if an employer believes an individual with disabilities is not protected by the ADA (either because he or she is unable to be reasonably accommodated, would be unable to perform the essential functions of the job even with accommodations, or is not in fact limited in a major life function), the employer still may believe that there is a risk of being sued by this individual. Moreover, individuals who end up not being covered may face reduced employment opportunities—because of employers' fear of lawsuits—yet ultimately not receive remedies when they do sue because they are not, in fact, protected by the ADA.

Kruse and Schur (Chapter 8) and Blanck, Schwochau, and Song (Chapter 9) argue that policymakers should only be concerned with the well-being of people with disabilities who are within the ADA protected class. However, uncertainties surrounding who is protected by the law (and who will sue, even if ultimately unsuccessful) suggest that the ADA could have an effect on individuals with disabilities who are not covered by the law. The ADA could likewise assist individuals who are not covered by the act. For example, accommodations, such as modifications to work environments, made by employers for protected workers may also benefit workers with disabilities who are not covered by the ADA, and may improve their employment outcomes. In either case, a narrow, legalistic view of the impacts of the ADA misses the larger population of people with disabilities of interest to policymakers.

THE A PRIORI CASE AGAINST THE ADA

Prior to passage of the ADA, several authors argued that the ADA would not lead to a better integration of working-aged people with disabilities into the labor force or improvement in their economic well-being. I review these arguments in this section.

In their critical analyses of the ADA, both Weaver (1991) and Rosen (1991) point out that the ADA differs from federal civil rights protections for minorities and women in that it not only bans discrimination but also requires firms to provide "reasonable" accommodations to its employees with disabilities. Further, they argue that the costs of accommodation would represent a barrier to increasing employment opportunities and would reduce the demand for disabled workers and thus the number of disabled people employed (Rosen 1991 p. 23; Weaver 1991, p. 11). Weaver also predicted that the ADA would lead to distributional effects as well; firms would have relatively greater incentive to employ workers with disabilities who require little accommodation.

Epstein (1992) argues, as part of a more general argument against all antidiscrimination legislation when applied to labor markets, that the ADA is not the best way to assist people with disabilities in the labor market. He contends that protected groups are better served by freedom of contract (employment at will) and competitive labor markets in which entry is unfettered. Employers would have no reason to avoid hiring impaired workers out of (the mistaken) fear that they are less capable given that they would be free to fire any worker, impaired or not, who does not work productively. Workers with impairments would have greater levels of employment—although with fewer guarantees of continued employment—while employers would gain greater experience at employing workers with impairments.

Burkhauser (1990) argues that the ADA would be less effective at inducing employers to provide accommodations for people with disabilities than would a tax credit (or other type of subsidy) to employers for such accommodations. However, he also argues that the mandated-accommodation approach of the ADA was favored politically because it was off budget; that is, it did not involve any budget outlay or tax offsets by the federal government.

Acemoglu and Angrist (2001) present a model in which the ADA could reduce employment of people with disabilities by increasing employer costs (including costs of accommodation and potential costs of litigation). However, they also show that the ADA possibly could increase employment of people with disabilities through its implicit hiring subsidy. This implicit hiring subsidy is caused by employers' fear that an applicant with a disability who is not hired may sue. Thus, it is may be less expensive to hire an applicant with a disability.

Therefore, on theoretical grounds, the ADA could have led to an increase or to a decrease in the employment of people with disabilities depending on the relative importance of accommodation costs, firing costs, and hiring costs. To measure the impact of the ADA, I turn next to a review of the empirical studies of the ADA's effects.

EMPIRICAL STUDIES—THE WEIGHT OF THE EVIDENCE AGAINST THE ADA

To date, two major studies have used national data sets to examine the employment effects of the ADA: DeLeire (2000b) and Acemoglu and Angrist (2001). The methods used in these studies are similar to those in studies that examined the impact of the Civil Rights Act of 1964; that is, they examine trends in employment rates of people with disabilities relative to people without disabilities around the time the ADA was passed. The literature measuring the impact of the 1964 Civil Rights Act on the economic status of blacks includes studies by Freeman (1973) and Brown (1984), both of which found an upward shift in relative black economic status following 1964. (For a complete discussion of this literature and of the effect of civil rights policy on black economic progress, see Donohue and Heckman [1991]). These studies all examine black-white earnings ratios over a period of time spanning the passage of the Civil Rights Act. Findings that relative earnings increased post–1964 are taken as evidence that the act had positive effects. It is important to note that the preponderance of the evidence from studies using this method is that the Civil Rights Act did reduce employment discrimination and increase the employment of blacks.

The empirical studies of the impact of the ADA, described below, have a similar design as those used to evaluate the Civil Rights Act. For the most part, they examine relative employment rates before and after the enactment or implementation of the ADA to infer its impact. Acemoglu and Angrist (2001) and DeLeire (2000b) also employ additional comparisons that help shed light on whether any changes in employment trends are the result of the ADA. Because the ADA was enacted (and implemented) for all people with disabilities simultaneously,[1] it is difficult to disentangle alternative explanations why disabled employment has fallen. In response to this problem, Beegle and Stock (2002) examine the employment impact of state disability laws that were implemented between 1970 and 1990. In this section, I review each of these studies.

Data Sources and the Definition of Disability

DeLeire (2000b) uses data from the 1986 through 1993 panels of the SIPP on a sample of men aged 18 to 64. These data contain information on whether each individual worked in the previous four-month period as well as a large number of demographic characteristics of the individuals. Disability is measured by a self-report of a "health impairment that limits the type or amount of work an individual can do." Acemoglu and Angrist (2001) use data from the Current Population Survey (CPS). Beegle and Stock (2002) use data from the 1970, 1980, and 1990 Decennial Censuses. As in the SIPP, the measure of disability available in the CPS and in the Census is a self-reported work limitation.[2] As discussed by Burkhauser, Houtenville, and Wittenburg (Chapter 2), although this is not an ideal measure for establishing the working-aged population with disabilities, employment trends in this population are not significantly different from those using other measures of disabilities.

The Employment Effect of the ADA: Evidence from 1990–1992

Both DeLeire and Acemoglu and Angrist examine employment trends around the time the ADA was passed and implemented to empirically assess the effect of the ADA. Both studies estimate empirical models of employment and interpret declines as evidence that the ADA had a negative impact on the demand for disabled employment. Acemoglu and Angrist, using the CPS, estimate linear regressions of weeks worked and control for a large set of demographic characteristics—age, race, education, and region all interacted with year dummies. DeLeire, using the SIPP, estimates probit models of employment and controls for age, education, marital status, race, industry, and occupation. Importantly, both studies use individuals without disabilities who have similar skill levels as a comparison group by which to measure the post-ADA experiences of those with disabilities.

Figure 7.1 illustrates the estimated effect of the ADA on relative employment rates of working-aged (18–64) people with disabilities. The top panel of Figure 7.1 plots the employment rate of men with and without disabilities from 1986 through 1995 using data from the SIPP. The bottom panel of Figure 7.1 plots the employment rate of men with

Figure 7.1 Employment Rates of Men With and Without Work Limitations Disabilities, Aged 18–64: SIPP Data

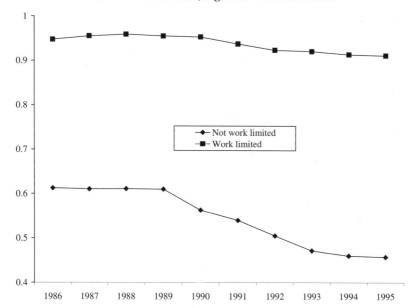

disabilities relative to that of men without disabilities. Neither panel controls for demographic characteristics. Although the employment of men without disabilities was slightly lower in the years following 1990, the employment of men with disabilities fell dramatically beginning in 1990, the year the ADA was passed. Empirical models of employment yield similar results and are reported in Table 7.1. I interpret Figure 7.1 as prima facie evidence that the ADA did not work as intended; rather than making it easier for people with disabilities to find employment, the ADA has made it more difficult.

Acemoglu and Angrist find similar results using the CPS when they examine weeks worked. There are, however, two differences between the findings from the CPS and those from the SIPP. First, Acemoglu and Angrist observe declines in weeks worked beginning only in 1992, the year the ADA became effective. Second, they observe steep declines primarily for men and women aged 21–39, and only slight declines for men aged 40–58, and they do not observe

Table 7.1 Summary of Empirical Studies of the Effects of Disability Discrimination Laws

	Employment rate (DeLeire)		Weeks worked (Acemoglu & Angrist)			Employment rate (Beegle & Stock)
	(1)	(2)	(3)	(4)	(5)	(6)
Disabled	−0.26	−0.24	−	−	−	−0.28
Post-law	−0.02	−	−	−	−	0.01
Post-law x disabled	−0.04	−	−	−	−	−0.12
1986 x disabled	−	−0.02	−	−	−	−
1987 x disabled	−	−0.03	−	−	−	−
1988 x disabled	−	−0.02	−0.41	−1.08	−0.49	−
1989 x disabled	−	−	2.00	0.67	−0.47	−
1990 x disabled	−	−0.03	−0.79	−1.33	−0.22	−
1991 x disabled	−	−0.06	−0.53	0.08	0.34	−
1992 x disabled	−	−0.06	0.57	−2.81	0.77	−
1993 x disabled	−	−0.07	−1.44	−4.37	−2.12	−
1994 x disabled	−	−0.07	−1.63	−5.00	−1.57	−
1995 x disabled	−	−0.07	−2.93	−3.93	−1.83	−
1996 x disabled	−	−	−2.68	−4.41	−0.75	−

NOTE: The data in this table can be interpreted as follows: Columns (1) and (6) show the difference in employment rates between people with and without disabilities in the first row, the change in employment rates for people without disabilities after the law was enacted in the second row, and the change in employment rates for people with disabilities (over and above the change for people without disabilities) in the third row. The first row of column (2) again shows the difference in employment rates between people with and without disabilities. Each row from the fourth onward shows the difference in the employment rate of people with disabilities relative to the employment rate of people without disabilities between the given year and 1989. For example, in the eleventh row, the −0.07 indicates that the employment rate of people with disabilities fell by 7 percentage point more than that for people without disabilities between 1989 and 1993. Columns (3), (4), and (5) show the difference in weeks worked between people with and without disabilities. For example, in the eleventh row, third column, the −1.44 indicates that the number of weeks worked by people with disabilities fell by 1.44 weeks since 1987 relative to the change in the number of weeks worked by people without disabilities.

SOURCE: Results from DeLeire (2000b, Table 4) are based on SIPP data for men aged 18–64. Results from Acemoglu and Angrist (2001, Table 2) are based on CPS data for men aged 21–39, women aged 21–39, and men aged 40–58, respectively. Results from Beegle and Stock (2002), Table 5, are based on census data for men and women aged 18–64. All studies measure disability as the presence of a work limitation and adjust for demographic characteristics.

declines for women aged 40–58. Their results change little when they add controls or employ alternative estimation methods.

Table 7.1 summarizes the results from DeLeire, Acemoglu and Angrist, and Beegle and Stock. All three studies conduct additional analyses comparing the relative employment declines across groups and across states. These analyses provide further evidence that the ADA—as opposed to some other policy change—is responsible for the employment decline for people with disabilities.

First, Acemoglu and Angrist control for the fact that Social Security Disability Income (SSDI) and Supplemental Security Income (SSI) recipiency rates increased over this period as well. They do so in three ways: they first examine employment trends only for nonrecipients; second, they control for the individual's SSDI and SSI receipt; and third, in each year, they control for the statewide fraction of individuals receiving SSDI and SSI. In no case do any of their results change substantially. That is, the declines in employment in the CPS following the implementation of the ADA are over and above those that could conceivably be the result of changes in SSDI or SSI policies. Acemoglu and Angrist also examine employment patterns by firm size. They found larger employment declines in medium-sized firms (those with 25 to 99 employees) than in smaller firms or larger firms. These findings are consistent with the ADA being the source of the employment declines because firms with fewer than 15 employees are exempt from the ADA, and very large firms are likely best able to absorb the costs of the ADA. They find no evidence, however, that the separation rate of people with disabilities fell, a fact they interpret as suggesting that the accommodation costs of the ADA might be a more important explanation for the decline in employment than the threat of lawsuits for wrongful termination. Finally, they find that employment, particularly of younger disabled men, fell more in states with a greater number of ADA-related EEOC charges than in other states.

State Disability Discrimination Laws

Beegle and Stock (2002) use data from the 1970, 1980, and 1990 Censuses along with data on state-level disability discrimination statutes to determine the employment effects of these state laws—all of which preceded the ADA. Because, unlike the ADA, these state-level antidiscrimination statutes were enacted in different states in different decades, it is easier to disentangle their effects on employment of people with disabilities from the effects of nationwide trends or changes in other policies. Some of these state laws were quite similar to the ADA, while others either had no accommodation requirement or did not cover mental impairments. In all cases, the resources dedicated to enforcement of these state laws likely were not as great as those of the EEOC to enforce the ADA.

How does the analysis of Beegle and Stock differ from those in DeLeire and Acemoglu and Angrist? The two latter studies, in their simplest form, compare employment rates of people with disabilities to those without disabilities before and after the act was passed. A potential concern is that something else, in addition to the ADA, happened around 1990–1992 that would affect employment rates of people with disabilities relative to employment rates of people without disabilities. Beegle and Stock use the variation in the timing of disability discrimination laws being passed in different states at different times. For example, Connecticut had a disability discrimination law in place by 1980 (enacted during the 1970s) while Rhode Island did not have a disability discrimination law in place until 1990 (enacted during the 1980s). Therefore, the authors can compare changes in employment rates of people with disabilities between 1970 and 1980 in Connecticut not only with changes in employment rates of people without disabilities between 1970 and 1980 in Connecticut, but also with changes in employment of people with disabilities between 1970 and 1980 in Rhode Island.

Beegle and Stock's findings are summarized in column (6) of Table 7.1. They find, as did the earlier research, that disability discrimination laws are associated with lower levels of employment of people with disabilities. Although the estimated effects of the state disability discrimination laws appear to be larger than the estimated effects of the ADA, the effects may not be comparable for several reasons. First, because Beegle and Stock use Census data, they measure the effects of the state laws over a longer period of time than do the studies examining the ADA. Second, the ADA was enacted on top of existing state disability discrimination law. Thus, the marginal effect of the ADA on employment rates might be smaller than would have occurred in the absence of these pre-existing laws.[3]

Are the Measured Employment Declines Real?

In a recent paper (summarized in Chapter 8), Kruse and Schur (2001) conduct an investigation of the trends in employment of people with disabilities in the early 1990s using data from the SIPP. The authors argue that disability can be measured in many different ways, both conceptually and using available data. The authors create 14 different measures of disability and show that, in contrast to the measures commonly used that show a decline in the employment of working-aged people with disabilities, some of these alternative measures show either no decline or an increase in employment. Because measures of functional limitations were available in the SIPP only beginning in the 1990 panel, Kruse and Schur estimate how employment (measured as the percentage of weeks worked) has changed since 1990. Because the ADA was passed on July 26, 1990, their data contain only a very short "pre-ADA" period with which to compare "post-ADA" employment. The authors conclude that studies that suggest that employment declined—in particular studies that suggest that employment declined as a result of the ADA—may be mistaken.

Although Kruse and Schur observe substantial declines in employment when the entire population of people with disabilities is used (based on either of the two broadest measures of disability—a work limitation or any functional "activity of daily living" (ADL) limitation), their preferred samples are based on specific subpopulations of people with disabilities. First, they exclude people with disabilities who report that they cannot work at all. Second, they use the population that reports a functional or ADL limitation, but not a work disability. These populations—in most of their specifications—represent less than one-half of the entire population of people with disabilities, based on a self-reported work limitation or any functional or ADL limitation.

The authors find that when people who are unable to work at all as a result of their disability are excluded from the sample of people with disabilities, there is no decline in employment. Moreover, when people who report a work limitation in addition to a functional or ADL limitation are excluded from the sample of people with disabilities (i.e., only those with a functional or ADL limitation but no work limitation are included), there is an increase in employment following the ADA.

One should not exclude individuals who say they cannot work as a result of their disability, however. Disability is not a medical condition, but rather the interaction of a medical condition with a person's environment. A person could report that "their health condition prevents them from working" because they did not receive reasonable accommodations or because they face discrimination. Therefore, unlike Kruse and Schur, I think it is incorrect to characterize individuals in this group as not being covered by the ADA because they are "not qualified" to work and, therefore, exclude them from analysis. In addition, excluding individuals with disabilities who do not work and who report that they are unable to work is essentially excluding the nonemployed—a major limitation in measuring the effect of the ADA on employment. Burkhauser and co-authors (Chapter 2) make a related point.

Nevertheless, the population who report a functional or ADL limitation, but not a work limitation, is an interesting one to study, and one that I examined in DeLeire (2001). These individuals do have health impairments that limit them in some way, but they self-report that their impairment does not limit the type or amount of work they can do. They are reporting that they are just as productive as they would be if they were not impaired, perhaps because they have already received a successful job accommodation or their impairment is irrelevant for their particular line of work.

Before extrapolating from the experiences under the ADA of this subsample of people with disabilities to those of people with disabilities as a whole, one should emphasize that the labor market experiences of this group are not typical. Even before the enactment of the ADA, people with functional or ADL limitations but no work limitations earned just 4 percent less than nondisabled individuals, controlling for observable characteristics such as experience and education, compared with almost 70 percent less for the remaining people with disabilities (DeLeire 2001).

According to Kruse and Schur (2001), individuals with any functional or ADL limitation but no work disability worked just 2.6 percent fewer weeks than nondisabled individuals in 1990, and worked 3.1 percent more weeks than nondisabled individuals in 1994. Although it is interesting and important to document that a significant subpopulation of people with disabilities earned just as much and worked just as much as people without disabilities even before the ADA was enacted, these were not and are not the typical experiences of a person with a disability. As has been documented in countless studies, including several in this volume, the low employment rates and low earnings of people with disabilities are problems that policymakers must address and that the ADA was intended to address.

A possible explanation for why employment rates increase for those who report a functional limitation and an ability to work is that members of this group do not require additional accommodations under the ADA. For example, DeLeire (2001) finds no wage gap for this group, suggesting that individuals with functional limitations but no work limitations require little in the way of accommodation. If so, employers would have little reason to avoid hiring them under the ADA. Alternatively, the ADA could be helping those workers with disabilities who are already employed and who have already received accommodation, and others with low accommodation costs, by providing them protection against unlawful terminations. However, the net effect of the ADA for individuals who are seeking employment and who require potentially expensive accommodations could be negative.

WHAT NEEDS TO BE DONE?

Economic studies have shown that antidiscrimination laws such as the Civil Rights Act of 1964 have reduced labor market discrimination, promoted integration of protected classes (i.e., blacks) into the labor force, and improved their labor earnings and economic well-being. However, economic theory does not unambiguously predict such success. Hence, the success of the Civil Rights Act does not assure that the ADA has achieved similar goals for working-aged people with disabilities.

This chapter argues that ADA's antidiscrimination and reasonable accommodation mandates have made workers with disabilities more expensive for employers to hire. This has had the unintended consequence of reducing their employment rate, rather than changing societal norms, reducing discrimination, and increasing their employment.

To achieve the goals of more fully integrating working-aged people into the labor force and reducing their dependence on disability-based transfers, it is important to understand why the ADA failed where the Civil Rights Act succeeded. More effort is needed in exploring why the negative incentives of the ADA outweighed the positive ones. One possibility is that, unlike the Civil Rights Act, the ADA requires potentially expensive accommodations for workers with disabilities. An exploration of the degree to which the costs of accommodating workers with disabilities deters hiring should be undertaken.

As Houtenville and Daly show (Chapter 3), there is great variation in the socioeconomic characteristics of working-aged people with disabilities, and there has been significant variation in employment rate experiences across subgroups during the 1990s. More work needs to be done to explain why some workers with disabilities fared better than others over this period, when the ADA was enforced. However, simply ignoring the losses for the majority of individuals with disabilities and focusing instead on the gains to the minority whose employment improved, as several authors in this volume choose to do, is not appropriate, either methodologically or from a policy perspective, if the reasons for the distinction between these classes relate to the policy under review. Nonetheless, it is important to show that for some subpopulations, employment improved during the 1990s. For example, my work suggests that individuals whose disability onset occurred as a result of a work-related injury did not suffer a reduction in their employment during the 1990s (DeLeire 2000b). Kruse and Schur, as discussed above, find that employment rates for some groups of people with disabilities did not fall during the 1990s. A recent paper by Carpenter (2002) finds that employment rates of individuals whose disability was related to obesity (to whom ADA coverage was extended under *Cook v. Rhode Island* in 1993) increased during this period. A more complete understanding of the reasons behind this variation in outcomes within the broader population with disabilities will help us design policies that better meet the ADA's goal of integrating people with disabilities into the labor force.

Notes

1. There are exceptions. Firms with 15 to 24 employees were not covered by the ADA until 1994. Also, in a 1993 federal court case, *Cook v. Rhode Island*, the ADA protected class was broadened to include workers with disabilities resulting from obesity (see Carpenter 2002).
2. In an unpublished paper, DeLeire (1997) also used the panel study of income dynamics to examine the impact of the ADA. Because the methods used and the findings were similar to those in DeLeire (2000b) and Acemoglu and Angrist (2001), they are not reported here.
3. It is still a challenge to distinguish the effects of disability laws from time trends, even with state variation in the timing of such laws. In an updated version of their study, Beegle and Stock (forthcoming) demonstrate this difficulty; one does not observe relative employment declines if one controls for disability specific time effects across states. These time effects reflect pre-existing trends for the 13 states which passed disability discrimination laws between 1980 and 1990, but may either reflect these trends or may reflect continued declines in relative employment resulting from the presence of disability discrimination laws for the 33 states that passed these laws between 1970 and 1980. In any case, the authors find declines in the relative earnings of people with disabilities regardless of whether these disability-specific time effects are controlled for.

References

Acemoglu, Daron, and Joshua Angrist. 2001. "Consequences of Employment Protection: The Case of the Americans with Disabilities Act." *Journal of Political Economy* 109(5): 915–956.

Americans with Disabilities Act. 1990. U.S. Code. Vol. 42, secs. 12101-213.

Beegle, Kathleen, and Wendy Stock. 2002. "The Labor Market Effects of Disability Discrimination Laws." Unpublished manuscript. Montana State University.

———. Forthcoming. "The Labor Market Effects of Disability Discrimination Laws." *Journal of Human Resources*.

Berkeley Planning Associates. 1982. *A Study of Accommodations Provided to Handicapped Employees by Federal Contractors: Final Report*. Washington, DC: U.S. Department of Labor, Employment Standards Administration.

Brown, Charles. 1984. "Black-White Earnings Ratios Since the Civil Rights Act of 1964: The Importance of Labor Market Dropouts." *Quarterly Journal of Economics* 99(1): 31–44.

Burkhauser, Richard. 1990. "Morality on the Cheap: The Americans with Disabilities Act." *Regulation* 13(2): 47–56.

Carpenter, Christopher. 2002. "The Impact of Employment Protection for Obese People." Unpublished manuscript. University of California, Berkeley.

Cook v. Rhode Island Department of Mental Health, 10F.2d 17, 2 AD 1476 (1st Cir. 1993).

DeLeire, Thomas. 1997. "The Wage and Employment Effects of the Americans with Disabilities Act." Unpublished Ph.D. dissertation. Stanford University.

———. 2000a. "The Unintended Consequences of the Americans with Disabilities Act." *Regulation* 23(1): 21–24.

———. 2000b. "The Wage and Employment Effects of the Americans with Disabilities Act." *Journal of Human Resources* 35(4): 693–715.

———. 2001. "Changes in Wage Discrimination against People with Disabilities: 1984–1993." *Journal of Human Resources* 36(1): 144–158.

Donohue, John, and James Heckman. 1991. "Continuous versus Episodic Change: The Impact of Affirmative Action and Civil Rights Policy on the Economic Status of Blacks." *Journal of Economic Literature* 29(4): 1603–1644.

Epstein, Richard A. 1992. *Forbidden Grounds*. Cambridge: Harvard University Press.

Freeman, Richard B. 1973. "Changes in the Labor Market for Black Americans." *Brookings Papers on Economic Activity* 1973(1): 67–120.

Job Accommodation Network. 1999. *Accommodation Benefit / Cost Data*. Available at: <http://janweb.icdi.wvu.edu/media/stats/BenCosts0799.html>. (Accessed: December 19, 2002.)

Kruse, Doug, and Lisa Schur. 2001. "Employment of People with Disabilities Following the ADA." Unpublished manuscript, Rutgers University.

Olson, Walter K. 1997. *The Excuse Factory*. New York: Free Press.

Reville, Robert T., and Robert F. Schoeni. 2002. "The Fraction of Disability Caused at Work." Unpublished manuscript. RAND, Santa Monica, CA.

Rosen, Sherwin. 1991. "Disability Accommodation and the Labor Market." In *Disability and Work*, Carolyn L. Weaver, ed. Washington DC: AEI Press, pp. 18–30.

Toyota Motor Mfg., KY., Inc. v. Williams, 224 F.3d 840 (Supreme Court).

U.S. Equal Employment Opportunity Commission (EEOC). 2001. *Equal Employment Opportunity Commission Americans with Disabilities Act of 1990 (ADA) Charges*. Available at: <http://www.eeoc.gov/stats/ada.html>. (Accessed: December 19, 2002.)

Weaver, Carolyn L. 1991. "Incentives versus Controls in Federal Disability Policy." In *Disability and Work,* Carolyn L. Weaver, ed. Washington DC: AEI Press, pp. 3–17.

8
Does the Definition Affect the Outcome?

Employment Trends under Alternative Measures of Disability

Douglas Kruse
Lisa Schur
Rutgers University

Has the Americans with Disabilities Act (ADA) affected the employment of people with disabilities? It was passed with hopes that outlawing disability discrimination and increasing workplace accessibility would increase job opportunities for people with disabilities, much as the Civil Rights Act improved economic outcomes for African-Americans (Donohue and Heckman 1991). As is often the case when new employment legislation is passed, detractors claimed that the legislation was an unwarranted encroachment on employer autonomy and would be counterproductive, possibly hurting the employment of people with disabilities owing to employer fears over lawsuits, concerns about accommodation costs, and lost productivity from complicated regulations (Epstein 1992; Janofsky 1993; Vassel 1994).

Assessing the economic effects of legislation is a tricky matter because there are always other economic or policy changes that may be affecting the outcomes of interest. Furthermore, the legislation itself often has accompanying effects that need to be taken into account (e.g., induced entry into the target population, or interactions with other programs). Assessing the effects of disability legislation is especially complicated given the difficult issue of defining the target population. The ADA offers protections to individuals with a "physical or mental impairment that substantially limits one or more . . . major life activities," or a record of such an impairment or being regarded as having such an impairment. In addition, Title I of the ADA offers protection against employment discrimination only to those who are "qualified" for employment positions. Ideally, all of these criteria would be measured in a straightforward way with little room for ambiguity, allowing employers, employees, job applicants, and researchers to know who is entitled to ADA protection. This, of course, is not the case—there is considerable room for disagreement over who has a disability. The disability population includes, at a minimum, nearly 8 million Americans who have been certified by the federal government as eligible for disability income (although most of these people would not be covered by Title I of the ADA because they are not "qualified" for employment). As an upper bound estimate, 53 million Americans of all ages report some type of functional or activity limitation or mental condition (McNeil 2001); when limited to those of working age, about one-fifth of Americans have an impairment or chronic health condition (see Burkhauser and coauthors, Chapter 2), although it is likely that many of these impairments do not "substantially" limit major life activities, preventing individuals from meeting the ADA criteria for coverage. Although ambiguity persists over who is covered, the courts have increasingly narrowed the ADA's definition and restricted the number of people who are covered (Lee 2003).

With such uncertainty over who is covered, how can the effects of the ADA be assessed? Given the evolution in the courts of the ADA's definition of disability, it is not surprising that there is no data set with a consistent measure of ADA coverage. Most studies have used the work-limitation measure, which is based on a reported health condition "limiting the kind or amount of work" one can do. An advantage of this question is that it has been asked in a fairly consistent way over time, in the National Health Interview Survey (NHIS), Current Population Survey (CPS), and Survey of Income and Program Participation (SIPP). Using this measure, DeLeire (2000) and Acemoglu and Angrist (2001) find a decline in employment following the ADA of people reporting work limitations, and Burkhauser and coauthors (Chapter 2) find that employment either decreased (among men) or was roughly stable (among women) throughout the 1990s. As will be discussed below, however, this measure has several limitations in assessing ADA coverage and the effects of the act, particularly in that it does not cover limitations in major life activities other than working, and in that it may be answered differently over time.

Study of the ADA's effects is also greatly complicated by the role of public disability income, and of possible differential effects of business cycles on people with disabilities. The Social Security Disability Insurance (SSDI) and Supplemental Security Income (SSI) programs provide income and health insurance to people with disabilities who are unable to engage in "substantial gainful activity," and the potential loss of such income and health insurance gives recipients strong disincentives for returning to work. The SSDI program expanded substantially in the 1990s, very likely playing a major role in the employment of people with disabilities (see Chapter 10). Researchers in this area have recognized that studies of the ADA must take into account the rise in disability income recipiency in the 1990s. In addition, workers with disabilities may have an especially procyclical employment pattern, being the first to be laid off in a recession and the last to be hired when conditions improve. This pattern holds true for African-Americans, another group with a history of substantial employment discrimination (Cherry and Rodgers 2000). The ADA was passed just before the economy entered a recession; therefore, any differential effects of recessions provide another competing explanation for the employment patterns of people with disabilities following the ADA.

In this chapter, we first review problems in defining and measuring disability, focusing on potential problems with the work limitation measure that has been the basis for most studies. The second section describes alternative measures of disability and what they reveal about compositional changes among those reporting work limitations at the time the ADA was being implemented. The third section reviews results from studies of employment of people with disabilities, looking at both employment patterns at the time of the ADA's implementation, and employment trends since that time. These results highlight the importance not only of disability income but also the reported ability to work; therefore, we briefly summarize efforts to validate that measure. Following a discussion of whether the employment of people with disabilities is procyclical, we present our conclusions.

PROBLEMS IN DEFINING AND MEASURING DISABILITY

No matter how disability is measured, people with disabilities are found to have low employment rates (whether using measures of work limitation, or specific impairments and other activity limitations) (see Burkhauser and coauthors, Chapter 2). In addition, longitudinal estimates show that employment declines after disability onset (see, for example, Burkhauser and Daly 1996; Krueger and Kruse 1995). These low employment rates are because of both high reservation wages associated with many disabilities (reflecting time and energy constraints, and the availability of disability income that is conditioned on not working), and low market wages, which can reflect both reduced productivity and employer discrimination. Reflecting some of these same factors, people with disabilities who do obtain employment are much more likely than nondisabled workers to be in contingent and part-time jobs, which are associated with low levels of pay and job security (Schur and Kruse 2001).

A main goal of the ADA was to expand job opportunities and raise the market wage for people with disabilities by eliminating the discriminatory component of wage differentials and increasing workplace accessibility. In addition, the substantial public attention to the ADA may have created an incentive for some employers to hire people with disabilities as a way of generating goodwill among customers and employees by showcasing a commitment to the goals of the ADA (which would tend to favor hiring people with very visible disabilities, such as wheelchair users). As noted, however, it has been argued that the law may have had a negative effect on employer demand for people with disabilities because of concerns about the costs of accommodations and potential lawsuits from terminated employees (Acemoglu and Angrist 2001). Acemoglu and Angrist also point out that fear of litigation could lead employers to hire more people with disabilities to avoid potential lawsuits from rejected applicants; however, layoffs are more likely to lead to lawsuits given that employees generally have greater stakes in existing jobs than do applicants in potential jobs.

A major problem in studying the employment impact of the ADA, as noted, is determining who is covered. The ADA protects only those who have a "physical or mental impairment that substantially limits one or more . . . major life activities," or have a record of, or are regarded as having, such an impairment. Whether an impairment does, in fact, substantially limit a major life activity depends not only on the definitions of "substantially" and "major life activity," but also on the person's environment and other characteristics. For example, in one major life activity—working—a wheelchair user may not be limited when working in an accessible law office, but would be substantially limited when performing many manual jobs or working in an inaccessible office. Also, a college graduate with a physical impairment may have many job opportunities, while a high school dropout with the same impairment may be substantially limited in finding employment. The variety of impairments, skills, personal characteristics, and environments in which major life activities are performed, and the question of whether limitations are "substantial," leave room for considerable ambiguity over who has a disability. Estimating employment trends is further complicated by the fact that disability is a fairly fluid category; not only do people's medical conditions deteriorate or improve, but environments and life circumstances change in ways that affect disability. For example, the increased availability of corrective technologies can mitigate the effects of an impairment, and increased workplace accessibility can remove barriers to working. Such developments may cause people to no longer consider themselves to be substantially limited in a major life activity.

The Work-Limitation Measure

The debate over the employment effects of the ADA has centered on results that use the work-limitation measure, based on a self-report of whether one has a health condition that prevents work or limits the kind or amount of work one can do. Burkhauser and coauthors (Chapter 2) show that about 8 percent of the working-aged population (varying between 7.3 percent and 8.9 percent) reported a work limitation in the March CPS during the past two decades. The employment levels of people reporting work limitations, relative to those without work limitations, declined around the time that the ADA passed and took effect, according to three studies. These studies use a difference-in-differences approach, which examines the difference over time in the difference in employment levels between working-aged people with and without work limitations, controlling for other personal characteristics. DeLeire (2000), using the work disability supplements of SIPP, finds a decline in the relative employment of people reporting a work limitation in 1990, which he attributes to the ADA given that it was passed and signed in July 1990. Acemoglu and Angrist (2001) use the work-limitation measure from the March CPS, and Kruse and Schur (2003) use this measure from the disability supplements of the SIPP, both finding that the relative average weeks worked by people reporting work limitations dropped in 1993, after the ADA took full effect in July 1992.

One difficulty that immediately presents itself in efforts to attribute these declines to the ADA is the difference in timing. Contrary to DeLeire, Acemoglu and Angrist find no relative decline in 1990 when the ADA was passed, while contrary to Acemoglu and Angrist, DeLeire's results indicate no significant decline in 1992 when the ADA was taking effect.[1] Although it is debatable whether the most relevant date for any changes in employer behavior should be the date of the act's passage or the full implementation date two years later, the disparate findings between the studies raise the question of whether the ADA was, in fact, playing a role in these results, or whether other idiosyncrasies of the measure and data sets were at work.

Apart from this, there are four potential difficulties in using the work-limitation measure to study employment trends, as we discuss in Kruse and Schur (2003). Each of these concerns changes in the composition of people reporting work limitations that may cause the measured trends to be misleading. First, Kirchner (1996) notes that the work-limitation measure may be affected by the success of the ADA in making workplaces more accessible, as people who obtain jobs would no longer say they are limited in the ability to work. This could particularly affect people with less severe disabilities, who are easily accommodated, removing them from the group reporting work limitations and leaving a higher concentration of people with more severe disabilities and employment problems in that population. This could cause measured employment of people with work limitations to decline as the ADA increases job opportunities among people with disabilities (measured broadly).

A second potential problem noted by Kirchner (1996), Schwochau and Blanck (2000, 2003), and Blanck, Schwochau, and Song (Chapter

9) is that many people reporting a work limitation may not be covered by Title I of the ADA, either because they are not qualified for work even with accommodations (removing them from Title I protection), or because they have impairments that do not substantially limit a major life activity (removing them from any ADA protection). Just as it may be overinclusive, the work-limitation measure is also underinclusive of ADA coverage in that it does not capture impairments that do not limit work but substantially limit other major life activities. The ADA's Title I protections may be just as (or even more) important for these individuals, who may face employer discrimination even though they believe their health conditions do not limit their capability for work. (It is noteworthy that many plaintiffs sue employers claiming nonwork disabilities, although it is possible they would still report having a work limitation on a survey.) The over- and underinclusiveness of the work-limitation measure makes it a very unreliable indicator both of the ADA-covered population at any one point in time and of changes in that population over time.

A third potential problem of the work-limitation measure concerns the historical stigma attached to disability (see, for example, U.S. Commission on Civil Rights 1983), which may cause people to underreport any type of disability. One of the major goals of the disability rights movement has been to eradicate the stigma attached to disability (Hahn 1985, 1987). Many policies and programs designed for people with disabilities over the years have been based on a paternalistic, charitable model, creating a "social construction" of people with disabilities as second-class citizens (Schneider and Ingram 1993). The rights-based approach of the ADA may have contributed to a new social construction of disability that reflects greater respect for and influence of people with disabilities. Perceptions of increased social acceptability and rights may have encouraged more people to identify themselves as having a disability following the ADA. It is plausible that this effect was greatest among those who were suffering the greatest stigma owing to a lack of employment, and thus increased reports of work limitation would lower the associated employment rate.

This last example relates to a fourth potential problem of the work-limitation measure, which is that the likelihood of reporting a disability may be intertwined with employment status (Currie and Madrian 1999). Among people with the same medical conditions, functional limitations, and other characteristics, those who are not employed may be more likely to say they have a work limitation as a way of justifying their lack of employment (referred to as the "justification hypothesis") (Baker et al. 2001). Those who obtain jobs may become less likely to cite a work limitation even if they have the same impairments and medical conditions as before (and, in fact, it can be argued that a work limitation may rightfully disappear when a new job provides an environment in which the impairment or condition no longer limits one's ability to work). It is especially likely that employment status will affect subjective measures, such as a self-reported work limitation. Baker et al. (2001) have found this to be true even for objective measures; their comparison of self-reports and medical records found that objective health problems are more likely to be overreported by nonemployed than by employed individuals.

As a result of these potential limitations, there could be compositional changes among people reporting work limitations that cause misleading trends in employment. Compositional changes are especially likely when the size of the group reporting work limitations is changing, but are very possible even when the size is stable. For example, a decrease in reports of work limitation owing to increased workplace accessibility may be counterbalanced by an increase in reports among nonemployed people who no longer fear the stigma of disability and would like to assert ADA coverage. Tight labor markets may also cause a decrease in reports of work limitation among people who gain jobs, but an increase in reports of work limitation among those who lose jobs and other nonemployed people in an effort to save face and to justify their lack of employment. This could result in an apparent worsening employment trend among those reporting work limitation even as labor markets grow tighter and more people with disabilities (measured broadly) are obtaining jobs.

Alternative Measures of Disability

What about other measures of disability? Are there measures that follow the ADA definition more closely, enabling a more reliable assessment of employment trends in the ADA-covered population? The Equal Employment Opportunity Commission (EEOC) regulations say that the "major life activities" referred to in the ADA's disability definition include functions such as "caring for oneself, performing manual tasks, walking, seeing, hearing, speaking, breathing, learning, and working." Although it is arguable whether several of these limitations are properly seen as disabilities, the EEOC regulations indicate that such limitations are likely to be used by judges as criteria for ADA coverage.[2] Also, it is undoubtedly true that each of these limitations would be regarded by most members of society as constituting a disability, given that most facilities and societal institutions have been set up assuming these basic abilities.

In Kruse and Schur (2003), we explore alternative disability definitions, using data from the SIPP disability supplements to create 14 measures of disability. The three basic measures are of work limitation, any functional or activity of daily living (ADL) limitation, and severe functional or ADL limitations. Functional and ADL limitations encompass difficulties in basic physical functions (seeing, hearing, walking, speaking, climbing stairs, and lifting and carrying) or in performing basic daily activities (such as eating, taking a bath, or getting around inside or outside the home). Severe limitations represent an inability to do a functional activity at all, or a need for help with an ADL.[3] The functional and ADL measures arguably capture ADA coverage better than the work-limitation measure given the wording of the EEOC regulations. (Again, it should be noted that Title I of the ADA is relevant to people with any type of disability given that employers may discriminate on the basis of a nonwork disability. It should also be noted that measuring those with any functional or ADL limitation is probably overinclusive, because some of these individuals would not be substantially limited.)

Because Title I of the ADA only protects people who are "qualified" for employment, we created three additional measures of disability that subtracted those who claim an inability to work from the three basic measures. Similarly, because disability income can play a major role in discouraging employment, we created three measures that subtracted disability income recipients from the three basic measures. Finally, we created three measures that subtracted both disability income recipients and those claiming an inability to work from the three basic measures (leaving people who may be considered "available to work," as described by McNeil 2000), and an additional two measures that subtracted all people reporting work limitations from the functional and ADL limitation measures. These 14 measures are listed in Table 8.1.

As discussed, changes over time in the work limitation measure may reflect a variety of factors that cause estimated employment trends to be misleading. Similar factors may be at work on other measures as well; for example, if the stigma associated with disability has decreased, people may become more likely to report functional limitations. Also, just as lack of employment may increase the likelihood of reporting a work limitation, a perceived lack of good employment prospects may increase the likelihood of reporting that one's health

Table 8.1 Alternative Disability Measures and Employment Change

Disability measure	Percent of working-aged population, 1991	Employment rate change as ADA implemented, 1991–93
1. Work limitation	10.4	–
2. Any functional/ADL limitations	12.6	0
3. Severe functional/ADL limitations	4.5	0
No SSI/SSDI and has:		
4. Work limitation	8.5	0
5. Any functional/ADL limitations	10.9	+
6. Severe functional/ADL limitations	3.3	+
Health condition does not prevent working and has:		
7. Work limitation	6.4	0
8. Any functional/ADL limitations	9.2	+
9. Severe functional/ADL limitations	2.3	+
No SSI/SSDI, health condition does not prevent working, and has:		
10. Work limitation	6.1	0
11. Any functional/ADL limitations	8.9	+
12. Severe functional/ADL limitations	2.1	+
No work limitation and has:		
13. Any functional/ADL limitations	5.4	+
14. Severe functional/ADL limitations	1.1	+

NOTE: – and + are negative and positive changes significant at the 95% level; 0 indicates change is not significant at 95% level. Results are based on difference-in-difference comparisons of employment changes among people without disabilities, controlling for demographic characteristics.

condition makes one unable to work. Although all the measures may be subject to such influences, those based on disability income and functional and ADL limitations are probably less affected because these measures are less subjective than judgments of whether a health condition limits or prevents work.

Arguments could be made in favor of any of these measures; however, we suggest that the best measure of ADA coverage is the one including those who have severe functional and ADL limitations (who are most likely to be substantially limited in a major life activity) and who claim an ability to work (thereby being qualified for employment). Some validation of the ability-to-work measure—concluding that it does measure changes in underlying health conditions that affect ability to work—will be reported (based on Chapter 6). Using these data, we address the questions of whether there was compositional change among those reporting work limitations during the early 1990s, and whether employment trends differed by definition of disability as the ADA was being implemented.

Were There Compositional Changes among Those Reporting Work Limitations?

Did the population reporting work limitations change in some important ways as the ADA was being passed and implemented? If so, could these compositional changes account for the relative decrease in employment of people reporting work limitations at the time?

Both DeLeire (1997) and Acemoglu and Angrist (2001) discount compositional changes as an explanation for their results. DeLeire examines whether there was increased reporting of impairments that are difficult to detect following the ADA and found that, among people reporting work limitations, there was no relative increase in reported mental impairments and bad backs (which are often difficult to verify). A compositional change is, however, suggested in his finding of a relative decrease in the most easily detected impairments (missing limbs, paralysis, blindness, and deafness); in addition, it is very possible that compositional changes may have occurred along other dimensions or in the severity of impairments reported. Acemoglu and Angrist use a matched CPS sample between March 1993 and March 1994, examining changes in reported weeks worked in the previous year to determine whether employment fell among a constant sample reporting work limitations in both years. Because the previous years were 1992 and 1993, a decline could be taken as evidence that employment declined as a result of implementation of the ADA. There is a serious problem with this method, however, in the disjuncture between the timing of the measurement of disability and of employment. There will naturally be a decline in average weeks worked using this method, given that some of the individuals reporting a work limitation in March 1993 and 1994 would have worked many weeks in 1992 prior to the onset of a disability. We find that 42 percent of workers who report a work limitation in a CPS March supplement during the 1992–2000 period did not report one in the previous March, indicating that many of the people reporting a work limitation spent much of the prior year without a disability (although measurement error also plays some role in accounting for the change in reports). As a result of this methodological problem, there is a decline in employment for all matched samples in the 1981–2000 period, with no larger decline in 1992–1993 than in other years.[4] Therefore, this method does not rule out the possibility that compositional change was a factor in the relative employment decline of people reporting work limitations.

Comparing reports of work limitation with reports of functional and ADL limitations, we find evidence strongly suggesting that compositional change was occurring among those reporting work limitations during the time the ADA was being implemented. The SIPP data show a significant increase in the percentage of people reporting work limitations between 1991 and 1993 (from 10.4 percent to 10.9 percent, consistent with CPS data reported by Burkhauser and coauthors in Chapter 2) (Kruse and Schur 2003). More important, among those reporting a work limitation, there was a statistically significant 2.8 percentage point increase in those reporting any of the measured functional or ADL limitations (from 68.5 percent to 71.2 percent), and a statistically significant 5.2 percentage point increase in those reporting severe functional or ADL limitations (from 32.7 percent to 37.9 percent). The increases were particularly strong in the percentages reporting they had difficulty walking one-fourth of a mile (4.5 percentage point increase) and those having difficulty with ADLs inside the home (7.2 percentage point increase), but the increases were also positive and significant across many other conditions.

It is also important to note that the 0.5 percentage point increase in reports of work limitation among all working-aged people was more than accounted for by significant increases in reports of receiving disability income (0.8 percentage point increase) and being prevented from working by one's health condition (0.6 percentage point increase). The increase in disability income was spurred by changes in SSDI program rules in the early 1990s, which relaxed the eligibility criteria and the use of continuing disability reviews (see Chapter 10). In addition, there was a significant tightening of eligibility for workers' compensation in many states (Spieler and Burton 1998), which probably led many workers who were injured on the job to apply for SSDI income, claiming an inability to work in order to qualify.

These findings clearly suggest compositional changes among people with work limitations in the direction of more severe limitations, reflecting either objectively more severe conditions or an increased willingness to cite such conditions to justify obtaining disability income or ADA coverage.

ESTIMATES OF EMPLOYMENT PATTERNS AND TRENDS

Employment Patterns as the ADA Was Being Implemented

Do these apparent compositional changes among people reporting work limitations make a difference in estimated employment trends? Using the work limitation measure in SIPP data, we find, as do Acemoglu and Angrist (2001), that there was a relative employment decline for people reporting work limitations between 1991 and 1993 (Kruse and Schur 2003). We also find, however, that there were nonsignificant, relative employment increases among people reporting any, or severe, functional and ADL limitations, and among people reporting work limitations but an ability to work. The basic results are summarized in Table 8.1.

Most strikingly, there were significant increases over this period in the relative employment of people with any or severe functional and ADL limitations who do not receive disability income, and among those with functional and ADL limitations reporting they were able to work. Among those covered by the arguably best measure of ADA protection (having severe functional and ADL limitations that do not prevent work), there is a strongly significant, relative employment increase of 5.9 percentage points in weeks worked from 1991 to 1993. It is unlikely that compositional shifts accounted for this result, given that there was no change in the percentage of the population covered by this measure. In addition, although Burkhauser and coauthors (Chapter 2) show that overall employment trends were more negative for men than for women with disabilities during the 1990s, we found that the pattern of results among our alternative disability measures during the 1991–1993 period was quite similar for men and women with disabilities.

The difference in employment trends among disability measures raises strong caution about the conclusions of DeLeire (2000) and Acemoglu and Angrist (2001) that the ADA caused a decline in employment among people with disabilities. The relative employment decline among people reporting work limitations at that time is fully accounted for by an increase in reports of disability income and an inability to work. DeLeire and Acemoglu and Angrist attempt to discount the role of disability income in various ways, but they do not address the issue of inability to work or other disability definitions.[5]

Employment Trends, Disability Income, and Reported Ability to Work During the 1990s

There was no overall employment growth among people with disabilities in the 1990s, according to Burkhauser and coauthors in Chapter 2, using several basic disability measures—work limitation, housework limitation, and other activity limitations.[6] The potential importance of disability income is indicated by the evidence of Bound and Waidmann (2000, p. 1) (see Goodman and Waidmann, Chapter 10, for a review), which "suggests that the expansion of [disability income] during the 1990s played a central role in accounting for the decline in the employment of the disabled during this decade."[7]

The lack of employment growth among people with disabilities in the 1990s is also statistically linked to increased reports of inability to work. Consistent with our findings, Kaye (Chapter 6), Burkhauser and coauthors (Chapter 2), and Louis Harris and Associates (2000) found increased employment among people who report work limitations with an ability to work. An important question is how to interpret reports of inability to work. Do these reports indicate severe impairments that truly make productive work impossible, or do they reflect the social environment? As examples of the latter possibility, people may have an incentive to report an inability to work to qualify for disability income, or may in fact be qualified for jobs but cannot obtain them owing to employers' fears of lawsuits or reluctance to make accommodations. If this is the case, the rising employment rates among those reporting work limitations with an ability to work may be very misleading, as those who cannot obtain jobs become more likely to say they are unable to work.

Some validation of the inability-to-work measure is provided by Kaye (Chapter 6), who analyzes National Health Interview Survey data. He finds that those reporting an inability to work, relative to those reporting a work limitation with an ability to work, are more than six times as likely to report poor health (31.4 percent compared with 5.4 percent), and have much higher averages of restricted activity days, bed days, need for personal assistance, and functional limitations. In addition, he finds that the growth in reports of inability to work during the 1990s is strongly linked to measures of worsened health and increases in functional limitations and need for help with daily activities. Just as the social environment can influence reports of work limitation (as discussed earlier), it is also possible that it influences self-reports of overall health, restricted activity days, need for assistance, and functional limitations. This evidence nonetheless provides some support for the idea that self-reported inability to work indicates a high likelihood of not being "qualified" for employment (i.e., unable to perform a job even with reasonable accommodations), such that one is not protected by Title I of the ADA. Consequently, the rising employment rate among people with disabilities who are able to work may represent real improvement in job opportunities among the ADA-covered population.

Employment Patterns across the Business Cycle

Apart from definitional issues and disability income, do business cycles help explain employment patterns among people with disabilities? Business cycles may, as noted, have different effects on the employment of people with disabilities, much as they seem to have different effects for African-Americans. Burkhauser et al. (2002) find that this may have been true in the 1980s, but not the 1990s. Among men with work limitations, employment decreased more in the 1980–1982 downturn, and increased more in the 1982–1989 growth period, than among their nondisabled counterparts. In the 1990s, however, their relative employment decreased in the 1989–1992 downturn, but continued to be worse in the 1992–1999 growth period. We explored different sensitivity to business cycles by using variation among states in labor market tightness, and found mixed results, which are sensitive to the issue of disability income. Measuring labor market tightness using state unemployment rates during the 1995–1999 period, we found that a 1 percentage point change in the unemployment rate is linked with only a 0.07 percentage point change in employment of people reporting work limitations, compared with changes of 0.98 percentage points among those without work limitations, and 1.83 percentage points among African-Americans in general (Schur and Kruse 2001). When excluding disability income recipients, however, the change is 1.18 percentage points among people with work limitations, indicating that they have somewhat greater sensitivity to labor market conditions than do people without disabilities. Similarly, in our examination of employment patterns in the early 1990s during a recession, people with disabilities appeared to have especially low employment levels when state unemployment rates were higher, indicating greater sensitivity to the 1991–1992 recession. This was particularly true among those with any functional or ADL limitation who did not receive disability income (Kruse and Schur 2003). Accounting for this extra sensitivity, however, made no noteworthy difference in the estimated overall employment trends of people with disabilities as the ADA was being implemented (there remained a 1991–1993 decline in employment of people reporting work limitations, and an increase in employment using several of the functional and ADL limitation measures). Also, the booming economy of the late 1990s did not appear to increase the overall employment of people with disabilities, countering the idea that their employment is especially aided by a tight labor market (Burkhauser et al. 2002, Chapter 2).[8] Disability income and reported ability to work remain more important factors in helping explain the overall employment trends among people with disabilities.

CONCLUSION

Assessing the employment effects of the ADA is very difficult because of problems in defining who is covered, and accounting for the effects of disability income. Although studies using the work-limitation measure appear to show worsening employment among people with disabilities since the ADA was passed, this measure has been criticized on a number of grounds, both for being over- and underinclusive of those covered by the ADA, and for being particularly sensitive to compositional changes related to employment status.

Disability measures do, in fact, make a difference in estimated employment patterns surrounding the implementation of the ADA, interjecting a strong caveat in interpretations that the ADA is harming employment of people with disabilities. In contrast to findings of decreased employment of people reporting work limitations as the ADA was being implemented, we found increased employment among people reporting functional and ADL limitations who do not receive disability income, or who report the ability to work. The greatest increase occurred among those who are arguably most likely to be covered by the ADA: people with severe functional or ADL limitations who report the ability to work. The employment declines among people reporting work limitations are linked to several indicators of compositional change in this population.

Disability income and the reported ability to work are important factors not only in estimates of employment patterns at the time the ADA was implemented, but also in subsequent employment trends during the 1990s. The rise in disability income recipiency statistically accounts for the declining overall employment of people reporting work limitations, and employment rates have actually improved among people with disabilities who report the ability to work. Although it is possible that the ADA played a negative role here (causing decreased job opportunities that led to increases in disability income recipiency or reports of inability to work), this interpretation is weakened by the fact that changed program rules were instrumental in the growth of recipiency during the 1990s (see Chapter 10), and by the validation of the inability-to-work measure based on other indicators of increased disability severity (see Chapter 6).

These results indicate a need for continual attention to disability definitions and measures. The current efforts of the federal government to develop better measures of disability should provide a stronger basis for estimating disability employment trends and the effects of public policies (Kruse and Hale 2003). Apart from these efforts, it would be valuable for researchers to closely examine what leads people to report work limitations, and whether these people are likely to be covered by the ADA. In particular, following the research of Baker et al. (2001), it would be useful to examine how employment status affects reports of work limitation as well as of more objective measures; that disability measures are intertwined with employment status creates thorny problems in estimating employment rates and trends among people with disabilities. An ideal research project would follow individuals over time, independently recording medical conditions and impairments, as well as self-reported work limitation status and ability to work, as people gain and lose jobs and labor markets become tighter and looser. Although such an ideal study is unlikely, there may be many ways in which creative researchers can disentangle employment status and disability measures. Such research would greatly help us better understand the effects of labor market conditions, public policies, and workplace accommodations on the employment prospects of people with disabilities, and lead to informed public policies that can enhance their employment prospects.

Notes

This chapter is based on a presentation at the Employment and Disability Policy Institute sponsored by Cornell University in Washington, DC, in October 2001. Helpful comments have been made by David Stapleton and Richard Burkhauser.

1. The SIPP disability supplements did not include the work-limitation measure before 1990; therefore, we were unable to assess changes before and after 1990 in our study.
2. Difficulty with several of these activities, such as walking, seeing, and hearing, would be regarded as functional limitations rather than disabilities in most disabil-

ity models (Altman 2001). In the standard paradigm, functional limitations become disabilities only if they cause a limitation in a major life activity, such as working, education, family life, or recreation.

3. Burkhauser and coauthors (Chapter 2) present an "other activities" limitation measure using SIPP data on difficulties with activities of daily living, but do not include difficulties in walking, seeing, hearing, speaking, climbing stairs, and lifting or carrying.

4. Based on computations by the authors and Andrew Houtenville, Cornell University.

5. DeLeire (2000) notes that disability income recipiency did not change substantially between 1990 and 1991 when he found a relative employment drop, while Acemoglu and Angrist (2001) using several methods to address this issue, conclude that it does not account for the 1992–1993 employment drop among workers aged 21–39, although it may help account for the drop among men aged 40–58 (there was no significant drop among women aged 40–58). Acemoglu and Angrist also employ other methods to examine the effects of the ADA, including comparisons by firm size (given that firms with fewer than 15 employees are not covered by the ADA) and between states with different levels of ADA charge rates. The 1992–1993 drop in employment was slightly, but nonsignificantly, larger in medium-sized (24–99) than small (>15) firms among men aged 21–39, but the apparent employment drop was just as large in small firms relative to medium-sized and large firms for women aged 21–39 and men aged 40–58, which provides little support for the idea that ADA protections were causing declining employment. Similarly, there is only weak evidence from state-level EEOC employer charge rates, which are not significantly associated with the relative employment levels of any of these groups when accounting for the endogeneity of charge rates using instrumental variables.

6. We analyze data only during the 1990–1994 period when the ADA was being implemented because the placement of the work-limitation and ability-to-work questions in the 1997 and 1999 SIPP disability supplements was changed in a way that seriously threatens comparisons. In these latter years, the two questions were asked in the core survey following questions about employment status, rather than in the disability supplement following questions about functional and ADL limitations. Perhaps not surprisingly, the reports of work limitation fell by more than 2 percentage points from 1994 to 1999, while CPS data show reports of work limitation to have slightly increased over this period (Burkhauser et al., Chapter 2). This strongly indicates that answers to the SIPP work-limitation question were affected by the placement of the question. Estimates using the 1997 and 1999 SIPP data show a dramatic decline in measured percentage of weeks worked among people reporting work limitations in these two years relative to the 1990–1994 results. Although this may reflect some employment decline among those reporting work limitations when using a consistent measure, it is also apparent that the changed question placement made a big difference, presumably because the stigma of reporting a work limitation (particularly among employed people)

was lower after they had just revealed functional/ADL limitations in the 1990–1994 supplements. The very different prevalence and effect sizes stemming from the changed placement of the work-limitation question show that estimates of disability employment trends are sensitive to the wording and context of the disability measure, often confounding the measures with employment status.

7. In addition, Autor and Duggan (2003) find that the expansion of public disability income in the 1990s lowered the overall unemployment rate by two-thirds of a percentage point, as low-skilled people were more likely to gain disability income and take themselves out of the labor market.

8. As noted earlier, reports of work limitation are likely to be intertwined with employment status, and it is even possible that a booming economy will lead to a lower measured employment rate of people reporting work limitations, as newly employed people no longer report work limitations, and job losers and other nonemployed people become more likely to cite work limitations to justify their lack of employment.

References

Acemoglu, Daron, and Joshua Angrist. 2001. "Consequences of Employment Protection? The Case of the Americans with Disabilities Act." *Journal of Political Economy* 109 (October): 915–957.

Altman, Barbara. 2001. "Disability Definitions, Models, Classification Schemes, and Applications." In *Handbook of Disability Studies*, Gary Albrecht, Katherine Seelman, and Michael Bury, eds. Thousand Oaks, CA: Sage Publications, pp. 97–122.

Autor, David, and Mark Duggan. 2003. "The Rise in Disability Recipiency and the Decline in Unemployment." *Quarterly Journal of Economics* 118(1): 157–205.

Baker, Michael, Mark Stabile, and Catherine Deri. 2001. "What Do Self-reported, Objective Measures of Health Measure?" NBER working paper no. 8419. Cambridge, MA: National Bureau of Economic Research.

Bound, John, and Timothy Waidmann. 2000. "Accounting for Recent Declines in Employment Rates among the Working-Age Disabled." Research report 00-460. Ann Arbor, MI: Population Studies Center, Institute for Social Research, University of Michigan.

Burkhauser, Richard V., and Mary C. Daly. 1996. "Employment and Economic Well-Being Following the Onset of a Disability." In *Disability, Work, and Cash Benefits*, Jerry L. Mashaw, Virginia P. Reno, Richard V. Burkhauser, and Monroe Berkowitz, eds. Kalamazoo, MI: W.E. Upjohn Institute for Employment Research, pp. 59–101.

Burkhauser, Richard V., Mary C. Daly, Andrew J. Houtenville, and Nigar Nargis. 2002. "Self-Reported Work Limitation Data: What They Can and Cannot Tell Us." Unpublished manuscript. San Francisco: Economic Research Department, Federal Reserve Bank of San Francisco.

Cherry, Robert, and William Rodgers, eds. 2000. *Prosperity for All? The Economic Boom and African Americans.* New York: Russell Sage Foundation.

Currie, Janet, and B.C. Madrian. 1999. "Health, Health Insurance, and the Labor Market." In *Handbook of Labor Economics,* vol. 3C, Orley Ashenfelter and David Card, eds. New York and Oxford: Elsevier Science, North-Holland, pp. 3309–3416.

DeLeire, Thomas. 1997. "The Wage and Employment Effects of the Americans with Disabilities Act." Unpublished Ph.D. dissertation, Stanford University.

———. 2000. "The Wage and Employment Effects of the Americans with Disabilities Act." *Journal of Human Resources* 35(4): 693–715.

Donohue, John, and James Heckman. 1991. "Continuous versus Episodic Change: The Impact of Affirmative Action and Civil Rights Policy on the Economic Status of Blacks." *Journal of Economic Literature* 29(4): 1603–1644.

Epstein, R.A. 1992. *Forbidden Grounds: The Case against Employment Discrimination Laws.* Cambridge, MA: Harvard University Press.

Hahn, Harlan. 1985. "Toward a Politics of Disability: Definitions, Disciplines, and Policies." *The Social Science Journal* 22: 87–105.

———. 1987. "Civil Rights for Disabled Americans: The Foundation of a Political Agenda." In *Images of the Disabled, Disabling Images*, Alan Gartner and Tom Joe, eds. New York: Praeger Publishers, pp.181–202.

Janofsky, J.C. 1993. "Whoever Wrote ADA Regs Never Ran a Business." *Wall Street Journal,* March 15, p. A-12.

Kirchner, Corinne. 1996. "Looking Under the Street Lamp: Inappropriate Uses of Measures Just Because They Are There." *Journal of Disability Policy Studies* 7(1): 77–90.

Krueger, Alan, and Douglas Kruse. 1995. "Disability, Employment, and Earnings in the Dawn of the Computer Age." NBER working paper no. 5302. Cambridge, MA: National Bureau of Economic Research.

Kruse, Douglas, and Thomas Hale. 2003. "Disability and Employment: Symposium Introduction." *Industrial Relations* 42(1): 1–10.

Kruse, Douglas, and Lisa Schur. 2003. "Employment of People with Disabilities Following the ADA." *Industrial Relations* 42(1): 31–66.

Lee, Barbara. 2003. "A Decade of the Americans with Disabilities Act: Judicial Outcomes and Unresolved Problems." *Industrial Relations* 42(1): 11–30.

Louis Harris and Associates. 2000. *2000 N.O.D./Harris Survey of Americans with Disabilities*. New York: Louis Harris and Associates.

McNeil, John. 2000. "Employment, Earnings, and Disability." Presented at Western Economic Assoc. International Annual Meeting. Available at: <www.census.gov/hhes/www/disability.html.> Washington, DC: U.S. Bureau of the Census.

———. 2001. "Americans with Disabilities, 1997." *Current Population Reports*, P70-73. Washington, DC: U.S. Bureau of the Census.

Schneider, Anne, and Helen Ingram. 1993. "Social Construction of Target Populations: Implications for Politics and Policy." *American Political Science Review* 87(2): 334–347.

Schur, Lisa, and Douglas Kruse. 2001. "Nonstandard Work Arrangements and Disability Income." Champagne, IL: University of Illinois at Urbana-Champaign, Disability Research Institute.

Schwochau, Susan, and Peter David Blanck. 2000. "The Economics of the Americans with Disabilities Act, Part 3: Does the ADA Disable the Disabled?" *Berkeley Journal of Labor and Employment Law* 21 (Winter): 271–313.

———. 2003. "Does the ADA Disable the Disabled? More Comments." *Industrial Relations* 42(1): 67–77.

Spieler, Emily, and John F. Burton, Jr. 1998. "Compensation for Disabled Workers: Workers' Compensation." In *New Approaches to Disability in the Workplace*, Terry Thomason, John F. Burton, Jr., and Douglas E. Hyatt, eds. Ithaca, NY: Cornell University Press, pp. 205–244.

U.S. Commission on Civil Rights. 1983. *Accommodating the Spectrum of Individual Abilities*. Clearinghouse publication no. 81. Washington, DC: U.S. Commission on Civil Rights.

Vassel, R.A. 1994. "The Americans with Disabilities Act: The Cost, Uncertainty, and Inefficiency." *Journal of Law and Commerce* 13: 397–411.

9
Is It Time to Declare the ADA a Failed Law?

Peter Blanck
University of Iowa, College of Law

Susan Schwochau
Dickinson Wright PLLC

Chen Song
Resolution Economics LLC

By some accounts, the track record of the Americans with Disabilities Act (ADA) appears dismal for improving the employment opportunities of individuals with disabilities. Several empirical studies report that, compared with employment of persons without disabilities, the employment of individuals with work disabilities has declined since the early 1990s (see Burkhauser and coauthors, Chapter 2). The authors of some studies conclude that the ADA has failed to achieve its goals and is, in fact, the likely cause of the employment declines (see DeLeire, Chapter 7).

In contrast to these studies, other research finds improvements in employment since the ADA was passed (see, e.g., Kaye 2002; Kruse and Schur 2003). This research defines "disability" outside the context of a self-reported work limitation, focusing as well on individuals' self-reported limitations in the activities of daily living. Some findings suggest those most likely to be considered disabled under the ADA—individuals with severe functional limitations who were not prevented from working—saw improvements in their relative employment between 1991 and 1993.

One clear difference between the research streams mentioned is how the authors define and measure disability. Of course, how researchers identify individuals with disabilities is fundamental to whether their findings on the ADA's effects are informative. To be sure, the ADA does not guarantee employment to individuals with disabilities. The law does not protect all individuals with disabilities from discrimination, nor does it provide all individuals with disabilities a right to reasonable workplace accommodations. Because it is possible that the ADA has had different effects on various subgroups within the population of individuals with disabilities, identifying and analyzing those subgroups becomes crucial to understanding the ADA's effects (Zwerling et al. 2003).

Obviously then, the answer to the question whether the ADA is causally related to the employment rates of individuals with disabilities requires close analysis of the *legally defined* group that the ADA is meant to protect—the "ADA qualified disabled." This analysis has not yet been done. We conclude that because studies claiming to show support for predictions derived from economic theory both exclude in their measure of disability individuals protected by the ADA and include those not protected by that law, claims that the ADA is a failed law are unfounded and premature.

In the next section, we describe two of the predominant economic models of discrimination and how the ADA's employment provisions may be tied to those models' forms of discriminatory behavior. We follow with an overview of the predominant economic models from which predictions are derived that the ADA will result in declines in the employment of individuals with disabilities. We also offer a description of studies that purport to provide support for those predictions.

In the final section, we discuss reasons why existing research does not allow for the conclusion that the ADA is, in effect, a well intentioned, but bad law, focusing on definitions and measures of disability used in that research. We identify questions and issues that extant research leaves unaddressed, in part to encourage researchers to continue to develop models that will enable assessment of the ADA's influences, and in part to caution policymakers of the limitations of the research and theories on which that research may be based.

We make no claim to resolving debates regarding either the ADA's employment effects or who should bear the costs associated with removing barriers to employment faced by those with disabilities. Instead, we identify questions, the answers to which will inform policymakers about whether any further or different steps in regard to the

ADA (aside from other policy issues) should be taken to reduce unemployment or labor market withdrawal of those with disabilities.

ECONOMIC MODELS OF EMPLOYMENT DISCRIMINATION

A fundamental purpose of the ADA is to reduce discrimination against those with disabilities and those perceived to have disabilities, and thereby enhance their employment opportunities. Whether the ADA has been successful, therefore, can be seen as a question of whether discrimination has been reduced, or whether the employment opportunities and wages of those it covers have improved over time. To date, the focus has been on the latter question, although recent efforts have been directed also to the former (see, e.g., DeLeire 2001).

In discussing discrimination generally, it is useful to distinguish between discriminatory behavior that occurs prior to an individual's entry into the labor market and discrimination faced after entry. Individuals with disabilities (whether covered by the ADA or not) who face premarket discrimination in education, for example, may obtain less, or inferior, education compared with individuals without disabilities (for a review, see Schwochau and Blanck 2000). Information from the Current Population Survey (CPS) indicates that individuals with disabilities have far lower levels of education than individuals without disabilities.

Postmarket discrimination occurs after entry into the labor market. This phenomenon may cause individuals with disabilities (again covered by the ADA or not) to receive lower wages and face fewer occupational choices, despite having equivalent amounts of human capital as individuals without disabilities. Postmarket discrimination also may influence individuals' decisions prior to entry into the labor market. If discrimination by employers, customers, or coworkers significantly reduces the wage received or the probability of obtaining employment, those individuals may choose not to invest in substantial amounts of education given that the return on this investment will be minimal.

Becker's Model of Postmarket Discrimination

Gary Becker has shown that one form of postmarket discrimination originates when employers display a "taste for discrimination" (Becker 1971). If individuals in the "majority" and "minority" groups are perfect substitutes for one another (i.e., they are equally productive), tastes for discrimination reflect employer perceptions that the cost of hiring those in the minority group is greater than the cost of hiring those in the majority group. This is "irrational discrimination"; there is no productivity-related reason for treating individuals differently. To hire an individual from the minority group, an employer with tastes for discrimination must deduct from that individual's wages the added cost associated with the "distaste" of including that person in the workforce. As a result, Becker argues, wages received by those in the minority group will be lower than the wages of the majority, despite productivity.

One prediction derived from Becker's model is that in perfectly competitive markets, tastes for discrimination are minimized in the long run if the firm's unit cost in production does not vary with output. So long as one firm exists with no discriminatory policy, market wages of the minority group should be equal to those of the majority group. This prediction relies on the profit-maximizing behavior of employers, which leads them to capitalize on the lower market wage of the minority group and hire only (qualified) individuals in that group. Because the nondiscriminating employer's costs would be lower as it expands its production, discriminatory employers would eventually be driven out of the market and one uniform wage would result.

Statistical Discrimination

Another model of discrimination relies on notions of employer decision-making in the context of imperfect information (see, e.g., Baldwin 2000). For example, when an employer seeks to hire a worker, the employer does not have full information regarding that individual's future productivity. Such information, moreover, is costly to obtain. Either the employer must spend resources on obtaining better information regarding the candidates prior to hiring, or hire from the pool of candidates (incurring the costs of doing so) and observe productivity thereafter. As a result, it is in the employer's interest to identify relatively cheap "indicators" of productivity (e.g., the number of years of education). These indicators may be identified through perceptions of past experiences with employees (e.g., workers with a college degree tend to have higher productivity than those without such a degree) or through other sources of information. The indicators used, if accurate predictors of productivity, lead to efficient decisions, on average.

Statistical discrimination results when employers use an indicator such as a disability to make predictions about individuals; that is, perceptions of the average employee with disabilities are used to make predictions about one individual (i.e., a stereotype) (Aigner and Cain 1977). Even if accurate, on average, the indicator may be inaccurate when applied to a particular individual. Thus, although an employer's past experiences with individuals with a particular applicant's disability has led the employer to equate that disability with higher costs owing to missed days of work, the particular applicant may not have a history of missing work any more than a nondisabled employee. The employer's rejection of the applicant, based on its perception of individuals with similar disabilities, would be statistical discrimination.

If the indicators used are inaccurate predictors (on average or for a particular individual), costly mistakes can be made. Discrimination (i.e., the differential treatment of equally productive individuals) may persist over time under this model because employers who act consistently with their perceptions may trigger responses from applicants and employees that confirm those perceptions (Blanck 1993; Schwochau and Blanck 2000).

Theories of Discrimination and ADA Title I

Both of the theories of discrimination identify how employer perceptions cause some individuals to be treated differently from others. Under Becker's theory, the crucial perceptions are wholly inaccurate; under theories of statistical discrimination, perceptions based on a stereotype are uniformly applied to all individuals within the group, again with the result that equally productive individuals may be treated differently.

Leaving aside for the moment the ADA's requirement that a firm make reasonable accommodations for its qualified disabled workers

(42 U.S.C. § 12112(b)(5)(A)), the law tracks the standard definition of discrimination: the differential treatment of those who are equally productive. Under ADA Title I (the law's employment provisions), qualified individuals with disabilities are to be treated the same as nondisabled individuals with respect to pay and employment decisions.

People falling within the second and third prongs of the ADA's disability definition—those with a past history of disability and those who are regarded as having a disability—may be closest to Becker's requirement of perfect substitutes given that they have no actual impairment that would affect their productivity (although some of these individuals certainly have impairments that do not rise to the level of disability as defined under the law's first prong). These individuals also may be the victims of wholly inaccurate stereotypes. The ADA's emphasis on a case-by-case analysis of whether individuals with disabilities are qualified for the job they seek likewise is consistent with an attempt to restrict the use of stereotypes (29 C.F.R. p. 1630 App.).

The addition of language requiring that employers make reasonable accommodations for disabled workers is a departure from standard definitions of economic discrimination (Krenek 1994; Burgdorf 1997). "Economic discrimination" typically refers to individuals with equal productivity not being rewarded with equal compensation (Aigner and Cain 1977). The implicit assumption underlying this definition is that compensation should reflect the entire "marginal cost" of employing the individual. The standard definition of economic discrimination does not take explicit account of employer expenditures directed at making at least some workers more productive than they would be in the employer's "pre-accommodation" work environment. Indeed, the technology used to produce a product or provide a service generally is taken as given in those models, as is the capital necessary to operate a facility (Schartz, Schartz, and Blanck 2002). Becker's assumption of equal productivity implicitly holds technology constant; an individual hired randomly from either the majority or minority group would be equally productive within the firm.

The ADA's accommodation provisions (42 U.S.C. § 12112(b)(5)) mandate that an employer provide benefits to (or take steps in response to the peculiar needs of) particular individuals in order that they may perform the essential functions of the job (Jolls 2000; Kelman 2001).

As such, the ADA imposes on employers a potential additional cost of hiring (or retaining) an individual with disabilities.

The ADA's definition of discrimination, which identifies both a failure to pay the same wage (broadly defined to include all forms of pay) and to make reasonable accommodations, therefore departs significantly from the prior concept of economic discrimination. Not only are individuals with disabilities entitled to be treated the same as others, but they have, by virtue of the ADA, a claim to resources that others are *perceived* not to have. The requirement that employers incur expenses to allow individuals to be productive on the job represents a focal point of economists' criticisms of the ADA (see, e.g., Oi 1991), and stands as a central element of public policy debates about the proper confines of the ADA's protection.

EFFECT OF ADA TITLE I

Pre-ADA Operation of Labor Markets

Because the ADA focuses on decisions made by firms, most models developed to assess its effects deal primarily with predicting the law's effects on labor demand (Rosen 1991). Standard economic models predict that firms combine labor and capital in ways dependent on the relative prices of the inputs to production (i.e., the price of labor and the price of capital), the demand for the product or service, and the technology available (see Ehrenberg and Smith 1991 for a general description of standard models of labor markets). In theory, a change in any one of these factors triggers responses that move the firm toward a new equilibrium. Thus, an increase in the price of labor may lead to a reduction in the amount of labor demanded, and in the long run, a change in the amount of capital used by the firm. Similarly, a change in technology (e.g., the invention of a more efficient machine, or new use of the Internet) may yield changes in both the amounts of labor and capital demanded.

The simplest of economic models assumes that all labor and all capital is identical; that is, each and every unit of labor offered is the same, and each and every unit of available capital is the same. These models also assume that all parties (individuals and firms) have perfect information and are perfectly mobile. They generally yield the expectation that a firm chooses the most profitable and efficient means of production, given the state of technology, demand for the product, and relative cost of capital and labor. If capital and customer buying behavior is fixed, the amount of labor demanded is a function of its costs, with the expectation that a firm will stop demanding additional labor at the point at which the marginal revenue product of the last unit of labor (the added revenue brought to the firm given what is produced) equals its marginal cost (the added cost associated with that unit). The demand for labor in a particular market is the number of workers (or units of labor) all the firms in the market would demand at given wage rates.

Thus, under the standard model, employers will hire an individual only if the marginal benefits of doing so at least equal the marginal costs. This is true for individuals with and without disabilities. Employers will incur additional employment costs (such as those associated with medical insurance, life insurance, and pensions) only if the benefits of doing so outweigh the costs of providing the added benefit. If, for instance, employers find that providing fringe benefits makes attracting and retaining employees cheaper and productivity greater, then they will supply fringe benefits (Weaver 1991).

In general, disabilities are expected (assumed) to reduce productivity on a particular job, or to restrict the individual's ability to be productive in a variety of jobs (Weaver 1991). Because profits only may be realized if pay given to employees is less than or equal to what the sale of their output yields, the pay of disabled workers will be less than nondisabled workers because individuals with disabilities are less productive.

In the absence of the ADA (or any other comparable legislation), the standard models suggest that an employer will provide a disabled individual with tools or a particular work setting if doing so is profitable (Rosen 1991; Weaver 1991). As in the case of fringe benefits, however, disabled individuals provided with such accommodations should expect their wages to be reduced accordingly. If no such reduction occurs, the net gain to the employer of hiring the disabled individual who needs accommodation will be less than the net gain of hiring an individual needing no such accommodation, and the employer will maximize profits by hiring the nondisabled individual (Donohue

1994). Under such a model of the employer's decision-making, the chronic unemployment of the disabled is owing, in part, to the fact that they cost more, causing employers to prefer nondisabled individuals (Weaver 1991).

Thus, disabled persons' wages are predicted to be less than the wages of nondisabled individuals for two primary reasons: lower productivity, and/or increased marginal costs owing to accommodation. Individuals with disabilities for whom the lower pay does not justify participation in the labor market (for instance, those for whom the expected wage is sufficiently low that the costs of labor market participation exceed its benefits) will drop out of that market or will never enter it.

Note that these principles yield the conclusion that the ADA is not necessary. Employers do, without the ADA, what is economically rational and efficient. Disabled individuals are hired, with or without accommodations, to the extent that doing so is profitable (Barnard 1992). They are matched to jobs throughout the economy in ways that maximize firm profits and individual utility.

Introduction of ADA Title I

With this picture of employer behavior as a starting point, predictions of the effects of the ADA focus on what the law forces employers to do differently (Barnard 1992). Viewing the pre-ADA environment as efficient overall, it should be no surprise that the ADA is predicted to lead to inefficiencies and to the imposition of costs on all, or virtually all, affected. Economists have tended to focus on the effects of two of the ADA's provisions: the "equal pay" requirement, and the reasonable accommodation requirement. Each is often predicted to have deleterious effects on individuals with and without disabilities, on firms, and on the economy (Weaver 1991).

The provision of the ADA that prohibits employers from discriminating against qualified individuals with disabilities with regard to compensation and other benefits of employment (42 U.S.C. § 12112(a) (1994)) is viewed as forcing employers to pay more for the labor of such individuals than they otherwise would. There are two components to the "otherwise would" aspect of this prediction. First, to the extent that two individuals, one disabled who needs no accommodation and one not disabled, are in fact equally productive, requiring that the employer pay each the same wage for the same work when it would not otherwise do so is an attempt to reduce discrimination of the type described by Becker (1971).

Second, although such a requirement may hasten the exit of discriminating employers from the market,[1] one may predict that forcing an employer to pay more than it otherwise would for labor perceived to be less beneficial will lead to a reduction in the employment of those individuals in the short run, as fewer persons are demanded in the face of increasing wages (Donohue 1986). This effect of the "equal pay" provision is not, however, the focal point of most discussions.

Instead, modelers tend to assume that the ADA-qualified individual with a disability is less productive than a nondisabled person without accommodation.[2] Given the assumed difference in productivity, the equal pay provision is seen as forcing employers to pay individuals with disabilities more than they are "worth" to the firm. The increase in pay is predicted to cost the employment of at least some individuals with disabilities, as fewer such persons are demanded at the higher wage (Acemoglu and Angrist 2001). Higher wages also would attract more individuals with disabilities to the labor market (Jolls 2000). However, because fewer persons are demanded, these new entrants will be unemployed.

The ADA's requirement that employers pay qualified disabled and nondisabled individuals the same compensation for the same work also has been said to harm all persons with disabilities in their attempts to compete in the labor market (see, e.g., Olson 1997). Epstein (1992), who advocates allowing labor markets to operate entirely free of governmental restraint, notes that laws such as the ADA, the Fair Labor Standards Act, and the Occupational Safety and Health Act, restrict a disabled person's ability to underbid their nondisabled competition by forbidding negotiation between the individual and the firm as to the conditions of employment.

Instead, so the argument goes, individuals with disabilities should be free to, for example, "waiv[e] their right to health and life insurance" and thereby "improve their prospects of getting a job without having to call into play the coercive power of the state" (Epstein 1992, p. 493; see also Friedland and Evans 1996). A variant of this argument focuses on the inability of individuals with disabilities to negotiate a reduction in their wage to compensate for the increase in the so-called "firing costs" realized by the employer when an individual with disabilities sues to challenge the employer's decision to fire the worker (Acemoglu and Angrist 2001).

The ADA's requirement that firms make "reasonable accommodations" for their employees and applicants with disabilities also is predicted to have negative effects on disabled individuals. By increasing productivity and removing the obligation to personally pay for accommodations, the ADA's accommodation requirement, Rosen (1991) argues, should increase the number of individuals with disabilities who seek employment at any wage. However, the increase in the supply of labor could well reduce the wages of nondisabled individuals, who will drop out of the labor market as a result (Rosen 1991).

On the demand side, as noted, the ADA is predicted to force firms to pay more than an individual is "worth" to the firm, and to do so at every wage. In short, the ADA's accommodation mandate is expected to force employers to provide accommodations they otherwise would not provide (i.e., those that are not profitable) and the ADA's equal pay requirement prevents the added expense to be transferred to the employee through a lower wage (Rosen 1991).

Thus, if employers comply with the ADA, the added labor costs associated with accommodating qualified employees with disabilities will result in lower demand for workers with disabilities (Weaver 1991; DeLeire 1997). Overall, negative effects on the employment of individuals with disabilities are predicted to be greater as the costs of accommodation increase. To the extent that firms make accommodations that do not yield net gains in profitability, the dollars spent in accommodations could be spent in areas having greater returns. Therefore, the expenditures represent a cost to society in the form of misspent resources. If employers compensate for the increase in labor costs by raising product prices, customers bear the ultimate burden (Weaver 1991).

In summary, the dominant economic models predict that, all else equal, employment of otherwise qualified individuals with disabilities will decline as a result of the ADA's implementation. This effect stems from the increased wages that must be paid to covered workers, and to the increased costs associated with mandated accommodations. This is not to suggest that employment of some subgroups within the disabled population will not increase, only that the number of people without jobs will be greater than the number gaining (or retaining) them (Weaver 1991).

Enforcement and Accommodation Mandates

Jolls (2000) departs from the standard models above in examining the effects of accommodation mandates on individuals with and without disabilities under different enforcement scenarios. Using a model that builds on the work of Summers (1989), Jolls demonstrates that whether qualified disabled or nondisabled individuals realize employment losses as a result of the ADA's accommodation requirement depends on the degree to which binding legal restrictions exist on employers' ability to pay different wages to individuals with and without disabilities (to have "wage differentials"), and to provide different employment opportunities to individuals with and without disabilities ("employment differentials").

In Jolls's model, the supply of labor of individuals with disabilities will increase at every wage by the value of the accommodations, on average, to disabled individuals. Employers' demand will fall at every wage by the cost of the accommodations to employers. The effect of these changes depends on whether the value of accommodations to individuals with disabilities exceeds the cost to employers, and on the degree to which legal restrictions are binding. Thus, where neither the pay nor the employment restriction is binding, relative wages are predicted to fall as a result of the costs of accommodating individuals with disabilities, and relative employment will rise, fall, or remain unchanged if the value of the accommodations to individuals with disabilities exceeds, is less than, or is equal to their cost to employers, respectively.

Jolls concludes that where only the ADA's equal pay requirement is binding on employers, individuals with disabilities can be expected to suffer relative employment losses and either flat or increased relative wages, and those workers will shoulder most of the costs of the accommodations. Where both restrictions are binding, she predicts that the relative wage of qualified individuals with disabilities is likely to rise or stay the same and the relative employment of those individuals will rise, in part because nondisabled individuals will shoulder some of the costs of the accommodation mandate.

Empirical Tests of the Predicted Effects of ADA Title I

Given the relative newness of the law, rigorous empirical tests of the ADA's effects on relative employment and wages are understandably few in number. The research streams of Acemoglu and Angrist (2001), and of DeLeire (1997, 2000, 2001) have received particular attention. Both streams are based on economic theory and attempt to assess the ADA's effects on the employment and wages of individuals with disabilities.

DeLeire (1997, 2000) employs seven panels of the Survey of Income and Program Participation (SIPP) data for men aged 18–64 to examine whether the ADA has affected the likelihood of employment and wages of individuals with disabilities. Acemoglu and Angrist (2001) use CPS data for men and women aged 21–58 for the 1988–1997 period to extend the standard economic model by incorporating concepts of hiring and firing costs. Within that model, hiring costs arise as firms reject applicants with disabilities, who with some probability challenge those decisions in court. Firing costs are incurred when employers terminate or lay off employees with disabilities, who with some probability challenge those decisions.

Because firms can avoid hiring costs by employing individuals with disabilities, Acemoglu and Angrist's model allows the prediction that the ADA may lead to increases in employment levels. The probability of detecting discrimination on the basis of disability, however, is much smaller for applicants than for current employees, and thus firing costs and the costs of accommodation together are likely to exceed hiring costs avoided. As a result, the law is predicted to reduce employment (hiring). The "equal pay" provision is expected to increase wages for disabled employees, creating involuntary unemployment.

Both sets of studies report findings that the authors contend support their models' general predictions (Acemoglu and Angrist 2001; DeLeire 1997). DeLeire (2000) summarizes his findings as indicating that the ADA has led to a 7.2 percent decrease in the probability of employment of individuals with disabilities, but to no change in relative wages. He attributes these findings to the costs to employers of complying with the ADA's accommodation requirement. Acemoglu and Angrist conclude that the ADA has had substantial disemployment effects on men with disabilities aged 21–58, and on women with disabilities under age 40. They find no clear evidence of a post–ADA change in relative wages of individuals with disabilities. Acemoglu and Angrist attribute their employment findings, in part, to the accommodation costs of the ADA and, in part, to the firing costs the law imposes.

Both sets of studies include a consideration of the effects of federal disability receipts. DeLeire does so by assessing possible changes in the level of benefits available, in eligibility, and in denial rates (DeLeire 1997, 2000). Reviewing data on these variables, he concludes that federal benefits are not likely to explain his results. DeLeire (1997) also considers the possible effects of the 1990–1991 recession. Using Panel Study of Income Dynamics (PSID) data, he investigates whether pre–1990 recessions led to widening gaps between employment rates of individuals with and without disabilities. Because those rates did not significantly widen in prior recessions, DeLeire concludes that the widening rates he finds after January 1991 are not from the downturn in late 1990 and early 1991.

Acemoglu and Angrist (2001) test whether receipt of federal disability benefits explain their findings. Because overall results allow for the same conclusions regarding fewer weeks worked by individuals with disabilities, the authors conclude that receipt of federal benefits does not account for most of the decline in employment found (Bound and Waidmann 2000). Having eliminated this alternative explanation, Acemoglu and Angrist, like DeLeire, conclude that the ADA has negatively affected individuals' with disabilities relative employment.

DOES THE ADA EXACERBATE THE EMPLOYMENT PROBLEM?

With authors using large national samples attributing to the ADA their findings of lower employment among disabled individuals, are we to conclude that the law has failed in achieving its goals? We believe the answer to this question is no for a number of reasons, the primary one of which is related to the definition and measure of disability employed in these studies.

Definition and Measurement of Disability

The definition of disability and the identification of those in that protected category obviously are critical to research addressing the labor market behavior of individuals with disabilities. If the purpose of the research is to examine labor demand and supply of those with disabilities relative to those without disabilities, using a measure that asks individuals whether they are "disabled," whether they have an impairment, or whether they have a disability that prevents or limits the work they can perform may be sufficient (but see Hale 2001; Kaye 2002).[3] The emphasis of this line of research could be on the general labor market experiences of individuals with disabilities, with an eye toward providing policymakers with an assessment of labor market barriers faced by those individuals.

However, such an approach, taken without regard to the ADA's language, is unlikely to yield valid conclusions if the goal is to assess the effects of that law (Hale 2001; Schwochau and Blanck 2000, 2003). Even if the relative employment of people with work disabilities fell during the 1990s (Burkhauser and coauthors, Chapter 2), the findings of DeLeire and Acemoglu and Angrist do not answer the question of whether the ADA has been effective since it was enacted because little to no consideration is given to whether the individuals captured by the selected measure of disability are, in fact, those covered by the ADA's provisions.

Those covered by the ADA's protections are people who have a substantial limitation on a major daily life activity who are "qualified"—that is, those who with or without reasonable accommodation can perform essential job functions (Blanck 1998). Thus, the ADA does not provide coverage to all persons with physical or mental limitations, or even to all persons with "disabilities" as the ADA defines that term. The law divides individuals with impairments into three groups: individuals with impairments that do not substantially limit a major life activity; individuals with substantial limitations who are qualified; and individuals with substantial limitations who are not qualified. The law provides protection to those in the second group, but not to those in the first or third group (Lee 1997).

Neither DeLeire nor Acemoglu and Angrist distinguish between these three groups. Instead, DeLeire divides his sample into disabled and nondisabled categories based on a question that asks respondents whether they have a physical, mental, or other health condition that limits the kind or amount of work that they can do (DeLeire 1997, 2000). This is the standard SIPP-based item used in tabulating broad indicators of labor force participation of individuals with self-reported, work-limiting impairments (McNeil 1993).

The item Acemoglu and Angrist use to categorize the disabled comes from the CPS March Income Supplement and asks whether individuals "have a health problem or disability which prevents [them] from working or which limits the kind and the amount of work [they] can do." Both definitions are narrower than the ADA's definition of disability in that they focus on impairments that limit working activity (rather than any major life activity). Interestingly, the U.S. Supreme Court has raised questions whether working is even a major life activity for purposes of the law (see *Toyota Motor Manufacturing, Inc. v. Williams* 2002).

The potential difference between the ADA's "major life activity" definition and the SIPP's work-disability definition is reflected in items in the SIPP survey that focus on functional and other limitations. From 1991 to 1992, 52.0 percent of individuals aged 21–64 with a disability were reported as employed, whereas only 42.5 percent of those with a work disability were employed (McNeil 1993). Although individuals with work disabilities were included in the overall disability category, the difference in figures suggests that at least some of those answering that they did not have a work activity limitation also indicated that they were limited in other areas (see also Kruse and Schur 2003).

Comparable figures for 1994–1995 were 52.4 percent (disabled) and 43.3 percent (work disability) (U.S. Census Bureau 2000) (see Burkhauser and coauthors, Chapter 2, for additional information regarding the employment rates of individuals with disabilities using alternative definitions of disability and alternative data sets). Unless individuals reporting themselves as disabled, but not as having a work disability, are those who would be considered without a substantial limitation under the ADA, the difference in the figures raises the possibility that some individuals who have substantial limitations on major life activities other than working were miscategorized as not disabled (Baldwin, Zeager, and Flacco 1994).

Within the category of individuals with disabilities, a problem arises when individuals who clearly are not qualified under the ADA are included (42 U.S.C. § 12111(8) (1994)). For example, DeLeire and Acemoglu and Angrist's disabled category includes those persons whose impairments prevent them from working at all (presumably, even with attempted accommodation). Individuals whose disabilities prevent them from working are considered not qualified, and therefore do not receive the protection of the ADA (see *Duckett v. Dunlop Tire Corp.* 1997). Information from the SIPP data for 1991–1992 suggests that 42.1 percent of individuals aged 16–64 with work disabilities were prevented from working (McNeil 1993). Because the studies rely on comparisons of the disabled and the nondisabled, including in the "disabled" category individuals who cannot work at all would depress coefficients associated with disability and make differences more likely to be found (Mashaw and Reno 1996).

Further, changes over time in the proportion of individuals within the disabled category who were unable to work would have implications for empirical results. For instance, increases in relative size over the period of interest of the "prevented from working" subgroup would over time increase the likelihood of finding significant differences between the disabled and those not disabled. Acemoglu and Angrist (2001) and DeLeire (1997) recognize that, as a percentage of the population, the number of disabled individuals increased during the time periods under investigation.

What those researchers do not consider, however, is evidence suggesting that the percentage of those with work disabilities who are unable to work also increased during the period of interest (Kaye 1998, 2002; Kaye et al. 1996; McNeil 1997; Burkhauser and coauthors, Chapter 2). The increase in the percentage of those unable to work has been greatest for individuals between the ages of 18 and 44, although a general trend upward is discernible for older workers (Kaye 1998, 2002).[4]

What a Difference a Definition Makes

Research conducted by Kruse and Schur (2003) demonstrates the potential usefulness of not only focusing on individuals with work disabilities, but also examining indicators of functional limitations on other life activities. Using SIPP data, Kruse and Schur tested variables measuring work disability (the same measure used by DeLeire), functional limitations or limitations on activities of daily living, and severe functional limitations or severe limitations on activities of daily living. In combination with other information, Kruse and Schur examined relative employment of individuals in those categories, and assessed relative employment of individuals who did not receive Supplemental Security Income (SSI) or Social Security Disability Insurance (SSDI) payments; indicated that their health condition did not prevent them from working; and indicated that they had functional limitations but did not have a work disability.

Kruse and Schur's findings with respect to those reporting a work disability were in line with DeLeire and Acemoglu and Angrist—the employment prospects of those individuals worsened after the ADA was passed. However, other results suggested that, by 1993 and 1994, the relative employment of individuals who had functional limitations or limitations on activities of daily living, but no work disability, improved. Some findings suggested that those most likely to be considered disabled under the ADA—individuals with severe functional limitations who were not prevented from working—saw improvements in their relative employment between 1991 and 1993. The findings reported by Kruse and Schur demonstrate, generally, that conclusions about the relative employment of individuals with disabilities depend very much on the how the disabled are identified (Kaye 2002; Stern 1989; Stoddard et al. 1998).

Policy Implications and Suggestions for Future Research

If unacceptably large numbers of individuals with disabilities are without jobs, will a law such as the ADA (or even an amended ADA) bring about enhanced employment? Or, will such a law only make employment more difficult for all individuals with disabilities to find and to keep? Do we need a law like the ADA, or should we, as some have urged (e.g., Epstein 1992), rely on market forces to sort those with disabilities into jobs?

Criticism of the ADA, at least as interpreted by the U.S. Supreme Court, is not restricted to those who see the law as unnecessary. Some fault the ADA's definition of disability as unduly restrictive and advocate that those with any limitation on a major life activity should be covered rather than merely those with a substantial limitation (see, e.g., Lee 2003). Amendment of the ADA is possible (but perhaps not politically feasible) to bring into the scope of the ADA a larger (but unknown) percentage of individuals with disabilities. Will such amendment worsen the existing employment problem?

The standard economic model would suggest "yes," and thus amendment or case law interpretation to broaden the ADA's coverage will only add to the problem. Broadening the coverage of the ADA will increase the number of possible legal challenges and may increase the success rate of ADA litigants (particularly those who will be able to pass the "disabled" threshold hurdle). This would be predicted to increase the employer's hiring costs and firing costs associated with ADA litigation (Acemoglu and Angrist 2001).

Expanding the scope of the definition of disability also will increase the number of individuals to whom employers will have accommodation obligations. To the extent that firing costs and the costs of accommodation are greater than the hiring subsidies, economic theory would predict that the net effect will be to increase the costs of employing workers with disabilities, and to reduce the wages and employment of individuals with disabilities (Acemoglu and Angrist 2001). Thus, applying the standard competitive model would predict that the employment of individuals with disabilities will decline further if the ADA's definition of disability is broadened.

Yet, determining whether a broader definition of disability will, in fact, have the deleterious effects predicted by economic theory will require that we learn more than we currently know about who reports they have a disability and why those individuals are, or are not, employed. We are far from knowing enough about the labor market experiences of individuals with disabilities to determine that the ADA should be amended, repealed, or more strictly enforced.

We simply cannot say why it is that individuals with work disabilities continue to face barriers to employment. Is it because of the

ADA's accommodation mandate, as DeLeire and Acemoglu and Angrist suggest? Is it because of premarket decisions of individuals? Or, is it because of other forces operating separately from the ADA, such as barriers to adequate and affordable health insurance or to economic disincentives in federal benefit programs (Blanck and Schartz 2001). Without the why, informed decisions regarding appropriate policy cannot be made.

Measurement issues

Getting to the why requires that researchers grapple with myriad issues surrounding the who—that is, how is "disability" to be measured and what are the characteristics of individuals captured by the measure selected. The study of individuals with disabilities brings numerous complications that do not exist in a study of individuals of different gender or races. Individuals' limitations differ in nature, severity, and age at onset. An individual's ability to work may vary over time because of the episodic nature of particular impairments (Silverstein 2002). Certain conditions may worsen with time, or fluctuate between severe and manageable (see generally Brief for Petitioner, *US Airways v. Barnett* 2001; Blanck et al. 2002).[5]

In addition, many work-related impairments, for example, carpel tunnel or back injury, require an individualized assessment. Because symptoms vary widely from person to person (*Toyota Motor Manufacturing, Inc. v. Williams* 2002), assumptions regarding disability status cannot be made from impairments individuals may state they have. Even creating a measure that is based on what may be called "objective" accommodation criteria—for example, the need for particular devices or products (a TTY telecomm device; voice-recognition software) or the need for assistance of another person to accomplish a particular task—may not yield what appear to be consistent answers over time (Berven and Blanck 1998).

Further complicating matters is that the ADA's definition of disability—"a physical or mental condition that substantially limits a major life activity"—is subject to varied interpretations by courts, policymakers, employers, and persons with disabilities. Critics of the ADA have noted the ambiguities within the law's provisions, identifying myriad difficulties associated with determining who falls into the ADA's definition of disabled (Weaver 1991; Barnard 1992). What is "a major life activity" under the ADA? What constitutes a "substantial limitation" on a major life activity?

The answer to these questions is not obvious, and an answer today may be in need of revision tomorrow. In 1999, contrary to prior interpretations of the ADA, the U.S. Supreme Court decided that factors that mitigate an individual's impairment—such as prosthetic devices or blood pressure medication—are to be considered in defining whether that person's impairment is substantially limiting for purposes of the ADA (*Sutton v. United Airlines, Inc.* 1999). In 2002, the Supreme Court concluded further that an individual is substantially limited in performing manual tasks for purposes of the ADA only if the impairment prevents or severely limits that individual from activities that are central to daily life (*Toyota Motor Manufacturing, Inc. v. Williams* 2002).

From Kruse and Hale's (2002) description of the efforts to find a reliable and accurate measure of disability, it may be concluded that merely asking individuals whether they have a physical or mental condition that substantially limits a major life activity likely will not reliably identify those covered by the ADA. Difficult measurement issues stem also from the ADA's basic focus on a physical or mental condition that limits one's activities; if an individual perceives him- or herself not to be limited, he or she will not respond affirmatively to questions focusing on "limitations" or "difficulties." This is undoubtedly a good thing from a policy and social perspective; it is not such a good thing if one is interested in measuring the effects of the ADA.

As Kruse and Schur (2003) point out, if the ADA is effective in eliminating barriers that historically have thwarted attempts of individuals with disabilities to work, over time fewer and fewer individuals will identify themselves as being limited in their ability to work. Technological innovations and the movement to achieve independence also will decrease the number of individuals identifying limitations in major life activities (Blanck and Sandler 2000).

In short, even if the law were responsible for changes in individuals' views regarding whether they are limited in the activities of daily life, and for the increased employment rates of those individuals, they would be treated as not disabled under our current measurement approaches using cross-sectional or longitudinal data. This would tend to increase the likelihood of obtaining empirical results that suggest the

ADA has had a negative, or no, effect on the employment of individuals with disabilities (Blanck 1997).

The task facing those attempting to identify an accurate and reliable measure of disability is, for these and other reasons, extremely difficult (Burkhauser and coauthors, Chapter 2). Kruse and Schur's (2003) work testing a functional limitation definition of disability should be viewed as encouragement to those faced with that task, as well as others who seek to devise or choose a disability measure to examine the effects of the ADA, because it demonstrates the potential benefits from using multiple measures of disability.

The use of measures of functional limitations in addition to measures that capture limitations on an individual's ability to work will enable further investigation into the reasons why results appear to differ depending on which measure is employed. Incorporating both would allow analysis of the large numbers of individuals reporting work disabilities but no other functional limitations. These individuals have had, arguably, the worst success rate in ADA litigation, as they are most likely to be forced to simultaneously argue that they are substantially limited in their ability to work in a range of jobs (or in daily life tasks), but are nonetheless qualified to do the job in question. Indeed, this issue was at the crux of the Court's *Toyota* decision.

In future analyses of either the labor force participation or employment status of individuals with disabilities, it is also crucial to examine measures of disability that go beyond the use of "yes/no" indicators of group membership (Collignon 1997). Such indicator variables treat those with disabilities as a relatively homogenous group, particularly given that a number of other individual characteristics often are left unmeasured. Research examining measures of severity and employment suggests that severity is, as may be expected, inversely related to the probability of working (Loprest, Rupp, and Sandell 1995). We have seen in prior research that measures of disability, limitations, and health each appear to explain variation in the phenomena being addressed (Blanck 2001; Stein 2000a).

Although all of the information desired is not likely to be contained in existing data sets, researchers must acknowledge the unique challenges that accompany the study of individuals with disabilities, and, until new measures are devised and expanded data sets are assembled, marshal the information that is available. The SIPP and CPS contain information that may allow those prevented from working to be identified (Schwochau and Blanck 2000, 2003; Kruse and Schur 2003). Surveys have asked individuals questions that provide the basis for a measure of severity (McNeil 1993). Only by examining many aspects of individuals' disabilities can we assess the extent to which the ADA has helped or hindered the efforts of those with disabilities to move into, and to stay in, the workplace, and ultimately understand the why underlying the results we obtain.

Effects of other individual and job characteristics

In addition to examining other measures of disability, it is important to incorporate into models of labor market behavior measures of individuals' productivity, such as education, job training, and work experience (Blanck and Schartz 2001). The lack of work experience has been described as among the principal reasons individuals with disabilities have difficulty finding employment (Collignon 1986). Some research reports that individuals with disabilities in the samples employed had more working experience, on average, but also more years of missed experience (Baldwin and Johnson 1995).

Results reported by DeLeire (2000) suggest that the probability of employment in some sectors and types of jobs declined by a greater degree than others. The effects of changes in the nature of jobs available in the economy may, in part, explain declining employment of individuals with disabilities (Yelin and Cisternas 1996). Stapleton, Goodman, and Houtenville (Chapter 4) have empirically assessed the possibility that jobs' requirements have changed over time in ways that make it less likely that those with disabilities will be able to compete for positions. Investigation into these sorts of questions will assist in identifying why individuals with disabilities face barriers to employment despite the ADA (Blanck and Sandler 2000).

Labor supply and productivity issues

Models of discrimination build on models of the functioning of labor markets. Within those models, individuals are matched with jobs as a result of their decisions and those of employers. Although researchers have theorized that the ADA will have the effect of increasing labor supply (see, e.g., Jolls 2000), empirical work to date has focused on the demand side of the market. To understand why individuals with disabilities still appear to face significant employment hurdles, we need to learn more about the labor force participation decisions of those with ADA covered disabilities[6] (Blanck 2000, 2001; O'Day, Schartz, and Blanck 2002; Zwerling et al. 2002), and human capital decisions of those individuals.

Under standard economic models, an individual's decision to look for employment reflects consideration of the value of time spent in work and in nonwork activities. How much available time the individual devotes to either activity depends on factors such as the value of an hour spent at work (usually taken as the wage rate), the value to the individual of that same hour in nonwork activities (e.g., household maintenance, child care, personal care, leisure, and so on), and sources of wealth that are not dependent on working for pay (Ehrenberg and Smith 1991). An individual will devote a positive number of hours to working for pay when the benefits of doing so (in terms of the wage rate, and the value of work as an activity) outweigh the costs (e.g., what is given up by spending time at work rather than in other activities, and the direct costs associated with going to work, such as transportation costs, clothing, and child care).

Kaye (1998) estimates that between 1990 and 1994, only 52 percent of 18–64-year-olds with "chronic health conditions or impairments" were working or seeking work. The factors noted above highlight some of the reasons why disabled individuals (covered by the ADA and not) may decide not to participate in the labor force. First, low wages may cause an individual to determine that the costs of working outweigh the benefits of doing so (Burke 1997). Second, with a fixed number of hours in a day, a disabled individual may find that there are fewer hours than can be dedicated to work, given the number of hours that must be devoted to personal care and other basic tasks (Oi 1991).

Oi (1991) describes how four aspects of disability are important in individuals' labor supply decisions: severity, age at onset of disability, anticipated duration of disability, and the disability's effect on expected length of life (see also Burkhauser and Daly 1996).[7] The ADA's equal pay and accommodation provisions have been predicted to affect the perceived benefits of working. Empirical examination of the probability that an individual was in the labor market (employed or actively seeking work for pay) would assist in isolating reasons why only some individuals with disabilities may be benefited by the ADA.

Research also has not yet examined empirically the effects of the ADA on decisions of individuals with disabilities to invest in human capital. Differences between persons with and without disabilities in areas such as life expectancies (length of one's working life), expected market wage, length of time needed to complete an educational or training program, and difficulties associated with acquiring skills and abilities lead to different decisions regarding the degree to which each group will invest in its own human capital. When an individual becomes disabled also will influence his or her decisions regarding human capital investment (Baldwin and Johnson 1995; Oi 1991). Less investment in human capital also may be the result of negative stigma toward individuals with disability. As Becker (1996, p. 147) states:

> A novel theoretical development in recent years is the analysis of the consequences of stereotyped reasoning or statistical discrimination. This analysis suggests that the *beliefs* of employers, teachers, and other influential groups that minority members are less productive *can* be self-fulfilling, for these beliefs may cause minorities to underinvest in education, training, and work skills, such as punctuality. The underinvestment does make them less productive.

The ADA, through its accommodation and equal pay requirement, has the potential to break this vicious cycle, thus narrowing the productivity gap between the disabled and the nondisabled. Younger individuals with disabilities may be less likely stay out of the labor force because of investments in education, if those investments are perceived to be associated with greater future benefits and have been made less difficult because of the ADA's provisions (Jolls 2000, 2001). Whether the ADA has triggered greater investment in education could be assessed by comparing years of schooling or training before and after the law's enactment. It may take a longer horizon than a decade, however, to capture the effects of changes in human capital decisions on employment.

Truly Difficult Policy Issues

The only way to assess whether the ADA is, overall, a beneficial or harmful piece of legislation is by assessing information regarding its influences (Blanck and Millender 2000; Blanck and Song 2001; National Council on Disability 1996). To be useful to policymakers, that information must be derived from rigorous study of the behaviors of primary actors affected by the legislation (Blanck et al. 2003). In the case of ADA Title I, these actors are qualified employees with and without disabilities and the firms that employ them. Researchers in different fields of study will approach questions regarding the ADA from distinct perspectives, and policymakers will gain a more complete picture of the ADA's influences if contributions to the pool of information represent a variety of approaches.

Undoubtedly, within that pool, some studies will conclude that the ADA has had harmful effects; others will conclude that the law has had beneficial influences; and still others will present a mix. Our concern here has been with studies based on economic theories of labor market behavior. It is crucial for policymakers and researchers to understand the limitations of these empirical studies (O'Day, Schartz, and Blanck 2002). In light of the flaws identified, we submit that existing empirical research provides little basis on which policymakers can make informed decisions regarding whether the ADA is the cause of employment declines and should be thus be amended, repealed, or left untouched.

Policymakers must concern themselves, however, not only with the validity of existing and future studies, but also with the limitations of the theoretical models on which those studies are based. Economic theory, because it allows us to focus on incentives and disincentives in the labor market, will undoubtedly assist in assessing what policy, if any, should replace the ADA. The assumptions and viewpoints embedded in that theory, however, may be argued to go beyond an emphasis on efficiency to perceptions of what efficiency means (Schwochau and Blanck 2000; Stein 2000a).

Under simple economic models, all nondisabled labor is identical, all disabled labor is identical, markets are perfectly competitive, and actors in those markets have perfect information.[8] Of course, in the real world, all labor and all capital is not identical, people do not have perfect information, and all markets do not operate efficiently in the absence of a law such as the ADA (Collignon 1986). However, even if variation and imperfect information are allowed within the labor and capital markets, it still may be argued that firms will do what is most efficient and most profitable, on average. Decisions will be based on information regarding the qualities of the average unit of labor or capital, the degree of variability in each respective market, and the expected costs and benefits of acquiring more information (Stein 2000b, 2000c).

For example, firms spend hundreds of thousands of dollars selecting a CEO, and this expenditure far exceeds the costs associated with selecting clerical workers. This difference, in part, reflects variation in the respective labor markets and the costs and benefits associated with gaining additional information about candidates for each type of position. The goal in each case, however, is to select the most productive individual, given the costs. Whether this goal is met is, of course, a matter of speculation at the time of hire. Over time, however, employers will make changes in their hiring practices (if the benefit of the change exceeds its costs) so that, on average, incorrect decisions will be reduced to tolerable levels.

Economic theory also generally would predict that an employer structures the firm's work environment to enable workers, on average, to attain the desired level of productivity (again given the costs and benefits associated with alternative orderings and available technologies). If the majority of workers are viewed as unimpaired, the work environment can be expected to build on assumptions that workers have no limitations on their abilities to see, hear, walk, climb stairs, lift, carry, grasp door knobs, write, speak, and so on (Burgdorf 1997). Because of employers' incentives to maximize profits, this environment becomes the baseline—the appropriate, efficient manner in which to order work and the work environment given the perceived characteristics of the average individual in the relevant labor markets (Rosen 1991). Accommodations, therefore, represent deviations from presumptively efficient status quo necessitated by the appearance in the candidate pool, or in the current workforce, of individuals with disabilities—individuals whose characteristics differ from those of the "model (able-bodied) worker" around whom the work environment was built (Krenek 1994).

The questions that the ADA's reasonable accommodation requirement poses are to which accommodations should individuals with disabilities be entitled, and who should bear the costs of those accommodations (Kelman 2001; *US Airways, Inc. v. Barnett* 2002). On its face, the ADA imposes on the employer the burden of paying for accommodations, a result that some have noted is justified on the basis of past decisions to structure working environments as they are (Kelman 2001).

Economic theory's predictions regarding the effects of the ADA on employment and wage of qualified individuals with disabilities can be seen as the market operating to transfer at least some of the employer's costs to individuals with disabilities (either through lower employment or lower wages). However, the labor supply and demand models deliver only a local equilibrium, not a global equilibrium from the social planner's point of view. Those models fail to realize that a person with a disability who chooses not to enter the labor market receives some form of transfer payment and the transfer payment comes from the taxpayers' pockets.

The question, therefore, is whether from a social perspective, it is more efficient for employers to incur the accommodation cost so that the individual with a disability works for pay instead of drawing on the transfer payment, or for taxpayers to support this individual. The answer depends on the wage rate, accommodation cost, the size of transfer payment, and value of output produced by the individual. A social planner will see to the enforcement of employer accommodation if the total social benefit (reduction in transfer payment plus increase in output) exceeds the total social cost (wage rate plus accommodation cost) (Wax 2003).

CONCLUSION

A benefit to assembling research from a number of fields is that differing perspectives, assumptions, priorities, and viewpoints are brought to the fore as results are compared and attempts are made to reconcile apparently conflicting conclusions. It is unlikely that one factor or phenomenon will explain the pattern of results that ultimately emerges. It may be that a combination of economic, social, and political incentives and disincentives and changes in the economy explains why employment of persons with disabilities seems to be declining (Blanck 2001).

We have identified some of the possible forces explaining the *why* question. Undoubtedly, more factors may be gleaned from the work of other researchers. We are beginning to investigate empirically questions regarding whether individuals who report a work disability or functional limitation continue to experience lower relative employment rates since the ADA was passed. We need to assess who those individuals are, and why they are or are not employed, before informed decisions about the effects of ADA's provisions and assessments regarding possible changes to the law's provisions can be made. If future research builds on the studies presented to date, we have the chance of obtaining at least some answers to these questions.

Notes

The views in this chapter reflect only those of the authors and not of any funding agency. This research was funded in part by the U.S. Department of Education, National Institute on Disability and Rehabilitation Research, for grants to the first author for: (1) the Rehabilitation Research and Training Center (RRTC) on Workforce Investment and Employment Policy for Persons with Disabilities, Grant No. H133B980042-99, (2) "IT Works," Grant No. H133A011803, and (3) "Technology for Independence: A Community-Based Resource Center," Grant No. H133A021801; and from the Great Plains ADA and IT Center, and the University of Iowa Law School Foundation. For most helpful comments, we thank Doug Kruse, Lisa Schur, Stephen Kaye, Nanette Goodman, David Stapleton, Rich Burkhauser, Bobby Silverstein, James Schmeling, Lisa Clay, and many of the participants at the Employment and Disability Policy Institute, sponsored by Cornell University, October 20, 2001, Washington, DC. For related projects see The Law, Health Policy and Disability Center Web site at <http://www.its.uiowa.edu/law>.

1. There is, of course, some debate on this issue (compare, e.g., Posner (1987) and Donahue (1986, 1987)).
2. The ADA's language may support this assumed difference in productivity. Because a qualified individual with a disability is defined as a person who is able to do the "essential functions" of the job (with or without accommodation), one may argue that individuals with disabilities who are able to perform only the "essential functions" are by definition less productive than persons able to perform all job functions (Weaver 1991).

3. Hale (2001) describes the problems associated with the CPS and SIPP data sets in examining the employment of individuals with disabilities. He suggests that the CPS, in particular, cannot be relied on to distinguish those with disabilities from those without disabilities. Kaye (2002) discusses these problems and proposes using alternative measures of employment rate, labor force participation, and unemployment. In addition, Kaye notes that the reported decline in the employment rates of persons with disabilities after passage of the ADA is mitigated when using these alternative definitions, and when considering the effect of the early 1990s economic recession and the coinciding rise in working-aged adults applying for and receiving federal disability benefits such as Social Security Disability Insurance (SSDI) and Supplemental Security Income (SSI). Burkhauser, Houtenville, and Wittenburg (Chapter 2) make note of "substantial increases" in SSDI and SSI program participation, particularly for men during the 1990s. Bound and Waidmann (2000) find that movement of men and women with disabilities out of the labor force and onto the SSDI rolls during the 1990s accounts for much of their decline in workforce participation, rather than the implementation of the ADA.

4. Although there may be a number of reasons for the increase over time in the number of individuals with disabilities who report themselves as unable to work, the ADA's provisions, by themselves, are not likely to be a direct cause (see Blanck, Clay, Schmeling, Morris, and Ritchie 2002). The more likely cause is the availability of SSDI and SSI benefits to those who are classified as unable to work under those programs' definitions. Until the U.S. Supreme Court's decision in *Cleveland v. Policy Management Systems Corp.*, 526 U.S. 795 (1999), a number of courts had held that receipt of SSDI or SSI benefits prevented an individual from asserting that he or she was a qualified individual with a disability under the ADA. Thus, it could be argued that those courts' interpretation of the ADA's provisions had the effect of forcing individuals with disabilities to choose between attempting to find work and obtaining SSDI or SSI benefits. If the latter was chosen, they ran the risk of being found not covered by the ADA.

5. By way of background, Robert Barnett worked at US Airways for 10 years. After suffering an on-the-job injury, he transferred into a mailroom position that effectively accommodated his disability. After serving in that position for two years, Barnett was informed that a more senior employee intended to bump him from the position, pursuant to US Airways seniority policy. Barnett requested accommodations that would allow him to perform other jobs, but US Airways rejected those suggestions. Barnett sued, alleging that US Airways had an obligation to engage in Title I's consultative interactive process. The Supreme Court held that because Barnett's requested workplace accommodation conflicted with US Air's seniority system, the accommodation was not "reasonable" and thereby not required (Blanck 1996; Issacharoff and Nelson 2001).

Similarly, Mario Echazabal worked at a Chevron oil refinery for 20 years as a laborer, plant helper, and pipefitter for various maintenance contractors. Twice during this period he applied for permanent employment with Chevron as a pipefitter/mechanic and plant helper. Although Chevron determined on both occasions that Echazabal was qualified for the positions, Chevron physicians refused to authorize an offer of employment, claiming that exposure to certain chemicals in the refinery might exacerbate Echazabal's Hepatitis C. After Chevron asked Echazabal's contracting employer to remove him from the facility entirely, Echazabal sued Chevron, alleging a violation of the ADA. The Supreme Court ruled that Chevron could limit the hiring opportunity of an ADA-qualified individual with a disability who the company believed might be harmed by exposure to their workplace environment. Chevron accomplished this goal by relying on a "direct threat to self" defense to discrimination charges, language set out in regulatory guidance by the Equal Employment Opportunity Commission (EEOC).

6. An additional factor regarding the definition of a qualified ADA individual has been introduced into the mix. In 2002, the U.S. Supreme Court upheld the validity of the EEOC interpretative regulations of the ADA to include an employer defense to the hiring of qualified individuals who pose a direct safety threat to themselves in the workplace (*Chevron U.S.A., Inc. v. Echazabal,* 2002, case facts described in endnote 5). The legal, and ultimately policy, question in *Chevron* is to what extent should employers or qualified individuals with ADA covered disabilities decide the degree of risk an individual with a disability can and should accept in performing a job. *Chevron* will have further implications for the definition of ADA qualified persons (see, e.g., *Chevron U.S.A., Inc. v. Echazabal,* Brief of the National Council on Disability 2002) and the employment of persons with disabilities as lower courts endorse the rule that employer qualification standards include the ability of an individual covered by the law to perform the job in question safely.

7. Silverstein (2002) adds four more aspects to the list of factors likely to affect individuals' labor supply decisions: 1) the macro-economic status during the reporting period (e.g., whether the country is in a deep or mild recession, in the beginning stages of recovery or full employment); 2) how other protected classes, e.g., minority groups, are fairing for the same period; 3) the race and ethnicity of the population and differences for subgroups, e.g., disabled African-Americans; and 4) an inventory of persons with hidden disabilities, e.g., epilepsy and mental illness, who may not self-report.

8. Thus, although applicants and employees may themselves be uncertain about whether they fall within the group of disabled individuals protected by the ADA, and employers may be similarly uncertain about whether a particular applicant or employee is an ADA-qualified individual with a disability, economic models of the effects of the ADA have not yet incorporated this uncertainty.

References

Acemoglu, D., and J.D. Angrist. 2001. "Consequences of Employment Protection? The Case of the Americans with Disabilities Act." *Journal of Political Economy* 109: 915–957.

Aigner, D.J., and G.G. Cain. 1977. "Statistical Theories of Discrimination in Labor Markets." *Industrial & Labor Relations Review* 30: 175–187.

Americans with Disabilities Act. 1990. 42 U.S.C. § 12101 et. seq.

Baldwin, M.L. 2000. "Estimating the Potential Benefits of the ADA on the Wages and Employment of Persons with Disabilities." In *Employment, Disability, and the Americans with Disabilities Act*, P.D. Blanck, ed. Evanston, IL: Northwestern University Press, pp. 258–281.

Baldwin, M.L., and W.G. Johnson. 1995. "Labor Market Discrimination against Women with Disabilities." *Industrial Relations* 34: 555–577.

Baldwin, M.L., L.A. Zeager, and P.R. Flacco. 1994. "Gender Differences in Wage Losses from Impairments." *Human Resources* 29: 865–887.

Barnard, T.H. 1992. "Disabling America: Costing Out the Americas with Disabilities Act." *Cornell Journal of Law & Public Policy* 2: 41–62.

Becker, G.S. 1971. *The Economics of Discrimination*. Chicago: University of Chicago Press.

———. 1996. *Accounting for Tastes*. Cambridge, MA: Harvard University Press.

Berven, H. M., and P. Blanck. 1998. "The Economics of the Americans with Disabilities Act: Part 2: Patents, Innovations and Assistive Technology." *Notre Dame Journal of Law, Ethics and Public Policy* 12: 9–120.

Blanck, P., ed. 1993. *Interpersonal Expectations: Theory, Research, and Applications*. New York: Cambridge University Press.

———. 1996. "Communicating the Americans with Disabilities Act: Transcending Compliance —1996 Follow-up report on Sears Roebuck and Co." Washington, DC: The Annenberg Washington Program.

———. 1997. "The Economics of the Employment Provisions of the Americans with Disabilities Act: Part I—Workplace Accommodations." *DePaul Law Review* 46: 877–914.

———. 1998. *The Americans with Disabilities Act and the Emerging Workforce: Employment of People with Mental Retardation*. Washington, DC: American Association on Mental Retardation.

———., ed. 2000. *Employment, Disability, and the Americans with Disabilities Act: Issues in Law, Public Policy, and Research*. Evanston, IL: Northwestern University Press.

———. 2001. "Civil War Pensions and Disability." *Ohio State Law Journal* 62: 109–249.

Blanck, P., L. Clay, J. Schmeling, M. Morris, and H. Ritchie. 2002. "Applicability of the ADA to Ticket to Work Employment Networks." *Behavioral Sciences and the Law* 20(6): 621–636.

Blanck, P., and M. Millender. 2000. "Before Civil Rights: Civil War Pensions and the Politics of Disability in America." *Alabama Law Review* 52: 1–50.

Blanck, P., H. Ritchie, J.A. Schmeling, and D. Klein. 2003. "Technology for Independence: A Community-Based Resource Center." *Behavioral Sciences and the Law* 21(1): 51–62.

Blanck, P. and L.A. Sandler. 2000. "ADA Title III and the Internet: Technology and Civil Rights." *Mental and Physical Disability Law Reporter* 24: 855–859.

Blanck, P., and H.A. Schartz. 2001. "Towards Researching a National Employment Policy for Persons with Disabilities." In *Emerging Workforce Issues: W.I.A., Ticket to Work, and Partnerships,* R. McConnell, ed. Alexandria, VA: National Rehabilitation Association, pp. 1–10.

Blanck, P., and C. Song. 2001. "With Malice toward None; With Charity toward All: Civil War Pensions for Native and Foreign-Born Union Army Veterans." *Transnational Law and Contemporary Problems* 11: 1–75.

Blanck, P., L.A. Sandler, D. Kutzko, M.L. Zaiger, D.R. Oelschlaeger, and S.J. Gayer. 2002. "Brief of the National Council on Disability as *Amicus Curiae* in Support of Respondent, *Chevron U.S.A., Inc. v. Echazabal*." Submitted to the U.S. Supreme Court.

Bound, J., and T. Waidmann. 2000. "Accounting for Recent Declines in Employment Rates among the Working-Aged Disabled." NBER working paper no. 7975. Washington, DC: National Bureau of Economic Research. Available at: <http://papers.nber.org/papers/w7975>.

Burgdorf, R.L., Jr. 1997. "'Substantially Limited' Protection from Disability Discrimination: The Special Treatment Model and Misconstructions of the Definition of Disability." *Villanova Law Review* 42: 409–509.

Burke, T.F. 1997. "On the Rights Track: The Americans with Disabilities Act." In *Comparative Disadvantages? Social Regulations and the Global Economy,* S. Nivola, ed. Washington, DC: Brookings Institution, pp. 203–231.

Burkhauser, R.V, and M.C. Daly. 1996. "Employment and Economic Well-Being Following the Onset of a Disability." In *Disability, Work and Cash Benefits,* J.L. Mashaw, V.P. Reno, R.V. Burkhauser, and M. Berkowitz, eds. Kalamazoo, MI: W.E. Upjohn Institute for Employment Research, pp. 59–102.

Chevron U.S.A., Inc. v. Echazabal. 2002. 122 S. Ct. 2045.

Cleveland v. Policy Management Systems Corp. 1999. 526 U.S. 795.

Collignon, F.C. 1986. "The Role of Reasonable Accommodation in Employing Disabled Persons in Private Industry." In *Disability and the Labor Market: Economic Problems, Policies, and Programs,* M. Berkowitz and M.A. Hill, eds. Ithaca, NY: Cornell University Press, pp. 196–241.

———. 1997. "Is the ADA Successful? Indicators for Tracking Gains." *The Annals of the American Academy of Political and Social Science* 549: 129–147.

DeLeire, T. 1997. "The Wage and Employment Effects of the Americans with Disabilities Act." Unpublished Ph.D. dissertation. Santa Monica, CA: Stanford University.

———. 2000. "The Wage and Employment Effects of the Americans with Disabilities Act." *Journal of Human Resources* 35: 693–715.

———. 2001. "Changes in Wage Discrimination against People with Disabilities: 1984–1993." *Journal of Human Resources* 36: 144–158.

Donahue, J.J. III. 1986. "Is Title VII Efficient?" *University of Pennsylvania Law Review* 134: 1411–1427.

———. 1987. "Further Thoughts on Employment Discrimination Legislation: A Reply to Judge Posner." *University of Pennsylvania Law Review* 136: 523–545.

———. 1994. "Employment Discrimination Law in Perspective: Three Concepts of Equality." *Michigan Law Review* 92: 2583–2612.

Duckett v. Dunlop Tire Corp. 1997. 120 F.3d 1222 (11th Cir.).

Ehrenberg, R.G., and R.S. Smith. 1991. *Modern Labor Economics: Theory and Public Policy* (4th ed.). Boston, MA: Addison Wesley.

Epstein, R.A. 1992. *Forbidden Grounds: The Case against Employment Discrimination Laws.* Cambridge, MA: Harvard University Press.

Friedland, R.B., and A. Evans. 1996. "People with Disabilities: Access to Health Care and Related Benefits." In *Disability, Work and Cash Benefits,* J.L. Mashaw, V.P. Reno, R.V. Burkhauser, and M. Berkowitz, eds. Kalamazoo, MI: W.E. Upjohn Institute for Employment Research, pp. 357–388.

Hale, T.W. 2001. "The Lack of a Disability Measure in Today's Current Population Survey." *Monthly Labor Review* 124: 38–40.

Issacharoff, S., and J. Nelson. 2001. "Discrimination with a Difference: Can Employment Discrimination Law Accommodate the Americans with Disabilities Act?" *North Carolina Law Review* 79: 307–358.

Jolls, C. 2000. "Accommodation Mandates." *Stanford Law Review* 53: 223–306.

———. 2001. "Antidiscrimination and Accommodation." *Harvard Law Review* 115: 642–699.

Kaye, H.S. 1998. "Is the Status of People with Disabilities Improving?" *Disability Statistics Abstract* 21: 1–4.
———. 2002. "Improved Employment Opportunities for People with Disabilities." *Disability Statistics Report* 17. Washington DC: U.S. Department of Education, National Institute on Disability and Rehabilitation Research.
Kaye, H.S., M.P. LaPlante, D. Carlson, and B.L. Wenger. 1996. Trends in Disability Rates in the United States, 1970-1994. Disability Stat. Center, Disability Statistics. Abstract No. 17.
Kelman, M. 2001. "Market Discrimination and Groups." *Stanford Law Review* 53: 833–896.
Krenek, S.A. (note). 1994. "Beyond Reasonable Accommodation." *Texas Law Review* 72: 1969–2011.
Kruse, D., and T. Hale. 2003. "Disability and Employment: Symposium Introduction." *Industrial Relations* 42(1): 1–10.
Kruse, D., and L. Schur. 2003. "Employment of People with Disabilities Following the ADA." *Industrial Relations* 42(1): 31–66.
Lee, B.A. 2003. "A Decade of the Americans with Disabilities Act: Judicial Outcomes and Unresolved Problems." *Industrial Relations* 42(1): 11–30.
Lee, M. 1997. "Searching for Patterns and Anomalies in the ADA Employment Constellation: Who Is a Qualified Individual with a Disability and What Accommodations Are Courts Really Demanding?" *Labor Lawyer* 13: 149–196.
Loprest, P., K. Rupp, and S.H. Sandell. 1995. "Gender, Disabilities, and Employment in the Health and Retirement Survey." *Journal of Human Resources* 30(5): S293–S318.
Mashaw, J.L., and V.P. Reno. 1996. "Overview." In *Disability, Work and Cash Benefits*, J.L. Mashaw, V.P. Reno, R.V. Burkhauser, and M. Berkowitz, eds. Kalamazoo, MI: W.E. Upjohn Institute for Employment Research, pp. 1–27.
McNeil, J.M. 1993. Americans with Disabilities: 1991–92. Current population rep. no. P70-33. Washington, DC: U.S. Department of Commerce.
———. 1997. Americans with Disabilities: 1994–95. Current population rep. no. P70-61. Washington, DC: U.S. Department of Commerce. Available at:<http://www.census.gov/hhes/www/disable/sipp/disab9495/ds94tl.html>.
National Council on Disability. 1996. *Achieving Independence: The Challenge for the 21st Century—A Decade of Progress in Disability Policy Setting an Agenda for the Future*. Washington, DC: National Council on Disability.
O'Day, B., H. Schartz, and P. Blanck. 2002. "Introduction: Disability Law, Research and Policy." *Behavioral Sciences and the Law,* 20(6): 537–539.

Oi, W.Y. 1991. Disability and a Workfare-Welfare Dilemma. In *Disability and Work: Incentives, Rights, and Opportunities*, C.L. Weaver, ed. Washington, DC: AEI Press, pp. 31–45.

Olson, W. 1997. "Comment on Burke." In *Comparative Disadvantages: Social Regulations and the Global Economy*, P.N. Nivola, ed. Washington, DC: Brookings Institute, pp. 146–181.

Posner, R.A. 1987. "The Efficiency and the Efficacy of Title VII." *University of Pennsylvania Law Review* 136: 513–521.

Rosen, S. 1991. "Disability Accommodation and the Labor Market." In *Disability and Work: Incentives, Rights, and Opportunities*, C.L. Weaver, ed. Washington, DC: AEI Press, pp. 18–30.

Schartz, K., H. Schartz, and P. Blanck. 2002. "Employment of Persons with Disabilities in Information Technology Jobs: A Literature Review for 'IT Works." *Behavioral Sciences and the Law* 20(6): 637–657.

Schwochau, S., and P. Blanck. 2000. "The Economics of the Americans with Disabilities Act, Part III: Does the ADA Disable the Disabled?" *Berkeley Journal of Employment and Labor Law* 21: 271–313.

———. 2003. "Does the ADA Disable the Disabled?—More Comments." *Industrial Relations* 42(1): 67–77.

Silverstein, R. 2002. "Issues Raised on Statistics on the Employment of People with Disabilities." Personal correspondence with Peter Blanck.

Stein, M.A. 2000a. "Labor Markets, Rationality, and Workers with Disabilities." *Berkeley Journal of Employment and Labor Law* 21: 314–334.

———. 2000b. "Empirical Implications of Title I." *Iowa Law Review* 85: 1671–1690.

———. 2000c. "Employing People with Disabilities: Some Cautionary Thoughts for a Second Generation Civil Rights Statute." In *Employment Disability, and the Americans with Disabilities Act: Issues in Law and Public Policy*, P.D. Blanck, ed. Evanston, IL: Northwestern University Press, pp. 51–68.

Stern, S. 1989. "Measuring the Effect of Disability on Labor Force Participation." *Journal of Human Resources* 24: 361–395.

Stoddard, S., L. Jans, J.M. Ripple, and L. Kraus. 1998. *Chartbook on Work and Disability in the United States*. Washington, DC: National Institute on Disability and Rehabilitation Research. Available at <http://www.infouse.com/disabilitydata/workdisability.html>. (Posted: March 29, 2001. Accessed: December 18, 2002.)

Summers, L.H. 1989. "Some Simple Economics of Mandated Benefits." *American Economic Review* 79: 177–189.

Sutton v. United Airlines, Inc. 1999. 527 U.S. 471.

Toyota Motor Manufacturing, Inc. v. Williams. 2002. 122 S. Ct. 681.

US Airways, Inc. v. Barnett. 2002. 122 S. Ct. 1516.
US Airways, Inc. v. Barnett. 2001. 228 F.3d 1105 (9th Cir. 2000), *cert. granted in part sub nom.* 121 S. Ct. 1600.
US Airways, Inc. v. Barnett, Brief for Petitioner, available at 2001 WL 747864. U.S. Supreme Court. 2001.
U.S. Census Bureau. 2000. *Americans with Disabilities, 1994–1995.* Washington, DC: U.S. Census Bureau. Available at: <http://www.census.gov:80/hhes/www/disable/sipp/disable9495.html>. (Posted: August 22, 2002. Accessed: December 18, 2002.)
Wax, A. 2003. "Disability, Reciprocity, and 'Real Efficiency': A Unified Approach." *William and Mary Law Review* 44(3): 1421–1452.
Weaver, C.L. 1991. "Incentives versus Controls in Federal Disability Policy." In *Disability and Work: Incentives, Rights, and Opportunities,* C.L. Weaver, ed. Washington, DC: AEI Press, pp. 3–17.
Yelin, E., and M. Cisternas. 1996. "The Contemporary Labor Market and the Employment Prospects of Persons with Disabilities." In *Disability, Work and Cash Benefits,* J.L. Mashaw, V.P. Reno, R.V. Burkhauser, and M. Berkowitz, eds. Kalamazoo, MI: W.E. Upjohn Institute for Employment Research, pp. 33–57.
Zwerling, C., P. Whitten, N.L. Sprince, C.S. Davis, R.B. Wallace, P. Blanck, and S.G. Heeringa. 2002. "Workforce Participation by Persons with Disabilities: The National Health Interview Survey Disability Supplement, 1994 to 1995." *Journal of Occupational and Environmental Medicine* 44(4): 358–364.
———. 2003. "Workplace Accommodations for People with Disabilities: National Health Interview Survey Disability Supplement, 1994–95." *Journal of Occupational and Environmental Medicine* 45(5): 517–525.

10
Social Security Disability Insurance and the Recent Decline in the Employment Rate of People with Disabilities

Nanette Goodman
Cornell University

Timothy Waidmann
The Urban Institute

During the 1990s, the Social Security Disability Insurance (SSDI) program grew rapidly. In 2000, the program provided cash and medical benefits to 5 million working-aged (18–64) adults with impairments that, according to eligibility criteria, prevent them from working. The SSDI rolls grew 67 percent from 1990, over five times faster than the working-aged population.[1] Because SSDI beneficiaries are essentially precluded from working as a precondition of benefits, this growth is consistent with the decline in the employment rate for people with disabilities, documented by Burkhauser, Houtenville, and Wittenburg (Chapter 2).

Based on findings by Bound and Waidmann (2002) and Autor and Duggan (2003), we conclude that the growth in the number of recipients can largely be attributed to two program changes: a period of liberalization in eligibility criteria, beginning in 1984, and a gradual increase in program generosity for low-wage workers. These changes interacted with the recession of the early 1990s to increase SSDI rolls while simultaneously decreasing labor force participation. Moreover, the findings suggest that these changes were the impetus for labor force withdrawal, rather than a result of people with disabilities withdrawing from the labor market for some other reason and turning to the SSDI program as a safety net.

Because virtually any factor that would reduce the employment rate for people with disabilities would also increase SSDI participation, a key question is whether it was a change in the SSDI program, rather than another factor, that caused the employment rate to decline. The work of Autor and Duggan (2003) and Bound and Waidmann (2002) reviewed in this chapter offer a wealth of evidence to suggest the causal relationship. The two sets of authors take different empirical approaches, but together provide strong support for the hypothesis that the changes in SSDI led to the decline in employment.

We will review the following findings, among others, to support this argument.

- Over the past three decades, the number of people receiving SSDI benefits has been responsive to changes in eligibility criteria and program generosity, and the trend in SSDI rolls closely tracks the employment rate of the insured population with disabilities (Bound and Waidmann 2002).

- The types of impairments for people with disabilities who increasingly report that they are unable to work are the same impairments that were most affected by SSDI eligibility expansions (Bound and Waidmann 2002).

- Workers without high school degrees, whose potential SSDI benefits are closest to their earnings, were more likely than workers in other educational groups to drop out of the labor force after the 1984 liberalizations (Autor and Duggan 2003).

- Based on state data, we can account for the entire rise in the fraction of the working-aged population that reports work limitations and is out of work by the rise in the fraction receiving SSDI benefits during the 1990s (Bound and Waidmann 2002).

- Low-wage workers who become unemployed were more likely to drop out of the labor force and apply for SSDI after the 1984 eligibility expansion than they were before the expansion (Autor and Duggan 2003).

This chapter is divided into three parts. The first section provides background on recent trends in employment rates, the SSDI program, and the historical context of recent expansions in eligibility and benefits. It also outlines a theoretical model of the decision to apply for benefits. The next section describes findings from the two papers, before discussing implications in the final section.

BACKGROUND

Trends in Employment Rates

As described in Chapter 2, the employment rate of men with disabilities, like that of other working-aged men, declined during the recession of 1990. However, unlike that of men without disabilities, the employment rate of men with disabilities continued to decline through the economic expansion of the mid and late 1990s.

Among women, employment rates were flat during the recession, but as the economic expansion took hold, the employment rate of women without disabilities continued its long historical growth. For women with work limitations, there is no such growth, and perhaps even some decline, in the employment rate.

Together, this implies that for both men and women, the employment rate of people with disabilities was falling relative to that of people without disabilities during the economic expansion of the mid and late 1990s. Rather than narrowing the employment gap, people with disabilities lost ground.

These trends are not simply an artifact of changes in the Current Population Survey (CPS); they are apparent in analyses using the Survey of Income and Program Participation (SIPP) and the National Health Interview Survey (NHIS) as well (see Burkhauser, Houtenville, and Wittenburg, Chapter 2). Nor is the trend merely a reflection of changing population demographics (See Houtenville and Daly, Chapter 3).

Social Security's Disability Programs

The Social Security Administration (SSA) provides cash benefits to people with disabilities under two programs: the SSDI program and the Supplemental Security Income (SSI) program. The medical requirements for eligibility are the same under both programs, and the same process is used to determine if a person's impairment meets the criteria. Eligibility for SSDI is based on prior work under Social Security, while SSI disability payments are means tested.

For SSDI, benefits are based on the worker's past earnings and are paid to the worker with disabilities and, in limited instances, to his or her dependent family members. To qualify, a worker must have worked in jobs covered by Social Security. The exact work requirement varies by age but, generally, a worker must have worked one-half of the ten years prior to disability onset.[2]

An SSDI beneficiary whose income (after counting SSDI benefits) and assets fall below SSI limits is eligible to receive SSI benefits in addition. In 2000, 4.8 million beneficiaries received SSDI benefits only, 1.1 million received both SSDI and SSI; and 3.4 million received SSI only (SSA 2001).

There is a five-month, postwork waiting period before SSDI eligibility can begin. Beneficiaries receive Medicare benefits after 24 months of SSDI eligibility. For SSI, benefits can begin immediately after work ends. Almost all SSI recipients are eligible for Medicaid, and in most states eligibility is automatic.

For both programs, the disability must be expected to last at least a year or result in death. The claimant must pass a strict definition of work disability defined as an "inability to engage in any substantial gainful activity (SGA)."[3] Whether an individual meets the definition is not always straightforward. State Disability Determination Services (DDS) determine if the claimant's impairment is "severe" and if the claimant has "residual functional capacity" to engage in any type of work, in an often complicated and lengthy process. Claims denied by the state can be, and often are, appealed to SSA's administrative law judges. In 2001, fewer than 56 percent of claims were allowed.[4] Periodically, beneficiaries undergo a "continuing disability review" (CDR) to determine if their impairment has improved sufficiently to enable the beneficiary to engage in SGA.

The evidence we present in this chapter focuses on SSDI program beneficiaries. Although the number of SSI-only beneficiaries of working age has also grown more rapidly than the working-aged population, SSI beneficiaries who are not SSDI beneficiaries are much less likely than SSDI beneficiaries to have substantial work experience. As a result, from a theoretical perspective, the relationship between declining employment rates and SSI alone is much less clear than the relationship between employment rates and SSDI.

Changes in Eligibility and Benefits: Expansions and Retrenchments in Historical Context

The SSDI program has undergone almost continuous change from its inception in 1956 (SSA 1986). From 1956 through the mid 1970s, Congress expanded eligibility for disability benefits dramatically and increased benefit levels. Originally, benefits were provided only for disability-insured workers between ages 50 and 65 with an inability to engage in SGA "by reason of any medically determinable physical or mental impairment which can be expected to result in death or to be of long-continued and indefinite duration." The 1957 regulations added consideration of such nonmedical factors as "the individual's education, training, and work experience" (SSA 1986).

In 1960, the minimum age requirement was removed, and in 1965 "long-continued and indefinite duration" was replaced with "expected to last for a continuous period of not less than 12 months." In 1967, concerned that the definition of disability had eroded, Congress directed SSA to "to reemphasize the predominant importance of medical factors in the disability determination." The Social Security amendments of 1967 added language to the definition to make it clear that a claimant may be found disabled, "only if his physical or mental impairment or impairments are of such severity that he is not only unable to do his previous work but cannot, considering his age, education, and work experience, engage in any other kind of substantial gainful work which exists in the national economy, regardless of whether such work exists in the immediate area in which he lives, or whether a specific job vacancy exists for him, or whether he would be hired if he applied for work" (SSA 1986).

In 1972, the waiting period from the end of work to the beginning of benefit payments was reduced from six to five months. In addition, the introduction of the SSI program, which replaced a wide variety of state programs, had the effect of eliminating the work history requirement for those without significant assets or other sources of income. The 1972 amendments also first provided Medicare and Medicaid protection for SSDI and SSI beneficiaries, respectively (SSA 1986).

During the early and mid 1970s, the size of the program increased dramatically, giving rise to concerns that expansion of eligibility and benefits encouraged persons with impairments to stop working and apply for benefits, and that the program was attracting individuals with nonsevere impairments.

Between 1975 and 1979, several proposals for disability reform legislation were introduced in Congress. At the same time, SSA tightened the disability determination process, making it more difficult to get benefits; initial acceptance rates declined from about one in two applications to one in three. Legislative activities intensified in 1979, culminating in the enactment of the Social Security Disability Amendments of 1980 (Mashaw and Reno 1996).

The 1980 amendments included a more stringent maximum family benefit calculation; greater work incentives for SSDI and SSI beneficiaries with disabilities; and increased authority for the Secretary of Health and Human Services to establish, through regulations, performance standards and administrative procedures to be met by the states, including the authority to overturn state allowances (Mashaw and Reno 1996).

The 1980 amendments also required SSA to conduct CDRs of all beneficiaries at least once every three years to certify their continuing eligibility. This replaced the practice of conducting CDRs only in selected cases in which the individual's condition was expected to improve or the individual had returned to work.

The 1980 amendments created a massive and highly controversial workload for SSA. Widespread concern over the effect the reviews and subsequent terminations were having on beneficiaries prompted more than two dozen congressional hearings. Questions were raised about the criteria for selecting cases for review, the effects that the enormous workload was having on the quality of adjudications, the adequacy of the medical evidence used in CDRs, and the standards applied in making such determinations. Concerns were also expressed that the criteria for establishing disability based on a mental impairment were too restrictive. During this period, federal courts were also issuing decisions requiring use of a medical improvement standard in CDRs and consistent application of particular standards (Mashaw and Reno 1996).

In 1984, Congress loosened the reins again, largely to address what were widely regarded as excesses in the benefit terminations of the early 1980s and to increase national uniformity in the program. Most of the major provisions of the 1984 Disability Benefits Reform Act involved the statutory standards for evaluating disability. The act made it harder to terminate a beneficiary, gave more weight to the assessments of the applicant's or beneficiary's physician ("source evidence"), and broadened the list of conditions considered to be disabling, most notably making it easier for persons with psychiatric impairments and chronic pain to qualify for benefits. In addition, the 1984 act provided that the combined effect of all of a person's impairments must be considered in determining eligibility, even if no single impairment qualifies as "severe." In subsequent years, further legislative changes and a series of court decisions gave additional weight to source evidence, thus expanding the de facto definition of disability for the SSDI and SSI programs (Mashaw and Reno 1996).

Replacement Rates

While regulations were directly affecting eligibility, an unintended consequence of the formula for computing benefits was also evolving. As Autor and Duggan (2003) explain, the effective replacement rate (the ratio of disability income to prior earnings) for low-skilled workers rose through the 1980s and 1990s.

Disability benefits are indexed to the mean wage in the economy. Given the increasing disparity between high- and low-wage jobs during the 1980s, most low-wage workers experienced lower than average wage increases. As a result, potential SSDI benefits increased faster than wages for this segment of the economy.

Examining the benefit formula illustrates this process. The formula starts with the calculation of the beneficiary's Average Indexed Monthly Earnings (AIME), which is essentially the worker's average wages over his or her work career indexed by national wage growth to account for wage inflation. In 2002, the Primary Insurance Amount (PIA), which is the monthly Social Security benefit for the worker, after rounding to the next lowest dollar, equals:

90 percent of the first $592 in AIME
+ 32 percent of the amount between $592 and $3,567
+ 15 percent of the amount exceeding $3,567.

The amounts of $592 and $3,567 are referred to as "bend points." The average wage growth in the economy is used not only to index the individual's monthly earnings but also to rescale these bend points.

Because the bend points rise each year with the average nominal wage, workers who would have had wage growth below this average have a larger fraction of the lost wage income replaced at 90 percent rather than 32 percent. In addition, because past earnings are inflated by national average wage growth to compute the AIME, this same worker's AIME is greater than it would be had past earnings been the growth rate of their own wages. These factors increase the effective replacement rate for individuals in the low end of the earnings distribution.

The actual value of SSDI is not limited to the cash benefit. All SSDI recipients (after a waiting period) receive Medicare coverage, one-fifth also receive SSI cash benefits, and many beneficiaries have dependents who receive cash benefits based on the worker's disability.[5] Autor and Duggan (2003) find that, although Medicare significantly increases the value of benefits, SSI does not affect the replacement rate even for recipients in the tenth percentile of the earnings distribution for workers.[6] They do not consider the influence of dependent benefits.

The replacement rate, with or without including the value of Medicare, is higher and has increased most dramatically for those at the low end of the earnings distribution (Table 10.1). In 1999, male workers aged 55–61 were able to replace 73 percent of their earnings with disability income, an increase from 52 percent in 1979, or a 21 percentage point increase. If we include the value of the associated Medicare benefits in the numerator of the replacement rate, and comparably add fringe benefits to the denominator, the increase is from 67 percent in 1979 to 104 percent in 1999, a 37 percentage point increase. By contrast, workers in this age group who were in the ninetieth earnings percentile saw an increase of only 4 percentage points (from 20 percent to 24 percent without Medicare, and from 19 percent to 23 percent with Medicare).[7]

Decision to Apply for Benefits

Autor and Duggan (2003) outline a model of the decision to apply for disability benefits in which the individual weighs his or her per-

Table 10.1 Potential SSDI Income as a Percent of Current Earnings for Nonelderly Males at Various Percentiles of the Wage Distribution, 1979 and 1999

Age	Earnings percentile	Cash income replacement rate (%)		Adding in-kind medicare benefit[a]	
		1979	1999	1979	1999
55–61	10	52	74	67	104
	25	45	54	48	63
	50	37	47	36	47
	75	27	32	26	31
	90	20	24	19	23
50–54	10	47	57	61	81
	25	41	47	44	55
	50	34	41	33	42
	75	26	32	25	31
	90	19	23	18	22
40–49	10	48	53	61	80
	25	41	45	44	55
	50	34	41	33	42
	75	26	33	25	32
	90	20	26	19	25
30–39	10	46	54	59	84
	25	41	46	44	58
	50	36	41	35	44
	75	29	36	27	35
	90	23	28	21	27

[a] Includes average Medicare expenditures and adjusts for average percentile-specific fringe benefits.
SOURCE: Autor and Duggan (2003). Reprinted with permission from the *Quarterly Journal of Economics* 2003, p. 165.

ceived chance of being awarded benefits and the value of those benefits against the net value of working. The net value is the wage minus the "disutility of effort," which is larger for people in poorer health.

An employed person must choose between working and applying for benefits. If the worker chooses to apply for benefits, he or she must first exit employment (either voluntarily or involuntarily) and wait five months before benefit eligibility begins. Further, the application process might take much longer than five months, even if benefits are ultimately awarded retroactively. This is a risky alternative because the applicant must forgo earnings, and there is a probability (based on the severity of the person's condition) that the individual will be denied benefits. Workers choosing this option are likely to have a low net value of working (either because of low wages or ill health) and are also likely to have severe work limitations.

An individual who might not choose to leave a job to apply for benefits might choose to apply in the event of an involuntary job loss. This is a key point in the Autor-Duggan model. If the worker is not employed and does not expect to be employed for an extended period of time, the opportunity cost of lost earnings during application is substantially reduced or eliminated. In this case, the individual compares the value of benefits (accounting for the probability of actually being approved) and the net wage of a new job (accounting for the odds of reemployment). People who lose their jobs involuntarily not only have a lower opportunity cost, they likely can expect to earn less in another job, if they find one, thereby raising the attractiveness of disability income.

Autor and Duggan (2003) refer to this second group as "conditional" applicants. They hypothesize that deteriorating labor market conditions in the recession of the early 1990s coupled with the post–1984 eligibility expansions greatly expanded the pool of potential conditional applicants, and increases in the value of benefits, especially for those with low past earnings, made application more attractive to those in this pool.

FINDINGS

The Number of DI Beneficiaries Is Responsiveness to Changes in Eligibility Criteria and Program Generosity

The decision model implies that individuals are more likely to apply for benefits if they think that their chances of being approved are high. This result is seen clearly in SSDI trends during the past three decades. During this period, applications and awards seem to mirror changes in eligibility standards.

SSA administrative data for men and women of all ages show a sharp growth in the number of applications per 1,000 insured workers between 1960 and 1974 (Figure 10.1). Awards per 1,000 insured follow the same pattern. The allowance rate—the percentage of applicants who are awarded benefits—stayed relatively constant during this period. This is a bit surprising. We would expect that an increasing number of applicants would include a greater number of marginal cases and result in more denials. The fact that the allowance rate remained constant suggests that the disability determination process was, de facto, relaxing the eligibility criteria (Bound and Waidmann 2002).

After the administrative and legislative tightening beginning in 1974 and culminating with the 1980 amendments, applications fell off sharply (Figure 10.1); the allowance rate declined and the number of new awards plummeted.

Figure 10.1 Applications Respond to Program Changes

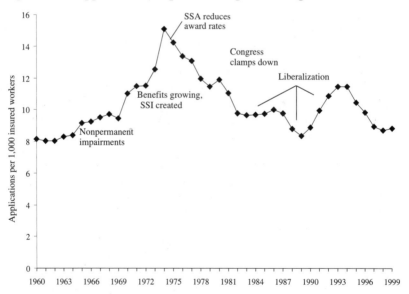

NOTE: Application data prior to 1982 adjusted using a consistent series on medical determinations (see Bound and Waidmann 2002).
SOURCE: U.S. Social Security Administration (various years). Reprinted with permission from the *Journal of Human Resources* 2002, p. 235.

After the liberalization in 1984, applications started to increase, but then declined again from 1987 to 1989 during the economic expansion. From 1990 to 1994, applications rose dramatically and then dropped in the latter half of the decade (Figure 10.1). The number of awards held steady as the allowance rate climbed from 1984 to 1999. The fact that the allowance rate climbed suggests another de facto expansion of eligibility standards. This is even more suggestive given the shifting profile of new applicants; they tend to be younger and more likely to suffer from mental impairments and musculoskeletal disorders than applicants in earlier years (Rupp and Scott 1998).

The number of beneficiaries per 1,000 insured grew substantially during the first period of program expansion, fell during the 1980s retrenchment, then began growing rapidly starting in 1990 and continuing through 1999 (Figure 10.2). The accumulation in the late 1990s

Figure 10.2 SSDI Applications, Awards, and Beneficiaries

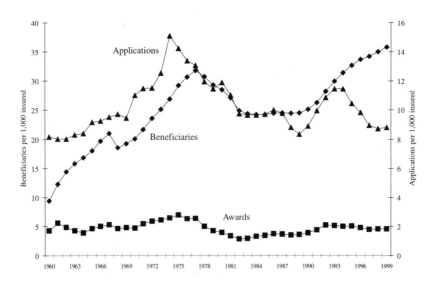

NOTE: Application data prior to 1982 adjusted using a consistent series on medical determinations (see Bound and Waidmann 2002).
SOURCE: U.S. Social Security Administration (various years), U.S. Department of Health and Social Services (various years), U.S. House of Representatives, Committee on Ways and Means (various years).

shows that fewer people were leaving the rolls than entering. Because being reclassified as retired or dying are the main reasons people exit the rolls (very few return to work), the growth in beneficiaries reflects the fact that newer beneficiaries tend to be younger and have lower mortality rates.

One critique of the hypothesis that eligibility expansions led to the decline in employment rates in the 1990s is that the timing is wrong. Although the 1984 legislation initiated the most recent eligibility expansion, the real increase in applications did not occur until 1990. There are, however, clear explanations for the delayed impact. One is that implementation of expanded criteria took many years, through revised listings for mental impairments in 1985 and numerous court decisions and regulatory changes in later years. Another is that it took time for potential applicants and their advocates to understand the changes fully. Perhaps most important, many newly eligible workers were likely conditional applicants, who stayed in the workforce during the economic expansion of the late 1980s, but applied when they lost their jobs in the recession of the early 1990s. These reasons for delay have made it easy to miss the role that eligibility expansions have likely played in the employment rate decline.

Trend in SSDI Beneficiaries Tracks the Employment Rate of People with Disabilities

Whatever the cause, clearly there has been a large increase in SSDI beneficiaries. The more salient question for this volume is whether this increase is reflected in the employment rate of people with disabilities. Using the NHIS, Bound and Waidmann (2002) compute the fraction of persons out of work and reporting work limitations. Because of major redesigns to the NHIS in 1982 and 1997, the analysis is restricted to the 1969–1996 period for men and 1982–1996 for women.[8]

The fraction of persons out of work and reporting work limitations corresponds well to the trends in the fraction receiving SSDI, especially for men. Findings are similar, but less clear, for women, reflecting the underlying growth in labor force participation for women. Figure 10.3, based on data from the NHIS, is limited to men aged 45–54, but the same patterns hold true for men of other ages. During periods when SSDI enrollment was expanding rapidly, the fraction of men

Figure 10.3 Work Limited and Not Employed and SSDI Enrollment (Men, aged 45–54) as a Percent of Population, 1969–1996

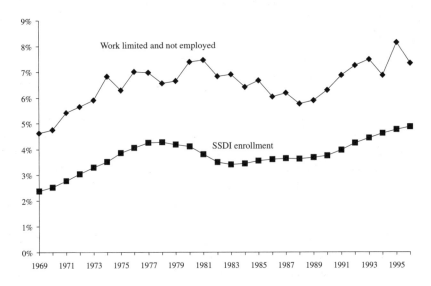

SOURCE: U.S. Social Security Administration (various years) and Bound and Waidmann calculations from National Health Interview Survey (various years).

identified as work-limited and not employed rose. During the late 1970s and early 1980s, when the size of the SSDI population shrank, so did the fraction of men out of work and identified as having work limitations. What is more, the size of the changes in these proportions are very similar, indicating an almost one to one correspondence between the numbers moving onto SSDI and the numbers showing up in the work limited and not employed category.

Bound and Waidmann (2002) develop a simple econometric model to predict the fraction of men who are work-limited and not employed from the fraction receiving SSDI benefits, using data from 1969 to 1989. Based on the estimates from this earlier period and SSDI data from 1990 to 1996, they forecast the fraction limited and not employed from 1990 to 1996.

Figure 10.4 shows the NHIS estimates and the Bound and Waidmann (2002) forecasts for men aged 45–54. The forecast is very close

Figure 10.4 Fraction of Men (Aged 45–54) with Work Limitations and Fraction Predicted by SSDI Enrollment 1969–1996

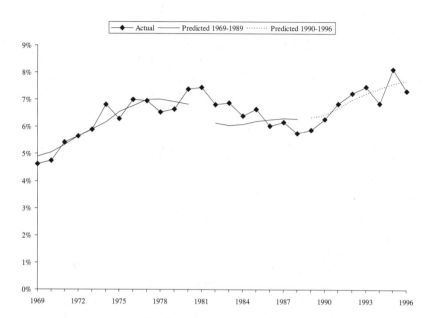

NOTE: The gap in the "predicted 1969–1989" line reflects the fact that SSA has never reported the number of SSDI beneficiaries for calendar year 1981. As a result, no prediction is possible.
SOURCE: U.S. Social Security Administration (various years) and Bound and Waidmann calculations from National Health Interview Survey (various years).

to the actual trend in the fraction of men who are work-limited and not employed. Estimates based on the other two age groups of men (30–44 and 55–59) also yield a very close fit (not shown in figure). Thus, we can account for recent trends in employment of men with work limitations by simply looking at historical trends in SSDI enrollment.[9] Although this tight relationship does not prove that SSDI program expansions caused the decline in the employment rate, we wonder whether such a tight relationship would be observed if the cause of the employment rate decline were external to the SSDI program.

Types of Impairments Cited by People with Disabilities Who Are Not Working Correspond to Impairments Affected by Program Changes

In previous sections, we analyzed the employment of people with work limitations. However, as Kaye notes in Chapter 6, the employment rate decline is associated with an increase in the proportion of people with work limitations who say they are unable to work at all. Kaye argues that there has been an increase in the prevalence of those impairments that are associated with the inability to work. A more plausible explanation is that this increase reflects a change in SSDI eligibility criteria.

A large fraction of the increase in the number of people identified as work-limited who also report that they are unable to work at all can be accounted for by an increase in the number of men and women reporting psychiatric or musculoskeletal impairments. These impairments represent an increasing proportion of SSDI beneficiaries. These are also the impairments that were most affected by the SSDI liberalizations, beginning with the Disability Benefits Reform Act of 1984 and continuing in the 1990s. We argue that these liberalizations increased the likelihood that individuals with psychiatric and musculoskeletal impairments would be SSDI-eligible. As a result, they are more likely to leave the labor force and report that they are unable to work at all.

The NHIS asked persons who reported a work limitation to identify the main cause of that limitation. Table 10.2 shows that, for younger men (aged 30–44), the increased prevalence of disabling mental and musculoskeletal conditions accounts for more than 60 percent of the total increase between 1983 and 1996. For older men (aged 45–59), these conditions account for approximately 90 percent of the overall increase. Among younger women, the increased prevalence of mental and musculoskeletal disabilities accounts for 72 percent of the overall increase. For older women, although the overall prevalence of work limitations increased only slightly, the prevalence of work limitations caused by mental and musculoskeletal impairments increased dramatically, and work limitations from all other causes declined.

When we compare these trends to similarly defined trends in the primary impairments assigned to current SSDI beneficiaries in 1986

Table 10.2 Change in Fraction (per 1,000) of Men Unable to Work, by Cause, 1983–1996

	Men		Women	
	Change	% of total	Change	% of total
All conditions				
Aged 30–44	19.6	100.0	15.0	100.0
Aged 45–54	15.4	100.0	2.6	100.0
Aged 55–59	14.9	100.0	0.7	100.0
Mental conditions				
Aged 30–44	4.8	24.5	5.5	36.7
Aged 45–54	3.3	21.5	3.5	131.1
Aged 55–59	1.8	12.0	3.4	498.9
Musculoskeletal conditions				
Aged 30–44	7.4	37.6	5.3	35.5
Aged 45–54	10.6	68.7	4.2	157.7
Aged 55–59	11.6	77.8	7.6	1,108.9
All other conditions				
Aged 30–44	7.4	38.0	4.2	27.8
Aged 45–54	1.5	9.8	−5.0	−188.9
Aged 55–59	1.5	10.2	−10.4	−1,507.7

SOURCE: Authors' tabulation using the 1983–1996 National Health Interview Survey.

(the earliest year for which SSA provides this type of data) and 1996, we find that mental and musculoskeletal conditions account for 73 percent of the increase in the fraction of the population receiving SSDI benefits for younger men (aged 30–44) and the entire increase for older men (aged 55–59) (Table 10.3). For women, these sets of diagnoses account for between 63 percent and 68 percent of the growth in SSDI recipients.

States with Larger Increases in the Percent of Their Population Receiving DI Benefits Saw Larger Increases in the Fraction of People Who Have Limitations and Are Out of Work

Although SSDI is a federal program, there was considerable cross-state variation in the growth of its population during the 1990s. For example, between 1989 and 1999, Wisconsin saw growth of 28 percent in the fraction of the working-aged population receiving SSDI benefits,

Table 10.3 Change in Fraction (per 1,000) on SSDI, by Diagnostic Group, 1986–1996

	Men		Women	
	Change	% of total	Change	% of total
All conditions				
Aged 30–44	7.2	100.0	7.2	100.0
Aged 45–54	13.3	100.0	14.4	100.0
Aged 55–59	15.2	100.0	22.4	100.0
Mental conditions				
Aged 30–44	3.9	54.3	3.8	52.6
Aged 45–54	7.6	57.0	6.0	41.9
Aged 55–59	4.9	32.1	5.3	23.6
Musculoskeletal conditions				
Aged 30–44	1.4	18.9	1.1	15.6
Aged 45–54	3.7	28.0	3.7	25.8
Aged 55–59	11.1	72.8	8.9	39.6
All other conditions				
Aged 30–44	1.9	26.8	2.3	31.8
Aged 45–54	2.0	15.0	4.7	32.3
Aged 55–59	–0.8	–4.9	8.3	36.8

SOURCE: Authors' tabulation using Social Security Bulletin Annual Statistical Supplement, 1997, 1987.

while Alaska saw 123 percent growth. Some of this variation may be explained by the recession in the early 1990s, which had different effects on state economies.[10] Local factors, such as cross-state differences in the administration of the DI award process, may also be a factor.

Bound and Waidmann (2002) capitalize on this variation to study the relationship between SSDI beneficiaries per capita and the fraction of the population identified as work-limited and not employed. They calculate the fraction of the 16–64-year-old population in each state receiving SSDI benefits from 1989 to 1999 using SSA administrative data and census population estimates. Using the CPS, they estimate the 16–64-year-old population in each state that was both work-limited and not employed.[11]

Their results imply that the increase in the fraction of the working-aged population receiving SSDI benefits can account for the entire rise in the fraction of the population that reports a work limitation and is not employed (Bound and Waidmann 2002).

High School Dropouts Are More Likely to Leave the Labor Force in States with High SSDI Growth

In a similar vein, Autor and Duggan (2003) use state-level variation to model the change in labor force participation of high school dropouts as a function of changes in the supply of benefits (SSDI and SSI recipiency), the average market wage, and other characteristics. Estimates were developed separately for the 1979–1984 period and the 1984–1998 period. Based on estimates for the 1979–1984 period, they found that a 1 percentage point increase in disability recipiency is predicted to reduce the labor force participation of male high school dropouts (regardless of disability status) by 3.2 percentage points. Because high school dropouts compose almost 31 percent of the disability recipient population (SSA 2000), a far larger percentage than their share in the workforce, this is an important finding. Despite the fact that the program was contracting in the 1979–1984 period and expanding thereafter, Autor and Duggan find that the estimated relationship between employment rates and disability recipiency levels is quite similar in the pre- and postreform eras. In other words, male high school dropouts were entering the labor force more rapidly in states with large reductions in the number of disability recipients during the retrenchment and leaving the labor force more rapidly in high disability growth states following the liberalization. This relationship between changes in disability recipients and changes in male labor force participation is much weaker for more educated workers, consistent with the fact that better educated workers are much less likely to receive SSDI benefits. Results for women were less precise, but again SSDI recipiency is negatively related to the labor force participation of high school dropouts; no relationship is found for females with a high school education or greater.

Additional Empirical Results Suggest that Program Expansion, Not Some Other Factor, Induced the Increase in SSDI Enrollment and the Decline in the Employment Rate

The research described above uses state-level variation to show that growth in disability benefits closely tracks employment rate declines. Bound and Waidmann (2002) establish that movement of workers with disabilities onto the SSDI rolls aligns with the increase in the percentage of the population that is work-limited and not employed. Autor and Duggan (2003) demonstrate that the labor force participation of high school dropouts is related to disability income recipiency.

Both empirical models predict employment as a function of SSDI recipiency, but SSDI recipiency is also a function of employment. Referring back to the theoretical model presented above, we can see that SSDI growth is driven by changes in both the supply of benefits and the demand for those benefits. The supply is defined by program characteristics (screening stringency and replacement rates). Demand—the number of people applying for benefits given screening stringency and replacement rates—is determined, in large part, by employment "shocks," or factors that would influence employer willingness to hire. The challenge is to show that a shift in the supply of benefits (i.e., a program expansion) caused an increase in the number of working-aged people with disabilities who demanded benefits and, consequently, reduced the number working. To separate the supply of benefits from the demand for benefits, Autor and Duggan (2003) exploit state variation in the replacement rate; because the SSDI benefit formula is progressive but not indexed to regional wage levels, workers in low-wage states have significantly higher replacement rates than those in high-wage states.

The theoretical model predicts that changes in screening stringency will have a larger impact in high-replacement-rate states compared with states with low replacement rates. Intuitively, if the replacement rate is extremely low, few people would be affected by a change in screening stringency because only those with extremely low earnings or who find work extremely onerous would choose to apply under any condition. If, on the other hand, the replacement rate is very high, more people would find SSDI participation to be a reasonable alternative to work, and would potentially respond to a program expansion. That is, for a substantial number of people with disabilities, the decision to apply will rest on individuals' perceived chance of getting benefits (i.e., screening stringency) and the generosity of benefits they would receive if their application were successful.[12]

Changes in Screening Stringency Have a Much Larger Impact on the Employment Rate in High-Replacement-Rate States than in Low-Replacement-Rate States

Autor and Duggan (2003) gauge the effect of the 1984 eligibility expansions by estimating the relative effect of screening stringency on the employment rate in high- and low-replacement-rate states before and after the 1984 liberalizations. The estimates indicate that the disability retrenchments during 1979–1984 increased the labor force participation of high school dropouts by 4.7 percentage points more in high-replacement-rate states than in low ones. The liberalization of the program after 1984 induced a similarly large, relative decrease in labor force participation in high-replacement-rate states compared with low-replacement-rate states. Although less precisely estimated, the data suggest that the labor force impact on female high school dropouts was about two-thirds as large. These data suggest that the eligibility stringency and the generosity of the program have an interactive effect on the labor force participation of low-skilled individuals, particularly high school dropouts.

Disability Program Applications Have Become Increasingly Sensitive to Employment Shocks

Autor and Duggan's (2003) model implies that eligibility expansions increase the sensitivity of SSDI entry and long-term labor force exit to an economic downturn. In the extreme, if eligibility is so stringent that anybody who can possibly work is denied with 100 percent probability, there would be no conditional applicants, and a downturn in the economy would have no impact on the number of beneficiaries. When large numbers of people who can work have some reasonable probability of being found eligible, a downturn in the economy will create many conditional applicants and have a substantial impact on the number of beneficiaries. Autor and Duggan confirm that disability program applications have become increasingly sensitive to employment shocks.[13] As Figure 10.5 indicates, for a given decline in the demand for labor, the increase in SSDI applicants per capita from 1993 to 1998 was almost seven times as large as the increase between 1979 and 1984.[14] In other words, the expansion in eligibility greatly increased sensitivity of applications to economic shocks. As a result, the program attracted more conditional applicants after the 1984 expansions.

High School Dropouts Are More Likely to Exit the Labor Force after a Job Loss Than They Were before 1984

Autor and Duggan (2003) also show that the labor force participation of adults who do not have high school degrees (those most likely to be affected by disability program expansions) is much more sensitive to the demand for labor now than before the 1984 reforms. More specifically, they find that workers without high school degrees are 60 percent more likely to exit the labor force after a job loss in the post–1984 period than they were before 1984. The recent growth in the high

Figure 10.5 SSDI Application per Population for a One-Unit Demand Shock, 1978–1998

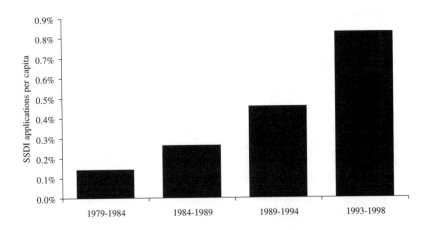

SOURCE: Calculations by Autor based on findings by Autor and Duggan (2003).

school dropout SSDI beneficiary population is consistent with this finding. In 1999, almost 60 percent of all nonelderly male adult high school dropouts who were not in the labor force were receiving either SSI or SSDI. Given that the population of nonelderly high school dropouts declined by 30 percent between 1984 and 1998, we would have predicted 550,000 fewer high school dropout recipients in 1998 than 1984. Instead the number rose by about 770,000. In fact, by 1998, more than one in seven high school dropouts were receiving either SSDI or SSI benefits (Figure 10.6).

Thus, the facts seem consistent with the hypothesis that SSDI expansions increased the sensitivity of labor force participation for low-skilled workers to economic downturns, thereby contributing to the employment rate decline. There is a second possible explanation for the finding that SSDI applications and labor force participation have become more sensitive to employment shocks, however. It is possible that, for other reasons, high school dropouts with disabilities who lose their jobs are finding it more difficult to find a new one, and are

Figure 10.6 Percent of Nonelderly Adults Aged 25–64 Receiving Disability Benefits,[a] 1984 and 1999

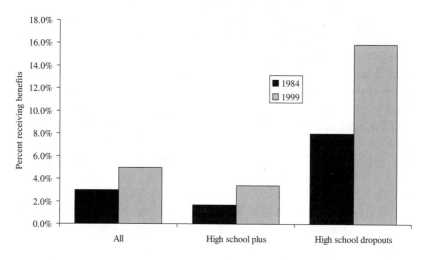

[a] Includes recipients of SSDI and SSI.
SOURCE: Calculations by Autor based on findings by Autor and Duggan (2003).

therefore more likely to apply for SSDI. Changes in required job skills could cause such a shift, although it seems likely that such a change would occur gradually over a long period. If the ADA discouraged employers from hiring people with disabilities, as others have argued (see DeLeire, Chapter 7, and Acemoglu and Angrist 2001), we would also expect to see increased sensitivity in both labor force exit and SSDI applications. The ADA could not, however, account for increases in the sensitivity of SSDI applications that occurred before 1990.

DISCUSSION

Clearly SSDI and employment are closely correlated. Although it is impossible to prove that SSDI expansions caused the employment rate decline rather than vice versa, we have presented a host of findings that are consistent with a causal relationship. In addition, other explanations of the employment rate decline do not fit the data nearly as well.

There is strong evidence that the eligibility expansions of 1984 increased the number of individuals applying for and receiving benefits. Prior to the 1984 expansions, there was a close, negative relationship between the employment rate of people with disabilities and the fraction of the population receiving SSDI. After 1984, there was a sharp increase in SSDI beneficiaries, and the eligibility expansions have been identified as a major cause. The SSDI expansion was matched by a parallel drop in the employment rate. This suggests that changes in SSDI were leading changes in the employment rate. Additional weight should be given to this evidence given the close correspondence between the growth in types of impairments of both people with disabilities who are not working and SSDI beneficiaries.

The evidence presented does not rule out the possibility that a factor other than SSDI liberalization is ultimately responsible for some of the observed labor force withdrawal, but among the competing explanations that have been put forward, SSDI liberalization seems the most compelling.

There is a growing literature suggesting that the ADA lowered the employment rate for people with disabilities by making employment less available (see DeLeire, Chapter 7; Blanck, Schwochau, and Song, Chapter 9). If true, this decline in job opportunities could lead to an increase in the number of people applying for SSDI benefits. It seems unlikely, though, that we would see such a close correlation between SSDI and the employment rate over such a long period if SSDI did not play an important independent role. Moreover, the ADA explanation fails to account for four other findings:

1) The employment rate began declining between 1989 and 1990. The implementation of the ADA's antidiscrimination provisions did not occur until the middle of 1992.[15]

2) An increasing proportion of SSDI recipients have musculoskeletal and psychiatric disorders—the same impairments cited by people with disabilities who are most likely to say they are unable to work at all. We could argue that employers are most wary of such impariments, and thus may be disproportionately affected by employers' fear of lawsuits,[16] but it is unclear why this would be the case.

3) Low-wage workers were more likely to drop out of the labor market than higher-wage workers, and the difference is greater in the 1990s than in the 1980s. To attribute these findings to the ADA, we would need to argue that employers are somehow more discouraged from hiring low-wage than high-wage workers. It is unclear why that would be the case.

4) If the ADA (or anything else reducing employment opportunities) pushed workers out of the labor market and toward applying for SSDI benefits, we might expect those with the most marginal disabilities to leave, and as a result, we would expect more rejected applications. However, this did not happen; award rates rose in the 1990s, which is consistent with a de facto expansion of eligibility.

Kaye (Chapter 6) presents an alternative theory that could explain the increasing number of applications coupled with a steady award rate. He argues that there has been an actual increase in the prevalence and severity of disabling conditions. Although we find this plausible, we find it hard to believe that it would have a sudden impact on employment in 1990. If the increase in the prevalence and severity of disabilities was sparked in large part by the recession, we should have seen an equivalent decline in employment during the recession of the early 1980s. We did not see this employment rate decline, we argue, because SSA had so severely restricted the SSDI program that dropping out of the labor market and applying for benefits was not an option.

A rise in the SSDI rolls in and of itself is not necessarily a positive or negative development. Clearly, if the growth indicates that individuals with disabilities are "trapped" in a cycle of dependence that is antithetical to the goals of the ADA and the independent living movement, the growth is troubling. If, on the other hand, the growth is a result of providing an increasingly meaningful safety net to individuals who cannot fully participate in the labor market because of their impairment, the growth may be desirable.

Analysts differ sharply when discussing work disincentives associated with expanding eligibility or increasing benefits. Some have argued that these are signs that people with disabilities are simply choosing not to work when they are capable. Others take strong exception to this belief, and argue that such work disincentives are often overstated (see Bound and Waidmann 1992 for a review). We hold a third point of view: people with disabilities are very responsive to changes in the structure of the SSDI program, but this does not necessarily indicate an abuse of the system. The appropriateness of the policy should be judged by the marginal recipients—do they have profound impairments that generate significant economic and health insecurity? If so, why is it a bad thing if they choose to take advantage of a program that is designed to meet their needs? Nevertheless, the system may benefit from a modification that would address the needs of recipients without requiring them to withdraw from the labor force.

Some interpret the expansion of the program beginning with the 1984 liberalizations as unnecessarily large. However, the retrenchment in the 1980s brought widespread hardship and was successfully challenged in the courts. There is no reason to think that this period represents an "appropriate" level of benefit availability. If we look over the entire time period and adjust for increases in the number of people eligible for benefits (see Figure 10.3), the growth does not seem so dramatic.

Nevertheless, the current system clearly has a significant work disincentive. There are undoubtedly some SSDI beneficiaries who can work above substantial gainful activity (SGA) but choose not to because of the loss of benefits that would entail. Put differently, if they could keep their benefits and work above SGA, they would. The system prior to 2002 basically prohibited this option to the detriment of both the individual with a disability and society. The individual loses the income (and the buying power that accompanies income) while society loses productivity.

There might be an optimum solution that allows beneficiaries to offset some benefits with earnings. Indeed, SSA seems to recognize this possibility and is piloting several efforts to ameliorate the disincentives under the 1999 Ticket to Work and Work Incentives Improvement Act. A more flexible program could well have allowed people with disabilities to share in the economic expansion of the 1990s. The desirability of such a program, however, depends significantly on how well the disability screening process operates. If those with severely reduced capacity for work are not easily identifiable by medical screening, then it seems possible that large numbers of able-bodied persons would take advantage of the SSDI program while continuing to work. The magnitude of this problem is obviously reduced as the ability to screen out the able-bodied is increased (Waidmann et al. 2002). Assuming that a satisfactory screening mechanism exists, it is possible that a reformed SSDI program would mean that people with disabilities do not have to miss the benefits of future expansions.

Notes

The authors would like to thank David Autor, John Bound, Richard Burkhauser, and David Stapleton for their comments on earlier drafts. Goodman's work on this chapter was supported by the National Institute on Disability and Rehabilitation Research (NIDRR) through the Cornell Rehabilitation Research and Training Center for Economic Research on Employment Policy for Persons with Disabilities, cooperative agreement No. 13313980038. The opinions we expressed are our own and do not represent official positions of NIDRR, Cornell University, or the Urban Institute.

1. Based on Decennial Census. Ages 18–65.

2. In order to qualify for SSDI a worker needs 40 credits, 20 of which were earned in the 10 years prior to becoming disabled. A worker can earn up to four credits per year with the earnings needed for each credit changing annually ($870 in 2002).
3. In 2002, an individual earning $780 per month ($1,300 if blind) is considered to be engaged in SGA.
4. Of the 1,988,425 determinations in fiscal year 2000, 38 percent were allowed at the initial level, 4.5 percent were allowed at reconsideration, 13 percent were allowed by administrative law judges, fewer than 1 percent were allowed by appeals council or federal court, 44 percent were denied.
5. In 1999, there was approximately one spouse or child dependent beneficiary for every three SSDI beneficiaries receiving benefits averaging $220 per month (SSA 2000, Table 5.E2).
6. Autor and Duggan calculate that individuals at the tenth percentile of the earnings distribution for workers, if they were to receive SSDI, would have cash benefits above the SSI threshold. A worker with earnings in the tenth percentile of the distribution would have received SSDI income of $592 in 1998 and $280 in 1979, above the SSI maximums of $480 and $208 for those years. As a result, although SSI may be important at the first through fifth percentiles of the earnings distribution for workers, it does not affect the replacement rates used in the analysis.
7. The replacement rate equals the SSDI benefit divided by the expected wage. When including the value of the Medicare benefits in the numerator, Autor and Duggan (2003) include an estimate of the value of fringe benefits in the denominator. The value of fringe benefits is estimated separately for each earnings decile. In the seventy-fifth and ninetieth earnings percentile, the estimated value of fringe benefits was higher than the estimated value of the Medicare benefit, yielding a replacement rate lower than if fringe benefits and Medicare were excluded from the computation. Further, that the calculated replacement rate increases even a small amount for people at the ninetieth percentile of earnings distribution (whose wages grew more than the average wage increase in the economy) is a consequence of the calculation methodology. Earnings used for the SSA indexation increased 20 percent more than the average wages for males aged 25–61 in the CPS. This is because SSDI benefits are calculated only on earnings subject to FICA. Because the FICA payroll tax cap rose substantially relative to real earnings in 1979–1999, this caused the replacement rate for high-income worker to rise. It is important to note that, for high-income workers, the replacement rate rose because high-income workers were paying more in SSDI taxes, not because the benefit formula became more generous (see Autor and Duggan 2003).
8. Prior to 1982, only men were routinely asked about their ability to work. In 1997, the entire questionnaire was restructured, including the sequence of questions on work limitations.
9. This exercise would be less useful for women for several reasons. First, the match between SSDI trends and employment trends in the 1970s and 1980s is more complex, when other social forces were making women's employment more the norm than the exception. In the 1990s, the percent of women who were limited

and out of work and the fraction of women receiving SSDI benefits were similar to trends seen for men. One plausible explanation for why the relationship was not as strong in the earlier years is that women's weaker attachment to the labor force in those years meant that women were less likely to be SSDI insured. Thus, a growing SSDI program was less salient in an era in which relatively few were covered by the program.

10. See Rupp and Stapleton (1995).
11. By using a linear regression, they hold constant state fixed effects.
12. Autor and Duggan apply an instrumental variable approach to identify the relationship between SSDI and employment. We have omitted many details and recommend that interested readers see Autor and Duggan, 2003.
13. The employment rate is affected by both the supply of labor and the demand for labor where the supply may be affected by SSDI enrollment. To isolate the exogenous labor demand shock, Autor and Duggan exploit cross-state differences in industrial composition and national-level changes in employment to predict state employment. See Autor and Duggan 2003, for details.
14. There is a one-year overlap in the last two periods to maintain three-year intervals in each group.
15. Bound and Waidmann (2002) added year-effects to their state level models and found little evidence consistent with a negative ADA effect. After controlling for DI enrollment, there is one increase (of about 0.5 percent) in the fraction out of work two years after the ADA went into effect that diminishes over time. If anything we would expect the ADA's effect to cumulate over time as employers make new hiring decisions, and we would expect continued divergence after implementation.
16. Most ADA lawsuits are for firing or refusing to accommodate rather than failing to hire.

References

Acemoglu, Daron, and Joshua Angrist. 2001. "Consequences of Employment Protection: The Case of the Americans with Disabilities Act." *Journal of Political Economy* 109(5): 915–956.

Autor, David, and Mark Duggan. 2003. "The Rise in Disability Recipiency and the Decline in Unemployment." *Quarterly Journal of Economics* 118(1): 157–205.

Bound, John, and Timothy Waidmann. 1992. "Disability Transfers, Self-Reported Health, and the Labor Force Attachment of Older Men: Evidence from the Historical Record." *The Quarterly Journal of Economics* 107(4): 1393–1419.

———. 2002. "Accounting for Recent Declines in Employment Rates among the Working-Aged Disabled." *Journal of Human Resources* 37(2): 231–250.

Mashaw, Jerry, and Virginia R. Reno. 1996. *The Environment of Disability Income Policy: Programs, People, History, and Context.* Washington, DC: National Academy of Social Insurance.

Rupp, Kalman, and Charles G. Scott. 1998. "Determinants of Duration on the Disability Rolls and Program Trends." In *Growth in Disability Benefits: Explanations and Policy Implications,* Kalman Rupp and David C. Stapleton, eds. Kalamazoo, MI: W.E. Upjohn Institute for Employment Research, pp. 139–174.

Rupp, Kalman, and David C. Stapleton. 1995. "Determinants of the Growth in the Social Security Administration's Disability Programs—An Overview." *Social Security Bulletin* 58(4): 43–70.

Social Security Administration. 1986. "History of the Social Security Disability Programs." Washington, DC: SSA. Available at: <http://www.ssa.gov/history/1986dib history.html>. Accessed: February 5, 2002.

———. 2000. "Annual Statistical Supplement, 2000." Washington, DC: SSA. Available at: <http://www.ssa.gov/statistics/supplement/2000/sipp2000.pdf>. Updated June 18, 2001. Accessed: June 12, 2002.

———. 2001. "Annual Statistical Report on the Social Security Disability Insurance Program, 2000." Washington, DC: SSA. Available at: <http://www.ssa.gov/statistics/di_asr/2000/ index.html>. Posted: October 2, 2001. Accessed: March 12, 2002.

Waidmann, Timothy, John Bound, and Austin Nichols. 2002. "Disability Benefits as Social Insurance: Tradeoffs between Screening Stringency and Benefit Generosity in Optimal Program Design." Paper presented at Social Security Administration Retirement Research Consortium Annual Conference, Washington, DC, May.

11
A Review of the Evidence and Its Implications for Policy Change

Richard V. Burkhauser
Cornell University

David C. Stapleton
Cornell University

Despite the promise of the Americans with Disabilities Act (ADA) of 1990, eight years of uninterrupted economic growth, and a series of government initiatives to integrate those with disabilities into the workforce, survey data tell us that the employment rates of working-aged men and women with disabilities declined substantially during the 1990s business cycle. In fact, the employment rate of working-aged people with disabilities was lower in 2000, the peak year of the 1990s business cycle, than at the bottom year of that business cycle (1992). At the same time, employment rates of those without disabilities grew. Concomitant with their fall in employment was a decline in their labor earnings, which were primarily offset by an increasing dependence on federal government income support benefits, namely, Social Security Disability Insurance (SSDI) and Supplemental Security Income (SSI). Labor earnings of those without disabilities grew markedly at the same time. This disconnect between the employment fortunes of those with disabilities and the rest of the population is in stark contrast to the 1980s business cycle, when the employment and earnings of those with and without disabilities moved in the same direction. What explains this change in employment trends in the 1990s? Did people with disabilities face greater discrimination in the workplace, despite or perhaps because of the ADA? Did workers with disabilities respond to the easing of disability eligibility standards and the increase in relative SSDI and SSI benefits and, forced to make an all or nothing choice, chose to leave the labor force and enter these programs at a greater rate? Or did the medical conditions and functional limitations among those with disabilities become more severe, making work less of an option for a growing number of them?

The previous chapters attempt to answer four sets of questions regarding the measured change in the employment rates of working-aged people with disabilities in the 1990s. The first two sets of questions focus on measurement issues:

- Did employment rates fall, or is this conclusion simply an artifact of flawed data?

- What population should be used to capture the employment trends of working-aged people with disabilities and evaluate the success of public policies aimed at this population? Should we measure employment for the full spectrum of people with disabilities, only those with disabilities who say they can work, or only those with disabilities who are targeted by the ADA?

The third set of questions focuses on causality:

- What caused these measured declines in the employment rate of working-aged people with disabilities in the 1990s: changes in the basic characteristics of the population with disabilities (sex, age, race, and education); changes in the nature of work that make it more difficult for people with disabilities to compete with others; the growing cost of health care and how it is financed; increases in the average severity of health conditions and impairments of those who have disabilities; unintended consequences of the ADA, which discouraged employers from hiring and, hence, increased discrimination against working-aged people with disabilities; or lowering of eligibility standards for the SSDI and SSI programs, as well as an increase in the relative value of SSDI benefits for low-wage workers, that encouraged a movement out of the labor force and onto the income support rolls?

The final set of questions focuses on what must be done in the light of this evidence:

- As we move into a new century and a new business cycle, what are the implications for public policy of the employment experiences of working-aged people with disabilities documented during the past two decades? Should we focus on inducing employers to employ those with disabilities rather than compelling them to do so via regulation? Should we shift from a predominately insurance-based disability support system to one that is more work oriented?

In what follows, we present our own answers to each of these questions, drawing on the evidence presented in the earlier chapters. Although we agree with many of the conclusions reached by the authors of individual chapters, we do not agree with them all. Indeed, we cannot agree with them all because some key conclusions are in direct conflict with one another.

Objective interpretation of the evidence provided in this book is difficult because of the emotionally charged nature of some of the issues it raises. On the one hand, those who believe that the social environment is the primary factor in determining the employment of working-aged people with disabilities are uncomfortable believing that the primary reason for the decline in employment in the 1990s was an increase in the severity of the health conditions and functional limitations of this population. Appeals to a medical model of this sort are difficult to accept for those who advocate for the full integration of people with disabilities into the workforce. This is particularly the case when much of the evidence for this view relies on the belief that the response of people with work limitations to a question asking whether they are able to work at all is solely influenced by the severity of their condition, and not by the social environment in which they find themselves.

On the other hand, those who see the ADA as the primary mechanism to more fully integrate people with disabilities into the workforce may fear that evidence to the contrary will lead to abandonment of the rights of this population rather than modifications of the law and its enforcement to more effectively achieve this goal.

Likewise, supporters of SSDI or SSI as mechanisms for providing insurance against lost earnings owing to a disability, or as a guarantee of minimum income support for all Americans with disabilities, might fear the political consequences of evidence showing how expansion of these programs resulted in the decline in the employment of working-aged people with disabilities. Such political consequences might include reforms that will increase the vulnerability of the population with disabilities in the name of improving their employment.

Finally, those who believe that market-based solutions are ultimately the most appropriate way to allocate resources are less than happy with evidence showing the inability of private labor markets to employ all those who are willing and able to work, at a living wage, and including health insurance benefits.

In other words, objective evidence is always controversial to those unwilling to allow their policy hopes to be tempered by reality. When public policy is subject to the scrutiny of social science, the outcome of that research is, by its nature, uncertain. Yet, an unflinchingly objective examination of the evidence is critical if we are to learn from the past and improve the employment opportunities of working-aged people with disabilities while maintaining appropriate income protection for those unable to work.

More controversial than the empirical evidence in this book, however, is the policy changes that it implies. Ultimately, policymakers must make the trade-off between the goal of increased employment and the increased economic independence that employment brings to those with disabilities, and the goal of a safe and secure income level for those with significant health conditions and functional limitations who are unable to work. Policymakers must also decide how to strike a balance between policies that directly intervene in the marketplace, such as regulations and quotas, and those that indirectly affect market outcomes via taxes, subsidies, or public investments to improve the productivity of people with disabilities (e.g., through education, rehabilitation, or job support).

Here, we review the evidence provided in the preceding chapters, weigh the sometimes contradictory nature of that evidence, and provide a first attempt at relating the body of this evidence to policy changes that should be considered by those interested in reversing both the decline in the employment of working-aged people with disabilities and their increasing dependence on government income support programs.

DID THE EMPLOYMENT RATE DECLINE?

All of the authors agree on the following three points:

1) The employment rate for working-aged adults with disabilities, broadly defined, has declined during the 1990s, both absolutely and relative to the rate for those without disabilities.

2) The proportion of people with disabilities who say they are able to work at all declined during the same period.

3) The employment rate for those with disabilities who say they are able to work at all increased.

We briefly discuss each of these points below.

The Declining Employment Rate of Working-Aged Adults with Disabilities, Broadly Defined

Using data from the Current Population Survey (CPS), Houtenville and Daly (Chapter 3) find that the employment rate of working-aged people with self-reported work limitations was 40.8 percent at the peak of the business cycle in 1989. By the peak of the next business cycle, in 2000, it had dropped by 8 percentage points, to 32.8 percent. By comparison, the employment rate of working-aged people without work limitations increased by 1.9 percentage points, from 86.3 percent to 88.1 percent over the same period. Thus, the gap between the employment rates of people with and without work limitations increased, by about 10 percentage points.

The validity of the CPS employment rate measure has been called into question because of the possible sensitivity of the size and composition of the population who consider themselves to have work limitations to changes in the policy and economic environment. Kruse and Schur (Chapter 8) provide an extensive discussion of this issue.

The work limitation measure of the working-aged population with disabilities leaves much to be desired, but Burkhauser and coauthors (Chapter 2) provide convincing evidence that the decline in employment in the CPS data among those reporting a work limitation is real, and not merely an artifact of that data set or the work limitation question. To arrive at this conclusion, they compare employment trends from the CPS with employment trends from the National Health Interview Survey (NHIS) and the Survey of Income and Program Participation (SIPP). NHIS and SIPP support a richer variety of disability definitions, including ones that we would expect to be less sensitive to the economic and policy environment. Although estimates of the size of the working-aged population with disabilities vary significantly across surveys, and across definitions of disability within surveys, in any given year, the authors find declining employment trends regardless of the survey used, and whether the working-aged population with a disability is defined broadly, based on a self-reported impairment, more narrowly as a limitation in any major activity, still more narrowly as any work limitation, and most narrowly as a work limitation that is reported in each of two interviews, one year apart.

If any doubt remains about whether the declines in the measured employment rates reflect real declines in employment, those doubts have to be dispelled by growth in the share of working-aged adults who receive SSDI or SSI (see Burkhauser et al., Chapter 2, and Goodman and Waidmann, Chapter 10). The tight relationship between the number of working-aged males who are not employed and who report work limitations, and the number of males receiving SSDI benefits, demonstrated by Bound and Waidmann (2002), is particularly compelling evidence that the survey measures are capturing a real phenomenon.

The Proportion of People with Disabilities Who Say They Are Able to Work at All Declined

This finding is perhaps not remarkable given the employment rate decline, but the magnitude of the decline is. For the population with work limitations, the CPS shows a decline in the proportion able to work at all, from 78 percent in 1988 to 73.2 percent in 1993, then, after a break in the series owing to a change in the CPS, an additional drop from 52.8 percent in 1994 to 45.4 percent in 2000. The NHIS shows a decline from 49.8 percent in 1988 to 40.7 percent in 1996, the last year of the data (Burkhauser et al., Chapter 2, Appendix 2C, Table C.4). Kaye (Chapter 6) finds similar declines using slightly different years of data and definitions of the population with disabilities.

The Employment Rate for Those with Disabilities Who Say They Are Able to Work at All Increased

Employment among the CPS male "able to work at all" population fell slightly during the recession, from 54.7 percent in 1989 to 51.7 percent in 1992, but then, after a definitional change in the series, increased from 61.6 percent in 1994 to 64.2 percent in 2000. The employment rate based on a similar measure from the NHIS fell from 85.1 percent in 1989 to 82.8 percent in 1992 and then increased to 86.3 percent in 1996, the last year of the data (Burkhauser et al., Chapter 2, Appendix 2A, Table 2A.5). Kaye (Chapter 6) finds similar increases using slightly different years of data and definitions of the population with disabilities. These increases are comparable to increases in the employment rate for people without work limitations.

WHICH MEASURE OF THE EMPLOYMENT RATE SHOULD WE FOCUS ON?

Although all authors agree that the employment rate of working-aged adults with disabilities, broadly defined, has decreased, and the rate for those who report being "able to work at all" has increased, there is disagreement about which measure is most relevant for purposes of understanding recent history and informing the public policy debate.

If we are interested in measuring the extent to which progress is being made toward the broad goals articulated in the ADA—greater inclusion of people with disabilities in major social activities, including work, and greater economic independence—we should be interested in the employment rate for all people with disabilities, regardless of whether they report they are able to work at all. To do otherwise ignores the aspirations for increased economic independence and social integration of a large share of people with disabilities.

Beyond this, however, is there something to be learned for policy purposes from analysis of the employment rate for only those who say they are able to work at all? Kaye (Chapter 6) argues that the answer depends on why the share of the population with disabilities who report being able to work at all has decreased. If the reason for the decline is an increase in the severity of medical conditions, then, according to Kaye, trends in the employment rate for those who are able to work at all tell us something meaningful about those for whom work is a realistic option. If, on the other hand, reports of inability to work are sensitive to the economic and policy environment, then looking at rates for only those who report being able to work at all misses an important, perhaps definitive, component of the effects of the economic and policy environment on employment (see Burkhauser et al., Chapter 2, and DeLeire, Chapter 7).

Kruse and Schur (Chapter 8) present an argument that is similar to Kaye's, although it is more focused on the ADA. They point out that the ADA was only intended to improve employment opportunities for those who are able to work at all, at least with reasonable accommodation. Therefore, for purposes of assessing the impact of the ADA, they would have us look at a narrower population, one that includes only those who report they are able to work at all.

If we can confidently rule out the hypothesis that change in the economic and policy environment affects the proportion saying they are able to work at all, then we can sharpen our understanding of the effects of the economic and policy environment by examining just those who are affected. But Kaye's evidence does not convince us that the proportion saying they are able to work at all is immune to the economic and policy environment. In fact, our understanding of that environment and reading of the evidence lead us to the opposite conclusion. We discuss why as we consider the evidence presented in this volume.

Concerning arguments that the ADA employment provisions only apply to a subset of the population, we echo the counterargument made by DeLeire (Chapter 7) and Goodman and Waidmann (Chapter 10): there is much ambiguity in the minds of employers, consumers, and courts about who is protected and who is not. Given this, it should not be surprising if the ADA affects employment outcomes for people who are not in its intended target population. We can hardly take comfort in the fact that the employment rate for people with disabilities who say they are able to work at all increased after the ADA unless we can rule out the possibility that the ADA contributed to the significant decline in the proportion of people with disabilities who say they are able to work at all.

In sum, we think it a mistake to rely on the employment rate of people with disabilities who say they are able to work at all as an indicator of the progress being made toward improving employment outcomes for people with disabilities. The evidence convinces us that the economic and policy environment has had an effect on the proportion of people with disabilities who say they are able to work at all.

WHAT CAUSED THE EMPLOYMENT RATE DECLINE?

The previous chapters consider the following possible explanations of the employment rate decline:

- Changes in the composition of the working-aged population of people with disabilities: Houtenville and Daly (Chapter 3) focus on the demographics and education of the population.
- Changes in the nature of work that affects the ability of people with disabilities to compete with other workers (Stapleton, Goodman, and Houtenville, Chapter 4).
- Growth in health care costs that, given the way health care is financed, make work less attractive for people with disabilities who have chronic, high-cost health conditions (Hill, Livermore, and Houtenville, Chapter 5).
- Increases in the severity of impairments and health conditions among those with disabilities (Kaye, Chapter 6).
- The ADA (DeLeire, Chapter 7; Kruse and Schur, Chapter 8; and Blanck, Schwochau, and Song, Chapter 9).
- Expansions of the SSDI and SSI programs, including both lowering eligibility standards and increasing the relative benefits for low-wage earners (Goodman and Waidmann, Chapter 10).

As we discuss below, the evidence presented by the relevant authors rules out changes in demographics and education as major causes of the decline. It also indicates that the growth in health care costs and changes in the nature of work cannot account for much of the decline, although they might have contributed to the decline for some. We find this evidence compelling.

At least one chapter supports as the single major cause each of the following potential causes of the decline:

- Increases in the severity of impairments and health conditions among those with disabilities (Kaye, Chapter 6);
- The unintended consequences of the passage and implementation of the ADA (DeLeire, Chapter 7); and
- Eligibility and benefit expansions in the SSDI and SSI programs (Goodman and Waidmann, Chapter 10).

In what follows, we summarize the evidence on the potential causes that we agree can be ruled out, and provide a more in-depth and critical review of the evidence on these three remaining potential causes.

Demographics and Education

Houtenville and Daly (Chapter 3) focus on the sex, age, race, and educational composition of the population (aged 25–61) with work limitations. Although there were substantial changes to the age and educational distributions of this population from 1989 to 2000 (mirroring changes in the general population), if anything these changes favored groups of adults with work limitations who have relatively high employment rates: those with at least some college education. Using a standard decomposition technique, they show that the decline of the employment rate for adults with work limitations would have been greater if the age, sex, race, and education composition of the population with work limitations had stayed constant, holding constant the decline within each age, sex, race, and education group.

A second finding from their analysis is that the decline in the employment rate is widespread, crossing all age, sex, race, and education groups, although it is greater for some groups than for others. The decline is particularly high for men. Based on the CPS, the employment rate for men with work limitations fell by 10.9 percentage points, from 44 percent in 1989 to 33.1 percent in 2000, compared with a 4.9 percentage point decline for women, from 37.5 percent to 32.6 percent. The larger decline for men reflects the substantial rise in the employment rate for women relative to men without work limitations. Hence, the size of the decline for men is perhaps a better indicator of the magnitude of the impacts of whatever force(s) caused the decline in the employment rate for people with work limitations than the decline for men and women together. Further, the smaller decline for women with work limitations is not an indication that the impacts of those forces were smaller for women.

Another notable feature of the decline in the employment rate is that it is greater for young adults (aged 25–44) than for older ones (aged 45–61), regardless of race, sex, or education. This is especially troubling because young adults have many more years than older adults before they would be expected to leave the labor force. We would also expect the decline in the employment rate for the younger group in the last decade to be reflected in future declines in the rate for the older group, as those in the younger group age into it.

The main point, however, is that the employment rate declined for all major demographic and educational groups. Thus, it seems likely that whatever forces have caused the decline are forces that affect all groups, but perhaps have their largest effect on those who are young.

The Nature of Work

Stapleton and coauthors (Chapter 4) consider how changes in the nature of work might have affected the ability of adults with disabilities to compete for jobs with other adults. From their perspective, the decline in the employment rate of people with work limitations relative to that of people without work limitations is viewed as a decline in the proportion of jobs that are filled by people with work limitations. That proportion was remarkably stable from the mid 1980s to the mid 1990s, and declined sharply during the second half of the latter decade.

Although changes in the nature of work are difficult to quantify, the authors provide evidence of some significant changes. In doing so, they distinguish between static job characteristics—those seen in a "snapshot" of a job at a point in time—and dynamic characteristics, particularly the frequency with which workers change jobs. Based on existing research about the nature of changing work, they conclude that changes in static characteristics of jobs are likely to disadvantage some workers with work limitations but be an advantage to others; that is, there is no reason to expect an overall positive or negative effect of changes in static characteristics on the proportion of jobs filled by people with disabilities. On the other hand, they expect that an increase in involuntary job loss is likely to disadvantage many workers with disabilities relative to those without disabilities because of the greater challenges they face in finding and starting a new job.

Although not entirely definitive, the evidence they present shows that changes in the nature of work seen during the 1990s began in the 1980s, if not earlier—and well before the start of the decline in the proportion of jobs filled by workers with limitations. Further, there is no evidence of an acceleration of change that could account for the sharp decline in the proportion of workers with limitations after the mid-1990s. Instead, the changes have been gradual and long-term. They do identify two changes that seem to be making it more difficult for people with disabilities to compete, on average, over the long term: a gradual increase in educational and skill requirements, and a gradual decline in job security, but the magnitude of these gradual changes is too small to contribute much to the decline in the proportion of workers with limitations. The main causes of the decline must lie elsewhere.

Health Care Costs

Hill and coauthors (Chapter 5) examine the effect that increases in health care costs, and concomitant changes in the way health care is financed, have on the employment rate. This explanation has considerable appeal given the rising cost of health care and the higher-than-average health care expenditures of people with disabilities. There is also considerable documentation that people with disabilities frequently cite access to health insurance as a main reason for not working.

The authors present two complementary analyses, and find mixed results. The first, using the 1987 National Medical Expenditure Survey (NMES) and the 1996 and 1997 Medical Expenditure Panel Surveys (MEPS), considers changes in employment rates from 1987 to 1996–1997 for individuals who have chronic conditions, regardless of disability, grouped by the costs of health care for those conditions. They find that the share of the population with high-cost chronic conditions increased over this period, and that the employment rate for those with high-cost conditions fell relative to that for those with lower-cost chronic conditions or without chronic conditions. This evidence is consistent with the hypothesis that growing health care expenditures contributed to the decline in the employment rate, but the authors note that it is based on all working-aged persons, not just those who report a disability. Comparability issues for the two surveys prevent them from making similar comparisons among those who report disability (e.g., work limitations) only.

They therefore turn to the NHIS. They are able to compare the employment rates of persons with work limitations with and without high-cost chronic conditions in 1984–1987 with those for the same groups in 1993–1996, using the high-cost condition group developed with the MEPS and NMES data. This analysis yields mixed results. For women with work limitations, the employment rate for those with high-cost chronic conditions fell relative to the rate for others, as we would expect if growing health care costs contributed to the employment rate decline. For men with work limitations, however, the employment rate for those with high-cost chronic conditions did not fall relative to others. If growth in health care costs explains the result for women, it is not apparent why the result for men would be any different.

Finally, as was done in some of the earlier chapters, these authors conduct a decomposition exercise. They find that, for both men and women, growth in the prevalence of high-cost chronic conditions combined with changes in the employment rate for those with work limitations who have such conditions, has depressed the employment rate for people with work limitations. The size of this effect, however, was small relative to changes in the employment rates for men and women that were observed during the same period (on the order of 10 percent).

Given the intuitive appeal of the hypothesis the authors have examined, it is perhaps surprising that they, and others, have not found evidence that growth in health care costs, and changes in financing, have contributed more substantially to the decline in the employment rate. Although it could be that data and methodological issues conspire to obscure the effect, another possible reason emerges from their analysis. Although people with work limitations, on average, have higher health care costs than others, those health care costs are concentrated among a very small share of people with work limitations; less than 7 percent of those with work limitations had high-cost chronic conditions in 1993–1996, based on Hill and coauthors' estimates. We suspect that growth in health care costs depressed the employment rate for those with high-cost chronic conditions, but this effect cannot explain much of the decline in the employment rate for people with work limitations because such a small share of people with work limitations have high-cost chronic conditions.

Severity of Health Conditions and Impairments

Kaye (Chapter 6) argues that changes in the type and severity of underlying health conditions can explain the decline in the proportion of people with disabilities who say they are able to work at all and, thus, the decline in the overall employment rate of working-aged people with disabilities found in the other chapters. All the previous chapters primarily used CPS or NHIS data to examine the employment rate of those who report a work limitation. In contrast, Kaye focuses on a somewhat broader population, those with "any major activity limitation" (including a work limitation). This is not, however, a critical difference; as shown by Burkhauser and coauthors (Chapter 2), the long-term employment rate trends for those with any activity limitation are quite similar to trends for those with work limitations only.

Kaye argues that:

- Responses to condition and impairment questions in the NHIS are not subject to social environmental factors, and, based on these data, the prevalence of conditions that are most commonly indicated as the cause of an activity limitation grew for the working-aged population from 1988 to 1996.

- For the conditions reported, the proportion of individuals with each condition who report an activity limitation, or say they cannot work, remained constant.

- If increases in the overall prevalence of disability or inability to work at all were because of environmental factors, such as disability benefits or the ADA, these proportions would have increased. Because they did not, neither of these two responses is influenced by the social environment. Instead, growth in the inability to work-at-all rate for those with activity limitations is caused by an increase in the prevalence of conditions that have low rates.

Although we agree that responses to questions about conditions and impairments are less likely to be affected by social environmental factors and that the prevalence of such conditions increased during part of the 1990s, we do not find the rest of Kaye's argument convincing. Part of the problem is that he focuses on activity limitation and inability to work rates for the working-aged population as a whole, rather than the proportion of those with activity limitations who are unable to work at all. This would be fine if activity limitation prevalence and inability-to-work rates were growing in lock step with each other, but they are not. That fact is not evident from the data unless we directly examine the proportion of those with activity limitations who are unable to work at all.

For the conditions in the NHIS checklist, Kaye provides estimates of overall prevalence, prevalence of activity limitations owing to the conditions, and prevalence of inability to work at all owing to the condition. Data on actual and predicted prevalence of activity limitations and prevalence of inability to work at all owing to these conditions (Chapter 6, Figure 6.15) seem to confirm the second and third points in the list. If, however, one considers the proportion of those with activity limitations owing to one of these conditions who report an inability to work at all, there is evidence of an increase (Figure 11.1), from 37.7 percent in 1988 to 41.1 percent in 1996—a 9.8 percent increase.[1] Further, as illustrated in the figure, Kaye's models for the prevalence of activity limitations and prevalence of inability to work at all do not predict this increase.[2] The increase in the proportion of those unable to work at all among those with activity limitations owing to a checklist condition is very comparable to the increase in the corresponding proportion for all conditions, as reported by Kaye; the proportion for all conditions increased from 39.9 in 1988 to 44.5 in 1996, an 11.5 percent increase.

In sum, growth in the prevalence of activity limitations owing to checklist conditions primarily reflects overall growth in the prevalence of these conditions, but the growth in the proportion of those with activity limitations who say they are unable to work at all is greater than expected, owing to growth in prevalence of these conditions alone. Put differently, Kaye's data are consistent with the following conclusion: it appears that changes in the policy and economic environment have not affected the rate of self-reported activity limitations from checklist conditions, but have increased the proportion of those with activity limitations who say they are unable to work at all.

Figure 11.1 Percentage of Persons with Affective Disorders Who Report an Activity Limitation or Inability to Work

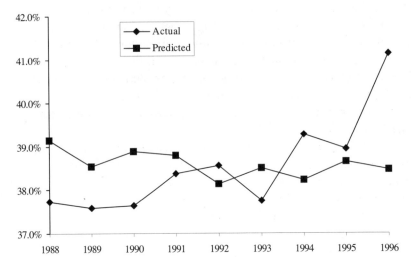

SOURCE: Calculations by the authors, using data provided by Kaye (Chapter 6). The actual series is the estimate of the proportion unable to work due to checklist conditions divided by the proportion reporting a major activity limitation due to the same conditions. The predicted series is the ratio of Kaye's predictions for the same series.

The above applies to the checklist conditions only, and does not apply to one very important condition that is omitted from the checklists: affective disorders (depression and bipolar disorder). Kaye does, however, provide some information on trends in prevalence of the condition, activity limitations owing to the condition, and inability to work at all owing to the condition, based on whether the respondent visited any physician (including psychiatrists, but excluding non-physician providers) because of the disorder in the past two weeks. We agree with Kaye that the 62 percent increase from 1988 to 1996 in this measure of the condition's prevalence is likely due, in substantial part, to the availability of new pharmacological treatments and a decline in stigma. What is more astonishing is the growth in reported activity limitations and in inability to work at all owing to these conditions, relative to growth in overall prevalence of the condition. Kaye's evidence indicates that the proportion of those with affective disorders who report an activity limitation roughly doubled, as did the proportion reporting inability to work at all. The evidence should be treated with caution because those with affective disorders that are most likely to limit their activities are perhaps also most likely to obtain new treatments. We would expect, however, that new treatments would reduce the real proportion of those with affective disorders who report an activity limitation, as well as the proportion reporting inability to work at all. This makes the growth in activity limitations and inability to work at all owing to these conditions even more troubling.

Kaye provides evidence on two possible causes of the increase in the prevalence of disabling conditions: growth in the prevalence of obesity and the recession of 1990–1991. It does seem likely that increased obesity has contributed to both activity limitations and the inability to work at all, although we think further work needs to be done to assess the size of its contribution.[3] We are not surprised that timing of growth in inability to work at all appears to be linked to the recession, but we think the mechanism for the link is probably quite different than the one that Kaye posits. When people lose their jobs in a downturn, they look for alternative sources of income. The SSDI program is a potential income source for people with disabilities, but to qualify, the applicant must claim to be unable to work for at least a year at any job. Although we are willing to accept the argument that job loss does damage the health of some individuals, as some research shows, it is much harder for us to believe that a recession could cause the large and sustained impact on health that Kaye reports.

Kaye's analysis ends in 1996, owing to changes in the NHIS. As Burkhauser and coauthors (Chapter 2) find, the decline in the employment rate for men and women with work limitations continued through 2000. Houtenville and Daly (Chapter 3) conduct an analysis for 1995–2000 that casts further doubt on the hypothesis that increases in the severity of impairments among those with work limitations is the principal cause of the decline in the employment rate. The CPS started to include a health status question in 1995. Houtenville and Daly find that, from 1995 through 2000, there is no trend in the distribution of the health status variable for those with work limitations, and the employment rate decline is as large, if not larger, for those who report relatively good health than for those who report relatively poor health.

Although health status and impairment severity are clearly not synonymous concepts, there is a strong statistical relationship between impairment measures and health status measures in the NHIS and other data sets where measures for both concepts are available. Hence, the findings of Houtenville and Daly would be surprising if the real cause of the employment rate decline among those with work limitations during the last half of the 1990s was an increase in the severity of their impairments.

Hence, we conclude that the main cause of the employment rate decline of working-aged people with disabilities lies elsewhere. Likewise, we conclude that the positive trend in the employment rate of the subset of working-aged people with disabilities who say they are able to work at all is a misleading indicator of the employment outcomes of working-aged people with disabilities because the declining share of this subset of the population is not driven by a purely exogenous decline in their health, but by changes in the social environment that all workers with disabilities face. Below we consider the two most important changes in that social environment in the 1990s.

The Americans with Disabilities Act

Is it possible that the ADA, intended to increase employment opportunities for people with disabilities and reduce their economic dependence, could have had the opposite effect? DeLeire (Chapter 7) would say yes, primarily based on evidence from his own work (DeLeire 2000a, 2000b, and 2001) and that of Acemoglu and Angrist (2001). Kruse and Schur (Chapter 8), however, say no, and Blanck and coauthors (Chapter 9) think it is premature to draw a conclusion.

It appears that the participants in this debate would all agree that the direction of the theoretical impact of the ADA on employment is ambiguous. On the one hand, the cost to employers of potential litigation from discrimination against people with disabilities ought to discourage unjust terminations. However, this same cost can be avoided through increased discrimination in hiring. As the authors point out, most ADA litigation is over termination; discrimination in hiring is much more difficult to detect, let alone prove, and perhaps much less likely to be reported. Therefore, it is possible that the ADA has tipped the balance against hiring people with disabilities and thus offset any gains from reduced terminations.

The ADA's requirement that employers provide reasonable accommodations increases the cost of employing a worker who needs an accommodation, whether an existing worker or a job applicant, again potentially discouraging employment. Although studies of accommodations have shown that many are inexpensive, as DeLeire (Chapter 7) points out, these studies do not consider the hard-to-measure costs of accommodations, such as flexible schedules, or the cost of accommodations that employers have been unwilling to make.

On the other hand, the implementation of the ADA was accompanied by a substantial effort to educate employers on accommodating workers with disabilities, and it provides some subsidies for that purpose. In general, the ADA advanced the expectation that employers take an objective look at what an individual with a disability can do rather than automatically discount the individual's ability.

As both DeLeire (Chapter 7) and Kruse and Schur (Chapter 8) point out, the consensus among economists is that the Civil Rights Act (CRA) of 1964 increased employment opportunities for African-Americans, and none dispute this conclusion—although, again, the direction of the expected effect was ambiguous. Two features of the ADA make it different from the CRA, however: mandated employer accommodations and the difficulty of determining who qualifies for ADA protection. The latter creates the possibility of lawsuits from many whom the law does not intend to protect.

Ultimately, the question of the ADA's impact on employment of people with disabilities is an empirical issue, and a very difficult one at that. DeLeire and others contend that the decline in the employment rate for people with disabilities, which began at about the time the ADA was passed and implemented, is evidence of a negative impact, just as growth in the employment rate of African-Americans in the latter half of the 1960s was evidence of the positive impact of the CRA. It is very difficult to draw this conclusion because of two other events: the recession that coincided with ADA passage and implementation, and expansions in the SSDI and SSI programs that began as early as 1984. Goodman and Waidmann (Chapter 10) argue that it is the combination of these latter events, rather than the ADA, that caused the employment rate to decline. Disentangling these competing effects is highly problematic.

Kruse and Schur argue that the evidence that the ADA caused the decline is flawed because the ADA was not intended to target the broad population with work limitations captured by the employment rate measures used by DeLeire and Acemoglu and Angrist (2001). They argue that the relevant group is the subgroup with health conditions or functional limitations that is able to work at all, an argument that is echoed by Blanck and coauthors (Chapter 9), and they find that the employment rate for those able to work at all increased.

DeLeire rejects this line of reasoning because he views disability as the outcome of an interaction between a medical condition and a person's environment. Some of those who consider themselves work-limited or unable to work at all in the absence of an accommodation might not think so when an accommodation becomes available. In fact, Kruse and Schur make this same point. More generally, DeLeire agrees with a point we have made previously: policy changes can, and do, have an impact on the proportion of people with disabilities who report they are unable to work at all. We would also add that the ambiguity of the ADA's disability definition, and its interpretation in the courts, leaves open the question of whether all ADA impacts are limited to its target population. In fact, Kruse and Schur allow for the possibility of this problem, but argue that it can ultimately be dismissed, and do so in their preferred results.

At the same time that we disagree with Kruse and Schur about their use of a narrow subgroup of people with disabilities to assess the impact of the ADA, we agree with their observation that measured compositional changes in those who report work limitations did occur, and that those compositional changes might help discriminate between the hypothesis that the ADA caused the overall decline in the employment rate of working-aged people with disabilities and the hypothesis that it was owing to expansions in the SSDI and SSI programs. We will return to this issue at the end of our discussion of the role played by those programs.

Blanck and coauthors also make a point about the ADA that is worth repeating. The ADA might have had a significant impact on the culture of disability, which could have long-term positive effects on employment. It has probably increased the visibility of people with disabilities who do work. It might have encouraged many people with disabilities to attempt work and to invest in their ability to work. Similarly, it might have encouraged educators, providers, and advocates to see work and independence as a desirable and achievable goal, and it might have encouraged employers and workers without disabilities to look more objectively at the capabilities of workers with disabilities.

SSDI and SSI Expansions

All of the evidence we have seen is consistent with the hypothesis that SSDI and SSI expansions interacted with the recession to cause a long-term reduction in the employment rate of people with disabilities. Goodman and Waidmann (Chapter 10) provide a comprehensive presentation of the evidence, primarily based on articles by Bound and Waidmann (2002) and Autor and Duggan (2003). In short:

- Increases in the SSDI rolls closely tracked the employment rate of those with disabilities who are insured for SSDI.
- Eligibility was primarily expanded by lowering the medical listings for the two impairment groups—musculoskeletal and psychiatric—that also account for a very large share of the increase in reported inability to work at all.
- Because of variation in wage growth and the way benefits are indexed to average wage growth, SSDI replacement rates increased for low-wage workers, and growth in the number of such workers on the SSDI rolls was much greater than for others.
- SSDI applications have become more sensitive to the business cycle, which is what we would expect from an expansion in eligibility. This is because eligibility expansion creates more "conditional applicants," that is, workers who might qualify if not working, and who seek benefits when they lose their job during a downturn. Benefit expansions for those with low wages also encourage them to apply (Autor and Dugan 2003).

Skeptics, however, offer two arguments. First, they argue that the timing is off—eligibility expansions occurred too early relative to the employment rate decline and growth in program participation. Second, they argue that the employment rate for workers with disabilities declined for some other reason, and SSDI and SSI participation increased as a response, as those who could not work or find jobs sought income support.

The timing argument reflects a lack of understanding about the nature of the expansions and how their impact on employment and program participation is related to the business cycle. As described more fully by Goodman and Waidmann (Chapter 10), although the eligibility expansion began in 1984, it continued for many years as regulations were developed and important cases worked their way through the courts. This is a well-documented fact, and is well known by program administrators. Further, strong economic growth during the late 1980s meant that many new conditional applicants had no need to apply for benefits until the recession of 1990–1991. Perhaps the strongest indicator of the eligibility expansion is that the allowance rate remained unchanged, or even increased, as the number of applicants grew rapidly. If an external force drove the rapid growth in applications, we would expect a decline in the allowance rate, as individuals with less serious impairments sought benefits. We find this evidence convincing.

It is more difficult to rule out the possibility that some external force caused both the decline in the employment rate and the increase in SSDI and SSI program participation. The two candidates for such an external force that are promoted by authors in this book are growth in the severity of impairments (Kaye, Chapter 6) and the ADA (DeLeire, Chapter 7). For reasons discussed above, we conclude that the evidence rules out increase in the severity of impairments as the cause. It is more difficult to discount the evidence for the ADA. Kruse and Schur (Chapter 8) and Blanck and coauthors (Chapter 9) argue that we should look only at the subgroup of the population targeted by the ADA. We are convinced, however, that the sensitivity to the social environment of self-reported inability to work at all, and the more overriding public policy perspective of considering the employment and economic well-being of all working-aged people with disabilities, requires us to focus on the broader population.

Hence, we are left with the question: Is the wide variety of evidence that appears in this volume more consistent with the ADA hypothesis or the SSDI and SSI hypothesis? Unfortunately, much of it is consistent with both. We agree with Goodman and Waidmann (Chapter 10) that some facts appear to favor the SSDI and SSI hypothesis. The three we find of greatest significance are:

1) The increase in the SSDI and SSI allowance rates. Eligibility expansions are expected to increase allowance rates, at least initially. If an external force such as the ADA induces SSDI and SSI applications, we would expect the average induced applicant to have a lower chance of allowance than the average applicant who would have applied anyway.

2) The decline in the employment rate is greatest for those with musculoskeletal or psychiatric impairments. These are the disorders for which SSDI and SSI eligibility standards are most relevant. We see no reason why the ADA would have its greatest impact on the employment of those with these disorders.

3) Employment rate reductions were highest among those with low earnings (Autor and Duggan 2003). This is the group that experienced a substantial expansion of their SSDI replacement rate. There is no apparent reason why the ADA would adversely affect this group more than others.

However, DeLeire points out three facts that appear to favor the ADA explanation:

1) Employment declines for workers with disabilities were greater in medium-sized firms than in small or large firms (Acemoglu and Angrist 2001). Small firms are exempt from ADA accommodation requirements, and there is good reason to believe that medium-sized firms would find ADA compliance more difficult than large ones. There is no apparent reason to think that SSDI and SSI expansions would reduce employment of people with disabilities at medium-sized firms relative to others.

2) Acemoglu and Angrist (2001) conclude that state employment rate declines for people with disabilities post-ADA are positively related to the number of Equal Employment Opportunity Commission (EEOC) charges in the state.

3) Acemoglu and Angrist (2001) find employment rate declines associated with the ADA's implementation even after omitting SSDI beneficiaries from their samples.

To date, proponents of one or the other of these public policies as the more important in explaining the decline in employment of working-aged people with disabilities in the 1990s have failed to reconcile the conflicts in the above evidence. Difficult questions that need to be addressed include:

- Are there reasons why the ADA would increase SSDI and SSI allowance rates?
- Are there reasons why the ADA would reduce the employment of people with musculoskeletal or psychiatric impairments more than those with other conditions?
- Are there reasons why the ADA would reduce the employment of those with low skills more than others?
- Are there reasons why SSDI and SSI eligibility expansions would reduce the employment of workers with disabilities in medium-sized firms more than in large or small ones?
- Does the cross-state association between EEOC charges and the employment rate decline remain after controlling for the cross-state variability in the effects of SSDI and SSI eligibility expansions in combination with the 1990 recession?
- How can we reconcile the Acemoglu and Angrist (2001) finding that the employment rate decline associated with the ADA remains even after omitting SSDI beneficiaries from the sample with the finding that the proportion of men who are unable to work at all owing to a health condition tracks very tightly with the number of male SSDI beneficiaries (Bound and Waidmann 2002)?

We do not have satisfactory answers to any of these questions, and it is not obvious that they will ever be answered to anybody's complete satisfaction.[4] Although our judgment to date is that the weight of the evidence favors the SSDI-SSI expansion explanation over the ADA explanation, our comfort level with that conclusion is not as high as we would like it to be.

We are convinced, however, that there has been a real, and substantial, decline in the employment rate of people with disabilities, and that it was caused by a change in public policy. If there were some other cause, why would the effect be observed across all demographic, education, and health groups? One possible answer to this question is growth in the severity of disabling physical and mental conditions, but, as discussed earlier, the evidence does not support this explanation. It seems very unlikely that several different factors coincidentally caused a substantial decline in the employment rate for people with disabilities that spanned all groups.

It is unlikely that there is some other major cause of the employment rate decline that we have somehow overlooked, although one has been suggested by Kruse and Schur: the tightening of workers' compensation eligibility and payment rules in response to the rapid growth in workers' compensation costs during the previous two decades. This is an intriguing suggestion, and one that is worth looking into further. It is possible that tightening of state workers' compensation programs induced more injured workers to leave their jobs and obtain SSDI benefits for lack of temporary or permanent-partial support. Tightening could also lead to the opposite effect, however, with injured workers returning to work earlier to support themselves and their families. We would be surprised if tightening of workers' compensation programs is *the* explanation for the employment rate decline, but perhaps it made a contribution. If so, however, we are still left with the conclusion that changes in public policy caused the decline. This explanation would also reinforce perhaps the most important finding from decades of research on the SSDI and SSI programs: the structure of income supports for people with disabilities has a substantial impact on their employment.

POLICY IMPLICATIONS

As discussed above, the evidence indicates that the widespread employment rate decline for people with disabilities is a consequence of public policies that were implemented in the late 1980s and early 1990s. The most important implication of this finding is that we are very unlikely to see substantial improvement in employment outcomes for people with disabilities in the near future unless we change public policy in very significant ways.

We are convinced that expansions of the SSDI and SSI programs played a significant role in the employment rate decline. Those expansions include both eligibility expansions and expansion in the value of benefits relative to wages for low-wage workers. Although we are not convinced that the ADA had a significantly negative effect on employment of working-aged people with disabilities, we also find no unambiguous evidence that it had a significant positive effect. At best, it may have increased the employment of the decreasing share of that population who report being able to work at all. This does not mean that we should roll back the clock to the policies that were in place before these changes. These changes were intended to address real, and serious, problems. Many people with severe disabilities were being denied SSDI and SSI benefits, in part because eligibility standards were increased from 1979 to 1981, before being lowered again in 1984. Similarly, the ADA was passed to address real discrimination in the workplace and elsewhere against people with disabilities. Many states did not have laws against such discrimination, and others found such laws difficult to enforce.

What the findings in this book lead us to recognize is that attempts to improve insurance protection against work loss owing to disability or to reduce discrimination in employment can have the unintended consequence of reducing employment. Hence, if we are to improve employment outcomes, we must make changes in the way we provide support for people with disabilities, and the way we protect their rights, that will minimize the negative employment effects, or, better, encourage employment, while maintaining a reasonable level of income protection and protection against discrimination.

Civil Rights

As discussed by DeLeire (Chapter 7), evidence of the positive impact of the 1964 Civil Rights Act on employment of African-Americans makes it clear that Civil Rights legislation can have a positive impact on employment. We think that the ability of Civil Rights legislation to induce employers to increase their hiring and retention of a protected class of workers critically depends on their assessment of the costs and benefits of compliance. Regardless of what the impact of the ADA has been on the employment of people with disabilities to date, policy changes that increase the benefits of compliance or reduce the costs for employers will improve the employment outcomes for people with disabilities.

Before considering how public policy changes could encourage compliance and improve employment outcomes, it is helpful to review how the employer's calculus of costs and benefits differs for existing employees and job applicants. With respect to existing employees, the main benefit of compliance is avoiding the cost of litigation and penalties from lawsuits over termination and other issues ("retention benefit"), and the main compliance cost is accommodation. With respect to potential employees (i.e., job applicants), the main benefit of compliance for employers is avoiding the cost of litigation and penalties from lawsuits over hiring issues. There are two components of an employer's compliance costs with respect to potential employees: accommodation costs, and the expected costs of lawsuits over future termination and other issues ("termination cost").

A critical feature of this calculus is that the litigation costs create a benefit for employers who comply in the case of existing employees (the retention benefit), but create a cost to employers who comply in the case of job applicants (the termination cost). Thus, if policy changes increase the employer's costs via lawsuits over termination, they will encourage employers to retain their current workers but discourage them from hiring new ones. Some of the evidence that the ADA reduced employment suggests that the reason is reduced hiring, not increased terminations (Acemoglu and Angrist 2001). The conflicting incentives created by the substantial numbers of lawsuits from existing employees, and the relative rarity of lawsuits from job applicants, could explain why.

Within this framework, the following three approaches to both improving ADA compliance and employment outcomes have considerable appeal:

1) Reduce the cost of employer accommodations through subsidies or technical support (e.g., providing better information about efficient accommodations),

2) Increase efforts to enforce compliance in hiring, and

3) Clarify who is protected, under which circumstances they are protected, and what constitutes reasonable accommodation.

We consider each of these approaches below.

Reducing the cost of employer accommodations through subsidies or technical support would reduce the employer's cost of ADA compliance for both existing employees and job applicants. As others have pointed out, accommodation provisions of the ADA are a feature that distinguishes it from the Civil Rights Act, and the compliance costs that these provisions impose on employers is an important reason why the two acts might have had opposite effects on the employment of their protected classes. The ADA uses a stick to encourage employers to hire people with disabilities. Although we consider how to increase the size of this stick (see below), we also consider some carrots to better achieve the goal of fully integrating working-aged people with disabilities into employment.

Increasing efforts to enforce compliance in hiring would increase the hiring of applicants with disabilities by increasing the benefit to an employer of compliance. Lawsuits concerning discrimination in hiring are relatively rare, for a variety of possible reasons. The first is that it can be very difficult for job applicants to detect discrimination, as they do not know how their abilities compare with those of competing applicants, and employers can usually offer plausible, seemingly legitimate explanations for not hiring any given individual. The second is that it is harder to establish that an applicant is capable of performing the required work than to establish that an existing employee can, because the latter is less likely to have performed it previously. The third is that the typical applicant who has been the victim of discrimination probably has less incentive to pursue a lawsuit than the typical victim who is an existing employee, for a variety of reasons (less chance of success, a desire to focus their energy on searching for other jobs, fear of creating a negative reputation for themselves, lack of support from fellow employees or employee organizations, and perhaps others). Clarifying who is protected, under what circumstances they are protected, and what constitutes reasonable accommodation would reduce the costs to employers of lawsuits from existing employees in a way that might significantly reduce their compliance cost for job applicants, without greatly reducing their compliance benefit for existing employees. The reason is that the costs associated with nonmeritorious lawsuits are likely to have a minimal effect on ADA compliance for existing employees. They do impose costs, and employers likely take actions to avoid those costs (e.g., retain an employee whom they have legitimate reasons to terminate), but those actions do not necessarily improve compliance, and could potentially harm it.

The main effect of nonmeritorious lawsuits might be to discourage the employer from hiring people who might bring such future lawsuits. Another potentially important effect is to undermine both employer and political support for the ADA in general. Of course, efforts to clarify these issues are already under way, through the judicial process, and it is possible that recent court decisions will have a significant impact on ADA compliance and employment outcomes for people with disabilities. There are significant problems with the court process, however. It is slow, expensive, and often haphazard. Legislative or regulatory changes might be less expensive, speed up the process, and lead to more desirable results. We believe, however, that successful efforts to clarify whom the ADA protects, under what circumstances, and what constitutes reasonable accommodation will significantly reduce ADA compliance costs and increase the employment of people with disabilities who are determined to be protected under the law—especially through new hires.

In this regard, it is important to note that the empirical evidence about the impact of the ADA on the employment of people with disabilities has focused on the period immediately before and immediately after its creation (DeLeire 2001) or implementation (Acemoglu and Angrist 2001). After more than a decade of judicial experience with the act, most scholars would argue that, although we now have a much clearer idea of who is protected by the act, the protected class has been much more narrowly defined than might have been expected at the time of its passage. (See Krieger 2000 for a fuller discussion of this point and the major court decisions that have shaped the current protected class under the ADA.) This suggests that the net effect of the ADA on the overall employment of working-aged people with disabilities, whether positive or negative, is likely to be much less than its impact as measured immediately after its passage, when the protected class was considered by employers and employees alike to be larger.

This judicial history has important implications for those who, in 1990, hoped that the ADA would have a dramatic effect on the overall employment of working-aged people with disabilities, and it returns us to a major point of disagreement with respect to the success parameters advocated by various authors in this book.

As ADA's protected class has been more clearly, but more narrowly, defined by the courts, it is possible that the employment rate of this narrowly defined class has increased over time, while at the same time the ADA has had a smaller impact on the overall employment rate of working-aged people with disabilities. The logic is the same as that of the success of the similarly shrinking population with disabilities that is able to work at all. This plausible scenario further adds to our concerns about the view that measures of the ADA success on employment should be confined to the population with disabilities that is covered by the law, most forcefully espoused by Blanck and coauthors (Chapter 9). More important, it suggests that the ADA as currently interpreted by the courts is unlikely to be the major vehicle for integrating working-aged people with disabilities into the labor market.

Pro-Work Support Policies

Historically, the federal government's approach to providing economic security for people with disabilities has been dominated by a caretaker approach, reflecting the outdated view that disability is solely a medical issue. A main premise of this model is that people with severe medical conditions are unable to work, and therefore cannot contribute to their own economic security. The government, at the insistence of advocates and others, has launched a multifaceted effort to change that, epitomized by the passage of the ADA, but also reflected in other legislation, such as the 1998 Individuals with Disabilities Education Act (IDEA), the 1999 Ticket to Work and Work Incentives Improvement Act (TW&WIIA), and in administration initiatives, such as the Clinton administration's Presidential Task Force on the Employment of Adults with Disabilities, and the Bush administration's New Freedom Initiative (NFI).

A glance at federal budgets, however, shows that we have a long way to go. Expenditures to support work as means to achieve economic security are paltry when compared with expenditures for income support and medical assistance. In fiscal year 2000, the federal and state governments combined spent $81 billion for income support (SSDI and SSI) and more than $84 billion for medical care (Medicare and Medicaid) for working-aged adults with disabilities—more than $165 billion in total.[5] In contrast, the federal appropriation for the Rehabilitation Services Administration in fiscal year 2000 was under $3 billion, and the appropriation for all Special Education programs was $6 billion.[6]

Much of the emphasis in the new pro-work policy initiatives is on increasing the investment in the "human capital" of people with disabilities (i.e., the skills they have), or in breaking down physical and institutional barriers to the use of their existing human capital. Increased investment in the human capital of children with disabilities, through increased educational opportunities, is a main thrust of IDEA, and most of the efforts encompassed by NFI could be reasonably characterized as either promoting human capital, or addressing physical barriers to use of existing human capital (e.g., through transportation initiatives and increased access to technology). The ADA also attempts to break down physical barriers to use of existing human capital, by addressing the problems of labor market discrimination and employer accommodation.

Increasing the investment in the human capital of people with disabilities and reducing physical barriers seem like sensible approaches to increasing the employment of people with disabilities and reducing their dependence on government benefits.[7] If the new policies succeed in increasing human capital and reducing the physical barriers to its use, they will likely result in some increase in the employment and economic independence of this population.

An important lesson from the evidence in this book, however, is that pro-work support policies will be much more successful if they go beyond investments in human capital. The decline in the employment rate of people with disabilities was not caused by less investment in their human capital or through the creation or reinforcement of physical barriers to its use; indeed, the opposite has occurred. Instead, the decline occurred because of changes in the social environment—reductions in individuals' incentives to work and reductions in employer incentives to hire them. We addressed the issue of employer incentives in the previous section. We now turn to incentives for people with disabilities.

Current income support policies, as well as many in-kind support policies, continue to be strongly conditioned on earnings; the more you earn, the less likely you are to be eligible for benefits, or the lower your benefit payments. The message these programs send to people with disabilities who can work is that "we will help you as long as you don't help yourself." That message must be changed to one of "we will help you, but we also expect you to help yourself as best you can, and we will reward you for doing so." If we are serious about changing the approach to economic security for people with disabilities to one that emphasizes using their abilities through employment, we need major changes in support policies. Support policies must create incentives rather than disincentives to work, and they must provide the supports needed to achieve greater independence. Instead, current support policies force people with disabilities to choose between a reliable monthly benefit check and other services, on the one hand, and supporting themselves through work that might generate more income, but that carries with it many challenges and risks, on the other.

TW&WIIA has several features intended to mitigate the work disincentives embodied in the SSI and SSDI programs and their links to Medicaid and Medicare. The Ticket to Work itself is intended to provide beneficiaries with more resources, and more control over resources, needed to return to work and become financially independent. It is also intended to give providers a stronger incentive to help beneficiaries do so. Expansion of the Medicaid buy-in program for people with disabilities and an extended period of eligibility for Medicare under the SSDI program are intended to weaken the link between access to these programs and earnings. The easy-return provision is intended to make it less risky for beneficiaries to give up their benefits in favor of employment. The legislation also includes provisions for SSA to experiment with other changes that would reduce disincentives to work, most notably the $1 for $2 SSDI benefit offset, under which beneficiaries would lose one dollar of SSDI benefits for each $2 earned above some threshold, rather than retain all benefits for as long as earnings are below the substantial gainful activity (SGA) level, then lose them all when their earnings exceed SGA by even a dollar.

Although TW&WIIA seems like a step in the right direction, it will only reduce, not eliminate the work disincentives associated with support programs. The $1 for $2 SSDI benefit offset makes this obvious. Even if it were implemented nationwide, rather than as a demonstration, beneficiaries would still face an implicit 50 percent tax on their earnings, as do current SSI recipients and as did Social Security retirement beneficiaries under age 70 until that long-standing feature of the retirement program was finally repealed in 2000.[8]

Although TW&WIIA seems like a major effort to address the incentive issue, it also seems small in comparison with the sweeping changes to welfare policy that were made in the 1990s, with a similar purpose: to encourage parents, especially single mothers, to support themselves and their families through work rather than welfare benefits. Although we think it is important not to take this analogy too far in its application to disability policy, it is also important to draw on the lessons of welfare reform to the extent that we can. Welfare reform has not been a universal success, but it has been much more successful than its early critics thought possible. There has been a clear increase in the employment, earnings, and economic independence of single-parent families, and the increase seems to be surviving the current economic slowdown. Most observers of welfare reform appear to agree that three features of the reforms have been critical.[9] One is early intervention—providing parents with emergency assistance when they have employment or other crises so that they can maintain an existing job, or find a new one, rather than become dependent on benefits. A second is the substantial expansion of the Earned Income Tax Credit (EITC). For those parents with low earnings, the EITC makes an additional dollar of earnings add substantially more than a dollar to income. A third is a change in expectations. Most parents are now expected to support themselves through work, and the government is expected to facilitate that effort.

The apparent successes of welfare reform are all the more remarkable when contrasted with the lack of success from earlier reforms. Earlier reforms emphasized investment in human capital, through education and a series of employment and training programs. However, whatever improvements in human capital were achieved were not converted into greater earnings and economic independence. The success of the more recent reforms suggests that the likely reason for the failure of earlier reforms is that welfare recipients did not have strong enough incentives to invest in, and use, their own human capital.

Perhaps we need a similar three-pronged change for people with disabilities: more assistance to help them stay in their current job, or find a new job when they lose it;[10] an earned income tax credit for those who work but have very low earnings;[11] and for at least a substantial share, an expectation that they will work and that government's role is to help them support themselves through work—an expectation that seems in line with the intent of the ADA.

Such a policy would complement efforts to increase the human capital of people with disabilities and break down physical barriers to its use. It not only would help ensure that increased human capital and reductions in barriers to its use would actually increase employment and reduce economic dependence, but would also create incentives for people with disabilities to invest more in themselves.

There are significant challenges to developing such policies, however. One is the "woodwork effect": workers who meet medical eligibility criteria for support, but do not rely on support, will have more incentive to seek support if they can obtain it without reducing their earnings. Although one might argue that these individuals are worthy of at least some support, the effect would be to increase program costs, perhaps substantially. A second challenge is determining who should be expected to work and who should not. Even if conceptual agreement can be reached, the practical problem of making actual determinations is enormous. A third challenge is determining how to provide support for work, and how much support to provide. The target population is a very heterogeneous one, as is their need for support. One size will not fit all. We are a long way from devising public policies that will simultaneously provide a reasonable safety net for people with disabilities, encourage employment, and provide sufficient job support to assure that those who are able to work are integrated into the workforce. We are convinced that such policies should be our goal, but policy change must go well beyond current initiatives if substantial progress is to be achieved. The first step in achieving these policy changes is recognizing that there is a problem with current policies. The bottom line of this book is that the unprecedented fall in the employment rate of working-aged people with disabilities in the 1990s was a direct effect of the unintended consequences of public policies. To better integrate working-aged people with disabilities into the workforce, increase their employment, and reduce their dependence on SSDI and SSI will require changes in these policies that make providing jobs less costly for employers and the relative gains from work over disability income supports greater for those with disabilities.

Notes

The authors wish to thank Ludmila Robka for her research assistance in updating the Burkhauser, Daly, and Houtenville (2001) tables used in this chapter as well as Andrew Houtenville for his help in assuring the accuracy of these values. We also thank the National Institute of Disability and Rehabilitation Research (NIDRR) and the Social Security Administration (SSA) for supporting our work on this chapter. We would also like to thank NIDRR's Ruth Brannon and our colleague Susanne Bruyère for their encouragement and guidance. The opinions we express in this paper are our own, and do not represent official positions of NIDRR, SSA, or Cornell University.

1. Kaye provides data on both the prevalence of disability and the prevalence of inability to work at all owing to just one of the individual conditions on the checklist: back problems (Figure 6.11). For that condition, inability to work increases from 10.3 percent of the former in 1988 to 11.4 percent in 2000, a 10.6 percent increase. This increase is not evident in the figure, which plots the two series separately, rather than plotting the ratio. It is apparent from the full series for the ratio that this change represents a trend, rather than just sampling error.
2. The relative change is missed when looking at Figure 6.15 because of the scale: Kaye shows two rates that are both very small and appear to move in parallel, but in fact they do not. Further, Figure 6.15 suggests that the two predicted series fit the actual series very well. They do when considered independently, but there is evidence of serial correlation in the prediction errors and an apparent negative relationship between the errors for the two models. In the early years, the errors for inability to work tend to be positive, while the errors for disability tend to be negative, and in the latter years the opposite is true.
3. The concern we have is that Kaye assumes a constant relationship between body mass index and work limitations. We think this relationship might have shifted because sources of growth in obesity are likely different from sources of cross-section variation in obesity. For instance, if reduced smoking has contributed to growth in obesity, the prevalence of inability to work among those with a BMI in the obese range might have declined.
4. One possible answer to the last question is that the application process takes months, and even years. During this period, there was a large surge in applicants, as reported by Goodman and Waidmann (Chapter 10). Therefore, even after excluding beneficiaries, the Acemoglu and Angrist (2001) sample likely includes

a large number of people who reported work limitations and were in the SSDI application process.
5. *Social Security Bulletin: 2001 Annual Statistical Supplement*, Washington, DC: Social Security Administration. In fiscal year 2000, the SSA spent $55 billion for SSDI and $26 billion for SSI. In fiscal year 1998, the Medicare program paid providers $24 billion for services provided to SSDI beneficiaries, and the federal-state Medicaid program paid $60 billion for services provided to working-aged SSI recipients.
6. U.S. Department of Education, Budget History Table. Available at: <http://www.ed.gov/offices/OUS/BudgetHistory/index.html>.
7. Intriguingly, evidence from a survey of private and government employers shows that lack of training and lack of related experience are the main barriers to employment and advancement of people with disabilities, not accommodation costs (Bruyère 2000).
8. See Song (2002) for evidence on the positive impact of this change on the earnings of persons aged 65–69.
9. See, for instance, Moffitt (2002) and Hotz and Scholz (forthcoming).
10. TW&WIIA includes provisions for SSA to develop and test early intervention strategies.
11. See Burkhauser and Wittenburg (1996) for a detailed discussion of the implicit taxes that disability income recipients face on their earnings, and how an earned income tax credit could offset those taxes.

References

Acemoglu, Daron, and Joshua Angrist. 2001. "Consequences of Employment Protection: The Case of the Americans with Disabilities Act." *Journal of Political Economy* 109(5): 915–956.

Autor, David, and Mark Duggan. 2003. "The Rise in Disability Recipiency and the Decline in Unemployment." *Quarterly Journal of Economics* 118(1): 157–205.

Bound, John, and Timothy Waidmann. 2002. "Accounting for Recent Declines in Employment Rates among the Working-Aged Disabled." *Journal of Human Resources* 37(2): 231–250.

Bruyère, Susanne M. 2000. "Disability Employment Policies and Practices in Private and Federal Sector Organizations." Unpublished manuscript. Ithaca, NY: Program on Employment and Disability, School of Industrial and Labor Relations, Cornell University.

Burkhauser, Richard V., Mary C. Daly, and Andrew Houtenville. 2001. "How Working Age People with Disabilities Fared over the 1990s Business Cycle." In *Ensuring Health and Income Security for an Aging Workforce*,

P. Budetti, R.V. Burkhauser, J. Gregory, and H.A. Hunt, eds. Kalamazoo, MI: W.E. Upjohn Institute for Employment Research, pp. 291–346.

Burkhauser, Richard V., and Wittenburg, David C. 1996. "How Current Disability Transfer Policies Discourage Work: Analysis from the 1990 SIPP." *Journal of Vocational Rehabilitation* 7: 9–27.

DeLeire, Thomas. 2000a. "The Unintended Consequences of the Americans with Disabilities Act." *Regulation* 23(1): 21–24.

———. 2000b. "The Wage and Employment Effects of the Americans with Disabilities Act." *Journal of Human Resources* 35(4): 693–715.

———. 2001. "Changes in Wage Discrimination against People with Disabilities: 1984–1993." *Journal of Human Resources* 36(1): 144–158.

Hotz, V. Joseph, and J. Karl Scholz. Forthcoming. "The Earned Income Tax Credit." In *Mean-Tested Transfer Programs in the U.S.*, Robert Moffitt, ed. Chicago and Cambridge, MA: The University of Chicago Press and National Bureau of Economic Research.

Krieger, Linda H. 2000. "Foreword—Backlash against the ADA: Interdisciplinary Perspectives and Implications for Social Justice Strategies." *Berkeley Journal of Employment and Labor Law* 21(1): 1–18.

Moffit, Robert A. 2002. "From Welfare to Work: What the Evidence Shows." Policy brief no. 13, Welfare Reform and Beyond. Washington, DC: The Brookings Institution.

Social Security Administration. 2001. *Social Security Bulletin: Annual Statistical Supplement*. Washington, DC: Social Security Administration.

Song, Jae G. 2002. "The Effects of the Removal of the Retirement Earnings Test in 2000." Working paper. Washington, DC: Social Security Administration, Office of Research, Evaluation, and Statistics.

The Authors

Peter Blanck (Ph.D., J.D.) is the Charles M. and Marion Kierscht Professor of Law, a professor of Psychology, and a professor of Public Health at the University of Iowa. He received his Ph.D. in psychology from Harvard University and his J.D. from Stanford Law School, where he served as president of the Stanford Law Review. Blanck is also the director of the Law, Health Policy, and Disability Center at the Iowa College of Law (see www.its.uiowa.edu/law). He has written over 100 articles and books on the ADA, received grants to study disability law and policy, represented clients before the United States Supreme Court in ADA cases, and testified before Congress. His work has received national and international attention. Blanck's recent books in the area include: *The Americans with Disabilities Act and the Emerging Workforce* (1998), and *Employment, Disability, and the Americans with Disabilities Act* (2000).

Richard V. Burkhauser (Ph.D.) is the Sarah Gibson Blanding Professor of Policy Analysis in the Department of Policy Analysis and Management of the College of Human Ecology at Cornell University. He received his Ph.D. in economics from the University of Chicago. He was a member of the Technical Panel of the 1994–1996 Advisory Council on Social Security and the 1994–1996 National Academy of Social Insurance Panel on Disability Policy Reform. He was a member of the Ticket to Work/Work Incentives Improvement Act Advisory Board from 2000–2002. Burkhauser has published widely in the area of United States and European social security retirement and disability policy. His current research interests focus on: the importance of the social environment on the work outcomes of people with disabilities; how disability influences economic well-being; how social security reforms will affect the work and economic well-being of older persons; and cross-national comparisons of the economic well-being and work of older persons.

Mary Daly (Ph.D.) is a senior economist at the Federal Reserve Bank of San Francisco and a visiting fellow at the Public Policy Institute of California. Her published research includes articles on health and labor market dynamics, income distribution, aging, and disability and retirement policy. She currently serves on the Advisory Board for the Rehabilitation Research and Training Center for Persons Hard of Hearing or Late Deafened, funded by the National Institute on Disability and Rehabilitation Research. Dr. Daly recently completed appointments with the Library of Congress Committee Assessing the Use of Vocational Factors in Determining Eligibility for Social Security Disability Benefits and with the National Academy of Social Insurance Committee Assessing the Costs and Benefits of Privatizing the Social Security

Program. Before joining the Federal Reserve Bank, Daly was a post-doctoral fellow at the Center for Policy Studies at Northwestern University. She holds a B.S. in psychology and economics from the University of Missouri, an M.S. in Economics from the University of Illinois, and a Ph.D. in economics from Syracuse University.

Thomas DeLeire (Ph.D.) is an assistant professor in the Irving B. Harris Graduate School of Public Policy Studies at the University of Chicago, and was the senior economist for labor, health, welfare, and education at the Council of Economic Advisers from 2002 to 2003 (on leave from the University of Chicago). He has published extensively on the effect of the ADA on the employment of people with disabilities. Dr. DeLeire graduated magna cum laude from Princeton University and received his Ph.D. in economics from Stanford University.

Nanette Goodman (M.S.) is a research associate at the Cornell Center for Policy Research. She is currently researching issues related to the employment of people with disabilities and working on a project for the District of Columbia to develop a Medicaid Buy-In for workers with disabilities. Goodman has also published on health policy issues affecting underserved populations. She received her M.S. in economics from the University of Wisconsin in 1988.

Steven C. Hill (Ph.D.) is a service fellow economist in the Center for Cost and Financing Studies at the Agency for Healthcare Research and Quality. Prior to joining the agency, he was a senior economist at Mathematica Policy Research, Inc. He received his Ph.D. in economics from the University of Wisconsin. His research focuses on managed care and disability, including topics such as plan choice, risk selection, managed care for people with disabilities, and the impacts of disability and health on employment and program participation. He has published in *Health Services Research*; *Inquiry*; the *Journal of Health Economics*; the *Journal of Human Resources*; the *Journal of Mental Health Policy and Economics*; and the *Review of Income and Wealth*.

Andrew Houtenville (Ph.D.) is a senior research associate with the Cornell University RRTC. He is responsible for analyzing economic information of people with disabilities from existing surveys, such as the Census 2000 Current Population Survey, National Health Interview Survey, Survey of Income and Program Participation, and the Panel Study of Income Dynamics. Andrew is an applied microeconomist with interests in the impact of disability and aging policy on employment and families in the United States and cross-nationally. In collaboration with Richard Burkhauser and Mary Daly, he investigates the impact of business cycles, demographic trends, and public policy on the employment and economic well-being of people with disabilities. Andrew's previous research includes: a comparative analysis of income mobility in the United States and Germany; a study of the impact of taxation and government spending on the geographic mobility of the elderly in the United States; and an analysis of the influence of public school resources on the allocation of educational resources within families with children.

H. Stephen Kaye (Ph.D.) is research director at the Disability Statistics Center, a NIDRR-funded Rehabilitation Research and Training Center at the University of California, San Francisco. Kaye received his Ph.D. from Stanford University. He has worked in the field of disability research since 1995; and his research interests have focused on changes in the social and economic status of Americans with disabilities since the passage of the Americans with Disabilities Act. He is principal author of the Disability Watch series of reports, the second volume of which was published in June 2001 by Disability Rights Advocates, Inc., a nonprofit disability advocacy legal organization based in Oakland, California. Dr. Kaye's main research at the Disability Statistics Center has focused on the employment status of people with disabilities and on their use of technology. His report, "Computer and Internet Use Among People with Disabilities," provided the first statistical evidence of the large impact of the digital divide on people with disabilities; this research was cited extensively in the media and by the White House, in support of former President Clinton's efforts to bridge the digital divide among the population with disabilities.

Douglas Kruse (Ph.D.) is a professor in the School of Management and Labor Relations at Rutgers University, and a research associate at the National Bureau of Economic Research in Cambridge, MA. He received his Ph.D. in economics from Harvard University. His research has focused on the employment and earnings effects of disability, and the causes, consequences, and implications of employee ownership and profit sharing. Dr. Kruse has been principal investigator for three U.S. Department of Labor grants, has testified three times before Congress, and served on the President's Committee on Employment of People with Disabilities.

Gina A. Livermore (Ph.D., M.P.H.) is the assistant director of Cornell University's Center for Policy Research in Washington, DC. Prior to joining the Center in 2001, Dr. Livermore was a vice president at The Lewin Group, where she conducted policy research and evaluation studies for seven years on health and welfare policy issues, including topics in disability, welfare, mental health, and substance abuse. Recently she served as co-principal investigator, with David Stapleton, to design the evaluation of the Ticket to Work program for SSA. She is also assisting the District of Columbia and the state of Massachusetts with research and technical assistance related to Medicaid Buy-In programs for people with disabilities. Other research experience includes: analysis of the impact of substance abuse and mental illness comorbidity on labor force participation; assessing barriers to and incentives for employment among persons with disabilities; study of the impact of health insurance availability on the employment of persons with disabilities; research on employment supports for people with disabilities; and assessments of the evaluation designs for two pilot tests of innovations to SSA's disability determination process. Dr. Livermore received her M.P.H. in epidemiology from Tulane University and her Ph.D. in economics from the University of Wisconsin.

Lisa Schur (Ph.D., J.D.) is an assistant professor in the Department of Labor Studies and Employment Relations at Rutgers University. She received her Ph.D. in Political Science from the University of California-Berkeley and a J.D. from Northeastern University. Her research focuses on disability, employment, and political participation—particularly non-standard work arrangements among people with disabilities and the effects of disability and employment on political participation. Her articles have appeared in *Political Research Quarterly*; *Political Psychology*; *Industrial Relations*; *Industrial and Labor Relations Review*; *Journal of Disability Policy Studies*; *Behavioral Sciences and the Law*; and other journals.

Susan Schwochau (Ph.D., J.D.) is currently an associate with Dickinson Wright PLLC in Lansing, Michigan. She received her J.D. from the University of Iowa and her Ph.D. in Labor and Industrial Relations from the University of Illinois. She has been a member of the faculty of the University of Iowa and the State University of New York at Buffalo.

Chen Song (Ph.D.) is an economist at Resolution Economics LLC. She earned a Ph.D. in Economics from the University of Chicago. Her areas of specialty include financial economics, econometrics, and labor economics. As a senior investigator for the Center for Population Economics (CPE) at the University of Chicago's Graduate School of Business, she has published numerous articles on disability politics under the Civil War Pension System. Her research interest lies in the fields of demography and labor market discrimination.

David Stapleton (Ph.D.) is the director of the Cornell Center for Policy Research, in Washington, DC. For the past 11 years, Dr. Stapleton's work has focused on programs for people with disabilities and their impacts on employment and economic independence. He and Gina Livermore led the SSA-funded effort to develop the design of evaluation for the Ticket to Work. Stapleton is also a co-PI for the NIDRR funded Cornell Research, Rehabilitation and Training Center for Economic Research on Employment Policy for People with Disabilities. Recent publications include articles on: the effect of health care access on employment of people with disabilities; transitions from Aid to Families with Dependent Children to Supplemental Security Income before the 1996 welfare reform; and the effect of an increase in the normal age of retirement on the Social Security Disability Insurance and Medicare programs.

Timothy Waidmann (Ph.D.) received his Ph.D. in economics from the University of Michigan. He is currently a senior research associate in the Health Policy Center of The Urban Institute. Waidmann's central research interests are the effects of health and disability on labor force behavior of older adults, as well as the health status and access to health care of vulnerable populations. He has worked extensively with the Health and Retirement Survey as well as other major U.S. health surveys. His work is published in major journals in gerontology, labor economics, and health services research. Prior to joining The Urban Institute, Waidmann held an appointment as an assistant professor at the University of Michigan School of Public Health and as a NIA post-doctoral fellow in the Population Studies Center and Survey Research Center.

David Wittenburg (Ph.D.), senior research associate at The Urban Institute, is a labor economist who specializes in quantitative public policy evaluation. He has applied econometric and microsimulation techniques using a variety of survey and administrative data sources to examine issues related to Social Security Administration disability programs, welfare reform, unemployment insurance, minimum wage increases, changes in the normal age of retirement, employment of people with disabilities, and job training. He has published his findings in peer-reviewed articles, book chapters, government reports, and policy briefs. Prior to joining The Urban Institute in July 2000, Dr. Wittenburg worked at The Lewin Group. He received his Ph.D. in economics from Syracuse University.

Index

The italic letters *f*, *n*, and *t* following a page number indicate that the subject information of the heading is within a figure, note, or table, respectively, on that page.

Accommodation costs, 17, 260–261
   critiques of, before ADA passage, 263
   difficulty of measuring, 320, 387
   economic efficiency, 328
   as explanation for employment rate decline, 269
   relation to seniority, 330*n*5
   and standard definitions of economic discrimination, 306–307
   subsidies to employers for, 395, 396
   survey of employers about, 404*n*7
   workers who do not require, 273
   See also Firing costs from ADA; Hiring costs from ADA
Activities of daily living (ADLs), 229, 230*f*, 231*f*
Activity limitations, 33
   relationship to inability to work, 383
   vs. chronic condition measures, 234
   See also Population with activity limitations
ADA. *See* Americans with Disabilities Act
ADLs. *See* Activities of daily living
Affective disorders (depression, bipolar), 236–238, 251–253, 384–385
Age as explanation for employment rate decline, 11, 378–379
Age group subpopulations, 89
   composition, 1980–2000, 116*t*, 117*t*
   decomposition of employment rate, 121*t*
   employment rate trends during 1990s, 96–97, 98*f*
   employment rates, 2000, 90*f*
   employment rates, 1980–2000, 118*t*, 119*t*, 120*t*

   population composition, 1980–2000, 91, 92, 93, 94*f*
   population shares, 1980–2000, 120*t*
   prevalence, 1980–2000, 115*t*
   prevalence of work limitations, 2000, 92*t*
Americans with Disabilities Act (ADA)
   a priori case against, 263–264
   assessing economic effects of, 279–281
   business cycle timing when passed, 281, 284
   comparisons with Civil Rights Act, 265, 273–274, 387, 394–398
   debate over its impact, 1, 5, 23–24
   definition of disability, 7, 33, 261–263, 302, 320
   effect of broadening its definition of disability, 319
   effect on human capital investment, 325
   effect on work-limitation measure, 284
   empirical studies, 265–273, 313–314
   empirical studies summary, 268*t*
   employment patterns when passed, 266–269, 288*t*, 291–292
   enforcement and accommodation mandates, 312–313
   as explanation for 1990s employment rate decline, 16–18, 363, 378, 386–389, 391–392
   and firm size, 147, 153–154
   goals, 23, 224, 259, 282, 303
   judicial interpretations, 316, 321, 330*n*5, 331*n*6
   labor market consequences, 259–260
   negative possible effects, 279, 397–399

413

Americans with Disabilities (cont.)
  pre-ADA operation of labor markets, 307–309
  provisions that impose costs on employers, 260–261, 309, 311–312
  reasons to call a success, 314–318, 387
  recommendations for improving it, 395–396
  state laws' effect on, 270
  success that looks like failure, 321–322
  theories of discrimination and, 305–307
  three categories of impairment, 315–316
  Title I, 306
  whether a failed law, 302
  See also Disability discrimination laws; Economic discrimination; Lawsuit risks from ADA; Policy implications for ADA; State disability discrimination laws
Arthritis, 238–239
Asthma, 233, 238–239

Back problems, 233, 235–236, 406n1
  and body mass index (BMI), 245, 246f
Becker's model of postmarket discrimination, 304
Bipolar disorder, 236–238, 384–385
Body mass index (BMI), 244, 403n3
Business cycle periods
  as explanation for employment rate trends, 293–295
  in 1980s and 1990s, 104
  See also Economic recession

Cardiovascular conditions, 233
  and body mass index (BMI), 245
  heart disease, 238–239
Carpal tunnel syndrome, 233

CCS. See Clinical Classification Software
CDPS. See Chronic Illness and Disability Payment System
Chronic condition cost categories, 194–196
  annual expenditures per person by, 201t
  correlation with employment rates, 203–206
  health insurance by, 202t
  prevalence of conditions by, 199t
Chronic health condition indicators, 190–191
  by costliness, 191, 194, 196
Chronic health conditions
  definition, 211n7
  increased prevalence, 198–200, 234–240
  relation with rising disability rates, 240–241, 242f
  See also Population with chronic conditions
Chronic Illness and Disability Payment System (CDPS), 194
Circulatory system conditions, 233
Civil Rights Act, comparisons with Americans with Disabilities Act, 265, 273–274, 388, 394–398
Clinical Classification Software (CCS), 194
College degrees. See Education level
Communication skills in jobs, 136
  See also Language skills in jobs
"Composition effect," 155–156
Compositional shifts
  in occupations, as explanation for employment rate decline, 128–129, 155–156
  in population with work limitations, 388
  See also Disability population composition shifts
Compressed work weeks, 144–145

Computer skills in jobs, 134, 135
Condition-specific disability rates, 238–239
Contingent work, 160, 282
Contract work, 144
Cost of accommodation. *See* Accommodation costs
Current Population Survey (CPS)
  about, 61*t*–63*t*
  debate over its usefulness, 5–7
  definition of disability, 29*t*–30*t*
  employment rates, 221–223
  household income of people with disabilities, 2, 3*t*
  internal inconsistencies, 44, 88–90, 147
  question about firm size, 147
  reasons for using, 88–89
  strengths and weaknesses, 27, 28
  variable definitions, 63*t* –69*t*
  work-limitation question, 38, 53–54

Data source inconsistencies, 28
  CPS, NHIS, and SIPP, 58*n*24
  CPS and DOT, 175*n*1
  CPS *vs.* NHIS and SIPP, 56*n*12, 57*n*21
  within CPS, 44, 88–90, 147
  in measures of ADA coverage, 280–281
  MEPS and NMES, 182–183, 198, 211*n*8
  MEPS and NMES *vs.* NHIS, 191, 197
  within NHIS, 56*n*9, 220
  within SIPP, 55*n*2, 55*n*5
Data sources
  chronic health conditions, 182–183, 190–191, 192*t* –193*t*, 234
  Current Population Survey, 2
  debate over, 5–7
  education levels, 162*n*14
  effect of health insurance on employment, 188–189
  empirical studies of ADA, 266
  employment rates for people with disabilities, 219–224
  job characteristics, 129, 160–170, 167–170
  national data sets, 8–9, 26–28, 61–63*t*
  recession effect on employment rates, 314
  state disability discrimination laws, 269
  See also Research methods
Dead-end jobs, 140*f*, 154, 169, 172*t*
Decomposition technique for employment decline, 101–102
Definitions of disability
  Americans with Disabilities Act (ADA), 7, 33, 261–263, 302, 320
  based on purpose, 28, 31
  Current Population Survey (CPS), 3*t*
  Current Population Survey (CPS) work-limitation question, 88–89
  from national data sets, 29–30*t*, 31, 266, 268
  problems with, 282–291, 320
  research questions about, 24–25
  review of, 315–318
  SSDI/SSI program, 343, 345
  used with CPS data, 221
  used with NHIS data, 219
  work limitation *vs.* able to work at all, 17
  See also Disability population
Demographic changes as explanation for employment rate decline, 10–11, 377, 378
Depression (psychological), 236–238, 251–253, 384–385
Diabetes, 238–239
  and body mass index (BMI), 245, 246*f*
Dictionary of Occupational Titles (DOT), 167–168
  merging with CPS data, 175*n*1
  replacement system, 176*n*4

Disability
  ambiguity over who has, 283
  body system causes of, 231–234
  conceptualizations, 32–34
  group membership measures of, 322
  medical model of, 7, 398
  prevalence, 34–36
  problems measuring, 282–291, 320–323
  stigma attached to, 285
  work-limitation *vs.* functional measures, 7–8
  from work-related injuries, 260, 274
  See also Definitions of disability; Impairment; People with disabilities
Disability Benefits Reform Act, 345, 354
Disability discrimination laws, 279–281
  evaluation of, 18
  unintended consequences, 394
  See also Americans With Disabilities Act (ADA); State disability discrimination laws
Disability population
  ADA definition of, 315
  broadening ADA definition, 319
  changes to ADA definition, 397
  clarifying ADA definition, 396, 397
  employment measures for, 219–224
  inclusion of individuals not qualified under ADA, 317
  reasons for low employment rates, 282
  size of, 280
  uncertainty about ADA definition of, 262, 263, 280, 285–286, 320–321
  which to measure, 9–10, 271–272, 375–377
Disability population composition shifts, 218–219, 224–234, 289–290
  as explanation for employment rate decline, 90–95, 96t, 101
  quantification of relative influence of, 101–102
Disability rates
  condition-specific, 238–239
  in early 1990s, 218
  by gender, 70t–71t
  increases, 231–234
  relation to chronic health conditions, 240–241, 242f
  risk factors, 242–253
Disability severity, 229–231
  as explanation for employment rate decline, 14–16, 17–18, 378, 382–386
  relationship to reporting work limitations, 56n16
  See also Population with chronic conditions
Discrimination. *See* Disability discrimination laws; Economic discrimination
DOT. *See Dictionary of Occupational Titles*
"Dynamic" aspect of work, 127

Earned Income Tax Credit (EITC), 401, 404n11
Economic discrimination
  ADA difference from traditional view, 306–307
  definition, 306
  possible ADA increase in, 386–387
  See also Disability discrimination laws
Economic models of employment discrimination, 303–307
  limitations of, 326–327, 328
Economic recession
  and chronic health conditions, 245–253, 385
  data sources for employment effects of, 314
  as explanation for employment rate decline, 281

Index   417

impact on SSDI program, 351, 390
link with mental health, 250
relationship with disability rates, 243
Education level
   disability subpopulations grouped by, 89
   as explanation for employment rate decline, 11, 377, 378–379
   job classification according to, 167t–168t, 171t
   required for jobs, 138–140, 151–152
   shift towards greater, 102
   and SSDI increases, 357, 360–362
   See also Human capital investment
Education-level subpopulations, 161
   composition, 1980–2000, 116t, 117t
   decomposition of employment rate, 121t
   employment rate trends during 1990s, 98, 99f, 100
   employment rates, 2000, 90f
   employment rates, 1980–2000, 118t, 119t, 120t
   population composition, 1980–2000, 91, 92, 93–94, 96f
   population shares, 1980–2000, 120t
   prevalence, 1980–2000, 115t
   prevalence of work limitations, 2000, 92f
Education-level variables, 176n5
EITC. *See* Earned Income Tax Credit
Employer size. *See* Firm size
Employer's compliance costs for ADA, 396
   See also Accommodation costs
Employment (definitions), 36, 86
   in CPS, NHIS, and SIPP, 68t
Employment differentials due to disability, 312
Employment discrimination models, 303–307
Employment levels *vs.* trends, 67n17
Employment rate decline in 1990s, 1–2
   areas of agreement about, 372–373
   chief three explanations for, 20
   explanations for, 10–20, 377–393
   four sets of questions regarding, 370–371
   and job market changes, 158, 160
   measures of, 3–5, 6t
   for men and women without disabilities, 42f, 43f
   for men *vs.* women with disabilities, 378
   for people with and without work limitations, 373
   during period ADA was implemented, 266–269, 288t, 291–292
   as policy success measure, 9–10
   as result of data and population choices, 25
   and SSDI beneficiary trend, 351–353, 390
   subpopulation trends, 45f, 46f
   for subpopulations of men and women, 38–41
   three factors looked at as cause of, 87–88
   whether a measurement aberration, 5–7, 36–41, 53, 271–273
   whether broad-based occurrence, 95–100
   See also Data sources
Employment rate of people with disabilities, 220t, 222t
   correlation with chronic condition cost categories, 203–206
   CPS, NHIS, and SIPP "Official," 68t
   how to measure, 375–377
   as measure of job opportunities, 217
   possible explanations for, 282
Employment rate trends
   across subgroups with work limitations, 95–100

Employment rate trends (cont.)
   as ADA was implemented, 291–292
   compared with prevalence of
      population with work
      limitations, 125–126
   by gender for population with work
      limitations and able to work, 76t
   by gender for subpopulations with
      disabilities, 72t–73t
   by gender for subpopulations without
      disabilities, 74t–75t
   individual subpopulation
      contribution to, 104, 105t, 106
   for men and women with disabilities,
      341
   during 1990s, 292–293
   of subpopulations with work
      limitations, 103t
Employment-related disabilities, 260,
   274
Employment-related health insurance,
   183–184
   employee contributions, 185
Employment shocks and SSDI
   applications, 359–360
Employment status, effect on self-
   reporting of disabilities, 286, 296
Employment variable, 198
Environmentally hazardous jobs, 142
Epilepsy, 233

Firing costs from ADA, 264, 311, 313
   effect on discrimination in hiring,
      386, 395
   See also Accommodation costs;
      Hiring costs from ADA
Firm size and employment of people
   with disabilities, 147, 148f,
   152–154, 172t, 269
Flextime, 144–145
Full-time and full-year (FTFY)
   employment, 143, 144f, 155,
   172t

Functional limitation measures of
   disabilities
   in addition to measures of work
      limitations, 322
   definition, 296n2
   SIPP questions, 64t
   vs. work-limitation measures, 7–8
Functional limitation severity scale, 229,
   230f

GED-Language skills for jobs,
   133f–134f, 152, 171t
Gender as explanation for employment
   rate decline, 11, 378–379
   See also Men with disabilities;
      Women with disabilities
Globalization of jobs, 133
Goal jobs, 169
Goods-producing sector, 129
Government expenditures and public
   policy, 398–399

Health care costs
   as explanation for employment rate
      decline, 12–14, 181–182, 377,
      380–372
   per capita, 185
Health care expenditures variable, 197,
   200, 201t
Health insurance, 145–146, 150–151,
   171t
   link with employment, 186–188
   percent unable to obtain, 184
   relation with disability rates, 243
   sources for people with disabilities,
      183–185
   subpopulations sensitive to, 208–209
Health insurance coverage variable,
   197–198, 200, 202t, 203
Health status of population with
   disabilities
   and ability to work, 289
   CPS questions regarding, 90

Index 419

as explanation for employment rate decline, 11, 108–110
and inability to work, 227–228
population share and employment rate, 1995–2000, 122*t*
relationship with impairment measures, 386
trends, 229–230
See also Chronic health conditions
Heart disease, 238–239
High-cost chronic conditions. *See* Population with work limitations and high-cost chronic conditions
High-mobility occupations, 169, 170
High school dropouts and SSDI, 357, 360–362
Higher education. *See* Education level
Hiring, increasing ADA compliance in, 396–397
Hiring costs from ADA, 264, 313, 367*n*16
See also Accommodation costs; Firing costs from ADA
Housework limitation measures of disability
in NHIS, CPS, and SIPP, 63*t*
Human capital investment
limitations of, 399–402
by people with disabilities, 325

IADLs. See Instrumental Activities of Daily Living
IDEA. *See* Individuals with Disabilities Education Act
Impairment
definition, 32
difficult to detect, 289
increased prevalence, 234–242
NHIS questions regarding, 67*t*
relationship with health status measures, 386
SSDI program changes concerning, 354–355
See also Disability severity
Inability-to-work measure, 293

back problem example, 403*n*1
relationship with activity limitations, 383
See also Population unable to work at all
Income, mean and median household, 2, 3*t*, 5, 6*t*
Income support increases during 1990s, 292–293
Income support policy changes
as explanation for employment rate decline, 18–19
vs. work support policies, 398–399
Individuals with Disabilities Education Act (IDEA), 398, 399
Industry shifts of jobs, 128–129
Instrumental Activities of Daily Living (IADLs), 229, 230*f*, 231*f*
International Classification of Disease, 190–191
International trade, effect on jobs, 133
Involuntary job loss, 156, 158, 159*f*, 379–389
and application for SSDI, 348

Job autonomy/control, 130*t*, 137–138, 155, 171*t*
Job benefits, 145–147, 150–151
Job characteristics
and ADA, 323
combined effects of changes, 155–156
data sources, 167–168
from *Dictionary of Occupational Titles,* 168–169*t*
effect employment rate decline, 126–127
as explanation for employment rate decline, 11–12, 377, 379–380
regression analysis, 148–150, 173, 174*t*, 175*t*
six dimensions, 129, 130–131*t*
Job complexity, 130*t*, 132–135
Job flexibility, 145
Job security, 157–158, 159, 160

Job tenure, 158, 159, 161
Jobs with environmentally adverse conditions, 142

Labor force participation decisions
    male workers aged 55 to 61, 346
    those with ADA disabilities, 324–325, 331n7
    vs. decision to apply for SSDI/SSI benefits, 346–348
Labor force participation rate in NHIS, CPS, and SIPP, 69t
Labor force participation trends for population with work limitations and able to work, 78t–79t
Labor market changes, 157–158
    effect on people with disabilities, 294
    pre-ADA, 307–309
Labor market success measure, 47–52
Labor productivity
    assumed lost because of disability, 310
    indicators, 305
    issues for the ADA, 323–235
    lost because of ADA, 279
    measures, 323
Language skills in jobs, 133–134f, 137, 152
Lawsuit risks from ADA, 262–263, 264, 269, 282
    most and least frequent sources, 367n16
    reducing, 396
Long-term disability insurance benefits, 146–147
Longer-term activity limitations, 32f, 34
Low-mobility occupations, 169
Low-skilled workers' SSDI replacement rate, 345, 346

Major life activities, 286–287
    and SIPP survey questions, 316–317
Managed care, 186
Medicaid health insurance, 184–185
    as an incentive not to work, 187–188
    managed care, 186
    need for further study, 208–209
    See also Supplemental Security Income (SSI)
Medical care support vs. work support policies, 398–399
Medical Expenditure Panel Survey (MEPS), 182–183
    for study of chronic health conditions, 189–190, 191, 192t–193t
Medical model of disability, 7, 398
Medicare health insurance, 184–185
    See also Social Security Disability Insurance (SSDI)
Men with disabilities
    effect of SSDI and SSI on earnings 1989–2000, 5, 6t
    employment rate compared to women's, 378
    employment rate trends by subpopulations, 38, 39f, 41, 72t–73t, 76t
    employment rate trends during 1990s, 4, 54
    health care costs, 13
    household income, 1989–2000, 2, 3t
    labor force participation trends, 78t
    prevalence of disability, 35
    prevalence rates by subpopulation, 70t, 81–82t
    SSDI/SSI beneficiary rate trends by subpopulation, 80t
    trends in proportions of, by subpopulation, 77t
    unemployment rate trends, 78t
    See also White men and women with disabilities
Men with disabilities who report activity limitations, 34–36
    employment rate trends, 36–37
Men with disabilities who report no work limitations
    composition by subpopulation, 116t

decomposition of employment rate, 121t
employment rates, 1980–2000, 119t, 120t
population shares, 1980–2000, 120t
Men with disabilities who report work limitations
  composition by subpopulation, 116t
  employment rate trends, 206, 207t
  employment rate trends during 1990s, 96, 97f
  employment rates, 2000, 90f
  employment rates, 1980–2000, 118t
  and high-cost chronic conditions, 204–206, 381
  population composition, 1980–2000, 91, 93f
  prevalence, 2000, 92f
  prevalence, by subpopulation, 115t
  SSDI/SSI benefits and labor market integration, 49, 51f–52
  unemployment rates, 47–49
Men without disabilities
  effect of SSDI and SSI on earnings 1989–2000, 6t
  employment rate during 1990s, 4
  employment rate trends by data source, 42f
  employment rate trends by subpopulation, 74t
  employment rates, 267f
Mental health conditions, 236–238, 384–385
  and disability rate increases, 252–253
  link with economic distress, 250
  and SSDI increases, 354
Mental health disability, 232f, 233–234
MEPS. See Medical Expenditure Panel Survey
Methods. See Research methods
Musculoskeletal system conditions, 221, 232f, 233

and body mass index (BMI), 244–245
and SSDI increases, 354

Nagi's conceptualization of disability, 33–34, 56n7
National Expenditure Panel Survey (MEPS), 182–183
  for study of chronic health conditions, 189–190, 191, 192–193t
National Health Interview Survey (NHIS)
  about, 61t–63t
  definition of disability, 29t
  employment rates, 219–221
  strengths and weaknesses, 26–27, 28
  for study of chronic conditions, 183, 190, 191, 192–193t
  variable definitions, 63–69t
National Medical Expenditure Survey (NMES), 182–183
  for study of chronic conditions, 189, 190, 191, 192t–193t
Nervous system conditions, 233
New Freedom Initiative (NFI), 398, 399
NHIS. See National Health Interview Survey
NMES. See National Medical Expenditure Survey
Nonstandard work arrangements, 143–145, 159
Nonwhites. See Racial subpopulations

Occupational shifts and employment rate decline, 128–129, 155–156, 167
One-year limitations, CPS questions, 65t
  See also Population with work limitations
Overweight and obesity, 243–245
  relation with disability rates, 243–245, 385
  relation with employment rates, 274

Panel Study of Income Dynamics
    (PSID), 314
Part-time employment, 143, 282
Partial work limitations
    CPS, NHIS, and SIPP questions, 66t
People with disabilities
    alternatives to ADA, 264
    employment rate during 1989 and
        1990s, 4
    household income, 1980–2000, 2, 3t
    incentives to work, 400–402
    labor supply decisions, 324–325,
        331n7
    predicted wages, 309
    1990s employment rate decline, 1–2
    See also Disability population; Men
        with disabilities; People without
        disabilities; Population
        subgroups; Women with
        disabilities
People without disabilities
    difference in household income, 2, 3t
    miscategorization of, 317
    See also Men without disabilities;
        Women without disabilities
Physical barriers at work, 399
Physical demands of jobs, 130t,
    141–142, 169t
Policy implications for ADA, 318–320,
    326–328, 393–398
    challenges for policymakers,
        371–372, 402–403
    pro-work support policies, 398–402
    public policies that discourage job
        searching, 49
    use of employment rate to define
        success, 9–10
Population able to work at all, 287
    advantage of using, 217, 289
    disadvantage of using, 17, 376–377
    employment rates, 223, 374–375
    impact of chronic conditions, 15, 16,
        381
    proportional decline in, 374

during 1990s, 292–293
See also Population with work
    limitations and able to work
Population unable to work at all, 41,
    218–219, 225f, 226f, 227f, 317
    by cause, 1983–1996, 355t
    impact of policy changes, 388
    reasons not to exclude from study,
        272
    See also Inability-to-work measure
Population with activity limitations
    (including work limitations), 15,
    35–36, 382–383
    characteristics, 32f, 33
    employment rate trends, 36–41
    prevalence by gender and
        subpopulation, 81t–82t, 83t–84t
Population with any functional/ADL
    limitations, 287, 291–292
    importance of studying, 318
Population with chronic conditions
    able to work at all, 15
    reasons for studying, 182
    See also Chronic health conditions;
        Disability severity
Population with functional/ADL but not
    work limitations, 272–273
Population with impairments,
    relationship to population with
    work limitations, 37
Population with longer-term activity
    limitations, 34
Population with major life activity
    limitations and a chronic
    condition, 15, 382
Population with severe functional/ADL
    limitations, 287, 288t, 291–292
    importance of studying, 318
Population with work limitations
    and autonomy/control in jobs, 155
    changes in employment rates,
        206–208
    composition by subpopulation,
        1980–2000, 116t, 388

Index   423

and dead-end jobs, 154
educational and training
    requirements, 151–152
employed in past two weeks, 205*t*
and employer size, 152–154
and employer-subsidized health
    insurance, 150–151
employment rate compared to that of
    people with disabilities, 125–126
employment rate decline, 373
employment rate trends by
    subpopulation, 1980–2000, 103*t*,
    105*t*–106*t*
employment rates by subpopulation,
    2000, 90*f*
employment rates by subpopulation,
    1980–2000, 118*t*
and full-year/full-time jobs, 155
and job repetitiveness, 155
and job strength requirements,
    154–155
NHIS sample definition, 198
not covered by ADA, 285–286
prevalence by subpopulation, 92*f*,
    115*t*
rate of failure in ADA litigation, 322
receiving SSDI and SSI benefits, 49,
    51*f*, 52, 80*t*
regression analysis, 148–150, 173,
    174*t*, 175*t*
relationship with population with
    impairments, 37
self-reported health status, 109*f*
sensitivity to labor market
    conditions, 294
unemployment rate trends, 47–49
Population with work limitations and
    able to work
    employment rate trends, 44–47, 76*t*,
        288*t*, 291–292
    employment rates, 220*t*, 222*t*
    labor force participation trends,
        78*t*–79*t*
    trends in proportion of, 77*t*
    unemployment rate trends, 78*t*–79*t*
Population with work limitations and
    high-cost chronic conditions,
    196–197
    prevalence, 199
    proportion, 381–382
    summary of findings about, 209–211
    switch from private to public health
        insurance, 203
Population with work limitations and
    SSDI enrollments, 1969–1996,
    351–353
Population without work limitations
    composition by subpopulation,
        1980–2000, 117t
    decomposition of employment rate,
        121t
    employment rate decline, 373
    employment rates, 220*t*, 221
    employment rates, 1980–2000, 119*t*,
        120*t*
    population shares, 1980–2000, 120*t*
    population shares and employment
        rates by self-reported health,
        1980–2000, 122*t*
Postmarket discrimination, 303–304
Premarket discrimination, 303
Private health insurance, 183–184
    and managed care, 186
Protective legislation. *See* Disability
    discrimination laws
PSID. *See* Panel Study of Income
    Dynamics
Psychological stress
    and disability rate increases,
        252–253
    from unemployment, 250–251
Public health insurance, 184
Public policy. *See* Policy implications
    for ADA

Race as explanation for employment rate
    decline, 11, 378
Racial subpopulations
    composition, 1980–2000, 115*t*, 116*t*

Racial subpopulations (cont.)
  decomposition of employment rate, 121t
  employment rate trends during 1990s, 98, 99f
  employment rates, 2000, 90f
  employment rates, 1980–2000, 118t, 119t, 120t
  population composition, 1980–2000, 91, 92, 95f
  population shares, 1980–2000, 120t
  prevalence, 1980–2000, 115t
  prevalence of work limitations, 2000, 92f
  See also White men and women with disabilities
Recession. See Economic recession
Relational or interactive nature of jobs, 130t, 135, 136, 137f
Repetitive nature of jobs, 133, 134, 135, 136f, 155, 164n29, 171t
Replacement rates, 345–346
Research methods
  to check robustness of subpopulation findings, 112n15
  construction of job characteristics, 129–132, 170, 173
  controlling for SSDI/SSI recipiency rates, 269
  debate over which population to use, 9, 10, 25
  decomposition technique for employment changes, 206–208
  decomposition technique for employment decline, 101–102
  to determine disability group measures, 322
  to find effect of health insurance on employment, 188–189, 208–209
  to isolate exogenous labor demand shocks, 367n13
  job characteristics, 170, 173
  pros and cons of self-reports, 218, 226–229, 285–286
  regression analysis of static job characteristics, 148–150
  selection bias problems, 57n17
  use of national surveys to measure disability, 7–8, 31
  use of subpopulations with disabilities, 18, 32–34
  usefulness of interdisciplinary research on disability, 328–329
  See also Data sources; Definitions of disability
Research results
  limitations, 326
  regression analysis of static job characteristics, 150–156
  still needed, 392
  three points of consensus, 9–10
Respiratory conditions, 233

Self-reports of disabilities or health, 218, 226–229, 285–286
Service sector, 129
Severity of disabilities. See Disability severity
SIPP. See Survey of Income and Program Participation
Skill requirements of jobs, 133, 151–152
Social environment
  as cause of employment rate decline for population with chronic conditions, 15, 382–383
  impact on population with work limitations and able to work, 47
  subpopulations most likely affected by, 34
  two most important changes in, during 1990s, 386–393
Social policies. See Policy implications for ADA
Social Security Disability Insurance (SSDI), 184–185
  about the program, 341–342
  allowance rate, 390, 391
  beneficiaries, 1980–2000, 350–351

"conditional" applicants, 348
controlling for recipiency rates, 269, 314
decision to apply for benefits, 346–348
effect on household income of people with disabilities, 5, 6t
effect on labor market integration, 49, 51f, 52
as explanation for employment rate decline, 18–19, 281, 339–340, 378, 389–393
history, 343–345
impact of employment shocks on applications, 359–360
impact of program changes on applications, 348–350
impact of program expansion on employment rate, 358–359
increases in benefit recipients by states, 353–357
reasons SSDI beneficiaries studied, 342–343
replacement rate, 345–346, 347t
screening stringency, 359
trends in receipts by work-limitation population, 80t
work disincentives associated with, 364–365, 400–401
See also Health care costs; Medicare health insurance
Specific vocational preparation for jobs, 133–134, 135f, 152, 171t
SSDI. *See* Social Security Disability Insurance
SSI. *See* Supplemental Security Income
Starter jobs, 140, 169–170
State disability discrimination laws, 268t, 269–270
State rates of SSDI increases, 353–357, 358–359
"Static" aspect of work, 127
Statistical discrimination, 304–305
Strength requirement for jobs, 141–142, 154–155, 171t

Stress
 and disability rate increases, 252–253
 from unemployment, 250–251
Subpopulations with disabilities, 18, 34
 affected by Medicaid thresholds, 188
 disability prevalence rates, 70t–71t
 employment rate change when ADA implemented, 288t
 employment rate trends, 72t–73t, 103t, 105t–106t
 employment rates, 37f
 with greatest change in employment, 102
 identification of, using CPS questions, 89–90
 with least change in employment, 102
 reasons to study, 274
 using to challenge employment rate decline, 271
 which ones should be studied, 376
Subpopulations without disabilities, employment rate trends, 74t–75t
Supplemental Security Income (SSI)
 about the program, 341–343
 allowance rate, 390, 391
 controlling for recipiency rates, 269, 314
 CPS and SIPP participation definitions, 69t
 effect of Medicaid threshold on recipients, 187–188
 effect on household income of people with disabilities, 5, 6t
 effect on labor market integration, 49, 51f, 52
 as explanation for employment rate decline, 378, 389–393
 Medicaid health insurance, 184–185
 trends in receipts by work-limitation population, 80t
 work disincentives associated with, 400–401
 See also Health care costs; Social Security Disability Insurance

Survey of Income and Program
    Participation (SIPP)
  about, 61–63t
  definition of disability, 30t
  questions about functional and other
    limitations, 316–317
  strengths and weaknesses, 27–28
  variable definitions, 63–69t

Task scope of jobs, 130t, 138–140
Taxpayers stake in ADA, 328
Team-based work, 135, 136, 137, 138
Technological changes in jobs, 133
Telecommuting, 144–145
Temporary employment, 143, 144
Terms of employment, 130t, 143–147,
    148f
Ticket to Work and Work Incentives
    Improvement Act (TWWIIA),
    185, 365, 398, 400–401

Unemployment
  and chronic health conditions,
    245–253
  and stress, 250–251
Unemployment rate
  CPS, NHIS, and SIPP, 69t
  due to involuntary job loss, 159f
  as measure of labor market success,
    47–49, 50f
  for population with work limitations,
    294
  for population with work limitations
    and able to work, 78–79t
U.S. Supreme Court interpretations of
    ADA, 316, 321, 330n5, 331n6

Variables
  chronic health condition, 197–198
  definitions from national data sets,
    63t–69t
  job characteristics, 129–132, 170,
    171t–172t, 173

Wage differentials due to disability,
    310–311
  and job loss, 312
Wage predictions for people with
    disabilities, 309
Welfare reform and disability policy,
    401–402
White men and women with disabilities,
    107
  See also Racial subpopulations
Women with disabilities
  effect of SSDI and SSI on earnings
    1980–2000, 5, 6t
  employment rate compared to men's,
    378
  employment rate during 1989 and
    1990s, 4
  employment rate trends by
    subpopulation, 38, 40f, 41, 73t,
    76t
  employment rates during 1996, 37f
  health care costs, 13
  household income, 1980–2000, 2, 3t
  labor force participation trends, 79t
  prevalence, 35
  prevalence rates by subpopulation,
    71t, 83–84t
  SSDI/SSI beneficiary rate trends by
    subpopulation, 80t
  trends in proportions of, by
    subpopulation, 77t
  unemployment rate trends, 79t
  See also White men and women with
    disabilities
Women with disabilities who report
    activity limitations, 34–36
  employment rate trends, 37f
Women with disabilities who report no
    work limitations
  composition by subpopulation, 116t
  decomposition of employment rate,
    121t

employment rates, 1980–2000, 119*t*, 120*t*
population shares, 1980–2000, 120*t*
Women with disabilities who report work limitations
composition by subpopulation, 116*t*
employment rate trends, 206, 207*t*, 208
employment rate trends during 1990s, 96, 97*f*
employment rates, 2000, 90*f*
employment rates, 1980–2000, 118*t*
and high-cost chronic conditions, 204–206, 381
population composition, 1980–2000, 91, 93*f*
prevalence, 2000, 92*f*
prevalence by subpopulation, 115*t*
SSDI/SSI benefits and labor market integration, 49, 51*f*–52
unemployment rates, 47–49
Women without disabilities
effect of SSDI and SSI on earnings 1989–2000, 6*t*
employment rate during 1990s, 4
employment rate trends by data source, 43*f*
employment rate trends by subpopulation, 75*t*
"Woodwork effect," 402
Work
disincentives, 364–365
incentives, 398–402
net value, 347
physical barriers to, 399
schedule flexibility, 145
See also Job characteristics
Work-limitation measure of disability
alternatives to, 286–289
and body mass index (BMI), 403*n*3
in CPS, NHIS, and SIPP, 63*t*
definitions, 33–34, 170
duration of work limitation, 290
limits to, 36, 37–38
partial work limitation, 66*t*

potential difficulties in using, 284–286
reasons to use, 373–374
significance, 52
use in studies of ADA, 283–284
vs. functional limitation measures, 7–8
See also One-year limitations; Population with work limitations
Work-limitation variable, 198
Work-related disabilities, 260, 274
Workers' compensation, 393
Working-aged people with disabilities. *See* People with disabilities
World Health Organization's conceptualization of disability, 33–34, 56*n*7

Depresin 384-5

About the Institute

The W.E. Upjohn Institute for Employment Research is a nonprofit research organization devoted to finding and promoting solutions to employment-related problems at the national, state, and local levels. It is an activity of the W.E. Upjohn Unemployment Trustee Corporation, which was established in 1932 to administer a fund set aside by the late Dr. W.E. Upjohn, founder of The Upjohn Company, to seek ways to counteract the loss of employment income during economic downturns.

The Institute is funded largely by income from the W.E. Upjohn Unemployment Trust, supplemented by outside grants, contracts, and sales of publications. Activities of the Institute comprise the following elements: 1) a research program conducted by a resident staff of professional social scientists; 2) a competitive grant program, which expands and complements the internal research program by providing financial support to researchers outside the Institute; 3) a publications program, which provides the major vehicle for disseminating the research of staff and grantees, as well as other selected works in the field; and 4) an Employment Management Services division, which manages most of the publicly funded employment and training programs in the local area.

The broad objectives of the Institute's research, grant, and publication programs are to 1) promote scholarship and experimentation on issues of public and private employment and unemployment policy, and 2) make knowledge and scholarship relevant and useful to policymakers in their pursuit of solutions to employment and unemployment problems.

Current areas of concentration for these programs include causes, consequences, and measures to alleviate unemployment; social insurance and income maintenance programs; compensation; workforce quality; work arrangements; family labor issues; labor-management relations; and regional economic development and local labor markets.